An Economic History of the Major Capitalist Countries

An Economic History of the Major Capitalist Countries

A CHINESE VIEW

Kang Fan with Zexing Song, Kelang Zhu, Wuxin Guo, and Yuanji Chi
Translated with an Introduction by Uldis Kruze

An East Gate Book
M.E. Sharpe, Inc.
Armonk, New York
London, England

An East Gate Book

80 Business Park Drive, Armonk, New York 10504

Available in the United Kingdom and Europe from M. E. Sharpe, Publishers, 3 Henrietta Street, London WC2E 8LU.

Library of Congress Cataloging-in-Publication Data

Chu yao tzu pen chu i kuo chia ching chi chien shih. English.
An economic history of the major capitalist countries:
a Chinese view / authors, Kang Fan with Zexing Song . . . [et al.];
translated with an introduction by Uldis Kruze.
p. cm.
Translation of: Chu yao tzu pen chu i kuo chia ching chi chien shih.
Includes bibliographical references and index.
ISBN 0-87332-711-X
1. Economic history.
2. Capitalism—History.
3. Marxian economics.
I. Fan, Kang.
II. Kruze, Uldis.
III. Title.
HC51.C4513 1991
330.9—dc20
91-25486
CIP

Printed in the United States of America
The paper used in this publication meets the minimum requirements of American National Standard for Information Sciences —Permanence of Paper for Printed Library Materials, ANSI Z 39.48-1984.

∞

MV 10 9 8 7 6 5 4 3 2 1

Contents

Preface to the 1973 Edition

We have compiled this book in order to give a concise account of the economic history of five major capitalist countries: England, the United States, France, Germany, and Japan. Our purpose is to explain the nature of the laws governing capitalism's birth, development, and demise. Finally, we hope to provide some relevant historical information for those readers who study Marxist works and who wish to understand the present international situation of class struggle.

The history of the birth and development of capitalism is a blood-stained history of the bourgeoisie's savage exploitation of its own working people and its ruthless plunder of the peoples of its colonies and semi-colonies. It is also a history of heroic struggles waged by the entire world's proletariat, oppressed people, and oppressed nations against capitalism, colonialism, and imperialism. The contradiction between the proletariat and the bourgeoisie is the principal contradiction of capitalist society. Presently, the proletariat and the bourgeoisie are locked in a fierce class struggle throughout the entire world. Understanding the economic history of the major capitalist countries will help us to better recognize the objective laws of the basic exploitative nature of the bourgeoisie and the inevitable replacement of the capitalist system by the socialist system.

Presently we are still in an era of imperialism and proletarian revolution. The specific characteristic of the current international situation is one of great turmoil. It is a manifestation of the intensification of the various basic contradictions in the contemporary world. The two superpowers—the United States and the Soviet Union—have evoked strong resistance from the Third World and the people of the entire world, and have also aroused strong dissatisfaction from the developed countries of the Second World. Understanding the economic history of the major capitalist countries as they have developed to this stage of imperialism will enable us to see that the root cause of this struggle for world hegemony lies in their rule by monopoly capital and is determined by their rapacious nature. Nevertheless, the history of imperialism demonstrates that anyone who wants to promote policies of aggresssion, expansion, and war in order to achieve world hegemony has, in the end, been unable to avoid a complete and ignominious collapse.

Imperialism is moribund capitalism. Chairman Mao has pointed out, "Imperialism has pushed the great masses of the people throughout the world into the historical epoch of the great struggle to abolish imperialism."[1] Presently, the people and countries of the Third World (Asia, Africa, and Latin America) have become the major force in opposing colonialism and imperialism, especially in opposing the two superpowers (the United States and the Soviet Union), and they are the revolutionary motivating force in pushing forward the wheel of world history. The broad historical tide of countries wanting independence, nations wanting liberation, and the people wanting revolution cannot be stopped. If we understand the history of the economic, political, and military expansion of the major capitalist countries, we can then comprehend that this great historical tide is in conformity with the laws of development of recent history. It is precisely the long-term economic exploitation and colonial oppression imposed by capitalism and imperialism on the vast masses of people of the Asian, African, and Latin American continents that forced these peoples to persistently fight an unyielding struggle against that very same colonialism and imperialism. The postwar rise and maturation of the Third World certainly has not been accidental, but has been the continuation and development of this great battle. If only the entire world's proletariat would unite with the oppressed people and oppressed nations of the world, and carry this struggle through to the end, then it certainly could completely bury imperialism and colonialism. This is an inevitable trend of history.

Understanding the economic history of the major capitalist countries will also assist us in following Chairman Mao's admonition to "read and study conscientiously, and develop a good grasp of Marxism." It will help us to understand the historical background referred to in the numerous Marxist classics, and will assist us in grasping the spiritual essence and historical basis of the numerous scientific statements of Marxism. As a result, it will strengthen our belief in the inevitable triumph of the proletarian revolutionary cause, raise our consciousness of proletarian internationalism, enable us to better comprehend and carry out Chairman Mao's proletarian revolutionary line, and help us to struggle bravely for the complete liberation of mankind.

To assist the reader in acquiring a comparatively comprehensive understanding of the history of capitalism's birth, development, and decay, we will first provide a general overview of the several historical stages of development of the entire capitalist system. Then we will give a separate account of each of the five major capitalist countries and of their specific process of economic development.

An Economic History of the Major Capitalist Countries

Translator's Introduction

I. Significance

How do scholars in the People's Republic of China view modern world history? How do they perceive the historical emergence and development of the major capitalist powers like the United States, Japan, and Germany? What contributions have they made to our understanding of world history, and to the writing of world history and political economy as seen from a Marxist viewpoint?

Kang Fan's *Economic History of the Major Capitalist Countries* (Beijing: People's Publishing House, 1973) is China's leading interpretation of world economic history, and represents an excellent case study of historical scholarship and political economy—its strengths and weaknesses—in the People's Republic of China. Initially conceived in the late 1950s to fill what Chinese scholars perceived was a void in Marxist-oriented writings on this topic, the *Economic History* was initially sponsored by the Institute of World Economics and Politics of the Chinese Academy of Social Sciences (CASS). The institute asked a number of prominent scholars to write a survey of the major capitalist country in which that person specialized. As an expert on American agricultural history, Professor Kang Fan, senior researcher at the institute, wrote the chapter on the United States that appears as chapter three in this translation. Acting as the general editor, she also contributed the Overview, which appears as chapter one. Zexing Song, professor of history at Liaoning University, wrote on England (chapter two). Kelang Zhu, professor of economics at Beijing University, contributed the chapter on France (chapter four). Professor Wuxin Guo of the Department of Economics of Wuhan University wrote on Germany (chapter five). Yuanji Chi, professor at Jilin University in Changchun, offered a critique of Japan (chapter six).

Although the book was written in the early 1960s, publication was delayed by the onset of the Cultural Revolution in 1966. The *Economic History* eventually emerged in print only in December 1973, and only as the result of Professor Fan's recall to Beijing in 1972 from her work on a state farm, or "May Seventh

Cadre School." As Professor Fan related to me in 1984 while she was visiting the United States, senior officials in the government wished to see the project come to fruition. They wanted her to return from the countryside at that time to lead and complete the academic project that had been launched in the late 1950s.

The publication of this book during the Cultural Revolution served an important dual role. As one of the few works on political economy published after the Tenth Party Congress (October 1973), the *Economic History* emphasized the theme that the forces of production, rather than class struggle, were the motivating force in the making of world history. As such, the book challenged the prevailing line of the Communist party that wanted to change the superstructure of Chinese society first, before China's productive forces could be liberated. This Maoist concept was embodied in the slogan "Grasp Revolution, Promote Production." Thus, the writing and publication of Professor Fan's book on world economic history and political economy in 1972–73 did not take place in a vacuum, but served an important political purpose, allowing the Zhou Enlai faction in the Chinese leadership to assert its own viewpoint regarding the primacy of economic growth. While the *Economic History* should be seen as an important academic contribution of Chinese scholarship in the 1970s, its political and ideological role in the polemical struggles of the Cultural Revolution and its immediate aftermath should also not be overlooked.

The end of the Cultural Revolution and the repudiation of the "Grasp Revolution, Promote Production" concept heralded a brisk market for the *Economic History*. After the Chinese Communist party formally embraced the doctrine of productive forces with its adoption of the "Four Modernizations" strategy in 1977, Professor Fan's work became required reading in every college course on political economy. And, despite its age, the *Economic History* has remained an important text even today (1991). Not only is it still on required reading lists at the university level, but it has become a widely read primer on the development of capitalism. It has been a best-seller, having sold 355,000 copies in four printings. The book has also gained an international readership, having been translated into Japanese, German, French, and Spanish editions. Professor Fan has subsequently written a sequel, *A History of the Rise and Fall of Capitalism* (Beijing: Beijing Publishing House, 1984), which elaborates on the themes that she introduced in her earlier work.

How could an American audience benefit from the full-length translation offered here? First, Professor Fan's work offers an extensive survey of American history as seen by an eminent Chinese scholar. As a "mirror" for our society, the book reveals us as others see us. Second, the *Economic History* also provides a critical and unsentimental analysis of American history from a Chinese Marxist perspective. As a text in political economy and economic history, it offers a methodological approach—historical materialism—that views historical change as the result of changes in the forces of production and the relations of production. In a sense, Professor Fan's work not only enhances our understanding of the

Chinese perspective on the history of capitalism's development, but contributes to the very history of that development itself.

II. A Survey of Publications on World Economic History and Political Economy in China

Where does Kang Fan's work stand in relationship to other Chinese publications in the field since 1949? Where does it fit into China's scholarly debates over trends in the economic history of capitalism? Here we need to survey China's contributions in this area.

The Institute of Historical Research of the Chinese Academy of Social Sciences published a *Bibliography of History Books, 1900–80* (Beijing: Chinese Academy of Social Sciences Publishing House, 1984) which listed twelve items on political economy and world economic history. This dozen (listed below in chronological order) has been supplemented by two books published after 1980, which were brought to my attention by Professor Weimin Zheng of CASS's Institute of World Economics and Politics (to whom I express my appreciation).

The first book published in the People's Republic of China on world economic history appeared in 1949. Xuehan Jiang's *The Capitalist Economy in Its Final Stage* (Shanghai: China Publishing House, 1949) launched China's fledgling endeavors in this field. Subsequent works include:

Liaoyi Xin, *Economic Circumstances of the Capitalist Countries* (publisher unknown, 1950);

Planning Commission of Northeast China, *The Economic Conditions of the Capitalist Countries* (Beijing: Commercial Press, 1951);

Zhizhong Sun, *On the Contemporary Stage of the American Economic Crisis* (Shanghai: The Study of Life Publishing House, 1955);

Zhihua Li, *The Birth, Development, and Decline of Capitalism* (Guangzhou: Guangdong People's Publishing House, 1956);

Mengjue Guan, *Questions Regarding the Economic Crises of Capitalism Since the Second World War* (Shenyang: Liaoning People's Publishing House, 1957);

The Political Economy Research Group of the Southwest China Institute of Politics and Law, *A Discourse on the Economics of Contemporary Capitalism* (Chongqing: Chongqing People's Publishing House, 1957);

Zexing Song, *Problems Concerning the Unequal Development of the Capitalist Countries* (Beijing: People's Publishing House, 1957);

Hainuo Wu, *Embryonic Forms of Capitalist Production in China* (Hubel People's Publishing House, 1957). The book is a comparative history of the development of capitalistic relations of production in Europe and in China.

Editorial Group of the Shanghai People's Publishing House, *The Economies of the Imperialist Powers since World War II* (Shanghai: Shanghai People's Publishing House, 1972);

Kang Fan, *An Economic History of the Major Capitalist Countries* (Beijing: People's Publishing House, 1973);

Kang Fan, *The Rise and Fall of Capitalism* (Beijing: Beijing Publishing House, 1984);

Qihua Qiu, *The Economy of Contemporary Monopoly Capitalism* (Beijing: Central Party School Publishing House, 1985);

Weimin Zheng, Su Huang, and Deyuan Jie, *The Postwar Economy of Capitalism* (Beijing: Ecnomic Sciences Publishing House, 1986);

These books essentially constitute the field of contemporary Chinese academic studies of world economic history and the political economy of capitalist societies. Professor Fan's work represents an important development in that field, but also reflects its shortcomings.

III. Salient Features of the *Economic History*

Professor Fan views history as driven by economic forces, and modern history as the story of capitalism's rise, development, and eventual demise. The book confirms and elaborates on the historical judgments on capitalism that have been made by Marx, Engels, Lenin, Stalin, and Mao, and in this sense becomes an extended commentary on their viewpoints. However, it does break new ground in evaluating the history of the political and economic challenges that confronted the major capitalist countries in the 1930s and up to 1945. Also, this work does not neglect the worker and peasant, especially in relating how the exploitative features of capitalism that eventually led to worker resistance and the emergence of communist movements. While focusing primarily on the major capitalist countries, it also introduces aspects of Chinese history: the impact of the opium trade carried out by the British in China in the nineteenth century, and the resistance to Japanese imperialism in World War II. It retains a polemical quality in criticizing not only scholarship that apologizes for capitalism, but also by targeting elements in the workers' movements that misled those efforts into reformism or capitulation.

The *Economic History* is not without shortcomings. Professor Fan and her colleagues carry their analysis of capitalism only up to 1945. The book therefore fails to confront the postwar economic revival of Germany and Japan, and the stunning prosperity enjoyed by the United States—including its working class—after World War II. Subsequently, this has been remedied by Professor Fan's *Rise and Fall of Capitalism*, which attributes capitalism's postwar prosperity, among other reasons, to its skillful application of new scientific and technological discoveries.

The *Economic History* lacks extensive documentation for the factual information it presents. The writings of Marx, Engels, Lenin, Stalin, and Mao dominate the footnotes, but we are given no information as to what other sources the authors relied upon to write this book.

IV. A Note on the Translation Itself

A translator's first priority must be placed on maintaining faithfulness to the original document. This has been my goal, and in this I hope I have succeeded. I have kept the English sentences short. Those in the Chinese language edition often run far longer than can easily be accommodated by a more literal translation making liberal use of relative pronouns and dependent clauses. China and Japan specialists should also know that I have placed Chinese and Japanese surnames last, in the accepted American usage. Thus, they will find Yuan Shikai in chapter six appearing as Shikai Yuan. I have done this to oblige a general American readership that may be confused by having some surnames come first and some come last. However, I have retained the Chinese word order in the case of Mao Zedong, whose writings are often cited in this text.

V. Acknowledgments

A translation project such as this could not be realized without a great deal of assistance from many people. Here I would like to acknowledge, with warm gratitude, the financial support of the Faculty Development Committee of the University of San Francisco. Their generosity made it possible to prepare this text for publication. Associate Dean Maureen O'Sullivan of the University of San Francisco provided word processing assistance from her office staff at a crucial moment in the development of this project. Professor Scott McElwain of the University of San Francisco read parts of the draft and made critical and valuable comments. Two dear friends, Tom Fergoda and Sue Johnson, offered encouragement and support, and also read parts of the manuscript. Professor Joyce Kallgren, who served as Chair of the Center for Chinese Studies at the University of California (Berkeley) in the 1980s, provided me with office space and a congenial environment in which to complete this project. Ben Baab, Manager of Academic and Research Computing at the University of San Francisco, helped me enormously with his timely assistance. Monica Roskos and Thuvan Le spent many hours working over my revisions and entering them onto numerous diskettes. To them I extend a warm thank you. Doug Merwin of M. E. Sharpe has been unfailingly supportive and encouraging in this venture. Finally, my family has been patient and understanding, and hopeful of the day when this project would be completed. To them I dedicate this book, with love.

1 Overview

The capitalist system, which began with the earliest appearance of capitalist relations of production in Western Europe and which has continued up to the conclusion of the Second World War, has passed through two great stages. The first stage has been that of free competition. The second stage has been that of monopoly. This book divides the development of world capitalism into the following four periods:

1. The period of primitive capitalist accumulation and the development of a workshop handicraft industry. This phase began in the sixteenth century and continued until the middle of the eighteenth century.
2. The period of the development of large-scale mechanized industry and the establishment of the capitalist system. This process began during the latter half of the eighteenth century and lasted until the 1860s.
3. The period of the transition to monopoly capitalism and the formation of imperialism. This phase began after the events of the 1871 Paris Commune and the 1873 economic crisis and ended with the October 1917 socialist revolution.
4. The period after the victory of the October 1917 socialist revolution in Russia. This event shook the foundations of the world capitalist system and opened a new era in world history. Capitalism now entered the stage of a general crisis.

1

Marx wrote, "The economic structure of capitalist society emerges from the economic structure of feudal society. The disintegration of the latter creates the essential factors for the former to achieve liberation."[1] This is to say that capitalist relations of production were engendered from within the feudal system.

Looked at from the perspective of world history, the disintegration of the feudal system and the birth of capitalist relations of production appeared earliest in Western Europe. Marx pointed out, "In the fourteenth and fifteenth centuries, the earliest sprouts of capitalist production had already sprung up here and there in some cities along the Mediterranean littoral."[2] The cities that Marx referred to were located in northern Italy: Venice, Genoa, Pisa, Florence, and Milan. Each had grown during the Middle Ages by monopolizing trade with the Near East. These cities had become centers of commerce by handling trade relations between Europe and the Near East. A commodity economy developed comparatively early in these places, and feudal controls there were relatively relaxed. As a result, these cities broke—at a rather early date—the bonds that the feudal guilds had maintained over the traditional woolen industry. At the same time, they gave birth to scattered—yet concentrated—capitalist handicraft workshops that were controlled by merchants.

However, if we consider Western Europe as a whole, the capitalist relations of production that emerged in these cities were but a small drop in a bucket, insufficient to mark the beginnings of a new era. Marx pointed out that "the era of capitalism only began with the sixteenth century."[3] The three hundred years spanning the sixteenth to the eighteenth centuries was a period when feudalism rapidly disintegrated in Western Europe. It was the period of primitive capitalist accumulation and the massive development of capitalist handicraft workshops. And it was also the period of transition from feudal society to capitalist society. This unprecedentedly significant historical transformation was the inevitable result of the development of contradictions between the forces of production and the relations of production in Western Europe's feudal society. It was also a transformation that received a powerful impetus from the great geographical discoveries that took place at the end of the fifteenth and early sixteenth centuries. Marx and Engles wrote, "The discovery of America, the rounding of the Cape, opened up fresh ground for the rising bourgeoisie. The East-Indian and Chinese markets, the colonization of America, trade with the colonies, the increase in the means of exchange and in commodities generally, gave to commerce, to navigation, to industry, an impulse never before known, and thereby, to the revolutionary element in the tottering feudal society, a rapid development."[4] The sanguinary process of primitive capitalist accumulation began in the various countries of Western Europe immediately after the discovery of new maritime routes. This was the origin and precondition for the birth of the capitalist mode of production. Bourgeois apologists with ulterior motives have said that the rise of the bourgeoisie was the result of its particularly abundant virtue of "hard work and thrifty habits." This is a fabrication of history. The basic preconditions for capitalist production were 1) the existence of many propertyless people having freedom in their persons but having lost access to any means of production and 2) the existence of vast monetary wealth necessary for organizing capitalist production. These two basic preconditions in fact were created by savage violence. Primitive capitalist accumulation occurred when the big landlords and the bourgeoisie used violence to separate the producers from the means of production. As a result, producers turned into hired workers, and money turned into capital.

Marx pointed out that "plundering the agricultural producers, that is, seizing the land of the peasants, formed the basis of this entire process. (Here Marx was referring to primitive accumulation.)"[5] This process was carried out most thoroughly and most typically in England. The discovery of new maritime routes caused the world market to expand suddenly. To meet the needs of this expanding domestic and foreign market in wool and grain, the English landed aristocracy and bourgeoisie employed violence and deception for three centuries to enclose the peasants' public lands and private lands. They turned these lands into large pastures and large farms which were then rented out to tenant farmers to manage. This forced the peasants to leave their home villages in droves. The state promulgated various kinds of sanguinary laws, including the use of flogging, imprisonment, and even capital punishment, to prohibit peasants from roaming about freely and to force them to become the hired laborers of capitalism. Although the other Western European countries did not forcibly seize the lands of the peasantry to the same extent as did England, they nevertheless all followed the same procedure, differing only in degree, methodology, and timing. Marx pointed out, "The history of this kind of plunder is written in blood and fire in the annals of humanity."[6]

The major element in primitive capitalist accumulation was the use of state power to plunder the colonies by using the cruelest force imaginable. Marx wrote:

> The discovery of the gold and silver mines of America, the extirpation, enslavement and entombment in mines of the aboriginal population, the beginning of the conquest and plunder of the East Indies, and the turning of Africa into an arena for the commercial hunting of black people all symbolized the rosy dawn of the era of capitalist production. These idyllic proceedings were the essential elements of primitive accumulation.[7]

After the discovery of the new maritime routes, the merchants and landed aristocracy from Portugal, Spain, Holland, England, and France each took—in turn—the path of colonial plunder. In this endeavor, they were supported by their own monarchs. And in this process, they wrote the darkest and most shameful page in human history.

The Portuguese and the Spanish were the first colonialists to take advantage of the opening of the new maritime routes. Asia and Africa became the principal targets for Portuguese plunder. After the discovery of a new oceanic route to India in the sixteenth century, Portugal created for itself a string of enclaves in Southeast Asia, India, Sri Lanka, China, and along the Sea of Japan. In addition, Portugal seized control over the Red Sea and the Indian Ocean littoral. Beginning in the middle of the fifteenth and up to the early sixteenth century, the Portuguese established a number of bases in Africa. First they began their activities along the west coast of Africa. Subsequently they expanded along the south coast, and finally reached Africa's east coast. In America, they took possession of Brazil. In the areas of Asia that they occupied, the Portuguese robbed the local nobility and imposed extortionate taxes on the citizens. They also used strong-arm measures to buy Asian products (such as spices, sugar, white rice, tea, indigo, silk, gems and jewels, handicraft arts, and other items) at bargain prices, then shipped these goods to Europe and sold them at prices seven to eight times more than the original cost. They shipped opium from India to China, and reaped huge profits from such transactions. In Africa, the Portuguese colonialists were predominantly engaged in either outright plunder or the exchange of inexpensive European commodities for gold and elephant tusks. In addition, the Portuguese hunted and kidnapped black people and shipped them to America to sell as slaves.

America was the principal target for Spanish colonial plunder. Beginning at the end of the fifteenth century and the first half of the sixteenth century, Spain first occupied Haiti, then took Cuba, Mexico, Peru, Chile, and Paraguay one after the other. Afterwards it expanded into all of Central and South America. Brazil became the sole exception to this process of expansionism. The towering crimes committed by the Spanish colonialists when they were subjugating Central and South America could not be duplicated by the most savage tyrants of any century. They slaughtered the Indians in droves, used every despicable method to either extort or loot the gold and silver treasures of the area, and forced the Indians to become slave laborers to open and cultivate plantations and to work the gold and silver mines. Within a few decades, the Indians of Haiti, Cuba, and the various islands of the Caribbean, were almost entirely exterminated as a result of the cruelty and enslavement by the Spanish colonialists. To make up for a shortage of labor power, the colonists began to ship kidnapped black people from Africa to America to work as slaves.

Brutal colonial plunder enabled Portugal, and Spain in particular, to become the most prosperous countries economically in Western Europe in the sixteenth century. Both experienced quite significant gains in commerce, oceanic trade, and in their workshop handicraft industries. However, the feudal systems in these two countries were comparatively secure, and the gold and silver wealth that entered from overseas was predominantly used to pay for the lavish expenditures of their parasitic feudal aristocracies, to maintain gigantic military bureaucracies, and to wage wars. Large amounts of gold and silver flowed into the purses of the foreign bourgeoisie, and didn't play a role in primitive accumulation in the home country. Portugal in the period from 1580 to 1640 was on the same level as Spain. However, the previously illustrious Spanish empire began to decline at the end of the sixteenth century. In 1588, its "Invincible Armada" was destroyed in the straits between England and Holland. This event proclaimed Spain's fall from the hegemony it had exercised over the oceans and over Western Europe.

Holland, England, and France—one after the other—rose to replace Spain and Portugal. What they plundered from their colonies in Asia, Africa, and America beginning in the seventeenth century would be no less and even more than what the Spanish and Portuguese colonialists took.

Holland was originally a part of the Netherlands.[8] As early as the period between the thirteenth and fifteenth centuries, the provinces of Flanders and Brabant in the southern part of the Netherlands and the provinces of Holland and Zeeland in the northern part were comparatively economically advanced areas in Western Europe. The discovery of new maritime navigation routes, and the subsequent alteration of global trading patterns, further promoted the development of this area. Antwerp, located in the province of Brabant, became the trading center of the world. Comparatively advanced handicraft workshops, a thriving commercial sector, and fishing, shipping, and shipbuilding industries all emerged in several northern provinces of the Netherlands—centered particularly in Holland—because feudal relationships and traditional guild privileges were relatively weaker there than in the south. By the first half of the sixteenth century, a bourgeoisie had emerged in the north. This class was headed by very wealthy merchants and exerted a relatively substantial amount of economic clout. However, at that time the Netherlands was ruled by the autocratic Spanish Hapsburg monarchy, and therefore suffered from the blows and persecution of this monarchy in politics, economics, and religion. In 1566, the people of the Netherlands launched a national uprising in opposition to Spanish rule and fought a war to gain their independence. In 1572, the northern provinces, headed by Holland and led by the bourgeoisie, proclaimed their independence. In 1579, they established a Republic of United Provinces. This was the earliest bourgeois revolution in history.

Not long after it gained independence, Holland began to plunder colonies. In the early seventeenth century, the wealthy merchant groups of Holland first established the East India Company and then created a West India Company. Both companies were invested with special powers by the government, having the right to mint their own money and to maintain a military organization capable of carrying out a policy of colonial aggression. In the first half of the seventeenth century, the East India Company forcibly occupied, one after the other, a chain of Indonesian islands. It grabbed a number of Portuguese bases in Southeast Asia and India, taking over the Portuguese monopoly on the spice trade with the East. In Africa, it seized some good vantage points. The West India Company also established its own colonial bases in North America. Marx exposed the bloody crimes committed by the Dutch colonists in Indonesia when he wrote:

> The history of the colonial administration of Holland—and Holland was the penultimate capitalist nation of the seventeenth century—"reveals a perfect panorama of treachery, bribery, murder, and sordid behavior." Most characteristic of Dutch behavior was their implementation of a criminal code on Sulaweisi Island in order to acquire slaves for Java. . . . Wherever the Dutch went turned into a depopulated wasteland.[9]

Plunder from the colonies provided a large amount of primitive capital accumulation for Holland's merchants and the owners of its handicraft workshops. It also established a firm basis for the economic prosperity that the Dutch enjoyed in the seventeenth century. Nevertheless, like Portugal and Spain, Holland's prosperity—historically speaking—was as short lived as a flower. What distinguished the development of Dutch capitalism was the fact that its foreign trade far and away dominated industry. As a result, the Dutch eventually became known as "the teamsters of the oceans." Not only did Holland monopolize trade with East India, but it also monopolized trade between southwestern Europe and northern Europe. Amsterdam was the world's commercial center at that time. This special characteristic of Dutch capitalism soon became a major weakness in its economic development. By the end of the seventeenth century, Holland's economic position in Western Europe and its maritime hegemony were taken over by England, which possessed a powerful workshop handicraft industry. Marx wrote that "the history of Holland's commercial supremacy and its path of decline is the history of commercial capital succumbing before production capital."[10]

Beginning at the end of the sixteenth and early seventeenth centuries, England carved out a series of colonies in North America, in the Caribbean, and in India. By the middle of the seventeenth century, France had accomplished the same. These events occurred after a unified, absolutist monarchy had been established in each country and after a workshop handicraft industry had developed. In the middle of the seventeenth century, after the victory of its bourgeois revolution, England intensified its plunder of overseas colonies. By the end of the seventeenth century, after waging three wars against the Dutch, England had supplanted Holland's position of superiority in maritime trade and colonial expansion. In the eighteenth century, England began its struggle with France for domination over a colonial empire. After the Seven Years' War of 1756–63, England was finally able to expel French power from North America and India, and established its own position of colonial hegemony. Even though the British subsequently lost their thirteen colonies in North America after the American War of Independence, their East India Company's brutal plunder and enslavement of the people of India yielded a colossal amount of primitive capital accumulation for the English bourgeoisie. It also created favorable conditions for England's Industrial Revolution (which began in the 1760s) and for its development into the premier industrial power of the world.

The slave trade, closely related to colonial plunder, was also a major source of Western Europe's primitive capital accumulation. Before the end of the eighteenth century, the capture and sale of black people was the basis of all colonial activities in Africa by Western Europe. The Portuguese colonists were slave traders at an early time (in the sixteenth century). After the seventeenth century, Holland, England, and France all participated—some early, some late—in an activity so evil that it makes one's blood boil. The hunting and kidnapping of black people expanded from West Africa to East Africa. Numerous black tribes were exterminated as a result of being pursued and attacked by groups of colonialist hunters; or these tribes became scattered and their members died from hardships suffered in the jungle. It is estimated that the number of black people shipped to America between the sixteenth century and the middle of the nineteenth century reached fifteen million. And the bloody slave trade caused an aggregate loss in Africa's population that is estimated at one hundred million people. Much of Western Europe's earliest capital, especially that which propelled the development of England's capitalism, came from the sun-bleached bones of countless black people.

Instituting a national debt, a modern system of tax collection, and protective tariffs were other important means of primitive capital accumulation used by the various Western European countries to plunder the working people of their own countries.

The various above-mentioned measures of primitive accumulation were exactly what Marx talked about when he said that "all used state power, as well as centralized, organized social forces to energetically promote the power of society to promote the transitional process from the feudal form of production to the capitalist form of production, and to reduce the period of that transition."[11]

In the period between the sixteenth and the eighteenth centuries, primitive accumulation played a powerful role in the gradual disintegration of the feudal system in Western Europe, enabling capitalist relations of production to develop gradually, and helping the workshop handicraft industry to make great progress. However, capitalist relations developed at an uneven rate in the various countries of Western Europe. This occurred because the extent and speed of primitive accumulation differed from country to country, because the strength of the feudal system and guild restrictions varied, and because the original industrial and commercial base of each country and the impact of changing world trade routes were not identical. As a result, the period of transition from feudalism to capitalism in each country occurred at different times, sometimes coming early and sometimes appearing late. Each country had its own unique characteristics.

2

By the latter half of the eighteenth century, the development of capitalist relations of production in Western Europe had reached a new turning point. Europe now awkwardly entered the era of the establishment of the capitalist system. The Industrial Revolution that first arose in England in the 1760s was the outstanding symbol marking the beginning of this period. This era covered approximately a hundred years of history, lasting up to the 1871 Paris Commune uprising, the outbreak of the 1873 world economic crisis, and the transitional period from capitalism to imperialism. This was the period of the development of a rising "free" capitalism, when the capitalist system attained a universal victory throughout the advanced countries of Europe and America.

The development of capitalist relations of production in Western Europe during the sixteenth through the eighteenth centuries encountered various kinds of restraints established by the feudal system. The contradiction between the newly rising bourgeoisie and the feudal ruling class sharpened daily. At the same time, the peasants' struggles against the feudal masters also became more violent following the intensification of feudal exploitation in the waning period of feudalism. The constant peasant uprisings dealt serious blows to feudal rule. The bourgeoisie, however, made use of the strength of the broad masses of the peasants to carry out its own revolution, overthrowing feudal rule and gaining political power.

The earliest bourgeois revolution occurred in Holland, but the first bourgeois revolution of world historical importance was the English bourgeois revolution of 1640–48. The victory of the English bourgeois revolution and the establishment of bourgeois political power symbolized the fact that human society was beginning to leave the era of feudalism and was now entering a new era of the bourgeoisie. Other bourgeois revolutions followed that of the English: the first success was in America in the latter half of the eighteenth century, the next in France at the end of that century. In Germany, the victorious bourgeoisie compromised with the feudal nobility after the 1848 revolution, carried out bourgeois reforms, and set up a political system based on an alliance of the landed aristocracy and the bourgeoisie itself. In Russia the czar abolished the serfdom system in the 1860s. The leaders of Japan's Meiji Restoration also instituted bourgeois reforms.

These victories swept away the obstacles that had impeded the development of capitalism. The bourgeois state, by playing its role in the superstructure, actively consolidated its own base, and vigorously fostered development of a capitalist economy. Many countries experienced an industrial revolution and carried out capitalist industrialization subsequent either to a bourgeois revolution or bourgeois reforms.

The Industrial Revolution replaced the handicraft workshops based on the skills of the handicraftsman with a factory system relying on machinery. Not only was this a technological revolution but also a great transformation in the relations of production. The appearance of a factory system that relied on machinery as its mainstay dealt a devastating blow to the independent handicraftmen. The final establishment of the capitalist system of hired labor created two completely separate and antagonistic classes—the capitalist class and the working class. Lenin pointed out:

> The transition from the handicraft workshop to the factory marked a basic transformation in technology, which does away with the craftsman's manual skill that has taken centuries to acquire, and this technical revolution is inevitably followed by the most thoroughgoing destruction of social production rela-

> tions, by a final split among the various groups of participants in production, by a complete break with tradition, by an intensification and extension of all the dark aspects of capitalism, and at the same time by a mass socialization of labor by capital.[12]

Scholars employed by the bourgeoisie have regarded the Industrial Revolution as merely a technological revolution. Moreover, they have argued that it was an accidental event in history and the result of inventions developed by a small group of geniuses. This is a reactionary viewpoint of historical idealism and obliterates the fact that the working people create history.

The Industrial Revolution was an objective demand of capitalist economic development. Subsequent to the gradual expansion of the world market, workshop handicraft production fell far short of being able to satisfy the ever-increasing need for industrial products. Only this objective demand produced the necessity for technical innovation. The Industrial Revolution was also the necessary result of a long historical development. First of all, the bourgeoisie engaged the feudal ruling class in a protracted struggle. The revolutions and reforms that they initiated swept aside the various obstacles to capitalist development and created favorable preconditions for an industrial revolution. Second, the lengthy process of primitive accumulation in the sixteenth through the eighteenth centuries provided the large number of free laborers and the colossal monetary wealth that was necessary for the establishment of a large-scale machine industry. Next, the development of a workshop handicraft industry over a long period of time brought about a gradual refinement in the division of labor, caused constant improvement and specialization in the tools of labor, and prepared the material and technological conditions for the transition to large-scale machine production. The various technological innovations that appeared during the Industrial Revolution were engendered precisely on the basis of the work experience accumulated by the working people over a long period of time. All of these technological innovations were inventions created collectively by the working people.

The timing, speed, and extent of each country's industrial revolution varied because the specific historical conditions of each differed. England was the first to begin its industrial revolution in the 1760s because it possessed the abovementioned historical preconditions at a comparatively early date. By the end of the 1830s, England's industrial revolution had basically been completed. By this time—a process that had taken approximately seventy to eighty years to accomplish—a factory system based on machinery enjoyed a clear superiority throughout all of England's basic industrial sectors. The United States and France began their own industrial revolutions in the early nineteenth century; Germany followed in the 1830s. These countries used the technical achievements and experience that England had acquired in order to achieve their own comparatively rapid industrial revolutions. Generally speaking, the United States had completed its industrial revolution by the end of the 1850s, France by the end of the 1860s, and Germany by the end of the 1870s. Japan's industrial development came last; it only began its own industrial revolution at the end of the 1860s. Nevertheless, vigorous sponsorship by the government and wealth pillaged from foreign wars accelerated its progress, and by the beginning of the twentieth century, Japan had also basically completed its industrial revolution.

As the industrial revolution proceeded, so also did capitalist relations of production rapidly develop in agriculture. The growth of a large-scale machine industry further promoted the commercialization of agricultural production and the fragmentation of the peasant economy. At the same time, innovative methods in agricultural production provided the material and technical conditions for the establishment and development of large capitalist farms. Moreover, the development of capitalist relations of production in agriculture and the growth of the forces of production in agriculture exerted a complementary effect in speeding up the development of a large-scale machine industry.

In England, capitalist relations of production in agriculture developed after the abolition of the system of serfdom effectuated by the "enclosure movement" that lasted from the sixteenth through the eighteenth centuries. It was a lengthy and thoroughgoing process that deprived the peasants of their land, and used force to eradicate the small peasant economy. It was on this basis that a large-scale, capitalist, tenant farming system developed. By the end of the eighteenth century, this large-scale, capitalist, tenant farming system in English agriculture had already claimed absolute dominance. In the other capitalist countries, just as Lenin pointed out, capitalist agricultural development followed two different roads: the "American model" and the "Prussian model."[13] The main characteristics of the former model can be characterized as follows: The bourgeois revolution thoroughly destroyed feudal land relations, and universally established land ownership by the peasantry in the process of breaking up the small peasant economy. The agricultural development of the United States presents the most typical example of this model. France's capitalist agricultural development also basically followed this road, though the process of fragmenting the peasant economy was more gradual than in the United States. The second model is best typified by the agricultural development of Eastern Germany. Its main characteristics can be summarized as follows: 1. The bourgeois reforms from above and below did not thoroughly destroy the feudal land relationships, and the land owned by the feudal landlords was not only preserved, but also expanded. 2. Stimulated by the development of a commodity economy, the feudal landlord economy gradually turned into a capitalistic enterprise employing peasants who were quasi-serfs. At the same time, a small number of rich peasants gradually emerged from within the peasant economy. 3. As a result, the broad masses of impoverished peasants suffered for a long period of time from the doubly heavy, cruel exploitation of both a landlord, rich peasant capitalism as well as from feudalism. Consequently, the "Prussian model" represents a path taken by capitalist agricultural development that preserved the remnants of feudalism. This was basically the path of agricultural development followed subsequently in Eastern Europe, Russia, and some other countries.

The social productive forces made great progress after the completion of the industrial revolution, the development of capitalism in agriculture, and after the final establishment of a capitalist system in various countries. In 1848, Marx and Engles wrote:

> The bourgeoisie, during its rule of scarce one hundred years, has created more massive and more colossal productive forces than have all preceding generations together. Subjection of Nature's forces to man, machinery, application of chemistry to industry and agriculture, steam-navigation, railways, electric telegraphs, clearing of whole continents for cultivation, canalization of rivers, whole populations conjured out of the ground—what earlier century had even a presentiment that such productive forces slumbered in the lap of social labor?[14]

All these achievements reveal the progressive nature of the capitalist form of production during its ascendant phase in history. Nevertheless, the various advanced capitalist states made use of the colossal economic forces generated by the Industrial Revolution to intensify their aggression against foreign countries and their exploitation of the colonial people. In this period, not only did they take additional steps to seize vast new colonies and spheres of influence in Asia, Africa, and Latin America, but they also turned these colonies into dependencies serving as markets for the sale of machinery and industrial products, as well as sources of agricultural raw materials. At the same time, the contradictions embodied in capitalism sharpened after the completion of the Industrial Revolution and the establishment of the capitalist system.

The basic contradiction in a capitalist economy is the contradiction between the socialized nature of production and the system of private ownership enjoyed by the capitalist. Although this contradiction existed as soon as capitalist relations of production appeared, it became completely exposed only after machine-based production developed as extensively as it did. Moreover, this basic contradiction created the inevitability of capitalism's periodic crises of overproduction. The first periodic crisis of overproduction in the history of capitalism occurred in England, in 1825, because it was then and there that the Industrial Revolution first made its surprising achievements. A crisis would subsequently occur approximately every decade. The basic phases in the development of such crises can be summarized as follows: Crises would become increasingly more acute and more global in nature as large-scale machine industry expanded in the major capitalist countries. Economic crises caused enormous destruction and waste in the productive forces of society. They brought high levels of unemployment, a decline in real wages, and other disastrous consequences for the working people. Economic crises caused the development of capitalist production to oscillate between alternating periods of boom and bust, of growth and retrogression, thereby reducing and slowing the overall speed of economic development. Economic crises revealed in a concentrated way the sharp contradictions inherent in the capitalist system, and demonstrated that capitalist relations had already become shackles on the development of the forces of production.

The modern proletariat was formed after the development of large-scale machine production. The contradiction between the proletariat and the bourgeoisie became the principal contradiction in society.

Capitalism is a system of hired slavery. "The production of surplus value or making money is an absolute law of this mode of production."[15] In order to extract the maximum surplus value, the capitalist would do anything to exploit the worker. In the hands of the capitalist, the machine became an instrument that cruelly enslaved the worker. Not only did the development of large-scale machine industry cause the ultimate formation of the proletariat, but moreover pushed it to the abyss of abject poverty. On the one hand, it caused the ruin of a large number of handicraftsmen, precipitating them into the ranks of the proletariat. On the other hand, it employed—at low wages—vast numbers of children and women, and discharged the men from the factories who then became a vast reserve army for industry. The women and children factory workers suffered inhuman working conditions in the various capitalist countries. The existence of a vast population of unemployed lowered the wages of those workers who were employed and also lengthened the time of work. Machine production also brought about an unprecedented increase in the labor intensity for workers, and work-related injuries occurred over and over again. Bad working conditions, coarse and terrible food, and crowded and dirty living conditions severely damaged the physical and mental health of the workers and shortened their life span. The extreme deterioration in the conditions experienced by the proletariat was a common phenomenon absolutely without exception in the process of development of large-scale machine industry in the various capitalist countries.

The growing strength of the ranks of the proletariat and its intensified impoverishment compelled it to struggle against capitalist exploitation. In the early period of the Industrial Revolution, the proletariat still did not understand that the source of its impoverishment was the capitalist system. The main target of its struggle was opposition to the use of machinery. Movements to destroy machinery became the earliest form of such spontaneous struggle. Only in the early nineteenth century did the proletariat begin to struggle to obtain improved living conditions and democratic rights, and only then did labor unions appear. It was at the same time that the utopian socialist trend of thought, represented by France's Henri de St. Simon and Charles Fourier and England's Robert Owen, achieved widespread dissemination. Utopian socialism exposed and criticized the various evils of the system of capitalist wage slavery, and played a certain role in enlightening and elevating the consciousness of the proletariat. However, the utopian socialists didn't understand the historical mission of the proletariat, and didn't recognize what constituted the social force that could destroy capitalism.

Because of this, none of the various proposals to transform society that they advocated and carried out experimentally could be realized.

By the 1830s and 1840s, the proletariat of England, France, and Germany had gradually matured, had become an enormous political force, and moreover had begun to turn from daily economic struggles to large-scale political struggles. In 1835, the English working class began to launch the People's Charter Movement. In 1831 and 1834, the workers of Lyons, France staged two uprisings. In 1844, the textile workers in Silesia, Germany staged an uprising. All these actions revealed the enormous power of the proletariat, and symbolized the fact that the proletariat had already stepped onto the stage of history and was beginning to attack the capitalist system with its own organized might.

Marx and Engels, the creators of scientific socialism and revolutionary teachers of the world proletariat, began their revolutionary and theoretical activities in the 1840s. They personally participated in the revolutionary movement of that time. They summed up the experience of the workers' revolutionary movement, and critically studied and absorbed English classical political economy, German classical philosophy, and French utopian socialist thought. Making a thorough study of the history of capitalism, they scientifically explained the exploitative nature of the capitalist system of wage slavery, revealed the laws of capitalism's emergence, development, and extinction, and proved that the historical mission of the proletariat was to serve as the gravedigger of the capitalist system. As a result, they established the exacting scientific world view and revolutionary theory of the proletariat: Marxism. In 1848, Karl Marx and Friedrich Engels published the great programme of the proletarian revolution—*The Manifesto of the Communist Party*—and scientific socialist thought began to achieve widespread dissemination in the workers' movement.

Marxism was established and developed in the process of repeated struggles with all thought and theories fundamentally inimical to the proletariat. Before and after Marx and Engels published *The Manifesto of the Communist Party*, they waged struggles with every type of feudal, bourgeois, and petty-bourgeois socialist theory and group. In particular, they sharply criticized and uncompromisingly struggled against the reformism espoused by France's Pierre Proudhon and the opportunism of Germany's Ferdinand Lasalle. Each of these two trends had previously exerted great influence in the workers' movement. It was precisely these struggles that gradually swept away from the worker's movement the influence of various kinds of spurious "socialist" trends of thought. These struggles established the leading position of Marxist thought in the international workers' movement and enabled the workers' movement of this period, centered on Western Europe, to grow enormously. The First International (i.e., the International Association of Workers) was established in 1864 under the leadership of Marx and Engels. For the first time, the struggles waged by the proletariat in various countries enjoyed leadership from an international organization. The workers' movement in Western Europe flourished in the 1860s.

3

In the first half of the nineteenth century, and particularly in the 1850s and 1860s, the rapid growth of a large-scale, capitalist, machine industry—and of agriculture, communications, transportation, foreign trade, and foreign colonial expansion—stirred up all the contradictions inherent in capitalism. The creation of the Paris Commune in 1871 and the unprecedentedly keen global economic crisis of 1873 were concentrated manifestations of the political and economic contradictions of capitalism during this period, and were the starting points that marked the transition from "free" capitalism to monopoly capitalism, i.e., imperialism.

Marx pointed out that the Paris Commune's "heroic movement of March 18 was the dawn of a great social revolution that would forever liberate humanity from class society."[16] It was the first attempt by the proletariat to overthrow the bourgeoisie and to establish a dictatorship of the proletariat. It symbolized the fact that the ruling position of the bourgeoisie was beginning to wobble, that the capitalist system was beginning its slide from prosperity to decline, and that the socialist revolution had been placed on the agenda for the day. Although the Paris Commune was destroyed, "the principles of the Commune are eternal, and cannot be extinguished."[17] The historical experience of the Paris Commune demonstrated that the proletariat must use revolutionary violence to seize political power, must demolish the bourgeois state apparatus, and must establish a dictatorship of the proletariat for it to achieve its own liberation. This has universal significance for the proletariat of every country.

The 1873 economic crisis that engulfed the various capitalist countries of Europe and America was the first profound crisis of a global nature. This crisis, and the depression that followed, continued for more than five years. This industrial crisis was also intermeshed with an agricultural crisis. The disruption in industrial and agricultural production, the serious extent of business bankruptcies and unemployment, and the atrophy of the financial markets all exceeded previous crises. The crisis increased competition among business enterprises and stimulated the concentration of production and capital. It was on this basis that monopolies appeared. The capitalist economy began its transition from the stage of free competition to the stage of monopoly.

The increasingly fierce competition among business enterprises, economic sectors, and the various capitalist states after the crisis of 1873 stimulated once again the appearance of a series of technical inventions in the capitalist world. Not only did this bring about further progress in the sectors of heavy industry that already existed (such as steel, coal mining, machine manufacturing, etc.), but it also gave rise to the sequential establishment and development of a series of new sectors of heavy industry (such as electric power, electric appliances, chemicals, oil, automobile and aircraft manufacture, etc.). By the end of the nineteenth century, heavy industry began to occupy the leading role in world industry. The further growth of large-scale, machine industry and the expansion of the capitalist economic system throughout the entire world also promoted the extremely rapid development of global steamship transportation, railroad construction, and international trade. The uneven nature of capitalist economic development became aggravated concurrently with these developments. Agriculture fell behind the development of handicraft industry, light industry fell behind heavy industry, the old industrial sectors lagged behind the new industrial sectors, and the old capitalist countries fell behind the newly rising ones. This intensified uneven development caused drastic changes in the relative rank held by each of these major capitalist countries in the world economy. In 1870, England held first place in world industrial production, but by the 1880s, the United States had overtaken England. In the early twentieth century, Germany also eclipsed England and took second place. France's share of world industrial production, like that of England, declined step by step. As a late arrival among the capitalist countries, Japan's share of world industrial production was initially very small; however, by the end of the nineteenth century and into the early twentieth, Japan's hasty efforts to catch up resulted in a rapid enhancement of its position.

The enormous progress made in technology in the last thirty years of the nineteenth century, the rapid development of industrial production (especially in heavy industry), and the intensification of competition all brought about a constant expansion in the scale of business enterprises, the widespread development of joint-stock companies, and the rapid concentration of capital and production. The concentration of production inevitably produced monopolies. After the outbreak of the 1873 global economic crisis, monopolies appeared one by one throughout the various major capitalist countries. By the end of the nineteenth century and the beginning of the twentieth, after almost thirty years of growth, the monopolies had become the basis for all economic life in each of the advanced capitalist states. At this time, monopoly capitalism took its final shape, and capitalism entered the stage of imperialism.

Because the degree to which production was concentrated and other historical conditions differed from country to country, the speed and extent of development as well as the organizational forms adopted by the monopolies also varied. If industrial production was concentrated to a comparatively high degree—such as in the United States and Germany which imposed protective tariffs—then the development of the monopolies was comparatively rapid, and the degree of monopoly comparatively high. However, if industrial production was concentrated at a comparatively low level—such as in England which had adopted a policy of free trade—then the development of the monopolies was comparatively sluggish, and the degree of monopoly was also comparatively low. The monopoly corporation in the United States mainly took the form of trusts working together in production. The German monopolies, however, predominantly adopted the form of cartels and syndicates unified on the basis of sales.[18] In reality these monopolies were identical, even though the principal organizational form they eventually adopted and their degree of ability to monopolize a market varied from country to country. They were all alliances among the big capitalists established for the purpose of controlling the great majority of production of sales of a certain kind or several kinds of commodities. They used every method to restrict the scale of production, to divide up markets, to control raw materials, and to fix monopoly prices. They exploited the great majority of people in their own country, and plundered the people of the colonies and semi-colonies. Moreover, they swallowed up small and medium sized companies, squeezed out the maximum in monopoly profits, and imposed their rule over the economic life of the entire society. As production and capital became further concentrated, the monopoly corporations in each country gradually developed into conglomerates,[19] forming a small number of large financial groups that controlled the entire national economy. Concentration and monopoly in industrial production stimulated concentration and monopoly in banking. By the early twentieth century, concentration and monopoly in the banking industries in the major capitalist countries had already reached an extremely high level. The role of banks also changed following this development. That is, the banks changed from their past role as the "middle-man" lender of funds to the role of omnipotent monopolists, controlling the monetary capital of the entire country and the operational activities of industry and commerce. In this manner, bank capital and industrial capital, though traversing different roads, eventually formed finance capital. Moreover, there appeared a small handful of financial magnates that not only controlled banking, but also ruled industry. The formation of finance capital and financial magnates and their control over the economic and political life of a country were the basic traits of imperialism. Lenin pointed out that "imperialism or the rule of finance capital is the highest stage of capitalism."[20]

The export of capital was a significant measure whereby imperialist countries carried out foreign expansion, and was an important basis for finance capital to exploit and control the whole world. Exports of capital took place before capitalism entered the stage of monopoly, but only when capitalism reached the stage of monopoly did it achieve a particularly vital significance. The conditions for investment existed when a small number of wealthy capitalist countries held large amounts of "surplus" capital, and when capitalist development had already drawn in the numerous backward countries into the sphere of the capitalist world market. Before the First World War, England and France were the two major capital exporting countries. Although Germany and the United States began their capital exports comparatively late, their expansion—when it did occur—was nevertheless quite rapid. By the early twentieth century, Russia and Japan also exported a small amount of capital. The main reasons why these imperialist countries exported capital to the colonial and semi-colonial countries were to make them become subsidiary sources of agricultural raw materials, and to make them into targets for exploitation and enslavement by finance capital.

Imperialism controlled Old China's financial and economic lifelines by the export of capital. It pulled the strings behind Old China's politics, and turned it into a poor and backward semi-colonial country. Currently, imperialism and social-imperialism vociferously spread the lie that their export of capital is "economic aid for backward countries," but history has already mercilessly unmasked the essence of this kind of "aid" as exploitation and plunder.

As the export of capital increased and as the monopolies expanded their ties abroad, the biggest monopolies intensified their contention for spheres of influence. To prevent competition, and to reduce the losses and damage that they inflicted on themselves, the monopolies frequently changed the form of their conflict, sought temporary compromises, entered into international agreements, formed alliances of international monopolies, and divided up the world on an economic basis according to the capital and power each possessed. However, these alliances and agreements were unstable. As their power relative to each other changed, conflicts would frequently break out among the monopolies of the various countries as each sought a larger share of the market. As a result, the emergence of international monopolies not only could not eliminate conflict among the monopoly capitalists of the various countries, but even caused these struggles to become more acute.

To guarantee success in the fierce international struggle and to squeeze out the maximum monopoly profits, the monopoly capitalists of the various countries always made every effort to seize and occupy even more colonies and spheres of interest. The role of the colony as producer of raw materials for the metropolitan country, as a market for commodities, and as a place for investment became even more important in the era of imperialism. While imperialism was making every effort to plunder the colonies, it was at the same time searching for a solution to alleviate its ever-sharpening domestic, class contradictions. While the imperialist countries were dividing up the world economically, they also launched fierce wars to divide up the world territorially. By the early twentieth century, this global division had been completed. Capitalism had swallowed up the whole world, and had formed a global system of capitalism. This system, however, embraced two antagonistic parts. On the one hand was a small number of imperialist countries that exploited and oppressed the colonies and semi-colonies. Among these, England had become the largest colonial empire—called the empire "on which the sun never sets." On the other hand were the colonies and semi-colonies that made up the great majority of the world's population. They constituted the basis for imperialism's continued existence.

After Lenin made a thorough analysis of the various basic characteristics of imperialism, he pointed out that "imperialism is capitalism in that stage of development in which the dominance of monopolies and finance capital has established itself; in which the export of capital has acquired pronounced importance; in which the division of the world among the international trusts has begun; in which the division of all territories of the globe among the biggest capitalist powers has been completed."[21] Because their specific historical conditions differed, each imperialist country exhibited its own unique characteristics. The United States was the model of a capitalist, imperialist state. Lenin said that "the American trusts are the highest expression . . . of an imperialist economy."[22] Lenin also characterized England as "colonial imperialism"; France as "a money-lending imperialism"; Germany as a "Junker-bourgeois imperialism"[23]; and Japan and Imperial Russia as "military-feudal imperialisms."

The moribund and parasitic nature of imperialism became ever more clearly revealed subsequent to the establishment of monopoly capital rule and following the expansion and intensification of the exploitation and enslavement of the people of the colonies and semi-colonies. Lenin wrote:

> Monopolies, oligarchy, the striving for domination instead of striving for liberty, the exploitation of an increasing number of small or weak nations by a handful of the richest or most powerful nations—all these have given birth to those distinctive characteristics of imperialism which compel us to define it as parasitic or decaying capitalism.[24]

This moribund and parasitic nature was revealed when the monopolies sought to maintain the highest monopoly prices and squeezed out the highest monopoly profits. They frequently limited the scale of production and destroyed "surplus" goods.[25] They failed to use new technologies which they had purchased to make up for losses sustained to their original equipment. This caused a colossal waste of material wealth. The moribund and parasitic nature of capitalism was also evident in the unprecedented increase in the number of idle people who relied exclusively on "clipping interest coupons" to enjoy an indolent life, in the constant growth domestically of workers employed in the service industry, and so on. The export of large quantities of capital and the cruel exploitation of many colonies intensified the phenomenon whereby a small number of the wealthiest and most powerful countries became leeches, sucking the blood of the people of the backward areas. In this period England and France were the most typical models of countries that behaved like leeches.

The moribund and parasitic nature of imperialism was also reflected in the workers' movement. In order to eradicate the struggle of the working class against monopoly capital, the monopoly bourgeoisie used two methods. On the one hand, it strengthened its control over the state apparatus and savagely suppressed the workers' movement. On the other hand, it used a small part of the colossal super-profits, obtained from exploitation of the colonies and dependencies, to bribe the upper stratum of the working class with high wages, to foster a worker aristocracy, and to destroy the workers' movement. The worker aristocracy was the social base for opportunism and revisionism in the workers' movement. England possessed an extremely large number of colonies at a comparatively early date, and moreover monopolized the world market for a long time. As a result, a stratum of worker aristocrats emerged after the middle of the nineteenth century. It was precisely on this social basis that revisionism flourished in the English workers' movement and exerted its deepest influence during the latter half of the nineteenth century. By the end of the nineteenth century and the early twentieth, a worker aristocracy bribed by the monopoly bourgeoisie had emerged in the various imperialist countries. This was the social and economic source of the Bernstein revisionism that appeared in the Second International of that time. Wearing the cloak of Marxism, the old revisionists, represented by Eduard Bernstein and then shortly afterwards by Karl Kautsky, cut the revolutionary soul out of Marxism, tampered with Marxism's theories on the proletarian revolution and the dictatorship of the proletariat, and advertised class cooperation and bourgeois reformism. In the period before the First World War, revisionism further degenerated into social chauvinism. Lenin waged resolute struggles against the revisionism of the Second International, thoroughly exposed its traitorous essence, and ultimately pressured it to its shameful collapse.

Imperialism is the eve of the proletarian social revolution. All the contradictions inherent in the capitalist world sharpened unprecendentedly after it entered the period of imperialism. Imperialism became a "paper tiger": outwardly strong but inwardly weak. Like someone perched on the mouth of a volcano, imperialism confronted grave problems.

The contradiction between the socialization of production and capitalist private ownership intensified within the imperialist countries. Economic crises flourished. The life of the proletariat worsened day by day. Politically, monopoly rule became ever more reactionary. This made domestic class contradictions increasingly acute, and strengthened the proletariat's struggle against monopoly capital.

The imperialist countries' increased exploitation and control of the colonies and semi-colonies intensified the contradiction that existed between the people of these colonies and semi-colonies and imperialism. It stimulated the people of these colonies and semi-colonies into resisting imperialist aggression, control, and enslavement, and aroused them to fight bravely for national liberation. This struggle, especially in Asia, surged forward after 1900. Lenin wrote in 1913 that "the new fountainhead of the vast storms sweeping the world has already gushed forth in Asia."[26] Moreover, he emphatically pointed out: "If the anti-capitalist struggle of the European and American workers does not unite most closely with the millions upon millions of 'colonial' slaves oppressed by capital, then in reality the revolutionary movement in the advanced countries is merely a fraud."[27]

As the unequal development of the capitalist countries intensified and the division of the world's territory was completed, the contradictions among the imperialist countries also sharpened increasingly. These contradictions revealed in a concentrated way that the imperialist powers were engaged in a struggle to redivide the world again, and to contend for world hegemony. Lenin pointed out that "a vital characteristic of imperialism is the struggle for hegemony waged by several great powers."[28] By the end of the nineteenth century and the early twentieth, Germany and England had formed two antagonistic, imperialist military blocs that contended for hegemony in Europe and throughout the world. Their violent contention finally led to the outbreak of the First World War that lasted from 1914 to 1918.

Kautsky, the chieftain of the old revisionism, invented the nonsensical "theory of ultra-imperialism" to cover up the profound contradictions among the imperialists. He maintained that the finance capitalists in the various countries could implement a kind of "ultra-imperialist" policy that not only would replace mutual struggle with international unity, but could realize a permanent, worldwide peace. Lenin strongly repudiated Kautsky's "theory of ultra-imperialism." He was quite accurate when he pointed out that its purpose was to cheat the masses by spreading "the hope that eternal peace could be achieved under the capitalist system" [source unknown]. The outbreak of the First World War thoroughly shattered Kautsky's shameless slander.

The imperialist war was an unprecedented disaster for humanity. Almost ten million people were killed on the battlefield. More than twenty million were wounded. The economies of many countries suffered enormous damage. The war also further intensified the uneven development of the capitalist countries in the postwar period, and caused even deeper contradictions and conflicts to flourish among them. At the same time, the contradiction between the people of the colonies and semi-colonies and imperialism became even more acute. Class contradictions and revolutionary crises also rapidly grew within the capitalist countries. Lenin pointed out:

> The tens of millions of dead and maimed left by the war—to decide whether the British or German group of financial marauders is to receive the most booty—and those two "peace treaties,"[29] are with unprecedented rapidity opening the eyes of the millions and tens of millions of people who are downtrodden, oppressed, deceived and duped by the bourgeoisie. Thus, out of the universal ruin caused by the war a world-wide revolutionary crisis is arising which, however prolonged and arduous its stages may be, cannot end otherwise than in a proletarian revolution and in its victory.[30]

War brought revolution. Four years of the great imperialist war greatly weakened the world capitalist system. It enabled the proletariat to break through the weakest link in the imperialists' line of battle, and to achieve victory in the socialist revolution by overthrowing the rule of the bourgeoisie initially in one country. The October 1917 socialist revolution in Russia achieved success under these conditions. The victory of the October socialist revolution opened up a new era in the history of humanity. It symbolized the fact that the history of humanity was beginning a fundamental turn from the old world of capitalism to the new world of socialism. The road of the October Revolution is the common road for the liberation of mankind.

4

The First World War and the victory of the October socialist revolution in Russia shook the foundations of the world capitalist system. Henceforth, the world capitalist system entered the stage of a general crisis.

The general crisis of capitalism was "comprehensive, embracing both the economic and political spheres"[31] of the world capitalist system. The evolving course of the general crisis of capitalism, dating from the conclusion of the First World War until the outbreak of the Second World War, can be divided into three periods:

The years 1918 to 1923 were the period when the capitalist system suffered a profound shock. During the Great War, the economies of the various European countries suffered serious damage. Germany immediately found itself in a chaotic situation after the conclusion of the war because it had to cede portions of its territory, pay an indemnity, and so on. The United States, England, Japan, and other countries experienced a brief stage of "prosperity" in this early period of transition from a wartime to a peacetime economy. However, the great mass of people lacked many daily necessities because of the war, and they had consumed the small stockpiles that existed. As soon as some industrial facilities and equipment that were urgently needed in the early postwar period were put back into operation, some countries blindly expanded their production capacity. Because this exceeded the narrow scope of the capitalist world market, a world economic crisis broke out in 1920–21. This crisis spread to many capitalist countries. Its destructiveness exceeded that of the repeated crises of the past.

Deeply influenced by the October socialist revolution in Russia, revolutionary movements surged forward in various countries during this period. Uprisings and revolutions broke out one after the other in Japan, Germany, Austria, Hungary, and many other countries. People's liberation struggles arose in Korea, China, Egypt, Syria, Morocco, India, Afghanistan, Iran, and other places. Massive strikes occurred in the United States, Italy, and other countries. The ruling groups of the various imperialist countries used every stratagem to suppress the revolution wherever it occurred. In addition, they launched an armed intervention against Soviet Russia. Only after 1924 did the revolutionary struggles in the various countries subside. However, with the support of the international proletariat, Soviet Russia smashed the imperialist armed intervention and the domestic counter-revolutionary disorders. It broke through the economic blockade of imperialism, consolidated the dictatorship of the proletariat, and even began to revive the national economy. All these events revealed the great vitality of the newborn socialist system.

The years from 1924 to 1929 were a period of relative economic and political stability in the postwar capitalist world. Its main characteristics were as follows: On the one hand, the economies of the various capitalist countries not only recovered, but also attained a certain level of development to the point where some progress was evident. On the other hand, the revolutionary movement became temporarily dormant.

The major factors enabling the capitalist world economy to attain a relative degree of stability were as follows: 1. The capitalist countries invested vast amounts of money to update the fixed capital which had sustained serious wartime damage. 2. Stimulated by intensified competition in domestic and foreign markets, a series of new industrial sectors (such as automobiles, electricity, chemicals, man-made fibers, etc.) made comparatively rapid progress. 3. The various capitalist countries, especially the United States and Germany, vigorously promoted a so-called "rationalization of production." These measures intensified the exploitation of the workers and increased their labor intensity, yet also raised their productivity. 4. In addition to these factors, some countries (like Japan) also artificially stimulated heavy industry (particularly the production of military goods) by either openly or secretly expanding the production of weapons. 5. During this period, the various capitalist countries returned—one by one—to the gold standard. This helped to stabilize their currencies. International trade also topped prewar levels, and expanded to a certain degree.

Nevertheless, capitalist economic development during this period also completely revealed its limitations and instability. This was largely manifest in the following areas: 1. Industrial enterprises often operated below capacity, and a large reserve army of unemployed walked the streets. 2. Sometimes the recovery or development of production was disrupted by partial declines or stagnation. 3. Agriculture fell into a chronic crisis and was unable to resuscitate itself. The relative overproduction of agricultural goods became ever more serious. 4. The problem of the world market became increasingly acute, influenced by the growth of national industry in the colonies and semi-colonies as well as the development of the national liberation movement. The increase in the amount of foreign trade carried out by the capitalist countries lagged far behind the economic growth in these countries themselves. 5. Because of intensified exploitation by monopoly capital, the living standards of the working masses of the various countries remained either the same or even dipped below prewar levels. As a result, a sharp contradiction arose between the narrow capacity of the international and domestic markets and the increasingly blind expansion of production. The elements of a crisis quickly ripened.

Contrary to the conditions in the capitalist countries, the national economy of the Soviet Union displayed the superiority of the socialist system by demonstrating sustained and stable development. During this period, the Soviet Union completed the work of resuscitating its national economy. In 1928, it began to implement the First Five Year Plan for developing the national economy. Socialist industrialization and agricultural collectivization surged forward, and served as a sharp contrast to the capitalist world engulfed in crisis.

The years from 1929 to 1938 were the period when the relative stability of capitalism collapsed and when its economy suffered an unprecedentedly serious crisis. It was also a period when the various contradictions in the capitalist world became extremely acute, and when there was a major resurgence of revolutionary struggles.

The great global economic crisis that began in the United States in October 1929 enveloped the entire capitalist world. This economic crisis arose on the basis of a general crisis of capitalism, and was the deepest, most protracted economic crisis in the history of capitalism. During the crisis (1929–33), industrial production in the various major capitalist countries fell drastically. In the United States and Germany, the economy contracted by more than half, and fell back to the levels achieved in the early twentieth century—or even the end of the nineteenth century! The number of unemployed in the entire capitalist world rose to 35,000,000. The rate of unemployment in some countries reached 30 to 50 percent. The agricultural crisis was also unprecedentedly severe. When large quantities of agricultural goods became "surplus," prices fell dramatically. The agricultural crisis became linked to the industrial crisis, with each harming the other. During the crisis decade, the level of world trade shrank even more than that of industrial production. Between 1931 and 1933, acute credit and monetary crises also broke out sequentially in the various countries of Europe and America. Many banks went bankrupt, and the entire credit system was on the verge of collapse. One by one, countries went off the gold standard and devalued their currencies. Because the metropolitan countries did their utmost to shift the burden of the crisis onto others, the blows suffered by the economies of the colonies and semi-colonies were especially catastrophic during the Depression years. The prices of agricultural products and raw materials exported from the colonies and semi-colonies plummeted, causing an even greater deterioration in the subsistence livelihood of the people of these areas.

The crisis brought unbelievable hardships for the working masses of various countries. Strikes, demonstrations, and farmers' struggles surged up anew. In order to suppress the revolutionary struggles of the people and to maintain the rule of monopoly capital, the financial oligarchs of the various imperialist countries began to cast aside the veil of bourgeois democracy, strengthened their direct control over the machinery of the state, and become even more reactionary politically. The financial oligarchs of Germany, Italy, and Japan set up the most reactionary, openly terrroristic, and fascist dictatorships. In addition, they put their national economies into the orbit of militarization, and intensified their preparations for war. In order to "resolve" the crisis, the other imperialist countries (like the United States, England, and France) also strengthened state "regulation" of the economy and developed a state monopoly capitalism that vainly sought a solution through arms expansion and preparation for war.

After the 1929–33 crisis, the capitalist world economy fell into a special kind of depression. That is, it languished in an economic depression that did not lead to an industrial resurgence. Generally speaking, production in the capitalist countries took a turn for the better only about 1935. However, after 1937, a new economic crisis—arriving with great ferocity—broke out in the United States, France, England, and other countries. The total number of unemployed workers in the capitalist world reached eighteen million in 1938. This crisis ended only because of the full-scale outbreak of the Second World War in 1939.

While the capitalist world economy of the 1930s faced an unprecedentedly acute crisis and depression, the socialist economy of the Soviet Union consistently grew quite rapidly. The Second Five Year Plan was completed in 1937 as envisioned and had successfully achieved socialist industrialization and agricultural collectivization. The strength of the socialist economy grew rapidly. This highlighted even more graphically the decadence of the capitalist system.

The appearance and rapid development of the socialist system after the First World War made a substantial impact on and profoundly shocked the world capitalist system. As the general crisis of capitalism deepened, it also made more acute the class contradictions within the imperialist countries, the contradictions between the people of the colonies and semi-colonies and imperialism, and the contradictions among the imperialist countries.

When we speak of the domestic situation in the imperialist countries, we can see that the further development of the monopolies, the astonishing profits derived from domestic and foreign exploitation, the strengthening of the reactionary rule of the financial oligarchies, and the deteriorating condition of the working class constantly stimulated the working class of various countries to resist monopoly capital. These struggles became particularly violent after the outbreak of the 1929 world economic crisis, and constituted a new revolutionary crisis. However, the revolutionary situation that existed in various countries in the early 1930s was undermined by the opportunists in the workers' movement and the treachery of the right-wing socialist parties. In particular, the working classes of Germany, Japan, and Italy lost all their rights and freedom under the tyranny of fascism, and suffered monopoly capital's unscrupulous oppression and enslavement. However, the revolutionary will of the broad working masses in the various imperialist countries could not be restrained, and it demanded the removal of the rule of monopoly capital. No matter how despicable the suppression imposed by the monopoly bourgeoisie, and no matter how shameless the treachery of the opportunists became, the struggles of the working people did not cease for a moment.

Because the issue of markets became more acute in the period between the two great wars, the various imperialist countries stepped up capital exports and used various methods to increase the economic exploitation and political control they exerted over their own colonies. Moreover, they intensified their penetration of the semi-colonial countries, and manipulated the financial and economic lifelines of these countries. Controlled by the power of foreign capital, agriculture in the colonial and semi-colonial countries continued its one-sided development, that is, their agricultural sector grew only a single product or several products for export. As a result, this intensified the chief characteristic of these countries as subordinate sources of agricultural and raw materials for imperialism. They suffered severe exploitation from imperialism's exchange of unequal values and catastrophic blows when imperialism passed along its crises to them. During this period, national industry in some colonies and semi-colonies (such as India, China, and so on) was one-sided and deformed despite achieving a certain level of development. In addition, national industry was always in turmoil from the interference and attacks of foreign capital. Like two colossal mountains, the cruel exploitation and oppression of feudalism and colonialism weighed heavily on the broad masses of people of the colonies and semi-colonies, and constituted the source of their backwardness and poverty.

On the other hand, a proletariat gradually emerged and matured as foreign capital investment in the colonies and semi-colonies increased and as national industries developed in these areas. Influenced by the October Revolution in Russia and the dissemination of Marxist-Leninist ideology, this proletariat began to form an anti-imperialist, anti-feudal political force that could not be ignored. The demands of the masses of impoverished peasants—squeezed by feudal landlords, usurious merchants, and by foreign capital and its representatives—to resist feudal and colonial oppression and to struggle for liberation became even more urgent. The consciousness of the patriotic national bourgeoisie, petty bourgeoisie, and intellectuals who demanded the removal of imperialist oppression and the achievement of national independence also grew daily. As a result, the contradiction between imperialism and the masses of people in the colonial and semi-colonial countries sharpened unprecendentedly and brought forth a powerful national liberation movement. Led by the great leader Chairman Mao and the Chinese Communist party, the Chinese people fought two lengthy and heroic revolutionary civil wars. Their direct goals were to oppose the oppression and rule of both imperialism and feudalism. The Indian people fought energetically three times between the two world wars for national independence. The national liberation movement made repeated gains in Egypt, North Africa, and Latin America. Despite being suppressed by imperialism and its running dogs, and despite the serious setbacks it suffered because of the betrayals and sellout tactics of the big bourgeoisie, the national democratic revolution in the colonial and semi-colonial countries during this period undoubtedly symbolized the fact that the colonial system of imperialism was already facing a serious crisis.

In the period between the two world wars, the contradictions among the imperialist countries also became more aggravated because of their increasingly uneven economic development. By the end of the 1920s, the United States—which reaped windfall profits during the First World War—had reached a pinnacle in its economic development. In 1929, for example, its economy accounted for half of the industrial production of the capitalist world. In the 1930s, however, America's economic status dramatically weakened under the impact of a profound economic crisis and a unique type of depression. England's economy began to decline after the First World War. It remained basically stagnant during the 1920s, and enjoyed a slight recovery and period of growth only in the latter half of the 1930s. Industry in France grew comparatively rapidly in the 1920s. By the 1930s, however, its economic situation gradually deteriorated under the impact of the economic crisis. In the immediate postwar period, the German economy was extremely chaotic. However, by the end of the 1920s, it had eclipsed France and England, having recovered and developed with the assistance of capital infusions from the United States. Although the German economy in the early 1930s also suffered from the severe blows of the crisis, its military-economic power grew rapidly after the fascists came into power. They energetically militarized the economy and expanded preparations for war. The power of Japan's military sector of the economy also increased noticeably during this same period because the government greatly augmented the size of the armed forces in order to carry out a war of aggression. These kinds of changes in relative strength inevitably led to unprecedented intensification of the contradictions that existed among the imperialist states.

Prior to the middle of the 1930s, the principal contradiction in the imperialist camp was always that between the United States and England. The two countries waged a fierce struggle with each other in contending for world hegemony. At the same time, the contradiction between England and France—both contending for hegemony in Europe—was also acute. In Asia, the United States and England sometimes contended with—and then sometimes colluded with—Japan, a nation that had suddenly emerged as a principal actor after World War I. In order to instigate Germany to become the sharp spearhead of attack against the Soviet Union, American and British imperialism adopted policies that actively fostered German monopoly capital. However, this was a self-defeating policy, like picking up a rock only to drop it on one's own foot. Following the speedy revival of German militarism, and especially after the establishment of the aggressive German-Japanese-Italian fascist axis, the interests of England, France, and the United States became threatened by a unified opponent. As the contradictions between the United States and England and between England and France abated, the contradictions between the two great imperialist groups—England, France, and the United States on the one hand, and Germany, Japan and Italy on the other—rose to become the principal contradiction. The contention for world hegemony among several imperialist powers finally led to the outbreak of the Second World War.

The Second World War was launched by the German and Japanese fascists, with the connivance of American and British imperialism. Japan's launching of an all-out war of aggression against China in July 1937 was the opening stage of this world war. After fascist Germany instigated a war in Europe in September 1939, a world war developed on a full-scale basis. In June 1941, the German fascists treacherously attacked the Soviet Union and spread the flames of conflict even further. Under the leadership of Comrade Joseph Stalin, the Soviet people and the Soviet Army fought well despite the difficulties that faced them, and eventually achieved a great victory in the war against fascism. Led by the great leader Chairman Mao and the Chinese Communist party, the Chinese people persisted in their own war of resistance, endured every sacrifice, and finally compelled the Japanese militarists to accept an unconditional surrender. The people of the various countries of the world also made their own contributions in the war against fascism. The utter defeat of German and Japanese fascism in 1945 created favorable conditions for many European and Asian countries to gain victory in their struggle for a people's democratic revolution. It also had an enormous impact on the development of the national liberation struggles of the people of the colonies and semi-colonies. The general crisis of capitalism became even more profound and sharper.

The Second World War was a profound disaster for the people of various countries. The losses far exceeded those suffered during the First World War. Sixty-seven million people were killed or wounded in the war. The destruction of material wealth totaled approximately 4 trillion U.S. dollars. The war dealt further blows to the imperialist camp. Germany, Japan, and Italy had been devastated in defeat. England and France had suffered serious damage. Only American imperialism drank its fill of fresh blood in the war. Its economic and military strength grew unprecedentedly. As a result, the United States replaced German and Japanese fascism and ascended to the position of ruler of the capitalist world. But the era when imperialism could arbitrarily carve up and enslave the people of the world had already gone, never to return. As soon as the war ended, enormous revolutionary storms arose in Asia, Africa, and Latin America. In 1949, the Chinese people's revolution achieved a great victory. Numerous countries in the Asian, African, and Latin American areas took the path of national independence. The old colonial system of imperialism rapidly disintegrated. The backyard of imperialism now became the front line of the anti-imperialist struggles, whose beacons linked together their common purpose.

2

England

Among the capitalist countries, England has a "brand name" reputation. When we consider the history of the development of world capitalism, we can see that England stands out as the model of primitive capital accumulation as well as pioneer of the Industrial Revolution. For a long time it monopolized world industry and the world market. Historically, the British controlled the world's largest colonial empire, and for more than two hundred years ruthlessly plundered and exploited the broad masses of people of the colonies and semi-colonies. However, it was also the first imperialist country to begin to decline.

1. The Emergence and Development of Capitalist Relations of Production

The Disintegration of the Serf System during the Fourteenth and Fifteenth Centuries: The Sprouts of Capitalist Relations of Production Begin to Emerge

Capitalist relations of production originated and developed in the process of the breakup of the feudal economy. At the end of the fourteenth century, the English system of serfdom had already disintegrated, and by the fifteenth century, capitalist relations of production gradually emerged. Serfdom became the predominant system throughout England after the Normans[1] conquered this country in the early eleventh century. In the twelfth and thirteenth centuries, the woolen textile industry located in Flanders on the European continent began to flourish, and as a result started to import large quantitites of wool from England. This promoted the development of sheep raising in England. The rise of cities as well as the growth of sheep raising destroyed the natural economy of the system of serfdom. The links between the peasants and the market gradually became closer. At the same time, the feudal lords' demand for money also increased. By the thirteenth century, the practice whereby the peasantry paid their rent with money rather than with corvee labor was gradually becoming more prevalent. By paying their rent with money, a segment of the serfs freed themselves from the feudal obligation of performing corvee labor on the manor (the land personally managed by the feudal lord), and as a result, these serfs came to enjoy a comparatively large degree of economic freedom. Consequently, the serf system began to disintegrate gradually in the aftermath of the development of a commodity economy and of money relationships in the villages.

Serf uprisings dealt the most serious blows to the system of serfdom. The widespread Black Death of 1348–49 reduced England's population by one third. Because of the extreme shortage of labor power, some of the feudal lords had to rent out their manorial land to prosperous peasants; or they had to turn the manorial land into pasture land, which not only economized on labor power but also could earn a profit. However, the feudal aristocracy was unwilling to easily discard the serf system. In order to ensure a supply of labor power for its estates, the aristocracy used every stratagem to fasten once again the exploitative system of corvee upon the serfs, and did everything it could to rescue this system from the crisis that it faced. This provoked the widespread serf uprisings that took place throughout England in the latter half of the fourteenth century. Among the largest in scale was the 1381 uprising led by Wat Tyler. The rebels demanded the elimination of serfdom, the abolition of corvee labor as payment for rent, and the abrogation of all feudal obligations. They even went so far as to demand the confiscation of church lands and their distribution to the peasantry. Although the serf uprisings were put down, they nevertheless shook the foundations of feudal rule in a fundamental way. They forced the feudal aristocracy to substitute money for corvee labor as payment for rent, and to gradually abandon the system of serfdom. In this way, "the system of serfdom no longer really existed in England by the end of the fourteenth century."[2]

After abandoning the system of serfdom, the feudal lords still retained monopoly rights over the land. While the serfs still rented the land from the feudal aristocracy, they nevertheless had freed themselves from the obligation of performing corvee labor, had achieved their personal freedom, and had become copyholders[3] paying a fixed amount of money for rent. By the fifteenth century, a broad stratum of yeomen[4], composed mainly of copyholders, was emerging in England's villages. A small peasant economy began to predominate. However, the impact of a commodity economy also created further class differentiation in the villages. For example, as some of the less affluent peasants became poorer and went bankrupt, they became hired hands. On the other hand, a small number rose to become rich peasants. These farmers rented seignorial manors, purchased the land tenancy rights from destitute peasants, employed hired labor, and gradually became the owners of tenant farms. Capitalist relations of production appeared in agriculture in this process.

The handicraft production of woolen goods was rather prevalent in England's villages and cities in the early period when serfdom predominated and when the sheep-raising industry was beginning to develop. By the fourteenth century, the wool-spinning industry had become rather sizable, and exports of woolen textiles grew continuously. Once the system of serfdom disintegrated, the peasantry became increasingly differentiated into various strata. Impoverished peasants desperate to make a living were forced to work in household handicraft production. By the fifteenth century, these types of semi-agricultural, semi-industrial, household handicraftsmen were becoming a common sight throughout England's villages. This opened vast opportunities for the merchants. At first, the household handicraftsmen cooperated with the merchants only in the marketing of their products, yet retained their independence in the production process. However, after the market in woolen fabrics grew larger and larger, the quantity of piece goods purchased from the hands of these small producers could not satisfy the needs of consumers. Merchants now began to provide wool to these household handicraftsmen to process in their local villages. And the merchants paid these people wages. In essence, the household handicraftsmen became hired workers who processed raw materials for the merchants. Subsequently, this "putting out" system (where the merchant-capitalist became a broker responsible for the purchase and marketing of these goods) gradually came to dominate the entire process of wool production—including spinning, weaving, warping, dyeing, and so on. This system now organized the household handicraftsmen (who had previously been scattered in various lines of work), and created instead a dispersed mosaic of handicraft workshops operating under the control of merchant-capitalists.

England's urban handicraft industry during the fifteenth century still remained under the control of the guilds. However, as industry and commerce grew, these guilds underwent a process of internal differentiation. A stratum of prosperous shopkeepers emerged who exercised leadership in the guilds and who kept the poorer shopkeepers under control. At the same time, it became increasingly more difficult for shop assistants to rise and become shopowners. Such assistants and apprentices gradually became the hired workers of the shopowners. As the various strata within the guilds became more highly differentiated, merchants and money-lending capitalists also intervened. They tried to control not only the poorer handicraftsmen, but also brought handicraftsmen from the villages into the cities to establish handicraft workshops there. As a result, capitalist employment relationships also gradually appeared in the urban areas.

Primitive Capital Accumulation and the Development of a Workshop Handicraft Industry in the Sixteenth and Seventeenth Centuries

The sixteenth and seventeenth centuries marked the period when England rapidly turned from feudalism to capitalism. It was a period characterized by the large-scale expropriation of land from the peasants, by overseas colonial expansion, and by primitive capital accumulation. It was a period when a capitalist handicraft workshop industry made great progress.

The expropriation of peasant land was the foundation for the entire process of primitive accumulation. In English history, peasant land was seized through a process called the enclosure movement. This enclosure of land began as early as the thirteenth and fourteenth centuries, and was linked to an expanding sheep-raising industry. During this process, a segment of the aristocracy forcibly appropriated the peasants' common lands, such as pastures, woods, wastelands, ponds, and so forth. Then they used palisades, fences, ditches, and other means to "enclose" the land, thereby transforming it into privately owned property. By the fifteenth century, and especially by the end of the 1400s, this type of land enclosure process had become quite common. It occurred in the aftermath of the growth of wool exports and the development of the woolen industry. After the great geographical discoveries, the world market suddenly expanded, and the woolen industries of Flanders and England grew vigorously. The price of wool shot up. Raising sheep had now become a particularly lucrative enterprise. At the same time, the flow of large quantities of inexpensive gold and silver from America into Europe stimulated a universal rise in prices that created the so-called "price revolution" of the sixteenth century. This caused a decline in the real income of the aristocracy, whose cash flow came from fixed money rents levied and collected according to custom. As a result, the aristocracy now initiated a large-scale movement to enclose land, and paid no attention to any resistance from the peasantry that they encountered in the process. At first the aristocracy enclosed and occupied the public lands that the peasants, and especially the cotters,[5] had depended upon for their livelihood. Next, they gradually destroyed the traditional regulations pertaining to land arrangements, and—using various pretexts—either seized the land of the copyholders or took it back from the other small tenant householders. They demolished the homes of these people, and turned their small plots of land into either large pastures or farmlands. Then the aristocracy either began to manage these farms by themselves or rented them out to tenants at a high price. As a result, many villages were wiped out. Many peasants, now bereft of land and housing, were left destitute and homeless. Wandering from place to place, they became beggars and vagabonds, and exemplified the so-called phenomenon of "men being eaten by sheep" that has been written about in English history.

Peasants living on the monastic domains of the church could not avoid this process of violent expropriation either. The Catholic church was a large feudal landowner in England, and owned one-third of the land of the entire realm. However, in the 1530s, the Tudor monarchy carried out religious reforms. It closed down thousands of Catholic monasteries and confiscated their lands. The Tudor monarchs did this in order to increase the income of the ruling house and to satisfy the demand for land of the new aristocrats and bourgeoisie. Ostensibly this was done to free England from its dependency on the Catholic Pope. The monarch granted a portion of these lands to favored ministers and trusted relatives. The other portion was sold at extremely low prices to members of the gentry and to land speculators, merchants, and entrepreneurs. These new landowners became a new aristocracy. First they evicted the tenant farmers who, for generation after generation, had originally lived on these parcels. Then they turned around and rented these very same properties to other tenants, but at higher prices. This process once again created a large number of destitute vagabonds.

The enclosure movement that forcibly separated peasants from their land 1. promoted the development of capitalist relations of production in the villages, 2. expanded the stratum of a newly bourgeoisified aristocracy, and 3. created a group of wealthy capitalist farm managers from people who had previously been prosperous peasants, merchants, and entrepreneurs. Sheep raising and agricultural production both recorded dramatic growth. However, the enclosure movement at the same time created a large number of jobless vagabonds. Pressured by a hostile environment, these vagabonds wandered about everywhere. Entire groups of people now became beggars and thieves, continuously fomenting disturbances and threatening the rule of the Tudor monarchy. As a result, the monarchy promulgated and enforced a series of "bloody laws" that embodied a dual purpose. On the one hand, these laws would assist the bourgeoisie in "subduing" these vagrants, and on the other hand, they would also force these people into becoming hired laborers on the capitalist farms and in the handicraft workshops. A law enacted in 1530 stipulated that only those persons who were either elderly or handicapped would be permitted to beg. These individuals would be issued a special permit that would enable them to beg for food. However, "sturdy vagabonds" were to be flogged and imprisoned. A law passed in 1536 stipulated that able-bodied vagabonds—immediately after their arrest—had to be paraded on the streets of the nearest city and flogged until blood was drawn. If they were caught a second time, half an ear was to be cut off in addition to the flogging. If caught a third time, the death penalty would be imposed. A 1547 law added the further stipulation that, if a person who refused to work was accused of being an idler, he would be sentenced to serve as a slave for the accuser. Slaves that had run away for a full fourteen days would be sentenced to serve as slaves for their entire lifetime, and the letter "S" would be branded on their forehead or face. If they ran away three times, they would be condemned to death. The bourgeoisie utilized these sanguinary laws enacted by the autocratic monarchy to transform the expropriated peasants into a huge army of hired laborers and to force these people to yield to the labor regulations and ruthless exploitation of capitalism.

Marx wrote:

> The spoilation of the Church's property, the fraudulent alienation of the state domains, the robbery of the common lands, the usurpation of feudal and clan[6] property, and its transformation into modern private property under circum-

> stances of reckless terrorism, were just so many idyllic methods of primitive accumulation. They conquered the field for capitalist agriculture, made the soil part and parcel of capital, and created for the town industries the necessary supply of a "free" and outlawed proletariat.[7]

If it can be said that the enclosure movement prepared a large number of hired workers and a domestic market for the development of English capitalism, then the plunder of foreign countries and colonial expansionism provided the development of English capitalism with colossal financial wealth and a foreign market. The major geographical discoveries and the change in the world's trade routes gave England an advantageous position with regard to overseas connections. In the sixteenth century, the mercantilist policy promoted by the Tudor monarchy provided an even greater incentive for merchants and aristocrats to invest in overseas commercial activity and enterprises involved in the plunder of colonies. England's foreign trade grew enormously because only British ships transported the products of all three continents of Europe, Africa, and America in the sixteenth century. Woolen textiles consistently ranked first among London's exports. At that time, the British boasted that at least half of Europe wore English clothing. Foreign trade brought England an enormous income. However, the ability of the English to ship products to the various countries of Asia was still quite limited because doing business there caused outflows of large quantities of gold and silver. This ran contrary to the bourgeoisie's desire to accumulate money.

Their boundless greed for gold and silver led English merchants and adventurers to become involved in piracy and plunder. In fact, in the sixteenth and early seventeenth centuries, the maritime trade of the various European countries largely resembled piracy. England at that time was called "a nation of pirates." The British robbed the Portuguese ships loaded with spices from the East, and looted the "Spanish white silver armadas" loaded with gold and silver from the Americas. These piratical actions were all looked upon as lawful activities; companies that engaged in this activity were chartered by the crown. Piracy enjoyed the active support of the English monarchs.

England's overseas trade and piracy were closely connected to its colonial expansion. After the discovery of new maritime routes and new continents, Portugal came to control East India, and Spain came to control the West Indies. Initially, England could use only trade and piracy to strike at Portugal and Spain economically. However, after the middle of the sixteenth century, as its economic and naval strength grew more and more formidable, England began to carry on an open war with both Portugal and Spain for the control of colonies. In 1588, the English government, with the powerful support of London's merchant community, routed Spain's "Invincible Armada," thereby eliminating the biggest obstacle to its maritime activities. England subsequently entered a stage characterized by its seizure of colonial territories. The East India Company that plundered India and monopolized trade with the Far East was established in 1600. It set up commercial outlets in Madras in 1620 and Calcutta in 1635, and established a beachhead for aggression against India. At the end of the sixteenth and the beginning of the seventeenth centuries, once London established its first group of colonies there, England's colonial power extended into North America and the West Indies. In addition, England carried out ruthless acts of aggression against neighboring Ireland when it seized vast areas of land from the Irish peasants. All of these activities not only brought enormous wealth to the English aristocracy and bourgeoisie, but also provided an immense amount of capital that enabled the domestic workshop handicraft industry to make great progress.

Up until the end of the fifteenth century, the English handicraft industry was comparatively backward. Wool produced in England mainly supplied the wool-spinning industry of Flanders. Woolen textiles that were intended for export were also mainly half-finished goods, and the final processing (the cutting and dyeing of the cloth) had to be carried out in Flanders. However, after the beginning of the sixteenth century, all the factors involved in primitive accumulation that have been mentioned above enabled England's workshop handicraft industry, and especially its wool-spinning industry, to achieve substantial progress. By the middle of the sixteenth century, the export of woolen textiles reached 120 thousand bolts, and by the first half of the seventeenth century, it had increased to an annual level of twenty-five thousand bolts. Wool-spinning became "an industry of all the people," common both in town and countryside. Not only did the scale of its production expand, but great progress was also made in its technological aspects.

Prior to the sixteenth century, England's wool-spinning industry was predominantly a semi-industrial, semi-agricultural household handicraft industry prevalent in the villages. A dispersed, capitalistic workshop handicraft industry emerged from those workshops which had fallen under the control of merchant-capitalists. After the sixteenth century—after many farmers had been dispossessed of their lands—these merchant-capitalists further extended their control over the household handicraftsmen living in the villages. The merchant-capitalist now supplied to the handicraftsmen not only their raw materials (such as wool), but also their tools (such as looms). In this process, the household handicraftsman became thoroughly subordinate to the merchant-capitalist, and became a hired laborer lacking any property. However, merchant-capitalists operating under this dispersed form of production also constantly faced the problem of getting the raw materials and tools into the hands of some hundred household handicraftsmen scattered over an area several tens of miles. At the same time, there was no way to supervise production. Raw materials and tools were easily damaged. The quality of the products was difficult to guarantee. The production of woolen textiles sometimes stopped during the agricultural busy season. For all these reasons, such a system could not satisfy the ever-increasing needs of the market. Therefore, centralized handicraft workshops established by these merchant-capitalists gradually emerged and developed after the middle of the sixteenth century—precisely at a time when there was an increase in the number of peasants who had lost their land. By the seventeenth century, handicraft workshops employing several hundreds of people were already quite common.

During the sixteenth century and up to the middle of the seventeenth, capitalist handicraft workshops also developed in industrial sectors such as mining, metallurgy, metal-working, salt, glass, paper, saltpeter, and beer. Many large-scale factories employing upwards of several hundred workers emerged in these industries. As handicraft workshops developed, the guild system gradually disintegrated. The guilds within many trades became the tools not only of the owners of the handicraft workshops who sought to control the handicraft workers, but also of the big merchants who sought to control the small handicraftsmen.

The Bourgeois Revolution of 1640–88

Important changes occurred in the class structure of English society as a result of the development of capitalist relations of production after the sixteenth century. A new exploitative group—a new aristocracy and a bourgeoisie—grew more powerful day by day. The new aristocracy was a bourgeoisified aristocracy, and originated largely from the middle and small aristocracy. However, during the sixteenth and seventeenth centuries, there were also quite a few well-to-do farmers and wealthy urban merchants who purchased land and entered the ranks of the new aristocracy. Some even received knighthoods conferred by the crown. After they enclosed the land of the peasants and made it into pasture land or farms, they either put into effect capitalist management practices, or leased that land to tenant farmers, and pocketed a capitalist land rent in the process. They also worked concurrently as both workshop owners and as merchants. Because of this, their economic interests were basically identical to those of the bourgeoisie. At the same time, they demanded relief from both the disadvantageous as well as advantageous feudal obligations they owed the king. However, the Stuart monarchy (which began its reign in the early seventeenth century) pursued domestic policies that increased the rent on land, established a monopoly on the sale of everyday consumer goods, and even went as far as to sell government positions and titles of nobility. The Stuarts wanted to strengthen their autocratic power to cope with their increasing expenditures. In foreign policy, the Stuarts compromised and arranged a marriage alliance with the autocratic ruling house of Spain. However, Spain at that time was England's principal competitor in foreign trade. Stuart policies brought strong disapproval from the bourgeoisie and the new aristocracy. In its ranks the bourgeoisie included prosperous merchants, financiers, merchant-capitalists, workshop owners, ship captains, and owners of large estates who rented out parcels of their land to others. Except for the wealthiest merchants who took the side of the monarchy (and who did so because they had received royal charters granting them monopolies on the sale of everyday commodities), the bourgeoisie in general demanded the abolition of the system of feudal autocracy, the establishment of a system of bourgeois democracy, and guarantees for the free development of industry and commerce. As a result, the various policies of the Stuarts to strengthen the system of absolute monarchy engendered a sharp contradiction with the interests of the bourgeoisie, a class whose economic strength was growing day by day. However, the bourgeoisie was neither politically nor economically as strong as the new aristocracy, and therefore allied itself with the new aristocracy in its struggle against the feudal dynasty.

The peasantry still constituted the largest segment of England's population prior to its bourgeois revolution, and the yeomen constituted the most extensive stratum within the peasantry. The enclosure movement had a direct, adverse impact on the yeomen, forcing them in large numbers to leave their land to become hired peasants or even beggars. They strongly opposed both the enclosure of land as well as feudal exploitation, and demanded guarantees for the right of land ownership. However, the cotters and hired peasants made further demands. They asked for the return of the common lands that had been previously enclosed and for some redistribution of additional land. For more than a hundred years, that is, from the first half of the sixteenth century until just prior to the English Revolution, peasants from different strata launched a series of uprisings in order to fight for the realization of these demands. These revolts dealt heavy blows to the feudal system and the enclosure movement. Afterwards, the yeomen became the main force in the bourgeois revolution. Engels wrote: "The initiators [of this revolution] were the urban middle class, but those who completed it were the self-supporting peasants who came from the villages."[8]

As capitalism developed, many small handicraftsmen and small merchants went bankrupt. They would then become workers in handicraft workshops, or serve as sailors, freight handlers, dock workers, or even turn into vagabonds. They faced great poverty, and usually spent between fourteen and sixteen hours daily at their jobs. As a result, the impoverished lowest stratum of urban residents constantly fought against such oppressive conditions, and sometimes their anger exploded into large-scale uprisings.

While the Stuarts did everything they could to protect the Catholics, they discriminated against the followers of Protestantism, a religion tinged with democratic aspects. This policy also aroused the dissatisfaction from people of various social strata.

All these constantly growing revolutionary forces mentioned above finally merged into a powerful, anti-feudal revolutionary torrent in 1640. A bourgeois revolution broke out, with the new aristocracy and bourgeoisie providing the leadership, and with the peasants and urban poor serving as the main army. However, the reactionary ruling class did not readily agree to end this stage of history. As a result, the English Revolution experienced a restoration and then a counter-restoration. Only after two major civil wars that took place from 1642 to 1646 and 1646 to 1648 was the feudal dynasty overthrown and King Charles I sent to the chopping block. Between 1649 and 1657, England became a Republic with neither king nor House of Lords. Beginning in 1653, Cromwell, representing the interests of the new aristocracy and bourgeoisie, imposed a dictatorship. In 1660, the feudal dynasty was restored. In 1688, the political party of the bourgeoisie carried out a coup d'état, the so-called "Glorious Revolution" of English history. Only this action enabled the results of the bourgeois revolution to be consolidated and a constitutional monarchy to be established under the joint rule of the bourgeoisie and new aristocracy.

The victory of England's bourgeois revolution marked the beginning stage of modern world history. It abolished the autocratic feudal system in England, established the rule of the bourgeoisie, and proclaimed the birth of a new social and political system. During the revolution, Parliament enacted legislation terminating the feudal obligations that the landed aristocracy owed to the king. It confiscated—and then later sold—the lands that belonged to the king, the Royalists, and the church. It transformed the system of landownership into a modern, capitalist system of private ownership from one that had previously been feudal in character. As a result, it destroyed the basis of the autocratic feudal system and swept away the obstacles hindering the further development of the capitalist mode of production. Nevertheless, England's bourgeois revolution was very conservative in nature. After the revolution, the political system formally retained backward elements of the monarchical system. A bourgeois republic was not set up. Economically there was no resolution of the land question faced by the farmers. On the contrary, a system of landownership dominated by wealthy landlords was consolidated and expanded, and the peasants' obligations to the landlords remained intact. The great majority of the land confiscated from the king, the Royalists, and the church fell into the hands of the bourgeoisie and the new aristocracy.

Capitalist Relations of Production Develop Further after the Bourgeois Revolution

After the victory of the English Revolution, the bourgeoisie and new aristocracy used the political power they had gained to open the road to the further development of a capitalist economy. Initially they accelerated their plunder of the peasants. Because of the rapid development of industry and commerce after the revolution, the urban areas' need for food increased sharply, and the price of wheat constantly rose. This set off an even more massive enclosure movement than had occurred before. Prior to the revolution, enclosures were regarded as violent actions perpetrated by individuals. However, beginning in the eighteenth century, enclosures became a "lawful" activity sanctioned by Parliamentary statutes. Nevertheless, violence and fraud still remained the particular features of this kind of "legal" enclosure of land. Large numbers of peasants lost access not only to the common lands, but also to their own strips of land on which they depended for their very existence. A large portion of these enclosed lands became concentrated in the hands of the wealthy landlords. These wealthy landlords then rented their properties to others to manage and operate. Marx wrote that

> in the last decades of the seventeenth century (in England), the yeomen (the independent farmers) still outnumbered those who rented their land. . . . Even the agricultural laborers still had access to the commons. About 1750, the yeomen disappeared. And by the last deacades of the eighteenth century, the final vestiges of the commonlands had also vanished.[9]

Of those peasants who had been robbed of their land, some died of hunger and poverty, some emigrated to England's colonies, some became small tenant farmers working without a fixed lease, and some became farm laborers hired by the managers of the large estates. However, the largest segment of these dispossessed peasants flooded into the cities to become either hired workers or serve as members of a reserve army for industrial production. As the urban population rapidly increased, agricultural production also grew. The favorable conditions created by the management of large estates also brought significant progress to agricultural technology. Farming became more efficient, the area under cultivation expanded, and the new "alternate" or "Norfolk" system of crop rotation replaced the old system of permitting the land to lie fallow every other year.[10] Improvements in agricultural technology and increased yields enabled the large capitalist farms to flourish, while at the same time these gains undermined the competitive possibilities of the small landowners and tenant farmers.

Once it had attained political power, England's bourgeoisie not only completed a bloody conquest of Ireland, but also adopted a series of policies promoting mercantilism and foreign expansion. Aiming to achieve hegemony over the oceans and to carve out new colonial possessions for itself, the British initiated a series of violent wars against other countries, beginning initially with Portugal and proceeding sequentially against Spain, Holland, and France.

In 1650, England launched a war against Portugal, a country already on the decline. In the aftermath of the war, the British obtained the right to trade with Portugal's colonies and to enjoy a schedule of preferential tariffs with them. In 1655, the British sent an expeditionary force to occupy Jamaica—Spain's colony in the West Indies—and to develop a plantation system based on slavery there. During the period 1650–63, the English government passed a series of maritime ordinances the purpose of which was to weaken Holland's trading position, to strike a blow at Dutch maritime strength, and to capture the colonial market for itself. The legislation included such stipulations as foreign merchants could not trade with Britain's colonies without receiving permission from the English government; commodities exported to England from its colonies could be transported only by English ships; commodities exported to England's colonies from foreign countries first had to be shipped to England to pay taxes, and only then would be permitted to be marketed in the colonies; and commodities exported to

Europe from the colonies also had to be trans-shipped through England to be allowed to be sold on the European market. England's struggle against Holland escalated from economic skirmishing to armed conflict. Only after waging three wars in the period between 1652 and 1674 could England force Holland to recognize its maritime ordinances, and only after these wars could it snatch from Holland's hands the colony of New Netherlands in North America. Subsequently, the British also squeezed Dutch influence out of India.

By the end of the seventeenth century, England began to contend with France for hegemony over colonies in India, North America, and the West Indies. England also developed sharp conflicts with France in competing for the monopoly rights to hunt and kidnap African blacks and to loot West Africa of its gold. Finally, the Seven Years' War (1757–63) broke out between the two countries. England relied on its superior naval strength and advanced industry and commerce to emerge victorious in the war. It seized from France a) all of Canada and its adjacent areas, b) the Lesser Antilles in the West Indies, and c) a part of Senegal in Africa. French influence in India was also pushed aside; France retained only five isolated cities there. Victory in the Seven Years' War had great significance for England's takeover of India. Marx pointed out that "the events of the Seven Years' War transformed the East India Company from a commercial into a military and territorial power. It was then that the foundation was laid of the present British Empire in the East."[11]

After conquering India by military means, the East India Company proceeded to openly carry out a policy of violent plunder. It looted the palace and national treasury, leaving nothing behind. It levied exorbitant land taxes, extorted tribute from India's ruling zamindar class, and held a monopoly over the sale of salt and opium. In short, it turned India into an important source of England's primitive capital accumulation. For example, the East India Company extorted from this country the equivalent of almost one billion English pounds in the years from 1757 to 1815. India became a poor, backward, and famine-stricken country after suffering from the ruthless plunder and bloody rule of the East India Company. One million people, or approximately one-third of the total population of Bengal, died in a single famine there in 1770. By 1789, even England's viceroy in India was forced to confess that "a third of the land owned by this company in India today is already a vast expanse of wasteland where only wild animals survive."

Beginning in the middle of the seventeenth century, English merchants and aristocrats began to make staggering—though bloodstained—profits from the slave trade. First they shipped black people who had been kidnapped in Africa to the Americas. There they sold them to slave owners to work the gold and silver mines and run the plantations. By the middle of the eighteenth century, England was the most extensively involved of any country in this evil commerce in slaves. For example, England's slave traders used almost 190 ships to transport 47,000 slaves in 1771 alone. Between 1686 and 1780, England shipped a total of

2,300,000 black African slaves to the Americas. And it ruthlessly exterminated several times this number of Africans in the process of kidnapping and transporting them. Liverpool was the center of the slave trade at that time, and its prosperity came from imbibing the fresh blood of the black people.

Trade wars with other countries, the looting of colonies, and the slave trade brought a continous flow of vast amounts of blood-stained foreign wealth into England. Marx pointed out:

> The colonial system ripened, like a hot-house, trade and navigation. . . . The colonies secured a market for the budding manufactures, and, through the monopoly of the market, assured increased accumulation. The treasures captured outside Europe by undisguised looting, enslavement, and murder floated back to the mother-country and were there turned into capital.[12]

In order to wage the wars that would enable it to compete for colonies with other foreign powers, the bourgeois government—in its domestic program—constantly increased taxes and floated bond issues. Statistics indicate that half of the income of the English working people in the 1730s was skimmed off by the government in the form of taxes on consumption. The government then channeled this money into the purses of the bourgeoisie, in the form of interest payments on the public debt. Established in 1694, the Bank of England played an important role in issuing government bonds, and was the government's major creditor. Increased bond issues not only enabled the financial bourgeoisie to receive huge interest payments each year, but also enabled them to reap windfall profits by speculative buying and selling of the bonds themselves. This also represented one of the important ways in which the bourgeoisie used state power to carry out primitive capital accumulation.

The workshop handicraft industry made even further progress after the bourgeois revolution and subsequent to the intensification of primitive accumulation. During this period, the woolen industry still retained its central place in English industry, and even throughout the entire national economy. During the seventeenth and eighteenth centuries, at least one of every five persons in England depended on the woolen industry for his or her livelihood. Woolen knitwear made up approximately one-third of England's total exports. At the same time, centralized, large-scale capitalist handicraft workshops increased in number. In 1736, a large woolen fabric mill would use a total of six hundred looms. In the eighteenth century, Great Britain—a country that once had exported wool in large quantities—had come to believe that its own supply of wool was now insufficient, and had to be supplemented by foreign imports.

Workshop handicrafts also made further progress in industries such as metallurgy, metalworking, salt extraction, beer brewing, silk weaving, and cotton weaving. Production technologies improved substantially. By the middle of the eighteenth century, the metalworking industry used more than five hundred different kinds of hammers. The division of labor within the handicraft workshop had also become much more sophisticated. For example, weaving work was divided up into eighteen different operations. A more advanced division of labor within the workshop not only brought about a large increase in the productivity of labor, but also simultaneously created the necessary technological conditions for the appearance of large-scale machine industry.

As its colonies grew constantly, England's foreign trade increased sevenfold during the entire eighteenth century. London became the center of world trade.

2. The Industrial Revolution: England Becomes "The Workshop of the World" and the World's Largest Colonial Empire

The Historical Preconditions and Course of Development of the Industrial Revolution

In the 1760s, the various major industrial sectors in England began, one after the other, to shift from handicraft production to machine production. The developing English system of capitalism entered the period of the Industrial Revolution.

England's society and economy experienced profound changes in the hundred years spanning the time from the victory of the bourgeois revolution to the middle of the eighteenth century. The establishment of bourgeois political power created favorable political conditions for the rapid development of a capitalist economy. The acceleration of the enclosure movement accomplished a thoroughgoing expropriation of the peasantry, and provided all the labor power as well as a domestic market for the development of a large-scale, capitalist industry. Defeating Portugal, Spain, Holland, and France one by one eliminated foreign competitors and secured England's position as maritime hegemon and center of world trade. The violent and fraudulent methods employed in its large-scale plunder of colonies and participation in the slave trade accumulated the money-capital necessary for the development of a large-scale, capitalist industry. The colossal progress made by the workshop handicraft industry prepared the necessary material and technological basis for the transition to large-scale, machine production. All of these factors were the historical preconditions that enabled England to be the first to experience an Industrial Revolution. As domestic and foreign markets expanded, production in the handicraft workshops could satisfy neither the ever-increasing needs of the market nor the bourgeoisie's greed in its search for profits. The handicraft workshop was a capitalistic enterprise that was based on handicraft labor. It could neither carry out large-scale production nor entirely force out the small producers from the basic sectors. These conditions instigated the bourgeoisie to seek a transformation in production and technology, and to replace handicraft production with machine production.

At this time, England's cotton textile industry was the industry most in need of technological innovation. It differed from the venerable woolen knitwear industry (which had monopolized the world market for a long time) because cotton textiles had become a new and developing industry in England only at the end of the seventeenth century. The cotton textile industry was regarded as the most dangerous competitor domestically by the woolen knitwear industry. As a result, cotton textiles had been subject to various kinds of restrictions and attacks while simultaneously having to face strong competition from high-quality, cotton textiles imported from India. On the other hand, it was also easier to carry out technological innovations in Britain's cotton textiles because it was a younger industry and therefore not hampered by old traditions. In 1733, a Lancaster watchmaker named John Kay invented the flying shuttle, and thereby doubled productivity in cloth weaving. Yarn became scarce for a long time as the utilization of the flying shuttle created a serious imbalance between spinning and weaving. Only in 1765, when James Hargreaves, a weaver and carpenter, invented the spinning Jenny[13]—a hand-operated spinning wheel that could move sixteen to eighteen spindles simultaneously—was this contradiction basically resolved. The spinning Jenny was a typical example of how a handicraft tool was turned into a machine. Engels pointed out that "the spinning Jenny reduced the cost of producing cotton yarn, thereby expanding its market and giving this industry its initial impetus."[14]

In 1769, Richard Arkwright, a barber, built a water-powered spinning machine, after stealing the idea from Louis Paul and David Bourn. Using this invention substantially reduced the cost of yarn, and also began to force out of business many individual spinners. Not only were water-powered machines extremely large, but they also had to be set up in specific locations with easy access to water power. The construction of factory buildings that centralized production established the foundation of the factory system. In 1771, Arkwright opened the first cotton yarn factory. Working between 1774 and 1779, Samuel Crompton (who had worked previously as a child laborer) combined the best features of the spinning Jenny with the water-powered machine. He made a machine called "the mule" (implying that it was a composite machine) that could spin delicate but durable yarn. After being improved by others, "the mule" eventually became an automatic yarn spinning machine that used water power to propel and operate between three hundred and four hundred spindles. As a result, the spinning of yarn was no longer carried out in a scattered fashion throughout family homes in various villages, but rather was done in rapidly expanding factories, centralizing its production.

The invention and improvement of the cotton spinning machine stimulated innovations in cloth weaving. Aided by carpenters and metal smiths, Edmund Cartwright, a parson, invented a water-powered loom in 1785. After others improved it, this machine could weave as many bolts of cloth as forty handicraft workers. Although the first factory that used Cartwright's loom was built in 1791, the machine came into common use only in the early nineteenth century after undergoing numerous improvements.

Because water power propelled the machines, the location of factories remained restricted by geographical conditions. However, in 1769, James Watt (who made teaching devices at Glasgow University) invented a single-stroke steam engine. This invention was based on the research he had performed on a steam-driven water pump that was originally built by Thomas Newcomen in the early eighteenth century. In 1782, Watt also built a reciprocating steam engine. By 1785, cotton spinning factories were beginning to use steam engines as their source of power. The steam engine was also used later in the cotton weaving factories. As the use of steam engines expanded, the factory system rapidly took root. Engels pointed this out:

> Division of labor, water power (and expecially the use of steam power), and the utilization of machines constituted the three great levers used by industry since the middle of the eighteenth century to rock the foundations of the old world.[15]

As cotton spinning and weaving became mechanized, and as steam engines were employed in the production process, other machines that cleaned, combed, bleached, and dyed cotton began to appear—one by one—in this industry. They constituted a network of machines, each with a specific task in a complex division of labor. The size of the factories constantly expanded, and the cotton spinning and weaving industry developed rapidly. In 1780, English cotton consumption was valued at only 5.5 million pounds sterling. By 1835, the figure reached 318 million pounds sterling. In that same year, the spinning and weaving mills counted nine million spindles and 110,000 looms, and included a work force reaching 237,000 people. By the end of the 1830s, the spinning and weaving of cotton by machinery had basically replaced that done by the handicraft system.

Stimulated and prodded by the cotton spinning and weaving industries, wool spinning, hemp spinning, silk spinning, and other light industries (such as papermaking, printing, and so on) slowly began their own transition from workshop handicraft industries to large-scale, machine-dominated industries. The invention and widespread use of machines in light industry also promoted technological innovations in heavy industry and transportation.

Iron smelting was one of England's most prized industries. Prior to the middle of the eighteenth century, charcoal was the fuel used to smelt iron. However, because the forests had virtually all been chopped down, and because pig-iron production fell to quite low levels, large quantities of charcoal had to be imported from Sweden, Germany, Russia, and other lands. In the early eighteenth century, Abraham Darby and his son (devoting two generations of their time to this work) conducted many experiments that sought to improve the smelting process. In 1735, they finally discovered a comparatively superior method that used coke mixed with unslaked lime to smelt iron ore. By the 1860s, the introduction of powerful blast equipment made the use of charcoal in the smelting of iron a far more economical technique, and therfore it came to be widely adopted. The first use of a steam-powered blast furnace in 1790 once again greatly decreased the consumption of fuel. Working on the basis of predecessors' efforts, and only after conducting repeated experiments himself, Henry Cort (an engineer) developed a "puddling and rolling" technique in 1783 and 1784. This procedure removed impurities and carbon from pig iron, and ultimately pig iron could be refined to produce wrought iron. This greatly increased the efficiency of forging iron. Although these technological innovations in the field of metallurgy appeared almost at the same time as the inventions of the spinning and weaving machines and the steam engine, it was only the widespread utilization of the latter inventions that promoted the universal dissemination of the new technologies in metallurgy as well as the rapid development of iron smelting. In 1740, England produced only 17,000 tons of iron. However, by the end of the eighteenth century, England had rapidly become a net exporter of pig iron rather than an importer. By 1835, pig iron production reached 1.02 million tons.

The widespread use of the steam engine and the development of the iron smelting industry also stimulated technological innovations in coal mining. By the beginning of the nineteenth century, steam-powered water pumps were already commonly used in mines. In addition, new technologies—such as steam-powered well-drilling machines, safety lamps, towing machines that replaced human porters, and so forth—appeared one after the other and were put into use. By 1835, coal production had rapidly increased to thirty million tons. England had become Europe's number one coal-producer.

In the early period of the Industrial Revolution, machines were not only made by hand, but the great majority of them were even made of wood. The use of steam-powered hammers and simple lathes to make metal parts began only at the end of the eighteenth century. Various kinds of forging presses and metal processing lathes were invented one after the other in the early nineteenth century, and machines gradually came to be used to make machines. By the 1830s, the machine manufacturing industry had become rather large in scale, and even exported large numbers overseas. A canal digging boom took place after the 1760s to meet the ever-increasing demand for the transportation of commodities, especially coal. By 1830, a nationwide water transportation network had been built. In 1807, Robert Fulton, an American, built the first steamship. After the British successfully manufactured a copy in 1811, England began widespread use of steamships for inland and coastal service. The successful crossing of the Atlantic Ocean in 1838 by the English steamships Sirius and Great Western catapulted England's oceanic shipping industry into a new era. In 1814, George Stephenson, the son of a miner, invented the locomotive. When England built the first railway from Stockton to Darlington in 1825, land transportation entered the railroad era. By 1840, a large part of England's major railroad network had already been constructed.

England's Industrial Revolution spanned a period of seventy to eighty years, beginning in the 1760s and reaching its basic completion by the end of the 1830s. The completion of the Industrial Revolution symbolized the fact that England was the first country to change from a predominantly workshop handicraft industry to one where a large-scale, machine industry was dominant. It also symbolized the fact that the capitalist system had achieved a complete victory in England.

England Becomes "The Workshop of the World"

The Industrial Revolution brought profound changes to England's society, politics, and economy. First of all, the social forces of production developed at an astounding rate, exemplified by the fact that large-scale, machine industry now enjoyed an absolute superiority in the production process. England established powerful textile, metal-working, coal, and machine-manufacturing industries to become the most advanced capitalist, industrial country in the world. Large-scale machine production increased labor productivity to an unprecedented degree. Between 1770 and 1840, the productivity of an English worker increased, on average, twenty times. Also, a dramatic geographical shift from England's southeast to the north occurred in the regional distribution of the industrial forces of production. New industrial centers appeared in Lancaster and Sunderland. Villagers moved to the cities in large numbers. Manchester, the center of the cotton textile industry, counted only ten thousand residents in 1770, but boasted a population of 353,000 by 1841. In 1750, England's population was approximately 7.7 million. By 1850, however, that number had soared to 27.5 million, half of whom lived in the cities.

The Industrial Revolution enabled the factory system to become the dominant force throughout British industry. The Industrial Revolution not only constituted a technological revolution, but at the same time revolutionized the entire mode of production. Marx pointed out that "machinery is merely a kind of productive force. Only the modern factory that uses machinery as its basis exhibits social relationships in production."[16] According to 1841 statistics, 68.7 percent of the workers in the cotton textile industry worked in factories, 50 percent of those in the woolen textile industry, and 40 percent of those in the silk weaving industry. If we stop to consider that the productivity of factory workers that used machinery in production was several times, and even several tens of times, higher than that of the handicraft worker, then the superiority of factory production becomes even more apparent. The factory system completely changed the social position of the worker. In the era of workshop handicraft industry, most of the handicraft workshop workers still maintained close ties with their village, and still retained the possibility of owning some simple tools and of becoming a small producer. However, the factory system of machine production completely severed the workman's links to the village. Once in the cities, these workmen became hired slaves forced to sell their labor power in order to survive. At the same time, machines compelled the skilled workers (who had superior skills and occupied a comparatively high status in production in the era of workshop handicraft industry) to become just like ordinary workers, the appendages of machines. As a result, the establishment of the factory system brought about not only the consolidation and development of the capitalist system of employment in industry, but also the formation of the modern proletariat. The struggle between the proletariat and the bourgeoisie constantly intensified.

The Industrial Revolution also promoted the further development of capitalism in agriculture. It brought about a further integration of the system of land ownership dominated by wealthy landlords with capitalistic management of large estates. After the Industrial Revolution began, the urban population grew rapidly, and the demand for staple foods greatly increased. As England began to change from a grain-exporting to a grain-importing country, the price of grain soared. Another upsurge in the enclosure of common lands (a process called "mopping up the land") occurred precisely during this period of the Industrial Revolution, in other words from the end of the eighteenth to the early nineteenth centuries. This movement expropriated the last parcels of land owned by the remaining yeomen, the cotters, and the small tenant farmers. This process once again enlarged not only the system of land ownership dominated by the big landlords, but also the cultivated acreage managed by the operators of the large estates. Capitalism achieved a complete victory in agriculture. At this time, three basic classes became clearly discernible in English agriculture: the large landlord, the manager of the large estate, and the agricultural worker. By 1851, England's agricultural workers already numbered 1.44 million.

The great achievement of the Industrial Revolution was to make England into "the workshop of the world," enabling it to monopolize the world's industry and trade. In 1850, England produced 39 percent of the world's total industrial output value, and enjoyed 21 percent of total world trade. England became the major supplier of industrial products for various countries, supplying not only industrial consumer goods, but also industrial capital goods. During the first half of the nineteenth century, exports of coal, iron, and machinery increased steadily. At this time, industrial revolutions were also beginning one by one in the various countries of Europe and America. These nations also came to depend—to varying degrees—on technical equipment imported from England. On the other hand, many countries also became—to varying degrees—suppliers of raw materials to England.

During the Industrial Revolution, the development of England's industry increasingly relied on an expansion of the foreign market. By the mid-nineteenth century, more than half of the industrial products were sold in foreign markets, and a majority of the raw materials and staple foods consumed domestically also relied on foreign suppliers. During this time, for example, 80 percent of England's cotton textiles were exported and all its raw cotton was supplied from abroad. Under these conditions, the venerable policy of protective tariffs had become an obstacle to England's industrial development and foreign expansion. As a result, England's industrial bourgeoisie in the early nineteenth century began a fierce struggle with the landed aristocracy, the financial aristocracy, and the big monopoly merchants to substitute a policy of free trade for that of protective tariffs. Gradually England's industrial bourgeoisie achieved victory.

In 1813, Parliament repealed the East India Company's right to monopolize trade with India. In the 1820s, England concluded bilateral tariff agreements with various major countries that granted them most-favored nation status. This legislation not only lowered Britain's tariffs on imported raw materials and industrial products, but also lifted the embargo on imported silk products as well as the restrictions that London had placed on products that could not be exported (such as machinery). In the 1840s, Parliament not only eliminated tariffs on several hundred types of commodities, but also lowered them on more than a thousand others. Particularly significant was the 1846 repeal of the Corn Laws,[17] statutes that had directly harmed the interests of the industrial bourgeoisie. Parliament subsequently also abolished the maritime ordinances which had been in force for almost two hundred years. By that time, England had become a country of free trade.

The policy of free trade was a policy of foreign economic expansionism that was adopted only after England's industry had achieved a monopoly status in the world. It played a very large stimulative role in the 1850s and 1860s when England's industrial development surged forward to make even greater gains. Marx wrote: "What is free trade in the present state of society? It is the freedom of capital. When you remove the few national fetters that still the advance of capital, you will have done nothing but give it entire freedom of action."[18]

The completion of its Industrial Revolution, the widespread use of machinery, a steady decline in commodity prices, and the comprehensive implementation of a policy of free trade all greatly augmented England's ability to compete with other countries. As railroad construction both within England and in other places greatly expanded, and as the various countries of continental Europe and America energetically promoted their own industrial revolutions after the 1840s, England now became the prime contractor for such current projects as well as the supplier of coal, iron, machinery, locomotives, and rolling stock for these activities. Demand for British goods stimulated a new upsurge in England's foreign trade and industrial production in the 1850s and 1860s. Engels pointed out:

> The previous astounding creations of steam and machinery dwindled into nothing compared with the immense mass of productions of the twenty years from 1850 to 1870, with the overwhelming figures of exports and imports, of wealth accumulated in the hands of capitalists and of human working power concentrated in the large towns.[19]

For example, in the period from 1850 to 1870, coal production increased from 49.8 million tons to 112 million tons. Pig iron production went from 2.24 million tons to 6.10 million tons. Cotton consumption increased from 590 million pounds sterling to 1.08 billion pounds sterling. In 1870, steel production reached 220,000 tons. Industrial technology also made substantial advances in this period. For example, many blast furnaces (some even eighty feet tall, capable of producing 450 to 550 tons of pig iron daily) made their appearance. The Bessemer steel smelting process (developed in 1867) expedited steel production. In shipbuilding, steam increasingly pushed aside sail to become the dominant force in the industry.

The 1850–70 period of high industrial growth in England coincided exactly with the years when the United States and Germany were hotly pursuing the British with their own rapid industrial development. However, even up until the 1870s, England still retained its leadership in world industrial production and world trade. In 1870, England enjoyed a 32 percent share of global industrial production, a decline from its previous position. However, it still retained its monopoly over several major sectors of industrial production. In 1870, England accounted for about half of the world's cotton consumption and coal and iron production. England's share of total world trade rose to 25 percent, almost equal to the combined shares of France, Germany, and the United States. It also held first place in the world in merchant ship tonnage, exceeding the combined tonnage of Holland, France, the United States, Germany, and Russia. England depended on a powerful ocean-going shipping industry to obtain cheap raw materials from various regions of the world, to control the trade patterns of other countries, and to pocket a colossal "invisible income." London became the center of international finance as various governments and companies from all over the world floated their bonds and sold their stocks there. England continued to export large quantities of capital (sums reaching 1.4 million pounds sterling by 1870) to Europe and America as well as to its own colonies. At this time, England's economic power was awesome, and far exceeded that of the other capitalist countries.

Capitalism's Contradictions Intensify and Class Struggle Becomes Acute

The establishment and development of a large-scale, machine industry exacerbated the basic contradiction of capitalism: the contradiction between the socialization of production and the private ownership of the means of production by the capitalist. This contradiction caused inevitable and periodic crises of overproduction.

England's first periodic crisis of overproduction occurred in 1825. This crisis was the inevitable result of the blind expansion of production stimulated by the Industrial Revolution and the extreme impoverishment of the working people.

During the crisis, production plummeted, prices skyrocketed, many banks and factories went bankrupt, and workers lost their jobs in great numbers. England experienced subsequent crises approximately every ten years. Each crisis led to further deterioration in the lives of the working class. As a result, while the Industrial Revolution gave a boost to the rapid development of a capitalist economy, it also sharpened capitalism's domestic class contradictions even more.

Profound changes in the class structure of English society occurred after the Industrial Revolution. The industrial bourgeoisie triumphed over the landed aristocracy. This class established its control over England's political and economic life after the parliamentary reforms of 1831 and the repeal of the Corn Laws in 1846.[20] While this was occurring, an industrial proletariat also came into being and grew in strength. The contradiction between the bourgeoisie and the proletariat now became the principal contradiction within England.

Engels pointed out that "the history of the English working class began during the latter half of the eighteenth century, in other words, from the invention of the steam engine and the cotton gin."[21] Large-scale, machine industry not only led to the further subordination of the handicraft worker (who toiled in the era of workshop handicraft industry) to capital, but also bankrupted many independent handicraftsmen and forced them into the ranks of the working class. For example, after the adoption of steam-powered looms in England, 800,000 handicraft weavers lost their jobs. Without an alternative, they could either starve or join the reserve army of industry and wait to become the hired slaves of a capitalist. Machinery was an expensive tool which only wealthy capitalists could afford. An unbridgeable chasm between capitalist and worker appeared. Two fundamentally antagonistic classes—the capitalist class and the working class—emerged in society.

Large-scale machine production not only created the modern working class, but also threw them into an abyss of poverty and misery. In this regard, both Marx in *Capital* and Engels in *The Condition of the Working Class in England* made trenchant observations and analyses.

Large-scale machine production threw large numbers of women and children into the labor market. Of 420,000 textile factory workers in England in 1839, women numbered 240,000; children and adolescent workers under eighteen years of age numbered 190,000. The factory system brought terrible disasters for women and children. Pregnant women could not ask for maternity leave without having their pay docked or even risking being fired. As a result, mothers either had to carry out abortions, or had to use opium or sleeping pills to drug the young babies who often were born right next to the machines that their mothers worked. Children often suffered fatal accidents after their mother had gone to work and there was no one at home to watch after them. Sons and daughters of workers began as child laborers at the age of six or seven. Even in the 1840s, when factory legislation began to appear, children generally "at nine years of age (were) sent into the mill to work 6 1/2 hours (formerly 8, earlier still, 12 to 14, even 16 hours) daily, until the thirteenth year; then twelve hours until the eighteenth year."[22] The oppression of child workers was even freer of restraints in those industrial sectors not restricted under the factory laws. For example, in the lace industry, according to a newspaper account of the time:

> Children of nine or ten years are dragged from their squalid beds at two, three, or four o'clock in the morning and compelled to work for a bare subsistence until ten, eleven, or twelve at night, their limbs wearing away, their frames dwindling, their faces whitening, and their humanity absolutely sinking into a stone-like torpor, utterly horrible to contemplate.[23]

Long and arduous work caused the bodies of child laborers to become deformed, their intelligence to be wasted, their morality to degenerate. Marx wrote: "British industry, which, vampire like, could but live by sucking blood, and children's blood, too."[24]

To extract the highest profit, the capitalist did his utmost to increase the speed of the machinery, thereby also increasing the labor intensity for the worker. To maximize the use of his machinery, and to bring out its full effectiveness, the capitalist did everything he could to lengthen the time that the worker actually worked. As a result, in the first half of the nineteenth century, it was very common for a worker to put in sixteen to eighteen hours every day. After the length of the work day was restricted under the Factory Laws, the capitalist engaged in " 'small thefts' of capital from the laborer's meal and recreation time"[25] in order to reap extra profits. These extra profits came from the surplus labor performed after the legally stipulated work time had been exceeded. The gruelling work greatly shortened the number of years that a worker could work. By the age of forty, a person was generally "over the hill," having lost his or her ability to perform.

The use of machinery threw large numbers of small producers into the ranks of the proletariat. However, the factories in reality absorbed far fewer workers than the people now available for work. The use of machinery, in short, created a large standing army of unemployed. The existence of these many unemployed people and the use of poorly paid women and children in factories brought about a continuous decline in the level of wages paid to workers. In 1810, the average weekly wage of an English textile worker was forty-two shillings, six pence. In 1821, it had declined to thirty-two shillings. By the time of the 1825 crisis, the average weekly wage had fallen even more and was down to twenty-five shillings, six pence. The tragic living conditions of the English working class can be seen from a parson's description of one of London's largest industrial areas in 1844:

> It contains 1,400 houses, inhabited by 2,795 families, or about 12,000 persons. The space upon which this large population dwells, is less than 400 yards

> (1,200 feet) square, and in this overcrowding it is nothing unusual to find a man, his wife, four or five children, and, sometimes, both grandparents, all in one single room of ten to twelve square feet, where they eat, sleep, and work. I believe that before the Bishop of London called attention to this most poverty-stricken parish, people at the West End knew as little of it as of the savages of Australia or the South Sea Isles. And if we make ourselves acquainted with these unfortunates, through personal observation, if we watch them at their scanty meal and see them bowed by illness and want of work, we shall find such a mass of helplessness and misery, that a nation like ours must blush that these things can be possible. I was rector near Huddersfield during the three years in which the mills were at their worst, but I have never seen such complete helplessness of the poor as since then in Bethnal Green. Not one father of a family in ten in the whole neighborhood has other clothing than his working suit, and that is as bad and tattered as possible; many, indeed, have no other covering for the night than these rags, and no bed, save a sack of straw and shavings.[26]

This was what the capitalist Industrial Revolution gave to the British workers!

The industrial upsurge of the 1850s and 1860s brought no improvement in the condition of the English working class. When Engels spoke about the condition of the broad working masses in this period, he wrote:

> But as to the great mass of working people, the state of misery and insecurity in which they live now is as low as ever, if not lower. The east end of London is an ever-spreading pool of stagnant misery and desolation, of starvation when out of work, and degradation, physical and moral, when in work. And so in all other large towns—an exception made only for a minority of privileged workers. . . .[27]

Britain's monopoly over global industry was founded on the blood, sweat, and bones of England's workers.

However, where there is oppression, there is also resistance. From an early date, the English working class struck at the capitalist system with constant attacks. The Industrial Revolution also was precisely the beginning stage of the modern workers' movement. Engels pointed out that "as a class, they first manifested oppposition to the bourgeoisie when they resisted the introduction of machinery at the very beginning of the industrial period."[28] In 1779, eighty thousand workers participated in the destruction of machinery in the Lancaster region. In the first fifteen years of the nineteenth century, the workers' struggle in opposition to the use of machinery (termed the "Luddite Movement") spread to every industrial region in England. These types of struggles, however, revealed that the working class at that time still did not correctly recognize the real source of their own misery. To suppress the resistance of the working class, the bourgeoisie mobilized troops to slaughter the workers. They enacted laws that included the death penalty for those convicted of destroying machinery. Parliament subsequently passed reactionary laws to prohibit strikes and workers' associations.

Once its ranks had expanded and once its consciousness had been raised, England's working class now began in the 1820s to fight for democratic rights. Pressured by the militancy of the workers, Parliament in 1824 repealed the laws prohibiting workers' associations. Labor organizations (labor unions) grew rapidly. And they provided outstanding leadership for the strikes that broke out during the crisis of 1825. In 1835, advanced workers led by William Lovett (a carpenter) and other groups of artisans established the London Working Men's Association. They drew up a People's Charter, and demanded various democratic rights such as the right of suffrage for all adult males, the use of the secret ballot in voting, annual Parliaments, the establishment of equal voting districts, the abolition of property qualifications that restricted the eligibility of candidates to run for seats in Parliament, and the payment of salaries for Members of Parliament. The bourgeoisie vigorously tried to suppress the Charter after it had been announced. The working class and the handicraftsmen then waged a mass struggle to attain the realization of their demands. Three massive waves—in which millions of people participated—surged forward, first in 1838–39, then in 1842, and finally in 1848. Although the Chartist Movement was defeated by the ruthless suppression of the bourgeois government, it did establish a model for subsequent workers' struggles. Lenin recognized that the English Chartist Movement was "the first widespread proletarian revolutionary movement, genuinely involving the masses of people and political in character."[29]

Confronted by powerful attacks from the working class, the English bourgeoisie adopted dual tactics in order to maintain its rule. On the one hand, it passed a series of "Factory Acts" in the 1830s and 1840s. For example, legislation enacted in 1833 prohibited textile plants from hiring children under the age of nine. The law also limited the workday for adolescent workers (those thirteen to eighteen years of age) to twelve hours. Children under thirteen could not work more than nine hours. (The legislation was subsequently revised in 1844 to restrict the workday to six and a half hours for those under thirteen.) The law also created a group of factory inspectors responsible for monitoring compliance with this legislation. An 1847 bill restricted women and adolescents working in textile factories to a ten hour workday. (During the 1850s and 1860s, this legislation was also successively expanded to include sectors outside the textile industry.) The English working class achieved these legislative victories only after waging several decades of arduous struggles, and only after it made use of the contradiction that existed between the landed aristocracy and the factory owners.

England Becomes the World's Largest Colonial Empire

The development of a large-scale machine industry demanded a rapid expansion of foreign markets as well as access to sources of raw materials. As a result, England began to intensify its foreign aggression and looting of colonies after 1800. Between 1800 and 1850, England's colonial empire expanded from 11.3 million square kilometers to 20 million square kilometers. By 1876, its empire claimed 22.5 million square kilometers and 251.9 million people. England had become the largest colonial empire in the world. In 1813, England began a new stage in its colonial exploitation of India after it revoked the East India Company's right to monopolize trade with that country. By shifting from plunder (primitive accumulation) to primarily exploitation (carried out by industrial capital), England gradually began to transform India into its biggest market for commodities and its source of raw materials. Between 1814 and 1836, England's cotton textile exports to India increased fiftyfold. By the mid-nineteenth century, England exported one-fourth of its entire cotton textile production to India. Like a barrage from heavy artillery, England's machine-made cotton products destroyed India's cotton textile handicraft industry (an industry which had been world-famous during the Middle Ages). As a result, millions of handicraftsmen lost their source of livelihood, and many starved to death. Cities which in the past had been centers of the handicraft industry and which had teemed with life now became desolate, deserted places. Even the Viceroy of East India at that time had to concede: "This kind of disaster is almost unprecedented in the history of commerce. The bones of the loom workers are bleaching everywhere on the plains of India."[30] The British colonialists also extended their devilish claws into India's many villages. They forced the peasants to pay agricultural taxes that took 50 to 70 percent of their total income. They compelled the peasants to grow cotton, jute, tea, and other crops, and turned India into Britain's agricultural subsidiary. The hunger and starvation resulting from England's ruthless exploitation finally led in 1857 to a massive uprising by the Indian people. Sweeping over the Ganges River valley and lasting for two years, this rebellion dealt a serious blow to England's colonial rule.

England also used India from the early 1800s to the 1860s as a springboard to launch a series of wars of aggression against other Asian countries such as Burma, Afghanistan, and Iran. It seized Aden, Singapore, southern Burma, and many other places. The English colonialists also carried on a shameful trade in opium, shipped large quantities of it to China, poisoned the Chinese people, and plundered that country of its silver, silk, and tea. When the Chinese people rose in resistance, the British then launched the first Opium War (1840–42) and militarily invaded China. They forced China to sign an unequal treaty, to cede Hong Kong, to open five ports to trade, to pay an indemnity of twenty-one million silver dollars, and to give England the rights of consular jurisdiction, most-favored-nation status, a tariff agreement, and so forth. All of these actions violated China's sovereign rights and interests. France, Britain's accomplice, then launched a second Opium War in 1856. The French marched into Beijing, sacked it, and once again forced China to pay an indemnity, cede territory, and open more ports for commerce. Tariffs on foreign products were limited to a maximum 5 percent ad valorem duty. Foreigners could freely propagate religion and engage in commerce in the interior, and they enjoyed other special privileges. As a result, China turned into a semi-colony of the Western capitalist powers. England also carried out military and economic aggression in Africa, Latin America, and Oceania.

One can see that the industrial prosperity that England has enjoyed since the Industrial Revolution has been the result of not only squeezing its own working people, but also of exploiting and plundering the people of Asia, Africa, Latin America, and Oceania.

Exploiting and plundering its vast colonies conferred on England the characteristics of imperialism far earlier than any other capitalist country. Lenin pointed out that "from the middle of the nineteenth century on, England had at the very least two major features of imperialism: 1. It had vast colonies; and 2. it enjoyed monopoly profits (because it monopolized the world market)."[31] England not only relied more heavily on its immense colonial empire for markets and raw materials than the other capitalist countries, but also revealed much earlier the parasitic and moribund nature inherent to capitalism.

This parasitic and moribund characteristic also was reflected in the workers' movement. After the middle of the nineteenth century, the bourgeoisie began to use a small part of the super-profits derived from their monopoly of the world market and exploitation of the colonies to buy over the top stratum of the working class, hoping thereby to stop the growing militancy of the working class against its exploitation. This tactic of cooptation led a portion of the most skilled workers to degenerate into "labor aristocrats." Lenin pointed out:

> In the middle of the nineteenth century, Britain enjoyed an almost complete monopoly in the world market. Thanks to this monopoly, the profits acquired by British capital were extraordinarily high so that it was possible for some crumbs of these profits to be thrown to the aristocracy of labor, the skilled factory workers.[32]

At that time, the labor aristocracy constituted approximately 15 percent of the total industrial work force, and its wages were double those of the ordinary worker. These labor aristocrats were representatives of the bourgeoisie in the workers' movement. They maintained a firm grip on the upper leadership posts in some major unions. By insisting that membership be contingent on a worker's ability to pay high union dues, they excluded the ordinary workers, keeping them outside the doors of the union. These labor aristocrats seriously damaged the English workers' movement because they pursued an opportunist line, undermined the militancy of the unions, and disseminated a variety of reformist illusions among the working masses.

3. A Relative Downturn in Economic Development after the 1870s and the Formation of Monopoly Capital Rule

A Slowdown in the Rate of Industrial Development and Loss of "Workshop of the World" Status

Before the 1870s, England monopolized the world's industrial, trade, shipping, and financial sectors, and possessed vast colonies all over the globe. As a result, England became known as "the workshop of the world" and "the empire on which the sun never sets." Yet, ironically enough, it was precisely this status that led England into an increasingly moribund and relatively backward position.

England's industrial strength had been established primarily in several older sectors such as textiles, coal, and iron smelting. Feeble growth and technological stagnation were their basic characteristics despite the fact that production in these sectors did increase, to varying degrees, in the period from 1870 to 1913. During this period, a large part of the machinery and equipment used in England's textile industry was a product of the Industrial Revolution era. The great majority of the coal that was mined still depended on hand labor. "Puddling" to smelt wrought iron was also still done by hand. Of the various major industrial sectors, only steel, machine manufacturing, and shipbuilding developed at a comparatively rapid rate. Stimulated by a wave of technological innovation that swept the entire capitalist world, England also began to establish a series of new industrial sectors, such as gas, electricity, automobiles, and artificial fibers. However, all these industries developed at a comparatively slow rate and on a comparatively modest scale. The majority of electrical and chemical products required domestically still depended on Germany for their supply. As a result, the growth of new industrial sectors could not compensate for the stagnation that now appeared in the older sectors, and therefore the speed of industrial development as a whole declined. Between 1850 and 1870, the average annual increase in English industry was 3.2 percent; however, between 1870 and 1913, that average annual increase was only 1.9 percent.

England lost its status as "workshop of the world" when its industrial development slowed down. When we speak of the capitalist world as a whole, we can say that the last thirty years of the nineteenth century and the early years of the twentieth century marked a period of great technological innovation and very rapid development in industrial production. In particular, industry in the youthful capitalist countries, like the United States and Germany, made a dramatic leap forward. This brought about an obvious change in the relative industrial rankings of England, Germany, the United States, and other countries in the years between 1870 and 1913. In this period, England's portion of the total value of the world's industrial production declined from 32 percent to 14 percent. By the 1880s, U.S. industrial production had eclipsed that of England. By the first decade of the twentieth century, Britain had fallen into third place, having been overtaken by Germany. England's decline was most evident in heavy industry. In 1870, England's iron, steel, and coal production was absolutely first rate, and the British maintained world leadership in these sectors. By the 1880s, however, all three industries were consecutively surpassed by the United States. In 1893 German steel production also caught up with England. By 1913, England's steel production was 7.78 million tons, only a fourth of the United States (31.3 million tons), and not half of Germany's (16.9 million tons). In the same year, the United States was able to command a 51.8 percent share of the total amount of machinery produced in the world; Germany had 21.3 percent; and England claimed only 12.2 percent. These statistics demonstrate that, by the end of the nineteenth century, England had completely lost its monopoly over world industry. In fact, as early as 1885, Engels had already pointed out that "the industrial monopoly enjoyed by England for close to a century was lost, never to return"[33] because the various countries of continental America and Europe now had access to steam power and machinery.

England's economy was extremely dependent on outside factors. Foreign trade was of decisive importance in the survival of England's economy. Therefore, the relative decline in English industrial production during this period strongly influenced its position in the world market. Conversely, a deteriorating position in foreign trade had a direct impact on the development of its industrial production. Beginning in the 1870s, English commodities encountered increasingly stiff competition in world markets from German and American goods. In the European market, German electrical, chemical, and machine products enjoyed an overwhelming superiority. In the U.S. market, America's own products became England's biggest competitors. In the past, the United States had been an important market for English machinery and textile products; however, at this time, England had not only lost its U.S. market subsequent to America's rapid industrial development, but even encountered increasingly keen competition from the United States in its Latin American, Asian, and other markets. In 1870, England's share of total world trade stood at 22 percent, but by 1913 it had fallen to 15 percent. While England still retained its leading role, it had, nevertheless, lost its monopoly status.

England's loss of its "workshop of the world" position was the inevitable result and manifestation of the increasingly uneven development of the various major capitalist countries. On the one hand, the newer capitalist countries, especially the industrial powers like Germany and the United States, were clearly making dramatic progress. On the other hand, England's own industrial development stagnated because various factors held it back. The main impediments were as follows:

1. England's early industrialization had resulted in technological backwardness and the obsolescence of fixed capital assets in major industrial sectors.

2. The fact that huge sums of investment were tied up in traditional industries made investors fear depreciation and the "writing off" of old equipment. This also hindered technological innovation and the renovation of fixed assets.

3. A massive export of capital (stimulated because profits on overseas investments were far higher than those generated within England) reduced domestic investment in both old and new industrial sectors.

4. The parasitic and moribund character of capitalism appeared at a much earlier date in England than elsewhere because of Britain's long-term monopoly over world markets and its exploitation of vast colonies.

5. England was unable to shift rapidly from a policy of free trade to one of protectionism because its economy was so heavily dependent on foreign markets.

All these factors increasingly weakened England's industrial competitiveness in international markets.

As industrial development—relatively speaking—lagged, English agricultural production fell sharply. During the last quarter of the nineteenth century, a chronic agricultural crisis enveloped the entire capitalist world. A glut of agricultural products from the Americas—from countries with vast areas of fertile, virgin land like the United States, Canada, and Argentina—continued to depress world agricultural prices. Cheap American grain flooded into Europe. In England big landlords monopolized landownership; the great majority of farms were rented, and the very high rents charged for land elevated English agricultural prices to levels higher than those in other countries. As a result, the dumping of cheap American agricultural products in Europe had the most disastrous impact on England's agriculture, and many small and medium-sized farmers went bankrupt. Between 1870 and 1910, England's wheat acreage and wheat production fell by half. Grain self-sufficiency declined from 79 percent to 35.6 percent. England's food supply and agricultural raw materials became more dependent on foreign imports. As a result, the exploitative income that England derived from the profits, interest, and commissions of its foreign investments became even more vital in order to compensate for its continuously expanding trade deficit.

Engels pointed out:

> England's industrial monopoly is the cornerstone of its present social system. The market could not cope with the rising productivity of English industry even at the time when it maintained its monopoly; as a result, a new crisis has occurred every decade.[34]

England's loss of its monopoly over world industry inevitably exacerbated the cyclical economic crises it encountered during this period. An unprecedentedly grave worldwide economic crisis occurred in 1873 in the capitalist countries. By

1874, England's economy began to show signs of stagnation. Subsequently, five crises broke out in 1878, 1882, 1890, 1900, and 1907. Their common characteristics were: 1. a sharp and prolonged drop in industrial production during each crisis; 2. a sluggish, long-term recession after each; and 3. a short-term, feeble recovery and upsurge. The increasingly acute crises caused even more massive damage to the social forces of production.

The loss of "workshop of the world" status and the prolonged economic slump threatened the profits of the bourgeoisie. As a result, the bourgeoisie attacked the working class, especially the vast pool of unskilled workers, and sought various pretexts to reduce wages. The condition of the working class deteriorated after the beginning of the 1880s. Workers were fired in large numbers. Unemployment frequently rose above 10 percent. By the end of the 1880s and the beginning of the 1890s, approximately one-third of the population of London was on the verge of starvation. At the beginning of the twentieth century, an English worker needed at least thirty shillings per week to maintain the most minimal living standard. However, at that time, only three-eighths of all male workers' wages reached this level, and the average woman worker took home only eight shillings as a weekly wage. In 1903, the leader of the Liberal party, Henry Campbell-Bannerman, confessed, "Approximately 30 percent of England's population don't get enought to eat, and find themselves on the verge of starvation . . . living in an iron grip of prolonged poverty" [source unknown].

The reality of a life of increasing poverty gradually reduced the ability of the "labor aristocrat"–controlled unions to deceive their rank-and-file membership. Many unskilled workers struggled to reorganize the older unions or to establish new ones. By the end of the 1880s, not only did unskilled workers in large numbers begin to participate in various unions, but many new unions—whose core membership consisted of the unskilled—also appeared. In 1892, Engels wrote:

> [The East End of London] has shaken off its torpid despair, has returned to life, and has become the home of what is called the "New Unionism," that is to say, of the organizations of the great mass of "unskilled" workers. . . . [T]he masses, whose adhesion gave them strength, were rough, neglected, looked down upon by the working class aristocracy. . . . And thus we see now these new unions taking the lead of the working class movement generally, and more and more taking in tow the rich and proud "old" unions.[35]

As the social composition of the unions changed and as their membership expanded, the struggles undertaken by the working class became even more organized and more mass-based in character. During the first decade of the twentieth century, longshoremen, railroad workers, sailors, and miners staged many large, nationwide strikes. All achieved great victories. In evaluating the six-month-long strike of English miners in 1911, Lenin wrote:

> [T]hose who are familiar with the British labor movement say that since the miners' strike the British proletariat is no longer the same. The workers have learned to fight. They have come to see the path that will lead them to victory. They have become aware of their strength. They have ceased to be the meek lambs they seemed to be for so long a time to the joy of all the defenders and extollers of wage-slavery.[36]

The Formation of Monopoly Capital Rule

After the 1860s, a trend toward capital accumulation and concentration in production gradually emerged in England following the development of large-scale machine industry and intensified competition. Joint-stock companies proliferated. The great depression that began in 1874 and its subsequent crisis intensified the competition raging among business enterprises, and stimulated a wave of takeovers. The development of joint-stock companies not only facilitated the establishment of large, capitalist enterprises, but also provided an advantageous method for expanding their capital and for swallowing up their competitors. In the 1890s, many comparatively large industrial enterprises, either capitalized independently or as partnerships, reorganized themselves as joint-stock companies. As stock companies, they initiated mergers and acquisitions, and thereby speeded up the concentration of production.

However, this concentration of production in English industry, both in speed as well as in extent, lagged behind that attained in the United States and Germany. This was particularly clear in some of the older industrial sectors. For example, by the mid-1890s, only a few large companies played decisive roles in the coal industries of the United States, Germany, and even France. On the contrary, England claimed 3,334 coal mines right up to 1913. The average work force in each mine did not exceed three hundred and most of the mines were individually owned. The same situation existed in the other older industrial sectors, primarily because the greater part of England's businesses were established during the period of the Industrial Revolution. Now they were hampered by obsolete plant facilities and technology as well as a smaller scale of operations. In addition, England's monopoly over colonial markets enabled such backward enterprises to retain their old equipment and yet stay in business. The investment of large amounts of capital overseas left insufficient funds domestically to renovate and expand England's fixed capital. This also influenced the concentration of production.

The development of monopolies in English industry also came later than that in the United States and Germany because of Britain's slow pace in concentrating industrial production. Monopolies developed on a large scale both in Germany and the United States after the crisis of 1873, and especially during the decade of the 1880s. However, this wave swept over England only in the 1890s, some ten to fifteen years later.

The larger monopoly corporations in England emerged mainly from sectors that were directly involved with military production. These monopolies generally arose from a small number of large enterprises that had already been in existence for some time. After mergers and reorganizations had augmented their capital, they became joint-stock companies which formed vertically integrated monopolies. These were based on the acquisition of those businesses to which they were related or linked to in the early or later phases of production. However, none of these industrial sectors (such as machine manufacturing, shipbuilding, or metallurgy) exhibited a high degree of horizontal monopoly, and in some industries such horizontal linkages were nonexistent. The vertically integrated monopolies were all created in the 1890s and in the early twentieth century. For example, the famous Armstrong-Whitworth and Vickers-Maxim companies emerged from the munitions and shipbuilding industries at this time. Not only did they produce munitions and build warships, but they also owned their own steel smelting, metalworking, and machine manufacturing plants. Famous companies like Nettlefolds, Baldwin, and John Brown also emerged in the field of metallurgy. These well-known, large corporations each linked together the various processes involved in metallurgy, and owned a series of installations that ranged from coal mines, iron ore mines, and coking facilities to steel smelting, steel rolling, metal processing, and shipbuilding factories.

Monopolies developed rather quickly in the new chemical industry where production was already comparatively centralized. For example, Nobel Industries, established in the 1880s, controlled the entire process of dynamite production. After a series of mergers, the United Salt Company came to control 91 percent of table salt production. By 1890, the United Alkali Company, also the end result of many mergers, controlled the entire process of producing bleaching powder. After a series of mergers and acquisitions, the Brunner-Mond Company controlled the great majority of soda production by 1895. By 1900 rather large monopolies also emerged in other sectors of the economy. An example was the Portland Cement Alliance Company, created by the merger of twenty-seven enterprises, which came to control 80 percent of cement production. In 1900, the Imperial Tobacco Company, also a result of mergers, agreed to divide up the English and American markets between themselves and the American Tobacco Company. In 1914, eleven British railroad companies reached an agreement that enabled them to completely monopolize all of England's railways.

Generally speaking, different types of monopolies had been created in all comparatively important industrial sectors in England by the end of the nineteenth and early twentieth centuries. The exceptions to this rule were such older industries as textiles, coal, and metallurgy. However, the number of British monopolies remained relatively small and their degree of control rather low compared to that of their American and German counterparts, a situation that was created first of all by England's stagnant industry and by the comparatively low degree of centralized production at that time. Second, England's policy of free trade also had a definite impact on both the speed as well as the shape of development of its monopoly capital. Lenin pointed out:

> In England—unlike other countries where protective tariffs facilitate the formation of cartels—monopolist alliances of entrepreneurs, cartels and trusts arise in the majority of cases only when the number of the chief competing enterprises is reduced to "a couple of dozen or so."[37]

The policy of free trade was a special impediment hindering the formation of business alliances aimed at dividing up a market. As a result, comparatively few syndicates and cartels emerged in England to control the sale of commodities. In general, England's monopolies faced fierce competition. One of the characteristics of these large corporations, created after mergers and reorganizations, was their formation of alliances based on production. Lenin pointed this out: "It is extremely important to note that in free-trade England, concentration also leads to monopoly, although somewhat later and perhaps in another form."[38]

Another characteristic of the development of English monopoly capital was the great energy it expended in monopolizing the production of raw materials in the colonies. This feature, of course, was related to England's possession of a vast colonial empire and its export of huge amounts of capital. For example, the De Beers Diamond Prospecting Company was one of the largest monopolies established to mine gold and diamonds in South Africa. In Southeast and West Asia, English and Dutch capital jointly set up the Anglo-Dutch Shell Oil Company in 1907. In 1909, the British-Persian Oil Company was established. Most of these companies were international monopolies. Moreover, English finance capital created many unique monopolies in India that controlled investment in that colony's industries, mines, and plantations. These monopolies were the "Agency Houses"[39] that held India's economic lifelines in their hands and squeezed the blood out from its people.

The degree of concentration and of monopoly in English banking exceeded that found in Germany and the United States because of the completely different industrial structures of these countries. From the middle of the nineteenth century on, many joint-stock banks appeared after England became established as the center of world trade and finance. The number of England's joint-stock banks fell from 250 in 1865 to 98 in 1900 during the fierce competition and merger mania that occurred after the 1870s. By 1913, their number had been further reduced to sixty-one, and bank deposits as a result became even more centralized. "The Big Five" monopoly banks (in other words, the Midlands Bank, the Westminster Bank, the Lloyd's Bank, the Barclay Bank, and the National Provincial Bank) had emerged by the end of the nineteenth and early twentieth centuries. They set up a domestic network of branches and sub-branches as if they were pieces on a chess board, and came to control all of England's financial matters. These banks sent their managers and directors to serve concurrently as directors of the Bank of England, the state central bank, and they participated at the highest levels in setting national monetary and financial policy, thereby influencing the political and economic life of the entire country.

Although bank capital in England was quite developed and extensive, it clearly was not up to the level of the United States and Germany in industrial capital. The vast majority of England's banking system was comprised of commercial banks. Most of these commercial banks had close links with foreign trade and foreign investment activities. Domestically, their main function was to absorb deposits to provide short-term credit for industry and commerce. As a result, the direct relationship between the commercial banks and industrial enterprises for quite some time was primarily limited to capital flows. However, by the end of the nineteenth and the early twentieth centuries, the contacts and links between bank capital and industrial capital began to gradually strengthen as the large banks carved out their own monopoly spheres of influence and as monopolies emerged in industry. For example, when a commercial bank permitted a company to constantly write overdrafts on its account, it was granting long-term credit in disguise. The commercial banks also expanded mortgage credit by using the stocks and debentures of companies as collateral. They increased their financial assistance to, as well as their control over, both investment brokers and investment companies. Personal ties between bank presidents and the heads of the industrial monopolies also developed. Quite often the directors of the major banks sat in the boardrooms of large and important industrial companies. Finance capital was beginning to take shape in England, and a wealthy financial oligarchy was emerging.

The Large-scale Export of Capital and Further Colonial Expansion

By the middle of the nineteenth century England was already exporting substantial amounts of capital. During its transition to imperialism, England further expanded its capital exports in order to intensify its exploitation and control over its colonies and semi-colonies, and to strengthen its own status as world hegemon. Lenin pointed out that "[England's] enormous exports of capital are bound up most closely with vast colonies."[40] By 1913, the total amount of England's foreign investment had already reached four billion pounds sterling, or one-fourth of England's entire national wealth. It also constituted half of the total foreign investment extended by all the various imperialist countries. More than half of England's foreign investment was located in its colonies or semi-colonies. England had become the largest international exploiter. The income from England's foreign investment (which was 194 million pounds sterling in 1911) exceeded not only its income from foreign trade but also from industry (which was fifty million pounds sterling in 1911). One can see that by this time England had already changed from being a model industrial country to one that was now a model parasite.

Colonies had a decisive influence on the development of English capitalism. From the beginning of the seventeenth century to the middle of the nineteenth century, England gradually established a colossal colonial system. However, England's plunder of its colonies began on a massive scale only after the 1860s. Lenin pointed out that "for Great Britain, the period of the enormous expansion of colonial conquests is that between 1860 and 1880, and it was also very considerable in the last twenty years of the nineteenth century."[41] It was not accidental that England frantically expanded its colonial empire during this period. First of all, England's economy—vitally dependent on foreign markets—gradually sank into a quagmire when it began to lose its monopoly over world industry. As a result, the British hoped to open new sources of raw materials and new markets by expanding their colonial possessions. Second, the living conditions of England's working people steadily deteriorated because of the emergence of monopoly capitalism and proliferating economic crises. As a result, working class militancy increased. The monopoly bourgeoisie calculated that they could use colonial expansionism to divert the attention of the working people from their domestic struggles, and use the huge profits derived from colonial plunder to co-opt and split the working class. In 1895, the big English capitalist and African colonialist Cecil Rhodes wildly clamored:

> I was in the East End of London [working-class quarter] yesterday and attending a meeting of the unemployed. I listened to the wild speeches, which were just a cry for "bread," "bread!" and on my way home I pondered over the scene and I became more than ever convinced of the importance of imperialism. . . . My cherished idea is a solution for the social problem, i.e., in order to save the forty million inhabitants of the United Kingdom from a bloody civil war, we colonial statesmen must acquire new lands to settle the surplus population, to provide new markets for the goods produced in the factories and mines. The Empire, as I have always said, is a bread and butter question. If you want to avoid civil war, you must become imperialists.[42]

During this period, England relied on its maritime supremacy and powerful military forces to undertake a series of colonial wars. It gobbled up large areas of Asia, Africa, and Oceania, and expanded its sphere of influence. Using India as its springboard for operations, it seized Malaya first, then took Upper Burma, and finally claimed North Borneo. It invaded Afghanistan again, and turned Iran into its protectorate. While these developments took place, England also actively participated—along with the other imperialist powers—in an effort to carve up and plunder China. England came to control the Yangtze River Valley, and claimed all of central China as its sphere of influence. In 1900, England's associates—the other imperialist countries—launched a large-scale war of aggression against China, and forced it to sign the humiliating Peace Treaty of 1901 which violated China's sovereignty. In 1904, England launched a military invasion from India into China's province of Tibet. In 1914, it took advantage of the

Simla Conference to fabricate the notorious and illegal "McMahon Line." England was also the most active participant among the imperialist powers in carving up Africa in the last twenty-five years of the nineteenth century. In 1875, England obtained the right to control the Suez Canal. In 1882, it occupied Egypt militarily. At the same time, England also extended its aggressive claws into Africa, reaching all the way from the Sahara Desert to South Africa. By the end of the nineteenth century, it had grabbed a vast colonial expanse that extended from the Nile River basin in North Africa, passed through the highlands of East Africa, and stretched all the way to the highlands of South Africa and the Gulf of Guinea in West Africa. By 1914, England's colonies accounted for one-fourth of the world's land mass, and comprised half of the colonial territories forcibly occupied by the various imperialist countries. However, England's own territory did not even account for 1 percent of the total area of the British Empire.

During this period, England's investments in its colonies and semi-colonies became important means for controlling, enslaving, and exploiting these areas. Its investments focused primarily on building roads and railways, and opening mines and plantations. The economic purpose of England's investments (other than to facilitate Britain's military and political control) was to turn these areas into markets for British commodities and sources of raw materials. For example, India and Egypt became England's sources of cotton supplies; Canada became England's granary; Australia became England's pastureland; and the area from the Sahara Desert to South Africa became England's crucial source of minerals and precious metals. Tightly squeezed by English finance capital, the broad masses of people in the colonies became appallingly poor. Take India as an example. In the last half of the nineteenth century, famines became ever more numerous and ever more serious. According to government records, twenty-four famines claimed altogether twenty million victims. On the eve of the First World War, the standard of living enjoyed by the Indian peasantry was only one-third that enjoyed by their parents' generation, and half that of their grandparents' generation. England's investments and loans in the semi-colonial countries not only extracted colossal profits, but were also an instrument for obtaining various privileges from the debtor countries and for controlling their political and economic lifelines.

The export of enormous amounts of capital and the ruthless exploitation of the vast colonies and semi-colonies intensified the parasitic and decadent character of English imperialism. The export of capital seriously affected domestic investment and the development of industry and agriculture. An endless income of super-profits and interest payments from overseas expanded the domestic stratum of the idle rich. By the early twentieth century, these idle rich numbered more than a million people. More and more manpower and financial resources were expanded to satisfy their parasitic spending habits. Large tracts of arable land were turned into hunting grounds for the enjoyment of the exploiters. The money spent annually on horse racing and fox hunting alone came to fourteen million pounds sterling. The proportion of nonproductive people engaged in such fields as commerce, finance, domestic service, and restaurant work constantly increased.

The stupendous income exploited from the colonies and semi-colonies gave the monopoly bourgeoisie the possibility of using a small part of it to pay the skilled workers comparatively high wages, to split the working class, and to foster a worker aristocracy. At the same time, they also enacted some so-called liberal, compassionate laws (such as compensation for work-related injuries, pensions, unemployment benefits, limits on length of the workday, and a minimum wage). These were implemented in order to moderate the workers' resistance, as well as to consolidate and maintain the bourgeoisie's system of exploitation. These cunning methods of the monopoly bourgeoisie produced an unhealthy influence on the workers' movement. As a result, an opportunist trend in the workers' movement also flourished—despite the strengthened organizational capability and increased militancy of the English working class during this period. The worker aristocracy held much of the leadership power of the labor unions in its hands. Their slogan was "honest work gets an honest wage." They advocated class cooperation, and were satisfied with the reformist measures of the bourgeoisie. They were termites in the workers' movement. Some so-called socialist organizations, like the Fabian Society and the Independent Labor Party, were established in the 1880s and 1890s. However, all of them were opportunist in nature. Their common characteristics were a. opposition to class struggle and to the dictatorship of the proletariat, and b. advocacy of parliamentary methods of political action, gradual reforms, and a peaceful transition to socialism. In 1900, the Trades' Union Congress (an alliance of various unions), the Independent Labor party, and the Fabian Society united to form the Labor Representative Committee, which changed its name in 1906 to the Labor party. This party basically was not a political party that represented the interests of the working class, but was the representative of the monopoly bourgeoisie in the workers' movement.

To sum up, opportunism in the English workers' movement was a product of the English bourgeoisie's policy of liberalism. It was the ideology of the worker aristocracy. Opportunism had deep social and economic roots in England.

4. British Imperialism's Economy Weakens during the First World War

The First World War was the result of intensified unequal development and sharpened contradictions among the capitalist countries. It was an imperialist war to redivide the world anew. In the early twentieth century, the principal contradiction among the various imperialist states was that between England and Germany. Germany's rapid development and frantic foreign expansion gravely threatened England. Germany's plan to build the Baghdad railway directly infringed on England's colonial interests in West Asia and India. Germany's aggressive ambitions in Africa and its policy of dumping cheap commodities in South America created sharp contradictions with England. Germany energetically expanded its navy, and contended for maritime supremacy with England. England, for its part, formed an anti-German alliance (called the Entente), reaching agreements with France in 1904 and Russia in 1907. England attempted to use warfare to eliminate the military and economic threat posed by Germany. It sought to consolidate its vested interests in its colonial empire, and it tried to seize even more colonies, especially the Arab countries with their abundant resources and important strategic position. In short, England was trying to restore its position as ruler of the world.

In the summer of 1914, the imperialist countries used the pretext of the Balkan question to provoke the First World War. Although England had for a long time prepared for such a contingency, nevertheless, its economic dependence on foreign markets and sources of raw materials, its obsolete industrial equipment, and its feeble heavy industry were no match for its newly risen opponent, Germany. Not long after the war began, Germany intensified its attacks on England's maritime shipping, and created shortages in England of raw materials and food.

In order to cope with the war as well as guarantee the profits of monopoly capital, the English government strengthened its management over the national economy as soon as open hostilities began. It implemented a series of measures that created a state monopoly capitalism. For example, the railroads were temporarily nationalized. Government agencies to supervise various sectors of the economy were established. Comprehensive controls were placed on the production, pricing, and distribution of industrial raw materials as well as on imports and exports. The English government froze wages, prohibited strikes, restricted workers from leaving or changing their jobs, forced women and children to work at very low, fixed wages, and so on. Everything the government did to regulate the economy proceeded from the interests of monopoly capital. For example, companies nationalized during the war and directly run by the state were guaranteed, by law, a profit 20 percent higher than their average prewar profit. The state provided special benefits and preferential treatment for the munitions monopolies in terms of raw materials, transportation, labor power, and loans. The government provided the capital to establish several hundred munitions companies, and, with the exception of the largest ones, handed them over to the monopolies to run. All these measures enabled England's monopoly bourgeoisie to reap a profit of four billion pounds sterling during the war. The profits of some large companies increased several times and even several tens of times. The monopolies expanded to unprecedented dimensions as they gobbled up state assets and acquired many small and medium-sized enterprises. The Federation of British Industries was founded in 1916, the result of a merger of eighteen thousand companies with a total capital value of five billion pounds sterling. It became the core of England's monopolies and the headquarters of the world of industry. It was called "the shadow government" because its actions influenced the policies of the English government.

A comprehensive militarization closely supervised by the government was the basic characteristic of England's wartime economy. For example, in the period from 1913 to 1918, the state budget increased twelvefold, with the vast majority of funds expended on military procurement. In addition, the state heavily subsidized the weapons monopolies (headed by the Vickers Company) as well as the metallurgical industry and the machine manufacturing sector of the economy. By 1918, more than twenty thousand companies were solely under contract to the government to produce military goods.

Because they directly served the war effort, the metallurgical, chemical, and automobile industries grew very rapidly under vigorous sponsorship by the government. Steel production increased from 7.78 million tons in 1913 to 9.69 million tons in 1918. However, industrial production as a whole constantly declined during the war due to shortages of raw materials, shrinking exports, and a decline in the consumer-oriented industries.

England's grain shortage became extremely acute during the war. Parliament appealed to the landlords and the managers of the great estates to turn their grasslands and pastures into cultivated acreage. It provided them with inexpensive farm machinery, and also guaranteed a minimum price for wheat and potatoes. Under the vigorous support of the government, English agricultural production achieved comparatively substantial growth after 1916. Grain self-sufficiency increased from about one-third prior to the war to about one-half during the conflict. However, as soon as the war ended, agriculture once again sank into difficulties.

The imperialist war brought severe hardships to the working class. The broad masses of workers endured military service and a grueling work schedule without respite. Because prices increased, workers' real wages decreased about 24 percent during the war. The tax burden carried by each citizen increased from 5.4 pounds sterling in 1913 to 19 pounds sterling in 1918. After the government imposed food rationing in 1916, working people found themselves in a state of semi-starvation.

After the Great War ended, England's monopoly bourgeoisie realized its predetermined goal of plunder. Germany's defeat enabled England to consolidate temporarily its leading position in Europe as well as eliminate Germany's challenge in the world market. Under the terms of the Versailles Treaty, England acquired many new colonies and took 75 percent of the world's petroleum reserves into its own hands.

However, the war caused far greater damage to England than any offsetting gains it might have achieved. In the first place, England lost 70 percent of its prewar shipping as a result of German naval attacks. Although England made the greatest effort to expand its shipbuilding capability during the war, production still fell below pre-1914 levels. The shipbuilding industry in the United States and Japan, however, seized the opportunity presented by the war and grew enormously. As a result, England lost the maritime supremacy that it had enjoyed for 250 years, and saw its naval power greatly diminished. Second, England's foreign trade situation deteriorated. In the period from 1913 to 1918, England's export trade, calculated by volume, decreased by half, sending its trade deficit soaring. During the war, England not only sold one billion pounds sterling of its foreign investments, but also fell into debt to the United States to the tune of 900 million pounds. This shifted the world's financial center to the United States. At the same time, the United States took advantage of this opportunity to occupy the markets of Europe and Latin America. Japanese goods also flooded into India, Southeast Asia, and other markets previously controlled by England. England's position in the world market deteriorated further.

In addition, national capitalism made certain gains in England's self-governing territories and colonies during World War I. As reliance on England's economy weakened, a national bourgeoisie and working class began to emerge and grow in these areas. Especially important was the great victory of the socialist revolution in October 1917 (November 1917 by the new calendar) in Russia which greatly encouraged the liberation struggles of the colonial and semi-colonial peoples. As a result of these developments, the foundation of England's colonial rule began to shake during World War I. Battered by the raging national liberation movements in the colonies, the era of England's trouble-free rule and unrestrained exploitation of the colonial peoples was gone, never to return. The British Empire that ruled the world for the previous hundred years was beginning to decline.

5. England's Economic Decline between the Two World Wars

The Long-term Economic Recession of the 1920s

As England entered the first few years of the era of the general crisis of capitalism, its political situation was unstable, and its economy was feeble. On the one hand, serious surpluses existed in military industrial production. On the other hand, serious shortages occurred in the production of consumer goods. When the government continued issuing paper currency to make up for its fiscal deficits, prices skyrocketed. The purchasing power of the English pound fell to one-third of its prewar level. In March 1919, England formally announced that it would abandon the gold standard.

At this time of economic chaos, the class struggle within England also sharpened to an unprecedented degree. A downsized military industry created large unemployment. Soaring commodity prices also caused real wages to plummet. The disastrous aftereffects of the imperialist war forced the working class to intensify its resistance to monopoly capital. The victory of the October socialist revolution in Russia gave even greater encouragement to the revolutionary fighting will of the English working masses. In the early postwar period, strikes broke out everywhere. The ruling class attributed this revolutionary wave of activity on the part of England's workers and the colonial peoples to the existence of Soviet Russia. As a result, England—in league with other imperialist countries—launched an armed intervention against Soviet Russia, hoping to destroy this revolution in its swaddling clothes. British imperialism's despicable actions met with strong opposition from the worker masses. They organized powerful and vocal demonstrations to protest the actions of English imperialism, and refused to transport and load weapons intended for the "White bandits" in Russia. The consciousness of the working class was raised in this struggle, and it strengthened itself organizationally. Union membership increased from 4.5 million in 1918 to 6.5 million in 1920. The Communist party of England was founded in this year.

After this political and economic instability calmed down, a temporary period of pseudoprosperity appeared early in 1920. However, within a year, England plunged into its first (1920–21) postwar economic crisis. This crisis was touched off by the contradiction that had existed between wartime shortages in the production of consumer goods and the demand for consumption. This demand had built up during the war, and was now released during this period of postwar pseudoprosperity. However, the postwar commercial prosperity was only a temporary phenomenon brought about by the change from a wartime economy to a peacetime economy. The real purchasing power of the citizenry was in fact quite low. As a result, a crisis of overproduction appeared as soon as industry had recovered somewhat. In addition to this, the United States and Japan also began to compete quite aggressively with England in international markets not long after the war ended. These two nations had reaped huge windfall profits from the war, and had seen their economic production expand to an unprecedented degree. Therefore, even after England's foreign trade position took a turn for the better, it once again quickly deteriorated when confronted with competition from America and Japan. The severity of Britain's crisis was unprecedented. Industrial production as a whole declined 46 percent from its previous high point. This went beyond any previous crisis in English history. Unemployment reached 14.8 percent. In order to shift the heavy burden of the crisis onto the backs of the working class, the bourgeoisie in 1921 lowered the average weekly wage to eight shillings for six million workers. The masses of workers bravely counterattacked this ruthless assault by the bourgeoisie. Strikes reached a scale never seen before.

An economic upsurge did not appear again in England in the 1920s even after this crisis had been surmounted. Rather, England found itself mired in a chronic recession. Up to 1929, total industrial production exceeded the prewar (1913) level by only 5.7 percent. However, the performance of each industrial sector varied. Generally speaking, the older sectors declined while the new ones grew to a certain extent.

England's traditional, basic industries numbered five: textiles, coal mining, steel, shipbuilding, and machine manufacturing (except for electrical goods). Prior to the war, these veteran industries accounted for approximately 50 percent of net industrial output value, and their exports accounted for 70 percent of total shipments. However, production in all these sectors (except for machinery, which grew to a certain degree) had declined when compared to their prewar situation. While steel production in 1929 was 9.79 million tons, this figure represented merely a return to the level already achieved in 1918. Coal, iron, shipbuilding, and textiles all slumped, to varying degrees, below their prewar levels. Moreover, the facilities in these sectors were all backward. In coal mining, for example, only 35 percent of coal cutting in England was mechanized by 1931, whereas 80 percent to 90 percent of that process was mechanized in the United States and Germany. In 1930, 42 percent of England's cotton textile machines had been produced prior to the 1870s and 1880s, and approximately 20 percent of these were often idle. Many coal mines lost huge sums of money and had to close down. Unemployment among coal miners averaged more than 16 percent in the period from 1925 to 1929. The shipbuilding industry had large amounts of surplus capacity because it was being squeezed out by new types of foreign vessels that used diesel oil. Unemployment in the shipbuilding industry averaged approximately 30 percent during the 1920s.

In contrast to the older industries, certain new sectors (such as automobiles, electrical goods, chemicals, and nonferrous metals) grew substantially in the 1920s. This expansion was due to temporary relief from German competition as well as the establishment of tariffs that protected these industries. For example, automobile production (including trucks) went from more than 30,000 units before the war to 240,000 units in 1929, or roughly equivalent to the number built in France. (Automobile production in the United States was 5.36 million units in the same year.) Aircraft construction, electric power generation, man-made fibers, and other new industries grew to a certain extent.

However, the development of these new industries could alter neither the backwardness of England's industrial plant and technology, nor its general pattern of chronic recession. As a result, England's share of the capitalist world's industrial production fell again from 14 percent in 1913 to 9 percent in 1929. The United States, on the other hand, increased its share from 38 percent to 48 percent.

England's industrial structure—created by its unique historical circumstances—and its obsolete plants and technology comprised one element that contributed to the sluggish economy of the 1920s. Another major factor that caused this chronic industrial recession was the adverse impact on Britain of the increasing competition for markets during the period of the general crisis of capitalism.

First of all, the national industries in England's colonies and self-governing territories took the opportunity that presented itself during the Great War to achieve a certain level of growth. After the war, the people of the colonies set into motion a revolutionary tide to attain their national liberation. The self-governing territories also waged a sharp struggle with England to achieve complete self-government and equality. These struggles forced England to make certain compromises, thereby weakening its economic control over its colonies and self-governing territories. As a result, the national industries in these areas expanded further, and became a competitive force in the marketplace with English commodities. For example, India's cotton textile industry made dramatic progress after the war. India's machine-woven cotton textiles now claimed more than 80 percent of the domestic market. This was in sharp contrast to the situation prior to the war when imports held more than 70 percent of the domestic market for machine-made cottons. In addition, some semi-colonial countries (such as China, Brazil, and others) also developed, to differing degrees, their own light industries, especially their cotton textile industries. All of these factors aggravated the shrinking foreign market for English industry's consumer goods, especially its cotton textiles.

Second, American and Japanese imperialism took advantage of the enhanced positions they had secured during World War I to launch an attack on England in various global markets. After the war, the great majority of Latin American countries now imported more American than British commodities. The United States also intensified its penetration of English imperialism's home market, and caused a gradual decline in the market share of imports that came from Britain's overseas possessions. Although Canada was nominally a self-governing territory of England, it now became—in reality—a market virtually monopolized by the United States. Japanese commodities undermined England's position even more by squeezing out British goods (especially textile exports) in the markets of Southeast Asia, India, China, and even Australia.

Third, the receptivity of foreign markets to England's traditionally substantial commodity exports (such as coal and cotton textiles) cooled because of the postwar development of new technologies. For example, the development of hydroelectric power, the widespread use of petroleum, the replacement of steam engines by diesels, and the emergence of various fuel-conserving inventions all greatly attenuated the demand for English coal. The rapid postwar development of man-made fibers also reduced the market for cotton textiles.

Finally, England returned to the gold standard in 1925 and pegged its currency at the prewar exchange rate, hoping thereby to regain its status as the center of international finance. This action, however, overvalued the real worth of the English pound and artificially increased the price of British exports which were calculated in foreign currencies. To a certain extent, this weakened England's own competitiveness vis-à-vis foreign products, and had an unfavorable impact on British exports.

These above-mentioned factors accelerated the steadily deteriorating export situation of England in the 1920s. Britain's share of total world exports slipped from a prewar 13.9 percent to 10.8 percent, and pushed England's industry, which relied on foreign markets to a critical extent, into a long-term recession.

England's agriculture also declined substantially in the 1920s because the government halted its farm subsidies, eliminated restrictions on grain imports, and permitted inexpensive foreign foodstuffs and animal products to flood the English market. Vast, cultivated areas once again became either wastelands or pasturelands. Agricultural production plummeted.

The industrial recession brought serious unemployment and deprivation to the English working class. While the rate of unemployment in the prewar decade fluctuated between 2 percent and 5 percent, the annual average in the 1920s stood at 12 percent, that is, upwards of a million workers unemployed. This chronic and massive unemployment forced many workers to leave their homeland and emigrate abroad. The bourgeoisie used this opportunity to frantically attack the working class, and did its utmost to reduce wages and lengthen the time of work. In June 1925, the English mine owners brazenly reduced wages by 10 percent, abolished the minimum wage, and subsequently extended the workday from seven to eight hours. In the face of this capitalist attack, the English working class resolutely worked out a concerted job action. A mammoth General Strike of miners, railway workers, and transportation workers finally broke out in May 1926. Almost four million workers participated at various stages of this militant strike. The General Strike paralyzed England's entire economy and revealed the fearless power of the working class.

Frightened by the heroic struggles of the working masses, and intimidated by the political and military moves initiated by the Conservative party government, the opportunist union leaders and heads of the Labor party took the road of capitulation. The treachery of the opportunist leaders caused the defeat of the General Strike. However, the brave miners sustained their struggle right up to December. The bourgeoisie began a new attack immediately afterward. In 1927, the Conservative party government enacted the Trade Disputes and Trade Unions Act which declared general strikes and sympathy strikes illegal. It stipulated that anyone who participated in an "unlawful" strike could be liable to penalties. It rejected the right of those unemployed to retain their jobs from their previous employers, regarded strikers as criminals, and so on and so forth. This law came to be known as the "Scab's Magna Carta." However, the opportunist union leaders fell on their knees in submission, initiated proposals to cooperate with the employers, and raised the slogan of "let's exert a common effort to improve industrial efficiency and elevate the workers' living standards." They held a joint conference in 1928 with the big industrial groups, and wanted the workers to submit to monopoly capital and take the road of class cooperation. This treacherous conduct of the opportunist leaders was fiercely resisted by the broad masses of workers.

The Economic Depression of 1929–32 and the Temporary Recovery of the Late 1930s

The chronic recession of the 1920s could not mitigate England's domestic contradiction between overproduction and underconsumption. On the contrary, this contradiction became increasingly acute as the broad working masses became more impoverished. The 1929 global economic depression immediately engulfed England because Britain's industry relied so heavily on foreign markets. The Depression appeared to hit England less severely than other countries only because the precrisis British economy was already not performing very well, and also because a comprehensive renovation and expansion of its fixed capital had not occurred. England's index of industrial production declined 23.8 percent when measured from its highest precrisis level to when it bottomed out during the Depression. (The U.S. index, in comparison, declined 55.6 percent.) However, diminished production was extremely serious in several important industries such as steel, shipbuilding, and textiles. Here the great majority of facilities sat idle. Unemployment was close to three million in 1932, and the average rate of unemployment reached 22.2 percent.

The crisis that enveloped the entire capitalist world maximized surplus production while simultaneously minimizing the capacity of the world market to buy these commodities. As a result, the Depression intensified the scramble for shares of the world market. England, however, suffered the greatest damage because it a) depended the most on foreign markets, b) remained comparatively weak in its overall competitiveness, and c) basically still followed a policy of free trade. England's exports fell 50 percent during the Depression, and its trade deficit grew quickly. Reduced income from foreign investments and maritime trade led in 1931 to England's first international balance of payments deficit that came to 100 million pounds sterling. England was forced to abandon the gold standard and devalue the pound in September of that year.

In order to extricate itself from the Depression and prevent further deterioration in its global position, the English ruling class enacted a series of measures to shift to others the burden of the crisis that broke out in 1929. First of all, the British ruling class implemented in 1930 a series of so-called domestic "austerity" measures that sacrificed the interests of the working class. That is to say, it substantially reduced funding for unemployment compensation, lowered wages, and imposed new taxes. These steps pushed the working masses to the brink of starvation.

Second, in order to protect the home market and stop competition from foreign commodities, the English ruling class completely abandoned its policy of free trade after 1932. It levied ad valorem duties ranging from 10 percent to 33.3 percent on all imported commodities, without exception. In addition, it tried to devalue the pound to stimulate exports. However, the effectiveness of these measures was quickly offset when the other countries abandoned the gold standard, devalued their own currencies, erected high tariff barriers, or restricted imports.

Third, England convened a Commonwealth Conference in Ottawa, Canada in 1931. London's purpose was to consolidate the market of the British Empire, and to strengthen its control over and exploitation of its colonies and self-governing territories. It eventually reached an "Agreement on Special Tariffs in the Empire" with the various self-governing territories and colonies. According to the agreement, England would grant preferential treatment—either abolishing or reducing tariffs—on commodities imported from the self-governing territories and colonies. In addition, it would restrict its own imports of agricultural goods coming from outside the Empire. Conversely, the self-governing territories and colonies would grant preferential treatment to industrial goods imported from England by reducing tariffs (generally, up to 20 percent of the value of the commodity) on these products. At the same time, they would increase tariffs on all imports from countries other than England. The purpose was to prevent other countries from penetrating the Empire's market. Finally, after abandoning the gold standard in 1931, England gradually organized a pound sterling monetary bloc. Britain did this to consolidate the role of the English pound as an international currency and to stop the United States from intruding on its sphere of influence. Currencies of participating countries maintained a fixed value vis-à-vis the English pound, and their rate of exchange with the U.S. dollar and other currencies was pegged according to the pound's value vis-à-vis the dollar. The foreign exchange reserves of participating countries were deposited in various London banks, and were used to clear international debts. In order to stimulate domestic investment, the English government also took steps to prevent capital flight, to lower interest rates, and to expand credit.

None of these measures mentioned above could basically alter or reverse the general tendency of economic decline. However, they did play a certain role in temporarily ameliorating the crisis.

After the 1929 Depression bottomed out in 1932, production once again began to rise—but only very slowly. This temporary economic revival, up to and after 1935, was achieved when the government expanded its intervention into the domestic economy and increased its military spending. By 1937, England's index of industrial production stood 23.7 percent higher than at its peak pre-Depression year in 1929. Steel production climbed from 9.79 million tons in 1929 to 13.19 million tons in 1937. Car production went from 240,000 units to 500,000 in that same time period. However, all these increases represented merely a partial recovery back to the already backward situation of the 1920s. In 1937, England produced only one-fourth of the steel and one-tenth of the automobiles that the United States did. However, U.S. production in 1937 in both of these sectors still had not returned to their 1929 levels.

Two important features characterized England's industrial production after the Depression: 1. British industry experienced comparatively large growth in the new industries as well as those sectors of heavy industry tied to military production. 2. The traditional industries such as coal, shipbuilding, and textiles still remained mired in a chronic slump.

The reason why the former sectors grew to such an extent (other than benefiting from protective tariffs, the renovation of their fixed capital, and increased domestic investment) was because the arms race artificially stimulated their expansion. After the 1929 Depression broke out, the imperialist countries pinned their hopes of extricating themselves from their crisis on initiating wars of aggression. Japan and Germany set up fascist political systems in their countries in the 1930s. When they energetically expanded their military forces and increased their aggressive activities, they further intensified the contradictions that existed among the imperialist nations. England actively abetted this fascist aggression in a frantic attempt to turn the spearhead of this attack against the Soviet Union. However, England also stepped up its own pace in preparing for war. Steep increases in the military budget after 1935 (in fact, 1937 expenditures were double those of 1935) stimulated the development of industries like steel, machine manufacturing, aircraft, automobiles, chemicals, construction, and so on.

However, even by 1937, the older industries like coal, shipbuilding, and textiles still had not regained their 1929 levels. Despite state intervention—which eliminated a great deal of obsolete equipment and closed many backward factories and mines in the name of rationalizing industry—plant capacity remained seriously underutilized, and unemployment still exceeded 20 percent.

The continued decline of the older industrial sectors was the direct result of a drop in productivity and a constant deterioration in the export sector. The establishment of a commonwealth system of preferential tariffs and a pound sterling monetary bloc strengthened England's position to a certain degree in the markets of the self-governing territories, the colonies, and the semi-colonies. However, England's exports had not regained their 1929 levels even by 1937 because of a shrinking global market and fierce competition from the United States, Japan, and Germany during this period. A continued reduction in income from foreign investments and maritime trade put England's international balance of payments account in the red almost every year.

The short-term industrial recovery of 1935–37 also did not bring a corresponding improvement to the lives of the working class. That is, there were still 1.5 million people unemployed when industrial production peaked during this period. Real wages for those still employed actually dropped because of inflation in the cost of living. One of every three households in London still lived below the poverty line. By the end of 1937, this temporary recovery had evaporated. Another crisis broke out in 1937–38. As a result, the ruling clique sought even greater relief by expanding preparations for war. For example, the military budget in 1938 was 50 percent higher than in 1937. Only the full-scale outbreak of World War II temporarily halted the downward trajectory embodied in this economic crisis.

England's agricultural production in the 1930s recovered to a certain extent as the government renewed its farm subsidies and protectionist policies, and as agricultural technology was significantly upgraded. After the 1932 Ottawa Conference, the English government levied across-the-board tariffs as well as set quotas on agricultural products that could be imported from other countries—with the exception, of course, of foodstuffs imported from the commonwealth's self-governing territories and colonies that were granted "preferential treatment." In order to guarantee a high income for its landlords and farm owners, the government provided "compensation" to these people if the market price on important agricultural commodities fell below a fixed level. This type of measure—using the government budget to take money from the wallets of consumers in order to line the pockets of the agricultural capitalists—was blatant plunder of the broad masses of the working people. The principal beneficiaries of these agricultural subsidies were the large farm owners—people who managed farms bigger than fifty acres and who operated comparatively advanced farm machinery. Despite all these measures, England's agricultural production in the 1930s still had not recovered to the level it had reached at the end of the First World War. More than 70 percent of domestic consumption still came from grain imports, and more than 85 percent of Britain's fat and meat was imported. The nature of England's colonial empire and the system of land ownership controlled by large landlords seriously hindered the development of agriculture.

In summing up, we can say that England's economy was stuck in a declining and volatile situation between the two world wars. The general crisis of capitalism was reflected on the body of this vast and venerable empire.

The Strengthening of Monopoly Capital Rule

Assisted by the central government and its various agencies, England's monopoly capital strengthened itself between the two world wars, and especially before the Second World War. Its aim was to rescue England's declining Empire as well as maintain its own control. First of all, the monopolies that had already emerged prior to World War I became the core of the developing industrial conglomerates. As a result of mergers and acquisitions both during and after the war, they were able to expand the scope of their operations and now came to control the new industries which enjoyed tariff protection from the government. For example, the Vickers Corporation (which had already staked out a monopoly in weapons manufacture even prior to the First World War) gobbled up quite a few companies both during and after World War I. In 1928, it merged with another weapons monopoly, the Armstrong-Whitworth Company, to create the Vickers-Armstrong Corporation. In 1929, Vickers and the Cammell-Laird Shipbuilding Company jointly founded a powerful metallurgical trust (the British Steel Smelting Company) and an automobile manufacturing trust (the Metropolitan Cammell Carriage and Wagon Company). As a result, Vickers became a huge combine focused on the production of weapons and machinery, and owned many domestic and foreign facilities that manufactured weaponry, military equipment, metals, ships, aircraft, and electrical goods. In the chemical industry, the Imperial Chemicals Company emerged as a huge concern created by the amalgamation of four large prewar monopolies: the Brunner Mond Company, the United Sodium Manufacturing Company, Nobel Industries, and the British Dyestuffs Corporation. Shortly after its founding, this company controlled 95 percent of England's production of basic chemicals, all of its synthetic nitrogen, and 40 percent of its dyes. It became the strongest competitor of Germany's Farben Company in international markets. As a result of post–World War I developments, six big monopolies in the automobile industry—Austin, Ford, Morris, Standard, Vauxhall, and Rootes & Standard—claimed almost 90 percent of England's auto production by the eve of the Second World War. The first three mentioned accounted for two-thirds of that production. All these huge concerns and companies further increased their power during the military expansion that took place in the late 1930s.

Second, after World War I—and especially after the Crash of 1929—monopolies began to emerge in some of the chronically depressed industries under the guise of "rationalization." Government intervention and promotion of these activities expedited the process, and constituted an important manifestation of the postwar development of Britain's state monopoly capitalism. For example, the Lancaster Cotton Textile Company, created by government support and the participation of the Bank of England, acquired 139 cotton mills in 1929. Then, under the pretext of "rationalization," the company closed down fifty-two obsolete plants in the early 1930s. In 1936, it once again purchased some small and medium-sized companies from the government—only to immediately destroy their existing textile machinery. This further strengthened the ability of the large corporations, with their relatively advanced equipment, to monopolize the textile industry. In shipbuilding, the National Shipbuilding Insurance Company (created by state intervention and financial backing from bank capital) also used the method of acquisition and divestment to destroy many small and medium-sized shipyards in 1930. This process thereby enhanced the control exerted by the large corporations over this sector. In the coal mining industry, the government enacted legislation in 1930 promoting the regional cartelization of coal mining operations. Each region would set quotas and minimum prices for coal. The government also established a Coal Mining Commission to promote mergers and "rationalization" of the industry. The British government enacted additional legislation in 1936 on compulsory mergers in the coal mining industry. It left no stone unturned in promoting the emergence of monopolies in this sector. Assisted by high protective tariffs and governmental support, five large steel monopolies (the United Steel Company, the British Steel Foundry Company, the Dorman Long Company, the Guest-Keen-Nettlefords Company, and the Lancashire Steel Company) emerged in the years 1929–30 in the field of metallurgy.

The founding in 1932 of the British Steel Corporation brought about the complete cartelization of the metallurgical industry. The ten biggest companies in this cartel controlled 47 percent of steel smelting capacity and 60 percent of steel blooming capacity.

The monopolies that controlled the extraction of raw materials from the colonies and semi-colonies not only continued to grow after the war, but also retained the greatest clout. For example, the Anglo-Persian Petroleum Company, the Royal Dutch/Shell Group, and the Burma Petroleum Company topped the list of England's monopolies when ranked by capital assets. These three petroleum giants controlled 76 percent of Middle East oil production in 1939, and were the biggest competitors of the Standard Oil Company.

Concentration and monopoly in the postwar banking industry also intensified. The strength of the "Big Five" banks grew enormously. The share held by the "Big Five" of total deposits in joint-stock banks increased from 40 percent in 1913 to 86 percent in 1938. The unprecedented increase in mergers between bank and industrial capital represented the biggest transformation in banking during this period. On the one hand, this was due to the chronic industrial recession and the sharp decline in the older industrial sectors. Industrial capital urgently demanded long-term credit support from the banks. On the other hand, the banks also became more enthusiastic about investing in industry. The turbulence in the postwar colonial system and the increased risks in the export of capital prompted the banks to become increasingly cautious about investing abroad. After the 1929 Depression, the collapse or financial insolvency of so many companies in the older industries (companies who owed substantial sums to the banks) directly threatened the interests of bank capital. As a result, a stock management trust, headed by the Bank of England, was established in 1929 to control the sale of industrial stocks. Assisted by the large commercial banks and investment houses, the Bank of England also created a "Bankers Industrial Development Corporation" in 1930 to provide not only financial help but also bank participation in the "reorganization" of industry. A huge wave of banking capital engulfed industry after these developments. The "Big Five" banks individually established close ties to and actively invested in the giant monopolies in the older and newer industrial sectors. The "personnel arrangements" between the leaders of the "Big Five" banks and of the industrial monopolies also became more closely intertwined by the expansion of interlocking directorates. In 1938, the one hundred directors who sat on the boards of the "Big Five" banks also concurrently held more than one thousand directorships in various joint-stock companies. These directors became the core of England's plutocracy.

Finance capital also completely controlled England's state apparatus. The great majority of the Conservative party members who sat in England's postwar Parliaments were people who were large stockholders, and half of them held executive positions in the big corporations. The prime ministers and other ranking ministers in the Conservative party cabinets—people like Stanley Baldwin,

Austin and Neville Chamberlain, and Addison—were all either large share holders or managers or directors of some large enterprise or big bank. The monopoly capitalists wormed their way into Parliament and into the cabinets in order to use the machinery of the state even more directly in suppressing the working people and to enable the monopoly capitalist groups to amass even greater profits.

The more intense the oppression, the stronger the resistance. By the mid-1930s, the English working class began to push aside the obstructions laid down by the opportunist leaders who occupied the top rungs in the labor unions. Roused to action by the humiliations they had suffered since 1926, England's working class now staged a series of continuous demonstrations and strikes, and struck a blow at the rule of monopoly capital. In 1935, the frightened and jittery mouthpiece of monopoly capital, *The Times*, cried out: "The spirit of the 1926 General Strike is once again appearing!" [source unknown].

6. England's Economic Strength Deteriorates Further during the Second World War: The British Empire Declines

Although the Second World War was launched by the fascist states of Germany, Japan, and Italy, England too was a supporter of the global rise of fascist power and pampered its foreign aggression. British imperialism deliberately attempted to make use of the hands of the German and Japanese fascists to destroy the Soviet Union, a country that it had always hated. However, Great Britain lifted a rock only to drop it on its own foot. England was forced to declare war on Germany in September 1939, after Hitler (who harbored ambitions of gobbling up the entire world) had occupied some countries on the European continent and had begun to point the spearhead of his attack against Britain itself. Not only did England participate in the war to strike at Germany, but also to rescue itself from its economic crisis, consolidate its colonial empire, and guarantee the highest profits possible for its monopoly capitalists.

After the war began, the government immediately intensified its intervention in and control over the entire economy by creating a wartime cabinet and economic regulatory agencies completely manipulated by monopoly capitalists. During the war, some 2,500 individuals who held leadership positions in the trusts came to control the governmental regulatory agencies, and turned these government offices into tools of monopoly capital that squeezed out the blood and sweat from the people. The heavy burden of the colossal military budget was shouldered entirely by the working people. They were the ones who paid for the war effort through higher taxes on rents, an increase in government bond issues, and inflation. Because disbursements were approved by governmental supervisory agencies controlled by the monopolies, money flowed endlessly into the wallets of the monopoly bourgeoisie. The mission of these regulatory agencies was to take charge of a) the procurement of military goods from the monopolies; b) the governmental allocation of investment, raw materials, and subsidies; c) budgetary decisions on the retooling of certain factories that could be profitable to monopoly capital; and d) the allocation of labor power. During the war, the government invested one billion pounds sterling in industry, half of which was used to set up state-run factories needed by the military. After the facilities had been built, they were turned over to private companies to manage. Afterwards, they were once again sold—quite cheaply—to the big monopolies. The other half of this billion-pound investment was directly used to expand the credit opportunities for privately run companies. The government also signed contracts with the monopolies to purchase military hardware. The total annual value of these contracts reached 500 million pounds sterling, and they guaranteed rich profits. Using military necessity as a pretext, the government also either shut down plants or transferred their ownership. For example, the government forced 2,800 companies in fifty-two different sectors of the economy to merge with the big monopolies. The rule of monopoly capital became strengthened to an unprecendented degree.

During the war, industrial production relied on military procurement to grow rapidly, and by 1944, had reached a zenith, surpassing its 1939 level by 25 percent. However, while production in military-related industry and heavy industry increased sharply, the production of consumer goods diminished, creating critical shortages in market supplies and a skyrocketing inflation. Except for those newly built or expanded companies involved in the war effort, very few other industrial facilities were either renovated or upgraded during the war. By compelling its workers to speed up production, the government not only added to the heavy wartime burdens they shouldered, but also caused serious deterioration in Britain's industrial plant and equipment. German aerial attacks also destroyed a portion of England's fixed industrial capital. By early 1945, England's industrial production began a general decline.

Governmental assistance enabled British agriculture to make some headway during the war. Cultivated acreage, farm mechanization, and grain production all grew to a certain extent. However, improved grain production did not compensate for the shortages induced by shrinking imports. From 1940 on, England rationed vital foodstuffs, and reduced food consumption by its citizens to the lowest possible level. Clothing also was rationed: adult cloth consumption in wartime was half that of the prewar amount.

The war seriously weakened England's economic strength. It claimed 410,000 lives. One-fourth of the nation's entire wealth went up in flames. Industrial technology and equipment became even more obsolete. England's rank in industrial production in the capitalist world declined further, and fell farther and farther behind that of the United States. In maritime strength, the total tonnage of the U.S. merchant and military fleets also far exceeded that of England. The era when "Brittania ruled the seas" was gone, never to return. English exports decreased by almost 70 percent during the Second World War, and its share of the capitalist world's trade also became overshadowed by the United States. Altogether, Britain's foreign investments shrank by 1.1 billion pounds sterling and its foreign debts increased to almost three billion pounds in order to pay for the military goods it had purchased from abroad during the war. Its wartime international balance of payments deficit reached four billion pounds. All of these factors seriously weakened England's international financial position.

As a result of the war, England's financial and economic life came to rely to a certain extent on the United States. Of England's wartime imports, 60 percent were American in origin. After the war had gone on for more than a year, the United States had squeezed England almost dry of its gold and foreign currency reserves. On the basis of the American Lend-Lease Act, the British subsequently brought in from the United States goods valued at twenty-seven billion dollars. The Lend-Lease Agreement contained many clauses intended to destroy England's hegemony over its imperial market. For example, some clauses demanded that England lower its tariffs, others that it should abolish its system of preferential tariffs. In addition, the United States also forced England to let it use many overseas air and naval bases in exchange for these lend-lease supplies.

The war also intensified to an unprecedented extent the centrifugal forces at work within the British Empire, and initiated the destabilization of that colonial system. England had little alternative but to develop some mining and processing industries in its colonies and self-governing territories during the war in order to satisfy its military needs as well as step up its plunder of these areas. At the same time, the national industries in its colonies and self-governing territories gained an opportunity to develop when imports from Britain fell off. On the one hand, this weakened the economic base that linked the British Empire internally. On the other hand, these developments also promoted the subsequent maturation of a national bourgeoisie and proletariat in these areas. England also ran up a huge debt with its colonies and self-governing territories—and refused to settle for a long time—when the raw materials it imported from them during the war far exceeded the value of the commodities it supplied. In reality, such an action not only placed the heavy burden of war-generated expenses on the backs of the people of the colonies and self-governing territories, but also intensified the contradiction between itself and its colonies.

England's weakened condition—as well as the penetration of its colonies and self-governing territories by the influence of American imperialism—greatly diminished its ability to control its empire internally. Also, victory in the global war against fascism, and especially the great victory of the Chinese Revolution, shook the entire imperialist camp quite vigorously, and encouraged the national liberation struggles of the colonial and semi-colonial peoples of the entire world. These events destabilized the postwar colonial system of British imperialism. They also produced a wave of activities on the part of the people of the colonies who broke away from Britain's direct rule. These people now set up their own independent, national political systems. The once-arrogant "empire on which the sun never sets" had now ended up like "the sun sinking quickly over the western hills." England was left without any hope of recovery.

3
United States

The United States is an imperialist superpower today. However, barely two centuries ago, the United States was not even an independent state but merely a group of colonies ruled by England. Only after they successfully defeated the British during the War of Independence in the 1770s did these colonies achieve their independence and establish a bourgeois republic: the United States of America. In the next hundred years after its founding this recent arrival among the capitalist states then grew rapidly. By the early 1880s, the United States had jumped so far ahead that it could claim industrial leadership over the capitalist world. Once it entered the stage of imperialism in the early twentieth century, the United States became an imperialist power where monopoly capitalism had developed to its highest level. The United States then reaped a fabulous bonanza from its participation in two world wars, and became the center of international financial exploitation as well as master of the world.

"Capitalism entered the world covered with blood and filth from head to toe."[1] The history of the development of American capitalism is precisely this history of filthy exploitation and bloodstained plunder. And, as Marx pointed out, capitalism grew in the United States under conditions more shameful than in any other country.

1. The Economy during the Colonial Period and the Revolutionary War of Independence (1775–83)

The Colonial Economy of the North American Settlements

The Indians were the original masters of the American continent. By the end of the fifteenth century, American Indian society remained at the stage of primitive communal settlements, and was organized into many tribal groups. After Columbus discovered America in 1492, this "new continent" became a target for exploitation. Various West European countries began to compete with each other to secure the spoils of primitive capital accumulation. For example, the Spanish, Dutch, French, and English each rushed to be the first to reach North America to plunder the new territories. They used the most savage methods to either expel or massacre the native peoples—the Indians. Then they confiscated their lands. England eventually defeated—one by one—the Spanish, Dutch, and French as soon as its own economy eclipsed each of these nations. In the seventeenth century, Britain founded thirteen colonies in North America in a narrow strip of land that stretched from the Atlantic coast on the east to the Appalachian Mountains in the west.[2] These thirteen colonies encompassed the extent of American territory during its revolutionary War of Independence. Its immigrant population numbered approximately 2.5 million—not counting the Indians, the original residents. Destitute workers from England, Germany, Holland, France, and other countries made up the bulk of this population. These people had come to North America to escape poverty, feudal tyranny, and religious oppression. They came to find a new path for their lives. However, the colonies were primarily organized by bourgeois merchants and prominent aristocrats. They managed the North American colonies like a financial venture: their goal, after all, was to make as much money as possible.

Initially the colonists were after gold and silver. However, when it was later discovered that the deposits of these two metals in North America were not as rich as those in Central and South America, the colonists then became involved in a predatory fur trade with the Indians. Here they made huge fortunes. Once colonies with fixed borders had been established, the settlers began to develop a colonial-type economy that served the interests of the metropole. The settlers now turned North America into an agricultural subsidiary of England. The colonies, however, each developed different economic arrangements in agriculture because each colony enjoyed unique natural endowments and each had been founded under special circumstances. Some colonies enjoyed a system of landownership dominated by farmers; some had a slave system; some even had feudal land relationships.

The colonies in the north were settled by groups of immigrant workers. These settlers would move in as a group, and after founding a village or town, would distribute the land there among themselves. As a result, small, self-cultivated farms were established throughout this region. However, the soil in the Northern colonies was poor and unproductive. Winters were rather long. The principal crops were corn, wheat, barley, oats, and potatoes.

In the colonies along the mid-Atlantic coast, the English king preserved a system of large landed estates. This system had originally been established by the Dutch in the Hudson River Valley. Now the British crown granted these estates to members of the English landed aristocracy, and thereby created a system of landownership in the mid-Atlantic colonies that was dominated by large feudal-type estates. The landed aristocracy then transplanted the European feudal system onto American soil. They divided up the land into small parcels, rented it to impoverished immigrants, and demanded payment requiring either goods or money. At the same time, they also brought over from Europe the rights of primogeniture, entail, and other accessories of the feudal system. Generally speaking, rents were not high because unclaimed land available for farming was plentiful throughout the colonies. Rents also remained low because the large estate owners competed with each other to attract renters to their land. However, the immigrants who had come to North America to seek a new life detested this kind of exploitation. They fought constantly against it, often withholding their rent payments or emigrating to a new area. The mid-Atlantic colonies also had many small, self-cultivated farms in addition to these large, landed estates. The natural environment in these colonies was comparatively better. Wheat, barley, and other grains grew in such abundance that the mid-Atlantic states came to be known as "the breadbasket colonies." Horticulture and animal husbandry also flourished.

The Southern colonies were run by landed aristocrats and wealthy merchant companies under charters granted by the British crown. The South enjoyed fertile plains and a warm climate, suitable for a simple, large-scale farm economy. In order to plunder the riches of this area, the British colonialists established a plantation economy here. They cultivated tobacco, grain, and blue indigo intended for sale in England. And they actually went so far as to reestablish a form of slavery that had vanished long ago. Slaves in North America came from two sources: white indentured servants[3] and blacks shipped from Africa. Prior to the revolutionary War of Independence, black slaves constituted the main work force on the plantations, and comprised roughly 50 percent of the entire population of the Southern colonies. By 1770, there were approximately 460,000 black slaves altogether in the thirteen North American colonies. Dutch merchants were the first to ship and sell black slaves to North America. After the middle of the seventeenth century, merchants from England and the North American colonies also began to get involved on a large scale in the slave trade. These slave dealers used worthless trinkets to exchange for black people who had been obtained from the hands of African tribal chiefs or local middlemen. These slave merchants then chained these black people together like livestock, packed them aboard shockingly crowded ships for the voyage across the Atlantic, and finally sold them to the plantations. This inhuman slave trade could make your blood curdle. For each black person who arrived in America, at least five others perished. These people died either when they were kidnapped in Africa or during the passage across the Atlantic. Black slaves were treated like cattle and forced to work hard. They expended their last bit of energy in tilling the soil on the plantations. Blacks not only remained slaves until their dying day, but their sons and daughters also became possessions owned unconditionally by the slave master. Marx said: "The sole natural basis of colonial wealth was the slave system."[4] Because land was readily available in the colonies, the worker had not been separated from the material conditions (the land) that sustained his work. As a result, the free labor necessary for capital to enrich itself was lacking. The capitalist had to resort to artificial measures to carry out exploitation, and therefore had to establish a system of forced slavery.

More than 90 percent of the colonial population was engaged in agriculture. Industry primarily consisted of household handicrafts. Small handicraft workshops flourished along the coastal areas where commerce was comparatively advanced. Handicraft factories that employed workers began to emerge in the eighteenth century. Small-scale handicraft factories employing several people—and even several tens of people—began to grow in shipbuilding, rum distilling, lumber, leather tanning, grain milling, iron forging, and other trades. These handicraft factories also used indentured servants or black slaves who were hired on an annual or monthly basis. With a winding coastline, many excellent harbors, and rich forest, and mineral resources, the Northern colonies constituted America's most advanced industrial area. Shipbuilding and aquaculture were the most advanced sectors.

As the economy developed and land and maritime transportation improved, the economic ties among the colonies also grew. The colonies eventually forged a common economic life. Of course, because they were colonies, the amount of trade between them was not great. However, their foreign trade was quite substantial. The South principally exported tobacco, rice, and blue indigo. The North emphasized fish, lumber, and nautical goods. And the mid-Atlantic colonies focused on grain as an export. Imports were primarily wool, iron tools, and other industrial products that came from England and Holland. Sugar, molasses, and other goods came from the Caribbean. The most lucrative commercial activity, however, was the so-called "triangle trade." This involved the purchase and sale of black slaves, and followed this pattern: Molasses was shipped from the West Indies to North America to be made into rum; the rum was sent to Africa to exchange for black slaves; black slaves were then shipped to the West Indies to be sold or exchanged for molasses; and the molasses was finally used in distilling the rum that was used to buy and sell the slaves. About thirty thousand slaves were transported annually to the Caribbean. Of these, approximately ten thousand were sent to the colonies on the American mainland. The slave merchants from England and the North American colonies made colossal—though bloodstained—profits from this inhuman traffic in slaves.

The Economic Contradictions between the Colonies and Great Britain and Their Relationship to the Revolutionary War of Independence

The British actively used their political power to control the economic life of the colonies and turn these colonies into economic appendages of England. During the initial years after their founding, the British rulers began to enact a series of legislative measures pertaining to colonial navigation, trade, industry, and finance. They did this in order to restrict the economic development of their North American colonies to limits demanded by the interests of the English metropole. For example, the Enumerated Commodities Act of 1660 stipulated that tobacco, sugar, cotton, indigo, and other commodities could be exported only to England. If such goods were to be shipped to other European destinations, then the cargo first had to be unloaded in England and then trans-shipped by English merchants. Subsequent regulations constantly expanded the categories of enumerated commodities, and eventually included virtually every export. The Staples Act of 1663 stipulated that all European commodities shipped and sold to the American colonies first had to be sent to England to pay taxes, and then could be sent forward only in British bottoms. In short, England monopolized the export and import trade of the North American colonies. In addition, Britain used this monopoly power to force down the prices of commodities it purchased from the colonies, thereby seriously obstructing their economic development. England also put restrictions on industry in the colonies. The Woolens Act of 1699 prohibited trade in wool and woolen goods. England also enacted the Iron Act in 1750 which prohibited the colonies from building or enlarging iron smelters or factories that made iron implements. The draconian controls exercised by the British colonialists over the industrial and commercial activity of their colonies created a sharp contradiction between England's colonial system and the independent economic development of North America. This was a major cause of America's revolutionary War of Independence.

The land question was yet another sharp contradiction that emerged between the colonies and the English metropole. In the process of colonizing North America, the English monarchs promoted a system of land ownership dominated by large estates. However, the farmers who worked on these large, landed estates opposed the exploitation involved when rents were paid in kind or money rather than in service. They emigrated westward en masse, cleared the land there, and began farming on their own. In order to preserve the interests of the landed aristocracy, the British monarchy then tried to prohibit the westward movement of these farmers seeking to own their own land. In 1763, the King of England announced that the land west of the Appalachian Mountains was the property of the British crown, and that the people of the colonies had no right to move there and settle down. This prohibition was directed mainly against the "westward push" of the farmers, which was essentially a movement directed against feudal oppression. The prohibition also engendered a conflict of interest with Southern plantation owners and merchants involved in land speculation. These people also demanded the westward expansion of the plantation-type land system. The British crown's laws and decrees aroused universal dissatisfaction from the people of the colonies and intensified their anti-British sentiments. As a result, the land question became yet another important element in the anti-British revolution, and gave the revolutionary War of Independence a striking anti-feudal character.

After the British had successfully concluded their Seven Years' War with the French, England—its treasury depleted—began to squeeze the colonies even more tightly. The Stamp Act of 1765 required Americans to pay taxes on all periodicals, legal documents, commercial receipts, and publications. The Currency Act took away the right of the colonies to issue paper money. After passing the Quartering Act, England sent military forces to North America to crack down on the colonies, and even forced the people to shoulder responsibility for providing the barracks and fuel supplies to the troops now stationed there. England also enacted other provocative regulations and statutes that squeezed the colonies. The economic exploitation and political oppression suffered by the Americans became increasingly severe.

The greater the oppression, the fiercer the resistance. Beginning in the 1760s, the people of the colonies became involved in a constant struggle against the English. On September 5, 1774, representatives sent from the various colonies convened the first Continental Congress. They were united in their resolute opposition to the British colonialists. In April 1775, the people of North America took up weapons, and heroically fought back against the troops sent by England to suppress them. The second Continental Congress convened in May 1775 formally declared war on England and elected George Washington as Commander-in-Chief. On July 4, 1776, the Continental Congress passed the Declaration of Independence. This document proclaimed the dissolution of America's subordinate relationship to the British crown and the establishment of an independent state—the United States of America. The people who had risen in armed struggle continued the battle. They fought a guerrilla war, and bravely attacked the English troops as well as the Loyalists among the big landed aristocrats, big slave owners, big merchants, and colonial officials who stood on the side of the British. After fighting seven long years, the people of North America finally achieved victory in their revolutionary war. England was forced to sign the Treaty of Paris in 1783 and to recognize America's independence. The North American colonies, with a population not quite three million and with extremely simple military equipment, nevertheless defeated Great Britain, the leading industrial power in the world at that time with a population of thirty million. The history of America's War of Independence fully confirms Chairman Mao's brilliant statement: "The people of a small country can certainly defeat aggression by a big country, if only they dare to rise in struggle, dare to take up arms and grasp in their own hands the destiny of their country. This is a law of history."[5]

The North American War of Independence (1775–83) was both a struggle to gain national independence as well as an anti-feudal bourgeois revolution. American victory in the war and the subsequent establishment of the United States overthrew England's colonial rule in North America. Domestically, it swept aside many feudal remnants, and it opened the road for the development of capitalism. For example, the American government (both during and after the war) confiscated the land of thirty thousand big landords who remained loyal to the British crown; it abolished the system of feudal land ownership and aristocratic titles; it abolished the system of corvee labor; and it abolished the right of primogeniture. The War of Independence ushered in a new era in the history of the development of American society. Lenin pointed out that "the history of modern, civilized America began with a great, truly liberating, truly revolutionary war."[6] The American people's struggle to gain independence and freedom also had a great impact on Europe's anti-feudal revolutionary movement. Just as Marx said, "The eighteenth century American War of Independence awakened the European middle class."[7]

Victory in the revolution was mainly achieved by relying on the strength of the farmers, workers, small handicraftsmen, small merchants, the lower strata of the bourgeoisie, and black people. However, the big bourgeoisie and the large plantation owners used the power of political leadership that they held in their own hands to steal the fruits of victory. After the victory of the revolution, the big bourgeoisie and the large plantation owners established a joint dictatorship. Although restrictions on westward migration were abolished, the land question—the most pressing demand of the vast numbers of farmers—was not yet entirely resolved. Although the evil system of slavery was either abolished in the North or limited in the mid-Atlantic states, it was still retained in the South and even legalized by the 1787 Constitution. Because the Constitution limited the electorate by imposing restrictions on voter qualifications, working people in reality found themselves politically disenfranchised. Blacks and Indians continued to be deprived of citizenship status altogether.

The masses of working people lost hope in the results of the revolution. In the days after the war, the burden of heavy debts and taxes once again weighed so heavily on them that they could scarcely catch their breath. As a result, the working people launched an uprising in 1786–87 under the leadership of Daniel Shays. The insurgents clearly reflected the interests of the impoverished farmers. They demanded that the government declare all land as common property, cancel all debts, and abrogate all land taxes. This impressive mass uprising frightened the bourgeoisie. In the name of preserving "God-given rights," the American government that had just proclaimed its independence ruthlessly put down the insurrection.

2. The Establishment of the Capitalist Mode of Production

Westward Territorial Expansion and the Settlement of Colonies

America fought the War of Independence in order to free itself from England's colonial rule. However, as soon as this newly founded bourgeois republic secured its freedom from the shackles of colonialism, it began to take the road of colonial expansion itself, and aggressively occupied vast territories in the West.

Beginning in the 1780s, the United States gradually wrested away from the hands of the Indians a huge tract of land between the Appalachian Mountains and the Mississippi River. The United States also annexed the English, French, and Spanish colonies in the western part of North America. It accomplished this by taking advantage of the Napoleonic wars that had plunged Europe into chaos, and of the anti-Spanish independence movements of the various Latin American peoples. In the 1830s and 1840s, the United States also gobbled up nearly half of the land of its newly independent neighbor, Mexico. By the middle of the nineteenth century, the United States had extended its borders to the shores of the Pacific Ocean. In 1776, at the time of the Declaration of Independence, the United States covered only 369,000 square miles; by 1860, however, it had expanded almost eightfold, and claimed an area of 3,022,387 square miles. The United States became a country vast in area and rich in resources, and possessed natural conditions far more advantageous to economic development than any other capitalist country.

Not only did the American government use coercion, bribery, and force to conclude treaties with other nations, but it also hatched various plots and schemes—and even frequently launched inhuman wars—to expand its territorial control. The settlement of the West was a process of bloody aggression, a process involving the removal as well as massacre of the Native Americans. Sayings like "savages must get out!" and "the only good Indian is a dead Indian" were common at that time. The U.S. government deployed its military forces in the early nineteenth century against the Indians, and often massacred them on a large scale. For example, American troops once suffered a defeat while conducting a military campaign against the Seminole Indians in Florida. At first, the American leaders enticed Chief Osceola of the Seminole tribe to enter into negotiations, and agreed to guarantee his safety. Then they treacherously doublecrossed Osceola, seized him, tied him up, and threw him into prison. When Andrew Jackson became President in 1830, he issued the Indian Removal Act which required that Indians be resettled west of the Mississippi River. President Jackson also sent troops in 1838 to round up the Indians and expel them under armed guard. This was one of the most heartbreaking migrations in human history. Thousands and tens of thousands of Indians died along the way. The Indians called this "the trail of tears." When this expulsion order was announced, the American government falsely promised the Indians that the new area where they were now being resettled "would be guaranteed theirs for as long as heaven and earth existed" [source unknown]. However, the eviction and massacre of the Indians also continued in the same manner in the areas west of the Mississippi River. For example, village after village of Indians was exterminated in the Gold Rush fever era after gold was discovered in California. In the decade between 1850 and 1860, for example, the Indian population of California fell from 100 thousand to around thirty thousand. The majority of Indians who lived in the Western territories that were eventually annexed by the United States was exterminated. The remainder were moved to desolate mountain regions which had been specially designated as "reservations." After the Civil War, punitive expeditions and land-grabbing still continued against the Indians. More than a thousand military operations were carried out. The savage deportation and slaughter of the Indians was one of the most shameful chapters in the history of the United States.

The vast lands of the West absorbed a flood of immigrants. More than five million foreigners came to the United States between 1790 and 1860. This seemingly endless flow of people became the principal force in settling the colonies. These immigrants came mainly from England, Ireland, Scotland, Germany, Sweden, and other European countries. In the early 1850s, Chinese workers, enticed by solicitors, began working in the mines, forests, farms, and factories in the western part of the United States. They participated in building California's main railroad and the western section of America's first transcontinental railroad, the Central Pacific Railroad. William Z. Foster (a leader of the American Communist party) once said: "The Chinese, and mainly Chinese workers, played a very great role in the history of America's West" [source unknown].

The natural increase in America's domestic population was quite rapid because revolution liberates the productive forces, and because America's territory was vast and its labor force small. The population of the United States really skyrocketed at this time. In addition to this natural increase, we must also consider the number of black people shipped from Africa to the United States in these statistics. In 1779, for example, America's population stood at 3,929,000. By 1860, it had reached 31,443,000. The population increased especially rapidly in the West. In 1790, only 3 percent of the total population lived west of the Allegheny Mountains. By 1860, that number had increased to 49 percent, indicating a population now divided almost equally between the West and the East. Twenty-three new states, in addition to the original thirteen colonies, were also founded in this period. Such statistics manifest the enormous scale and speed involved in the settlement of the Western colonies.

America's westward colonial expansion demonstrated the following striking characteristics: 1. The geographic contiguity of these colonies with the original thirteen states facilitated their economic development. 2. A vast immigrant labor force could rapidly open up Western lands. 3. The extremely rapid settlement of the West fostered a speedy fusion of these colonies with the original thirteen states to create a unified economic system. These circumstances helped consolidate the American colonial empire and strengthen its strategic economic position.

America's Industrial Revolution

America's modern industry did not achieve any dramatic gains in the period immediately after the revolutionary War of Independence. Although the United

States had gained its political independence, it still remained economically dependent on England. After the war, trade relations between the United States and Britain quickly resumed. After England had embarked on its own industrial revolution, London began to dump large quantities of inexpensive goods in the United States. The first tariff bill enacted in the United States in 1789 carried an ad valorum rate of only 5 percent to 15 percent, not enough to protect its own industry. America's fledgling industrial sector—just beginning to develop during the war—now suffered a setback. In addition, substantial profits existed in land speculation in the West as well as in commercial activity, and the great majority of capital flowed in these directions. When war broke out in 1793 between England and France, the United States used its neutral status to make quite a few business deals. As a result, its maritime shipping and foreign trade sectors made considerable gains. By this time, the United States could claim the world's second largest merchant fleet, and took about one-third of world trade into its own hands. The American bourgeoisie used the war to feather their own nests.

If England had never been reconciled to America's attainment of independence, then America's territorial expansion and its flourishing maritime trade now became even more detestable in its sight. England made every effort to strike at America's economic strength, and conveniently took advantage of the naval blockade it imposed during its war with France to constantly intercept and seize American vessels. To counter this blockade, the United States passed its own Embargo Act of 1807. It prohibited American vessels from leaving their home ports, and it cut off trade with both England and France. With an embargo piled on top of a blockade, Anglo-American relations became unusually tense. Conflicting economic interests over maritime trade finally led to warfare between England and the United States between 1812 and 1814. In 1814 Britain felt pressured to sign a peace treaty with the United States and reaffirm America's independence because it was preoccupied in coping with a tense European war, and because it confronted domestic opposition from its own people.

The Embargo Act of 1807 and the War of 1812 with England marked turning points in America's industrial development. Once the embargo took effect, imports were cut off, and the United States had to rely on its own manufacturers for all its industrial products. At the same time, once maritime shipping became restricted, the great majority of capital flowed into industry. Factories sprang up throughout the country like bamboo shoots after a spring rain. After the War of 1812, the United States finally took the road of independently developing its capitalist industry. America began its industrial revolution at this time.

By this time, the United States had the prerequisite conditions for launching an industrial revolution. The bourgeoisie had already accumulated a large amount of capital from a) interest on the wartime national debt, b) land speculation in the West, and c) fraudulent commercial activity, foreign trade, and the slave trade. A constant stream of destitute farmers and foreign immigrants supplied free labor power. The settling of new lands in the West after the War of Independence as well as a rapidly expanding population opened a vast market for American capitalism. At the same time, the bourgeois government adopted policies that energetically fostered domestic industrial development. Beginning in the early nineteenth century, the government continuously raised the customs duty. For example, while tariff rates ranged from 7.5 percent to 30 percent in 1816, their average increased to 40 percent in 1824 and had risen again to 45 percent by 1828. Protective tariffs enabled American industry to avoid foreign competition and develop smoothly.

America's industrial revolution—like England's—also began in the cotton textile industry. In 1790, Samuel Slater, an English-born textile worker who had emigrated to the United States, built a copy of Arkwright's water-powered spinning jenny and set up America's first cotton mill in Rhode Island. By 1800, eight cotton mills with almost twenty thousand spindles were hard at work. A machine-powered cotton spinning industry developed rapidly once the self-imposed embargo act took effect and, by the end of the 1820s, had already pushed aside handicraft cotton spinning. In 1830, there were 1.25 million machine spindles, a number which grew to 5.23 million by 1860. Mechanization of cloth weaving began relatively late. Prior to 1814, yarn spun in factories was still "put out" to families who would weave it into cloth by hand. Once the power loom was invented in 1814, both the spinning and weaving operations could be combined in one factory. The dyeing process also became mechanized quite rapidly. As soon as the spinning, weaving, and dyeing operations were mechanized, they were quickly linked together in one factory. This occurred because the United States traditionally lacked a powerful guild system that could have obstructed such a development. The entire textile production process could now be accomplished in one location.

A factory system that used machinery greatly increased the productivity of labor. A worker spinning yarn by hand could spin only four skeins daily. In 1825, however, any textile worker in a factory who looked after two hundred spindles could produce one thousand skeins daily. With such an enormous economic superiority, the machine-powered cotton textile industry clearly overwhelmed the handicraft mode of production. By the eve of the Civil War, the factory system had became the dominant force in cotton textiles.

Major industries such as woolen textiles, iron manufacturing, flour milling, food processing, and lumber also began to construct factories equipped with machinery. A modern machine manufacturing industry began to be established in the early nineteenth century, and some factories were already building steam engines by 1817. Beginning in the 1840s, steam engines began to replace water power on a widespread basis throughout industry. America's machine manufacturing industry developed quite rapidly. Except for those that were copied from English imports, the United States invented on its own many different kinds of machines. Examples of American inventiveness were such items as a large variety of agricultural machines, the sewing machine, and a shoe-making machine. Prior to the Civil War, America had already established—on an initial basis—a native and modern machine manufacturing industry.

Road building, such as the construction of the 834-mile Cumberland Road, represented the earliest phase in America's transportation revolution. In 1807, Robert Fulton built the first steamboat and tested it successfully. Beginning in the 1820s, steamboats made regular runs on the major river systems, and became an important mode of national transportation prior to the large-scale construction of railroads in the 1850s. Several large canals were dug during this perod which linked together the Great Lakes region with the ports along the East Coast. Construction began on the first railroad in 1828. Railroad construction made rapid gains in the 1850s, and by 1860, America's rail net extended 30,626 miles and carried two-thirds of the nation's goods. The construction of railroads on an extensive scale boosted the development of heavy industry in the East (such as metallurgy, mining, machine manufacturing), promoted agricultural growth in the West, and played a very stimulative role throughout the entire economy.

Industrial production grew rapidly under the impetus of an industrial revolution. In the fifty years spanning 1810 to 1860, the total value of industrial production increased almost tenfold. United States industrial production was now third in the world, ranking closely behind that of England and France. A bourgeoisie and a proletariat also emerged as the two basic classes in American society, once a large-scale factory system had been established. Class contradictions and class struggle developed gradually. The contradictions embedded in capitalist production also dramatically sharpened and became apparent in the three economic crises that broke out in 1837, 1848, and 1857. The 1857 crisis had a particularly adverse impact on industry. This crisis cut pig iron production by 20 percent, industrial cotton consumption by 27 percent, railroad construction by 50 percent, and shipbuilding by 75 percent.

By the eve of its Civil War, the United States had completed the basic stages of its industrial revolution. This becomes apparent if we examine the phases of its industrial revolution, the growth of its capitalist industrial production, and the appearance of cyclical economic crises. A capitalist factory system had now essentially been established in the United States. However, America's industrial revolution also exhibited an uneven pattern of regional growth. Large, modern factories had been built in large numbers througout the Northeast. Household handicraft industry prevailed throughout the newly settled West. At the same time, however, capitalist industrial development was extremely backward in the South where a plantation system based on slavery flourished. A capitalist factory system achieved victory on a nationwide basis only after the Civil War.

Prior to the Civil War, capitalist industry in the United States still had achieved only initial success. The United States remained an agrarian nation with the great majority of its population residing in villages and only 20 percent residing in cities. In 1859, industry accounted for only 36.2 percent of the combined net output value of industry and agriculture while agriculture claimed 63.8 percent. The vast majority of exports (80.5 percent of the total) were agricultural products, and more than half of America's imports were industrial goods. If we look at the context of Anglo-American relations during this period, we can see that the United States remained the target of British capital investment, the safety net for its emigrants, and the supplier of its raw materials and food stuffs. Marx said: "The United States today (1866) must still be regarded as Europe's colony."[8]

The ranks of the proletariat gradually expanded following the establishment and development of a capitalist factory system. While industrial employment (including processing, extractive industries, and construction) did not quite reach five hundred thousand in 1800, by 1860, however, 1.3 million were employed in the processing industry alone. Under the capitalist system of wage slavery, the exploitation that workers suffered became increasingly more severe. The workday was very long, commonly ranging from twelve to fifteen hours. Wages frequently did not guarantee the most minimal standard of living. According to an investigative report done in 1851, the weekly living expenses required to support a family of five came to $10.37. The weekly wages in any industry other than construction could not meet this level. In fact, weekly wages in some industries fell 25 percent—or even 50 percent—short of this standard. Factory owners employed women and children in large numbers due to a shortage of labor power. In 1832, for example, child laborers comprised approximately two-thirds of the total work force in New England's processing industries. However, their wages were generally only a tenth of that earned by adults. During an economic crisis, production would shrink, and many workers would lose their jobs. Life for these workers then became unbearable. The bourgeoisie's "American Paradise" then became a real hell for the workers.

The contradiction between the proletariat and the bourgeoisie constantly intensified. The working class fought more and more fiercely to oppose capital's merciless exploitation and to improve its own working conditions. Many labor organizations were established throughout the United States, and strikes frequently erupted after the 1830s. The first nationwide union, the National Trades' Union, was founded in 1834. By 1836, its membership had increased to more than three hundred thousand. However, the National Trades' Union collapsed under the attack of the bourgeoisie during the 1837 economic crisis.

Utopian socialism was widely propagated and tested in the United States from the 1820s to the 1840s. Several tens of "utopian" communities were established. However, these utopian plans all quickly failed. After the defeat of the 1848 revolutions in Europe, a number of European revolutionaries emigrated to the United States and spread the ideas of scientific socialism among the workers. A typical example was Joseph Wedemeyer, a friend of Karl Marx. He criticized the petty bourgeois illusion ("going West" to set up a homestead) that existed among the workers. On the contrary, he propagated the idea that workers should organize themselves and carry out their struggles on a collective basis. The first Marxist organization in the United States—the Proletarian League—was founded in New York in 1852 under his leadership. A nationwide organization—the Communist Club—was founded in 1857. This organization subsequently joined the First International. Marx and Engels maintained constant links with Wedemeyer—and other American Marxists—and paid close attention to the development of the American workers' movement. As a correspondent for the *New York Daily Tribune*, Marx himself became a leader in the movement to abolish slavery.

The credo of capital is to squeeze out the maximum in profits. In pursuit of this goal, capital has stretched out its bloody hands to every part of the globe. Even during the early period of its development, American capitalism adhered to this rule and ambitiously began to expand its aggressive operations abroad.

Latin America was its first target. In 1823, President James Monroe announced the Monroe Doctrine, proclaiming that "America was for the Americans." Looked at superficially, the Monroe Doctrine protected Latin American interests and opposed Europe's meddling in the region. However, its real purpose was to enable the United States—at some future date—to exert sole control over the entire continent. John Quincy Adams, Secretary of State at that time, revealed the real intentions behind the plan when he said that Cuba and Puerto Rico were "natural appendages" of the North American continent, and that "it was necessary to incorporate Cuba into our Union to sustain and complete it" [source unknown]. And, just as could be expected, the U.S. government made its first move against Cuba, then gradually expanded its aggressive operations throughout the Americas once its own strength had increased by the latter half of the nineteenth century.

China also became a target of American greed from quite an early date. During the 1840s and 1850s, special envoys from the United States, and others revealed America's rapacious desire for China's vast market. They said that China was "a vast territory for American enterprise, an unlimited market for American commerce" [source unknown]. "If only the entire interior were opened up, then China would become America's most valuable market for its industrial goods. Its value would be greater than the sum total of all other markets where the United States presently is involved" [source unknown]. The United States waited for a favorable moment to intrude into China. An opportunity finally presented itself. Using the pretext of maintaining diplomatic equality with France and England, the United States took advantage of the two defeats China suffered during its opium wars with England to force the Qing government to sign the Treaty of Wangxia in 1844 and the Treaty of Tianjin in 1855. In these treaties, the United States secured from China most-favored-nation status, the right of extraterritoriality, and the right of passage on internal waterways. The treaties forced China to relinquish its rights over setting customs duties and to open eight ports to trade with the United States. The United States then used these special privileges to expand its exports to China and sent merchants and missionaries to penetrate that country and engage in acts of aggression against it. During the Taiping revolutionary movement, the United States organized the notorious "Ever-Victorious Army" to assist the Qing government in its violent military suppression of the revolutionaries. From quite early on, the United States harbored wild ambitions for China's province of Taiwan. An American fleet, bent on aggression, sailed there in 1857. The United States also participated in Japan's intervention in Taiwan in 1873–74.

Washington also stretched out its aggressive, bloodstained hands toward Japan. In 1853, the United States used gunboats "to open Japan's door." It forced Japan to sign treaties permitting the United States to establish consulates there and to enjoy extra-legal rights. The treaties also permitted American ships to carry on trade or replenish their food supplies at Japanese ports.

The "American Model" of Capitalist Agricultural Development

American agriculture in the colonial period did not have to contend with a feudal system as deeply rooted as that in the European countries. The Revolutionary War of Independence completely destroyed any feudal land relationships that had remained and established in their place a system of land ownership dominated by farmers. Unhampered by the shackles of feudal relationships, capitalist farming took root and grew as the cohort of small farmers spontaneously evolved into a new social hierarchy in agriculture, with some individuals becoming wealthy, some middling in assets, and some poorer. This was a prime example of the capitalist agricultural development that Lenin called the "American model." Lenin pointed out that two possibilities objectively existed in capitalist agricultural development: the "Prussian model" and the "American model."

> In the first case (the "Prussian model"), a feudal landlord economy slowly evolves into a bourgeois, Junker landlord economy, which condemns the peasants to decades of most harrowing expropriation and bondage, while at the same time a small minority of *Grossbauern* ("Big Peasants") arises. In the second case (the "American model"), there is no landlord economy, or else it is broken up by revolution, which confiscates and splits up the feudal estates. In that case the peasant predominates, becomes the sole agent of agriculture, and evolves into a capitalist farmer.[9]

The opening of the West after the Revolutionary War of Independence gave the "American model" even broader opportunities for development. As the West was settled, the American government announced that all the land—without exception—that had been claimed by the state would be sold to immigrants to farm. The first Land Ordinance of 1785 stipulated that 640 acres was the smallest parcel of land that would be sold, and set its price at a dollar per acre. In

1796, the price was raised to two dollars per acre, and payments scheduled on an installment plan had to be concluded within four years. Many specialized companies organized by wealthy individuals became involved in land speculation once the land ordinances were enacted. Impoverished immigrants lacked the financial means to purchase land in such big parcels, so they ignored the law, "squatted" on the land, cleared it, and farmed it. The farmers' land hunger forced the government to revise subsequent land ordinances, and to reduce the minimum size of the parcels it offered. In 1800, the minimum was reduced to 320 acres. In 1804, it was lowered to 160 acres. In 1820, it was once again reduced to eighty acres, and concurrently, the price was lowered from $2.00 to $1.25 per acre. In 1832, the minimum size was again reduced to forty acres. To moderate the farmers' militancy, the government enacted legislation in 1841 clarifying farmers' rights regarding land claims. The law now stipulated that "squatters" had priority rights to buy the land that they had already been farming. Developments like this fostered the widespread growth of independently run farms throughout the West.

However, a farm economy based on individual labor could not be stable. The development of capitalist industry and transportation rapidly ensnared the farmer's product within a capitalist market, and consequently sped up the fragmentation of the farming community into different classes. Therefore, even as a small farm economy became established throughout the West, it also underwent a constant process of class differentiation. That class differentiation eventually led to the emergence and growth of capitalist farmowners who rose from the ranks of the more prosperous farmers. Even though capitalist agricultural development still remained at a comparatively weak stage during the first half of the nineteenth century, agriculture as a whole—whether in the North or in the South—was evolving along a path that was creating class distinctions among the free farmers.

The "American model" exerted a comparatively beneficial influence on economic development. Without the shackles of feudal relationships, the growth of capitalist relations in agriculture and the development of the forces of production both proceeded far more rapidly than those under the "Prussian model."

Because vast areas of "free" land could be settled and farmed in the West, agricultural development in the United States enjoyed some uniquely advantageous conditions:

1. No private monopoly over land existed in the West prior to the end of the nineteenth century. Only at that time had all the "free" land been claimed. Agriculture could avoid the burden of absolute land rent. As a result, prices of American agricultural products were low and the speed of accumulation in agriculture comparatively rapid.

2. Not only was the price of land in European countries comparatively high, but it also rose constantly. It was common to withdraw large amounts of capital from agricultural operations to use in buying and selling land. Because there

was a large amount of "free" land in the United States, and its price was extremely low, one could invest comparatively more capital in agricultural production.

3. The newly opened virgin territory was extremely fertile, which enabled expenditures on production to be kept to a minimum.

Because American agriculture possessed such advantageous conditions for its development, technological progress and increased production also became quite rapid. People were constantly inventing and using improved tools and machinery. Horse-drawn implements began to be used in sowing wheat, weeding, reaping, threshing, bundling, and mowing. American agricultural machinery was the most advanced in the world at that time. In competitions held at the 1855 Paris International Fair, an American-made harvester took first place, using only twenty-two minutes to cut an acre of oats while the English machine required more than double that amount of time to accomplish the same feat. The American thresher could do the work of 120 people, and similarly outperformed both English and French machines to win first prize. However, agricultural production in this period still relied mainly on human power. Machines were still not commonly used. Regional specialization in agricultural production was gradually emerging, with some areas specializing in intensive animal husbandry, or vegetable cultivation, or fruit tree cultivation. The total value of agricultural production increased more than sixfold in the first sixty years of the nineteenth century. In 1860, American grain production was about 30.96 million tons.[10] With a population at that time of 31.44 million, the United States produced almost a ton of grain for each person. Grain and cotton exports increased rapidly during this period.

The capitalist system brought about a substantial development in the forces of production in American agriculture. However, all these achievements were accomplished under preconditions. These included the slaughter and plunder of the native Indian population, territorial expansionism, and the constant socioeconomic fragmentation of the farming community. In addition, the development of capitalist agriculture also engendered colossal waste and led to the plunder of natural resources.

The Southern Plantation System Based on Slavery

The American South, with its flourishing slave plantation system, differed from the North. This slave plantation system was a product of British colonialism. However, not only did it continue to exist after America gained its independence, but it even gained access to new domains in the southwest after Americans expanded into that region. The slavery system then found a profitable avenue in the cultivation of cotton. This occurred when England's Industrial Revolution began, and the requirements of its cotton textile industry for raw cotton dramatically increased. The invention of the cotton gin in 1793 led to a hundredfold increase in the efficiency of removing the seeds from the cotton. This, in turn, promoted the speedy development of cotton growing. Such factors brought about an upsurge in the slave-based economy of cotton cultivation in the American South during the first half of the nineteenth century. For example, the first census taken in the United States in 1790 revealed a population of 697,000 slaves, a number which had increased to 3,953,580 by 1860. While cotton production in 1790 stood at three thousand bales (one bale was equivalent to 477 pounds), it had increased to 3.84 million bales by 1860 and comprised close to four-fifths of the total value of the South's industrial and agricultural production. Cotton exports in 1860 constituted 60.7 percent of the total value of goods exported from the entire United States that year.

Because it was so profitable to use slaves in growing cotton, the plantation owners regarded them as "yum yum trees" that were a ready source of great wealth. As a result, the price of slaves quickly shot up. For example, the average price of a slave was $250. By the middle of the nineteenth century, that price had climbed to $800, and sometimes even as high as $2,000. The purchase and sale of slaves became an extremely lucrative business. Despite a government prohibition in 1808 against the importation of slaves, an illegal slave trade still flourished. Ship owners and merchants from the North were heavily involved in smuggling operations, transporting vast numbers of black people from Africa to the United States. Most contemptible was the greed that led the "civilized" American bourgeoisie to collude in the propagation of slavery, and enabled them to reap enormous profits from the bodies of slaves. Southern states like Maryland, Virginia, and Kentucky—whose land had been exhausted and was no longer fertile—specialized in "producing" slaves and selling them to the newly opened plantations in the southwest.

In 1860, black slaves in the United States numbered almost four million, of whom three-fourths worked on plantations. In general, slave plantations encompassed seven to eight hundred acres and had several tens of slaves. Large plantations could have upwards of ten thousand acres and several hundred slaves. Many smaller ones, though, had only a few.

The living and working conditions that slaves confronted on the plantations were so arduous that they did not differ greatly from those of the draft animals. The slave owners hired poor white people to act as overseers to supervise the work of the slaves. Because the overseers' wages were determined by the amount the slaves produced while under their supervision, the overseers were consequently always thinking up new ways to make the slaves work harder. Usually working from sunrise to sunset, sometimes for as long as sixteen to eighteen hours, countless slaves shed their blood and poured out their sweat under the boots of the overseers. The slave owners gave their slaves only the most meager food and clothing. The amount expended to maintain one slave was usually much less than spent on a jailed criminal, and did not amount to even half of the dole granted to welfare recipients in northern poor houses. Excessive work and inhumane living conditions caused great suffering for the black slaves, and ultimately destroyed them. Often the life of a slave was cut short after only seven years of work. Countless black people shed their last drop of blood and sweat dying on American soil so that the plantation owners could amass a fortune.

Slaves were deprived of all human and political rights. Like draft animals, they were merely the property of the slave owners. They had no family rights. Marriage and divorce were entirely up to the wishes of the owner. If the owner sold a slave, then the family was dissolved. Black slaves were prohibited from reading and writing, and could not leave the plantation on their own. It was illegal for more than seven black people to walk around in a group. Slaves had no recourse but to suffer obediently through the floggings and other acts of violence perpetrated by their owners. The punishment suffered would be even more savage if there was the slightest resistance. Any white man could kill a runaway slave after catching him. Every southern state had a code of harsh punishments for slaves, including penalties such as cutting off an ear, amputating a hand, branding the cheeks, strangling, and so on.

The slaves, however, did not put up with the abuse and oppression they suffered from their owners, but fought a constant battle of resistance. At least 250 black revolts and uprisings have been recorded in the history of black slavery in the United States. The uprising led by John Brown in 1859 was a glorious page in the annals of the struggles waged by the black people. The rebels led by Brown occupied an arsenal, captured several slave owners, and liberated some slaves. Even when surrounded by the army of the slave owners, they stood their ground and fought to the end.

Marx made a profound analysis of the economic nature of the slave plantation system. He wrote that the economic system of slavery went through several stages: "It has evolved from a system of slavery operated chiefly to satisfy the individual needs of a patriarchal system, to one that has now become a genuinely colonial plantation system working consistently to serve a world market."[11] "In this second type of colony, whose commercial endeavors are geared to a world market, one sees the appearance of capitalist production. However, this appearance is merely one of form. Because black slaves are excluded from receiving wages for their free labor, the economic basis of capitalist production is also eliminated."[12] This is to say that the economy of the American slave plantation was a genuine slave system in every sense of the word. It possessed the basic characteristics of a system where slavery constituted the mode of production:

1. Like any other means of production, the slaves—the direct producers—belonged to the plantation owners and were entirely under their control.

2. The slaves worked at forced labor, threatened by clubs, boots, and other forms of violence.

3. The slave owners not only exploited the surplus labor of the slaves, but also expropriated a very substantial part of their necessary labor. The slaves received only shabby clothing and poor food—and even that was given at the whim of the slave owner.

Nevertheless, the American slave plantation system was a product of capitalism and was used by the capitalists to produce commodities for a capitalist world market. As a result, it also embodied some characteristics of capitalism.

The slave system played a rather important role in the growth of world capitalism. Marx pointed out that "the system of direct slavery was the basis of bourgeois industry. Without the slave system there would be no cotton; without cotton, a modern industry would be unimaginable. The slave system made colonies valuable. Colonies gave rise to a world market, and a world market was a necessary prerequisite for large-scale industry. One can see that the slave system was extremely important in the domain of economics."[13] English and American capitalism both rose and flourished by relying on the slave trade and the slave system. Without the American slave plantations to provide cotton, England's machine cotton textile industry—and even its Industrial Revolution—could not have achieved the rapid growth that occurred. The shipping and textile industries in America's North were also built directly on the foundations of the South's slave system.

Economic Contradictions between the North and the South and their Relationship to the Civil War

The slave plantation system of the South and the capitalist economy of the North were ultimately two different economic systems, and generated conflicts of interest both politically and economically between the two regions. The capitalist economy of the North demanded a vast domestic market for the sale of commodities, free labor power, a protectionist tariff system, and a centralized federal state. However, the slave plantation economy of the South restricted the supply of free labor power and the expansion of a domestic market. It demanded that cotton be exported directly to England, and advocated lower tariffs to facilitate the import of cheap industrial goods from England. As a result, the South demanded free trade and secession from the North. The contradictions between the North and the South were focused even more intensely on the question of who would establish control over the West. The North demanded that the land be given to the bourgeoisie and the farmers to settle and farm, and to set up "free states" that would prohibit slavery. The Southern plantation owners demanded that the slave owners take possession and establish "slave states." The conflict would become exceptionally fierce each time a new territory was settled and requested statehood. The Compromise of 1820 drew a line of demarcation between free and slave labor at a latitude of 36°30′. South of this line, slavery was permitted to expand; north of it, chattel slavery was prohibited.

The rapid development of the capitalist economy in the North by the middle of the nineteenth century intensified its feeling that slavery constituted an obstacle. On the other hand, the economic and class contradictions in the South were also becoming increasingly acute. Cotton production had plummeted. Slave resistance was everywhere. The slave owners therefore did everything in their power to expand the system of slavery in order to rescue it from its decline. When a new state north of the 36°30' parallel was admitted to the Union in 1854, the slave owners attempted to use force to expand slavery to that area, and touched off an armed conflict between North and South. When Abraham Lincoln, a Republican who represented the interests of the northern bourgeoisie, was elected President in 1861, the South rebelled and the Civil War broke out. In this war, the northern bourgeoisie represented the forces of progress and received the active support of vast numbers of people, especially black people. In the South, however, black slaves frequently rebelled, ran away in large numbers to the North so they could fight in the war, and posed a grave political threat to the slave owners. The North was also far more powerful economically than the South. The North claimed twenty-three states with a population of twenty-two million people; the South had eleven states with a population of nine million. The North's industry was advanced and its food supply abundant. The South lacked self-sufficiency in both food and daily necessities. Political and economic superiority rested with the North. The Civil War finally ended in 1865 with the North victorious.

The American Civil War, which lasted from 1861 to 1865, "was a struggle between two social systems, a struggle between the slave system and the system of free labor."[14] It was the second bourgeois revolution in American history. During the war, the Federal Government in the North distributed land under the Homestead Act of 1862 without charge to farmers. The Emancipation Proclamation of 1863 abolished the slave system. After the war, the bourgeoisie eliminated the slave owners as a class and took sole political power. This created the conditions for the rapid development of capitalism throughout the whole country. Of course, this revolution also lacked the thoroughness and displayed the hypocritical characteristics of all bourgeois revolutions. Although slavery was abolished, the slaves themselves received no land. "After the American bourgeoisie 'emancipated' the blacks, they made every effort to restore everything that could possibly be restored, did everything that could and could not be done, to achieve the most shameful and despicable goal of oppressing the black people on the basis of a 'free,' democratic capitalism."[15] The slaves were not really liberated either politically or economically. Racial discrimination against blacks continued to flourish, and has continued to exist until today. The struggle of the American black people against racial oppression has also never let up. Today, the struggle of black people in the United States has become an important force in the worldwide united front against American imperialism. Chairman Mao paid extremely great attention to the struggles of black people in the United States, pointing out that "the just struggles of American black people will certainly be victorious under the support of more than 90 percent of the people of the world. The hateful systems of colonialism and imperialism that flourished on the enslavement and sale of black people will inevitably come to an end with the complete emancipation of the black people."[16]

3. The United States Becomes the Archetypical Monopoly Capitalist Country

The Development of a Capitalist Agriculture

During the Civil War, the Federal Government passed a law regarding land distribution—the Homestead Act—the purpose of which was to attract large numbers of people willing to fight against the slave owners. This law permitted immigrants to take up to 160 acres of wilderness as their own land, and yet pay only a $10 processing fee for it. A veritable flood of immigrants, attracted by the Homestead Act, now surged toward the West. Immigration statistics skyrocketed. Between 1861 and 1914, more than twenty-seven million people came to the United States, supplying America with a vast pool of labor power. Between 1860 and 1914, the number of American agricultural workers increased from 6.2 million to 13.58 million. The area under cultivation also more than doubled, going from 410 million acres to 910 million acres. Marx pointed out: "It was European immigrants who enabled North America to carry out large-scale agricultural production."[17]

Contrary to what is said by certain bourgeois scholars, the implementation of the Homestead Act did not make the United States a "paradise" for the small farmer. The bourgeoisie still grabbed vast areas of land through the railroad companies or through groups of speculators. They either became involved in land speculation or set up large capitalist farms. However, farmers who had acquired land under the Homestead Act very quickly became differentiated into richer or poorer strata. This class polarization occurred because of the competition that these farmers faced from the larger farms, and also because of the myriad layers of exploitation that fell upon them from the banks, railroads, and industrial and commercial capitalists. The Homestead Act, however, made certain that American agriculture would evolve along the "American model" on a national scale. Beginning in the 1880s, the process of class polarization in the farming community became extremely obvious, and occurred irrespective of region—whether in the older states or in the new ones in the West. Capitalist relations in agriculture took a big step forward.

Capitalist relations in agriculture appeared in three forms: 1. as a system of capitalist land rent; 2. as a system of mortgage payments;[18] and 3. as a system of hired labor. According to 1910 statistics, tenant farms in the North and in the West constituted 26.5 percent and 14 percent, respectively, of all farm households. One-third of all farm households had fallen into debt, with their farms mortgaged to the banks. Capitalism's classic form—hired labor in agriculture—had also made considerable headway. By 1910, hired agricultural hands reached 3.38 million, one-fourth of the entire agricultural work force of 13.55 million. More and more farmers became destitute, went bankrupt, and lost their land. The large capitalist farms came to occupy an increasingly important position in agriculture. Although they constituted approximately one-sixth of all farm households, large capitalist farms produced more than half of the value of agricultural goods of the entire country in 1910. Capitalist relations were already clearly becoming the dominant economic form in this sector.

Although slavery was abolished in the South after the Civil War, the "emancipated" black people received no land. Empty-handed and stone broke, they still had to depend on the plantation owners by renting land from them and also by borrowing seeds, tools, livestock, and fertilizer. One-third to one-half of their harvest would then be turned over as rent. This tenancy system was called sharecropping and was a remnant of the system of slavery. Lenin called this kind of tenancy "a semi-slave *sharecropping system*."[19] Farm households living in this type of tenancy arrangement comprised about half of all farm households in the South and 24 percent on a nationwide basis. In general, poor black sharecroppers were able to maintain their families' living standard only at an impoverished, semi-starvation level. Faced by such a multitude of problems, tenants frequently owed the landlord a good deal of money and had to perform some labor in order to wipe the slate clean. A system of merchant money-lending also flourished in the South. Black tenants who fell into financial difficulties would either buy goods on credit or borrow from a merchant. They had to put up their harvest as collateral, or reach an agreement with a merchant who would then sell their harvest on a consignment basis. As a result, the tenant farmer was exploited by the merchant in a variety of ways. Blacks were severely exploited economically. Politically they had no rights. Culturally they remained extremely backward; nearly half (44.5 percent) of the black population was illiterate. In addition, blacks faced racial discrimination, persecution, and lynchings carried out by the Ku Klux Klan. Southern blacks found themselves extremely oppressed and utterly humiliated. Illiteracy among Southern whites was also more than double the national norm. Lenin said: "The American South is like a prison for the 'emancipated' blacks who are confined, deprived of education, and lack even a breath of fresh air."[20]

The Southern plantation owners did little to improve production techniques because they relied on exploiting the cheap labor of black people to make money. The increasing use of machinery in agriculture in the North and West followed both the development of industry as well as capitalist farming. This period was characterized by the semi-mechanization of American agriculture. Agricultural machinery in this context primarily meant improved farm tools and horse-drawn implements. Animal power still remained the principal motive force. 1905 saw the earliest use of a steam-powered tractor in agriculture. By 1910, the United States had only a thousand tractors, which represented an insignificant number in agriculture. (The gasoline-powered tractor gradually replaced animal power after 1920.) Because the United States during this period was still in the process of industrializing and its heavy industry base remained comparatively weak, the transformation of agricultural technology only attained a level of semi-mechanization. The adoption of improved tools and machinery increased labor productivity in agriculture, and the number of agricultural workers as a percentage of the total number of American workers gradually decreased. In 1860, agriculture claimed 59 percent of the nation's labor power; by 1910, however, that proportion had declined to 31 percent. Of course, the absolute number of agricultural workers was still constantly increasing during this period, expanding from 6.2 million in 1860 to 13.55 million in 1910. The number of agricultural workers gradually declined after reaching a peak in 1916 with 13.63 million.

The opening of vast and fertile lands in the West, a huge influx of immigrants that provided labor power, improvements in agricultural technology, and the development of large-scale capitalist farms enabled American agricultural production to achieve rapid growth. Wheat production almost quadrupled, corn production went up about three-and-a-half-fold, and cotton production grew roughly fivefold during the latter half of the nineteenth century. In 1900, wheat production reached 600 million bushels (or 16.32 million tons), corn weighed in at 2.7 billion bushels (68.58 million tons), and cotton rose to ten million bales (2.17 million tons). America's vast areas of arable land not only served as huge natural range lands but were conducive to the cultivation of grasses and corn which could be used as animal fodder. As a result, the livestock industry became quite advanced. This became a special characteristic of American agriculture. Throughout the entire nineteenth century, the output value of the livestock industry was more than half that of crops. An advanced livestock industry played an important role during the entire process of agricultural development and throughout the life of the economy. Because the livestock industry was so advanced, butchering and meat packing became important sectors of American industry, and ranked second in American industrial output value in 1900. The United States was the world's foremost grain producer at that time as well as the biggest grain exporter. By the end of the nineteenth century, approximately one-fourth to one-third of the wheat produced was exported, while more than 60 percent of total cotton production went abroad. The dumping of large quantities of cheap American agricultural products on the world market brought about Europe's agricultural crisis in the 1870s.

The United States Becomes the World's Foremost Capitalist Industrial Power

After the Civil War, the United States swept aside the obstacles to the development of capitalism, and industry entered a new period of swift development. According to official United States statistics, the output value of the American processing industry increased nineteenfold during the period from 1859 to 1914. Prior to 1860, light industry dominated industry as a whole. The post–Civil War period was the era of heavy industry's rapid development, and its rate of growth far exceeded that of light industry. Between 1860 and 1913, for example, the cotton textile industry grew about sevenfold, yet steel, iron, and coal production increased several tens of times during the same period. Pig iron production went from 840,000 tons to 31.46 million tons. The amount of coal mined increased from 18.18 million tons to more than 500 million tons. Steel production in 1860 amounted to only twelve thousand tons, but by 1913 had reached 31.8 million tons. By the end of the nineteenth century and the beginning of the twentieth, the newly emerging heavy industrial sectors such as electrical goods, chemicals, automobiles, petroleum, and others also developed quite rapidly. For example, the automobile industry began regular industrial production only around 1895. Production was merely 4,200 vehicles in 1900. By 1914, however, that figure had increased to 573,000 units. The structure of America's industrial sector underwent a transformation as a result of the rapid development of heavy industry. For example, the foremost industrial sectors in 1860—ranked by output value—were in light industries such as flour milling, cotton textiles, lumber processing, footwear, and others. The foundry and machine manufacturing industries took fifth place. By 1900, however, the rank order now put steel first, with butchering and meat packing, foundry and machine manufacturing, lumber processing, and flour milling following behind in that order. In short, steel and machine manufacturing had jumped ahead to take first and third place, respectively, in industrial production. Heavy industry was now beginning to play the leading role in industry. Of course, the output value of light industry still exceeded that of heavy industry. For example, even up to 1900, it outperformed heavy industry by a factor of 1.5 to 1.

Railroad construction developed rapidly under governmental encouragement and assistance. In 1865, the United States had built 35,000 miles of railroad tracks. By 1900, this mileage had increased to 259,000. By 1913, total mileage reached 380,000, and comprised half of the world's total trackage. Five cross-continental railroads were built one after the other in the last half of the nineteenth century. Large-scale railroad construction promoted the opening and settlement of the West, and was especially important in directly stimulating the development of such heavy industrial sectors as steel, coal, machine manufacturing, and so on. It can be said that railroad construction was at the heart of America's nineteenth century economic development. Railroad construction in the United States was also a model of the greed, waste, deception, and larceny typically practiced by capitalist enterprises. To encourage railroad construction, the American government agreed to give to the railroad companies ten miles of land on each side of the roadbed, and a subsidy ranging from $16,000 to $48,000 for each mile of track that they laid. To acquire more land and receive larger subsidies, the railroad companies intentionally made the lines unnecessarily tortuous in order to extend their length. The bourgeoisie reaped a fabulous bonanza from railroad stocks and land speculation.

Industry developed faster than agriculture in the latter half of the nineteenth century. Beginning in the 1880s, industry replaced agriculture as the most important source of national wealth. Net industrial output value surpassed agriculture for the first time in 1884, and comprised 53.4 percent of the combined net output value of both agriculture and industry. By 1899, it constituted 61.8 percent of that combined net output value. If calculated according to the total value of production, industry was approximately triple the size of agriculture during this time.

America's capitalist industrialization was basically completed by the turn of the twentieth century when the United States was transformed from an agricultural to an industrial country. In this period, industry became the most important sector of the American national economy. Heavy industry played the leading role in industry, and could basically satisfy the technological demands of the various sectors of the national economy. It took more than eighty years to build the United States into a capitalist, industrial power, if we calculate that its industrial revolution began after the War of 1812 with Britain.

In this period, the speed of American industrial development far exceeded that of such veteran capitalist countries as England and France. By the early 1880s, American industry had already vaulted into first place in the world. By 1913, American industrial superiority was even more evident and claimed 38 percent of the entire world's industrial production. It even slightly exceeded the total combined industrial production of England (14 percent), Germany (16 percent), France (6 percent), and Japan (1 percent). American production in such important industrial sectors as steel, coal, machine manufacturing, and electrical goods had also jumped ahead to take first place in the world in the 1880s and 1890s. The example of American development clearly proves the law of the increasingly unequal political and economic development of capitalist countries in the era of imperialism.

Why could American capitalism achieve such rapid growth? It certainly was not—as some bourgeois scholars argue—because the American capitalist system was "exceptional." American capitalism, just like any other capitalism, developed on a foundation of ruthless domestic exploitation and overseas colonial aggression. The reasons why it developed faster than other capitalist countries were due to America's specific historical, economic, and natural conditions.

First of all throughout its history, America never developed a deep-rooted feudal system. Also, its bourgeois revolution was comparatively thorough in eradicating whatever feudal relationships did exist. The development of capitalism therefore was not greatly hampered by the impediments of a feudal system. Economically, feudal relations were thoroughly eliminated in agriculture. Industry lacked the old inherited burdens and such fetters as guild traditions and conservative production methods. Politically, America experienced two bourgeois revolutions—the War of Independence and the Civil War—which completely eliminated the political forces that restricted the development of capitalism. The bourgeoisie, in sole possession of political power, adopted comprehensive policies that fostered capitalist development. For example, in the latter half of the nineteenth century after the Civil War, the American government consistently maintained a policy of protectionism, and imposed tariff rates ranging as high as 40 percent to 50 percent.

Second, the existence of a vast domestic market was an important element in American capitalism's speedy growth. After the Civil War, the abolition of slavery, the unification of North and South, the opening of the West, the influx of large numbers of European immigrants, the construction of railroads on a massive scale, and the development of a capitalist agriculture enabled the United States to form a vast, unified market unsurpassed by any other capitalist country.

Third, a capitalist agriculture (which enjoyed advantageous natural conditions and developed rapidly along the lines of what Lenin called "the American model") became a favorable precondition and solid base for industrial development. Neither England, France, Germany, nor any other nation could match the United States on this point. England fostered a system of landownership dominated by big landlords. France retained its small farm economy. Germany remained strongly influenced for quite some time by the remnants of the Junker landlord economy. As a result, the agricultural base in these three countries was comparatively weak. England was a particularly striking case because it relied mainly on foreign imports both for its food supply as well as its agricultural raw materials.

Fourth, the United States enjoyed a superior geographical location and possessed rich natural resources. America was far away from the European continent, its neighbors were all weak countries, and it was surrounded by two oceans. Geographically, the United States was in the safest possible location. After the Civil War, the United States never again experienced the destructiveness of a war on its own soil. At the same time, its territory was vast, replete with rich mineral, water, and forest resources. All of these natural and geographical conditions were extremely advantageous for America's economic development.

Fifth, as a newcomer among the capitalist countries, the United States made full use of the technological achievements, capital, and labor power of other nations. Compared to England, America's industrial revolution began rather late. This enabled the United States—during the early period of its own industrial revolution—to borrow extensively from England's technological accomplishments and experience in production. The amount of foreign capital absorbed by the United States was also rather considerable, reaching $2 billion in 1880, $3.5 billion in 1890, and $6.7 billion in 1914. America borrowed and used foreign capital to speed up—in depth as well as in breadth—capitalism's growth. Immigrants played a particularly important role in the development of American capitalism. According to official statistics, more than half of the total number of American workers in 1914 were immigrants. Immigrants made up 58 percent of the work force in the steel industry and 62 percent in the mining and textile industries. In the preface to the 1882 edition of the *Manifesto of the Communist Party*, Marx and Engels said: "Immigrants enabled the United States to tap its stupendous industrial resources, and provided the impetus whereby America could quickly eliminate the monopoly over industry that Western Europe, and especially England, had enjoyed up to that time."[21]

Finally, another important reason for the rapid development of American capitalism was its reliance on extensive overseas expansion and its predatory methods. First came the plunder of the native Indians. Then, at the end of the nineteenth century, the United States began to carry out aggression and expansion in regions like the Caribbean, the Philippines, East Asia, Central America, and South America. In discussing the characteristics of America's path of industrialization, Stalin wrote: "Only after thirty and forty years of arduous efforts—and only after relying on foreign loans, using long-term credits, and plundering its neighboring countries and islands—was the United States, the mightiest of the capitalist countries, able to establish its own industry after its Civil War."[22]

During these hundred years of its rule, the American bourgeoisie created enormous forces of production, greater than all the forces of production brought into being in all previous epochs. However, "even though these colossal means of production and methods of exchange of contemporary bourgeois society have been created as if by magic, the wizard now cannot control the demons that he himself has called into existence."[23] Despite the fact that the United States raised its forces of production to an unprecedented level, it also suffered from especially severe and acute crises of overproduction. Six economic crises (beginning in 1866, 1873, 1882, 1893, 1903, and 1907) broke out in the United States in the period after the Civil War and prior to the First World War. Each crisis, if viewed from the performance of the major industrial sectors, caused a one-year to four-year regression in American industrial output. The 1873 crisis was one of the most severe in the premonopoly period of capitalism. For example, railroad construction was cut in half, and shipbuilding fell by 60 percent during the first year of the crisis. Pig iron production declined 27 percent, petroleum went down by 16 percent, and coal production and cotton consumption in the cotton textile industry both decreased by 9 percent. Forty-seven thousand companies went bankrupt, and more than three million people lost their jobs. This crisis was of a very long duration. Production continued to decline for one-and-a-half to two years, and the recession lasted up to 1878. The 1907 crisis broke out after America had entered its stage of monopoly capitalism. The drop in production was precipitous. For example, steel and iron production—the core sectors of industry—declined 40 percent and 38.2 percent, respectively. On the eve of the First World War in 1914, the American economy was once again on the verge of another crisis. The steel industry was operating at only 50 percent of capacity. Steel and iron production both fell from thirty million tons to twenty-three million tons. Other industries were also correspondingly sluggish. The United States was able to shake off this crisis only because the war played a stimulative role in reviving the economy.

The United States: A Nation of Trusts

"One of the most typical features of capitalism is the extremely rapid process whereby production is concentrated in larger and larger corporations precisely when there is a boom in industrial development."[24] This trend—an expansion of the scale of production—had already emerged in American industry prior to the Civil War. However, both during and after the Civil War, the bourgeoisie reaped sudden and fabulous profits from an enormous and growing public debt, land speculation, and shady commercial deals. This produced not only a group of financial oligarchs who had made their fortunes from the Civil War, but also created a rapid concentration of capital. Because the economic crisis of 1873 bankrupted many medium and small-sized companies, the concentration of capital and production became even more accentuated. In an 1882 article ("On the Accumulation of Capital in the United States") specifically written on this issue, Engels pointed out that "in the United States, *capital accumulation was going forward at a surprising speed.*"[25] An example selected by Engels was the plutocrat Cornelius Vanderbilt, "a king whose property in railroads, land, factories, and so on amounts to about *$300 million United States dollars.* As Americans say, he is 'worth' $300 million."[26] Engels also listed the names of twenty-one other plutocrats—whose wealth ranged from $5 million to $100 million—to explain the large-scale accumulation of capital in the United States. By the early twentieth century, the concentration of both capital and production had become even more pronounced as a result of the extremely rapid development and fierce competition that took place within industry at the end of the nineteenth century. In 1904, large corporations with output value above one million dollars numbered about 1,900 and constituted 0.9 percent of the total number of enterprises. The workers they employed, however, made up more than a fourth (25.6 percent) of the total number of industrial workers, and their output value constituted more than a third (38 percent) of total ouput value. Five years later, the process of concentration had advanced even more. There were now 3,060 large corporations, and they made up 1.1 percent of the total number of American companies. However, their combined output value now constituted 43.8 percent of total industrial output value. In elaborating on the process of development of monopoly capitalism, Lenin pointed out that "the concentration of production is even more rapid in the United States, another advanced, modern capitalist country."[27] "About half of the total output value of all the enterprises of the country is produced by one per cent of these corporations! These 3,000 giant enterprises operate in 258 industrial sectors."[28]

The high degree of concentration in industrial production in the United States occurred because:

1. American industry was established on the most up-to-date technology available. Because many corporations were already quite large from the moment they were established, their competitive edge enabled them to rapidly buy out the smaller and medium-sized companies and concentrate production in their own hands.

2. American industrial growth, especially in heavy industry, was extremely rapid during this period. Because industries were comparatively concentrated, competition became extraordinarily fierce, resembling that of hand-to-hand military combat.

3. During the last thirty years of the nineteenth century, the economic crises America faced were more severe than those confronting other countries. These crises made mincemeat of many small and medium-sized enterprises and speeded up the phenomenon whereby "the big fish eat the small fry."

"One can say that as soon as concentrated production has developed to a certain stage, it will then naturally and necessarily lead to monopoly."[29] The "pool" was the earliest form of monopoly in the United States, and appeared at the end of the 1860s.[30] Pools developed in the major branches of industry and mining, and particularly in the railroad sector, after the crisis of 1873. Of course, these types of associations were temporary and unstable, and they fell apart when a change occurred in the relative strengths of their participants or when changes occurred in market conditions.

The Standard Oil Company was the first trust to emerge in the United States in 1879. By the 1880s, trusts had been organized in industries such as oil drilling, sugar refining, match manufacturing, tobacco processing, meat packing, coal mining, brewing, aluminum smelting, and so on. In order to earn high monopoly profits, the trusts frequently resorted to various kinds of despicable methods. These methods not only harmed people's lives, but even the interests of those within their own trade. Such activities stimulated anti-monopoly movements among the people. Pressured by public opinion, the American government hypocritically enacted the Sherman Anti-Trust Act of 1890. This legislation outlawed the monopolization of either inter-state commerce or foreign trade. In reality, the anti-trust laws were not harmful to the monopolies. On the one hand, the courts always shielded the trusts. On the other hand, the big capitalists now used the "holding company"—with an altered name and organizational form—to maintain their monopolies.[31] As a result, by the 1890s, monopolies had already become common in the areas of industry, mining, transportation, and urban public utilities. In 1899, trusts produced two-thirds of the nation's total value of manufactured products.

The 1898 Spanish-American War and the postwar seizure of colonies stimulated the development of the American economy. Mergers and monopolistic activities proceeded as never before. The years from 1898 to the early years of the twentieth century were of decisive importance for the development of the monopolies. In 1904, there were 318 trusts in American industry, of which 236 were established in the period after 1898. During the early twentieth century, America's major industrial sectors had generally become monopolized by one, two, or several trusts. So-called "kings" (such as Henry Ford, known as the automobile king; John D. Rockefeller, the oil king; and J. P. Morgan, the steel king) ruled these industries. United States Steel, Ford, General Motors, Chrysler, DuPont, General Electric, American Tobacco, American Telephone and Telegraph (ATT), and other large and world-famous trusts were organized. The degree of monopoly control over the railroad industry had also become quite high. The big trusts controlled these shares of production in the following industrial sectors: petroleum—95 percent; steel—66 percent; chemicals—81 percent; metallurgy—77 percent; aluminum—85 percent; sugar—80 percent; and tobacco—80 percent. Trusts had become the controlling force in America's economic life and held the nation's economic lifelines in their hands. The United States Steel Corporation and the Standard Oil Company became models of the largest industrial trusts.

The Standard Oil Company, founded in 1870 and run by John D. Rockefeller, was America's first large corporation. It was capitalized initially at $1 million. In 1879 it bought out fourteen other large oil companies and formed a trust. The Standard Oil Company trust was also the majority stock holder in twenty-six other oil companies. It controlled the railroads in the oil producing areas and built a vast oil pipeline network. It owned its own oil storage facilities, piers, and more than a hundred ocean-going tankers. The Standard Oil Company trust concentrated 90 percent of America's oil production in its own hands. Nominally its capitalization was put at $70 million, but $46 million of that was held by nine people, headed by Rockefeller. Standard Oil's monopoly position in the petroleum industry enabled it to rake in high monopoly profits. For example, dividends increased from 5.25 percent to 30 percent in the period from 1882 to 1898.

The United States Steel Corporation was a trust organized in 1901 by J. P. Morgan. By the end of the nineteenth century, only the four most powerful steel-producing groups remained in the American steel industry as a result of increased concentration in production. These four groups competed fiercely with each other. Finally, the confederation of steel companies led by Morgan—relying on the enormous wealth of the Morgan family—reached agreements with the other largest companies, bought them out, and created the United States Steel Corporation in 1901. The United States Steel Corporation was American's biggest and best-equipped trust. It was a colossal, comprehensive operation that had its own iron and coal mines, rolled steel plants, and companies that produced finished steel products. It also owned more than a thousand miles of railroads, as well as upwards of a hundred ocean-going ships and inland-waterway-vessels. In 1907, more than 210,000 people were employed in companies owned by this steel trust. During the early period of its establishment, United States Steel controlled 60 percent of the nation's iron ore production, 66 percent of its steel production, and almost 50 percent of its ready-made steel products. In 1910, its steel production reached fourteen million tons and its iron production came to 122 million tons. Its average annual net income was $112 million in the period from 1901 to 1910.

The trust was the most common form adopted by America's monopolies. The high degree of concentration in production—which occurred when a small number of large, technologically advanced companies rapidly achieved a dominant position—was the basis for the development of an advanced form of monopolistic trust. The United States had now become a land of trusts. Lenin said: "The American trusts are the highest expression of an imperialist economy or a monopoly capitalist economy."[32]

Concentration and monopolies also emerged in banking, just as they had in American industry. For example, twenty large banks dominated the American banking industry in 1900. By 1913, however, the two large bank cliques—headed by J. P. Morgan and William Rockefeller—controlled the entire world of banking. These large banks were transformed from ordinary intermediaries into all-powerful monopolists. They had now expanded the scope of their activities to include the provision of long-term credits to industrial corporations and invested more and more capital into production. The union of bank capital with industrial capital created finance capital and financial oligarchs. The fusion of the two was also accomplished in other ways. It also occurred when industrial monopolies acquired a controlling share of a bank's stocks, or if they directly created a bank under their control. This type of amalgamation moved ahead rapidly in the United States after the 1893 crisis. By the early twentieth century, the United States was ruled by finance capitalists. They were represented by eight large financial groups (the Morgan, Rockefeller, Kuhn-Loeb, Mellon, DuPont, Chicago, Cleveland, and Boston groups) and sixty families.[33] The Morgan and Rockefeller groups were America's two largest finance capital groups. They were also model examples of the amalgamation of industrial capital with bank capital.

The Morgan group originated in the 1860s as an agency dealing in negotiable securities. During the period of rapid economic growth after the Civil War, it became America's most powerful bank in issuing railroad stock certificates and government bonds. J. P. Morgan and eleven other associates subsequently organized Drexel, Morgan and Company in 1871, and gradually took over many large banks and insurance companies to become the nation's biggest bank. And Morgan continued to extend his power into industry and the railroads. The creation of the United States Steel Company in 1901 was a decisively significant act whereby J. P. Morgan, the banker, became J. P. Morgan, the financier. In addition to these activities, J. P. Morgan also served as a trustee of many other large companies. He served on the boards of twenty-one railroads, three insurance companies, General Electric, Western Union, Pullman, and many others. International Harvester, AT&T, and other big trusts were also under the control of the Morgan group.

The Rockefeller family exemplified the model of the industrial capitalist becoming the financier. After he took control of the oil industry in 1870 by founding the Standard Oil Company, John D. Rockfeller then proceeded to extend his control over the coal gas, electrical, zinc, lead, and steel refining industries. In the 1890s, William Rockefeller, his brother, shifted his industrial capital to banking, and—along with his associate Stillman—founded the National City Bank of New York. He used this bank to reinvest his capital. He would create other monopolistic corporations in industry and the railroads, or buy stocks in other companies to gain control over them.

According to materials released by America's House of Representatives in 1912, the Morgan and Rockefeller groups held a combined total of 341 trustee seats in the boardrooms of 112 large corporations. Moreover, the total amount of capital under the real control of these more than a hundred large corporations was in excess of $22 billion. There is a passage in *The Truth About the Trusts*, written in 1904 by the bourgeois scholar John Moody, that revealed the way in which finance capital ruled America. He wrote:

> Therefore, viewed as a whole, we find the dominating influences in the Trusts to be made up of an intricate network of large and small groups of capitalists, many allied to one another by ties of more or less importance, but all being appendages to or parts of the greater groups, which are themselves dependent on and allied with the two mammoth or Rockefeller and Morgan groups. These two mammoth groups jointly (for, as pointed out, they really may be regarded as one) constitute the heart of the business and commercial life of the nation, the others all being the arteries which permeate in a thousand ways our whole national life, making their influence felt in every home and hamlet, yet all connected with and dependent on this great central source, the influence and policy of which dominates them all.[34]

The monopoly capitalists not only controlled the entire national economy, but pulled the strings in government. They controlled all of America's political life and directed its domestic and foreign policies. Every administration was composed of representatives of the monopoly capitalists, or the monopoly capitalists personally took charge and grabbed the leading positions in the government. Let us take President McKinley's cabinet of 1900 as an example. Secretary of State

John Sherman was Rockefeller's spokesperson. Secretary of the Interior Cornelius Bliss was the Chairman of the Board of Trustees of the Morgan group's Equitable Life Insurance Company. Secretary of the Army Luther was Morgan's legal adviser. The Secretary of the Navy, Philander C. Knox, served in succession as Chairman of the Board of Trustees of a number of Mellon-affiliated banks. Joseph Hodges Choate, the Ambassador to Great Britain, was the most powerful legal adviser to Rockefeller. The people selected to hold various posts in McKinley's cabinet clearly reflected a coalition of the various finance groups. The American Congress, with its so-called peoples' representatives, was merely "a millionaires' club," just like the American people have called it. Lenin made a special appraisal of the American Congress in 1918 when he said: "Capital rules everything in both Switzerland and the United States. . . . In no other parliament is the power of capital as great as in these two countries. The power of capital and the stock exchange is everything; the Congress and elections are merely puppets and marionettes."[35]

A political characteristic of imperialism is its totally reactionary nature. For example, in the United States, a small number of plutocrats arrogantly controlled everything. There was open corruption within the government, and an endless series of cases of large-scale bribery and deceit occurred. The plutocrats, however, imposed various restrictions on the political rights of the people. They ruthlessly suppressed the workers' movement. They implemented a policy of racial discrimination against black people. They plundered, destablized, and intervened militarily in the economically underdeveloped countries. Lenin said:

> The United States of America is one of the world's most democratic Republics. However, there is no other country where the rights of capital and the control over society that is exerted by a small handful of plutocrats is as unconstrained as in the U.S. There is no other country where bribery is as rampant. (Anyone who has been there since 1905 probably understands this point.)[36]

The Impoverishment of the Working Class and Its Struggle against Monopoly Capitalism

"Not only is a system of hired labor a system of slavery, but this kind of slavery also becomes more ruthless as the productive forces of labor and society become more developed."[37] In the United States, the working class and the laboring masses brought material production to a highly advanced level. However, not only did the working and living conditions of the working class fail to improve, but the exploitation the working people suffered became more severe and their living conditions steadily deteriorated.

In their search for high profits, the monopoly capitalists promoted what Lenin called "blood and sweat systems." These were "the Ford system," "the Taylor system," and other "speed-up systems" that increased the workers' labor intensity to the utmost degree. The surplus value extracted by the capitalist from the worker's labor steadily increased. The degree of exploitation suffered by the worker became more severe. Increased unemployment was the only reward received by the working class for raising its labor productivity. The average annual unemployment rate for workers was 10 percent during the period from 1897 to 1914. The statistics for part-time employment are even more startling. Almost half of the workers could not find full-time employment. A report by the U.S. Industrial Relations Board in 1909 said that from half to two-thirds of workers' families lived below acceptable standards, and about one-third of these households lived in dire poverty. Workers' living conditions became even more tragic during periods of crisis. American newspaper accounts of the crisis of 1873 reported that entire families were starving to death in the big industrial centers every day. During the winter, police stations would be packed full every night with workers and their family dependents looking for a place to sleep, and begging that they be sentenced to serve time in a "workers' reformatory." Immigrants made up more than half of the total number of workers. Strangers in a new country—some not even speaking English—these people were even more severely exploited by the factory owners. Blacks constituted the lowest strata of workers. In 1910, there were 550 thousand black workers, and the great majority of them worked at the most onerous jobs. They received wages which were a third to a half less than white workers doing the same job.

Working conditions were extremely poor. Factories and mines lacked the most essential safety equipment and safety measures that could afford protection for the worker. Occupational illnesses and work-related accidents were both extremely prevalent. At the beginning of the twentieth century, an average of seventy-five thousand workers died annually as a result of industrial accidents. Of these, thirty-five thousand died on the spot. In other words, in the United States, one worker died at the side of his or her machine every sixteen minutes.

The monopoly capitalists not only ruthlessly exploited the masses of workers and farmers, but they also constantly shoved aside the small and medium-sized capitalists. As a result, they polarized the United States into a society characterized by a huge gap between the rich and the poor. In 1914, a small handful of plutocrats—constituting 2 percent of America's population—owned 60 percent of the nation's wealth. However, the working masses, who comprised 65 percent of the population, owned merely 5 percent of the nation's total wealth. The plutocrats lived in the lap of luxury and whiled away their time. In their boredom, they degenerated so far that they even gave banquets for dogs and dolled them up with collars worth $1500. At that time, the annual living expenses for a working class family of five came to only $700. This was the so-called "American living style"! Lenin condemned this kind of situation in the United States when he wrote in 1914:

> America today is extremely well-off. Not only can it immediately triple its own wealth and triple the productivity of its workforce, but it can guarantee the implementation of a shorter workday—a six-hour workday—to each working class family, as well as an income that each person should reasonably receive.
>
> However, what we see is quite different because of the existence of a capitalist system. On the one hand, there exist horrifying levels of unemployment and poverty throughout America's cities and towns, and where the individual's labor is sucked bone dry by exploitation. And on the other hand we can observe the plutocrats (that is, those wealthy individuals owning countless possessions) enjoying a life of unprecedented luxury.[38]

As class contradictions became more acute, the struggle of the working class against monopoly capital intensified. Strikes became frequent and took place everywhere. Some massive strikes even became famous. For example, the 1874–75 anthracite coal miners' strike has been recorded in the annals of history as the famous "long strike." In 1877, railway workers staged a big strike to oppose a reduction in their wages. This job action represented the first nationwide strike. On May 1, 1886, workers in Chicago launched a nationwide general strike to obtain the eight-hour work day. They achieved a great victory. In 1889, the Paris Conference of the Second International declared May 1 as "International Labor Day." More than a thousand strikes occurred annually in the United States during the period from 1886 to 1914, and these work stoppages frequently escalated into armed conflicts.

The frequency of strikes in the United States and the degree of their militancy were comparable to those taking place in Europe at this time. The working class displayed a tenacious fighting spirit in these struggles. However, the American working class was immature organizationally and ideologically. Comparatively healthy unions had not been organized. A mass-based, Marxist proletarian political party also had not yet been established. Opportunist thinking exerted substantial influence on the worker's movement. The bourgeoisie systematically co-opted the worker aristocracy. The national identity of the proletariat was complicated because of the large numbers of immigrants in its midst. The attraction and availability of "free" land in the West corroded the unity of the proletariat. These factors temporarily hindered the development of the American workers' movement.

American Imperialism Pursues a Policy of Foreign Aggression and Expansionism

The export of commodities can be compared to imperialism's heavy artillery. It served a vital role in achieving economic expansion abroad. As American capitalism matured, its export of commodities increased rapidly. Beginning in 1876, the United States became an exporting nation, and was no longer the importer which it had been for quite some time. By 1900, the United States ranked second in total international trade, next only to Great Britain which had monopolized the world market for a long time.

In addition to continuing its exports of large quantities of cotton, wheat, and other agricultural products, America's finished and semi-finished industrial goods (not including food products) gradually increased, and by 1913 comprised almost half (48.8 percent) of total exports. American commodities were chiefly exported to Western Europe and Canada. Exports to Latin America and Asia began to increase rapidly and significantly by the end of the nineteenth century. Prior to the First World War, the United States had already squeezed out English and German influence in the markets of Central America and the Caribbean to take the leading role in these regions. Its share of China's total foreign trade was second only to that of Great Britain. In order to contend for the commodity markets of the world, American monopolies participated extensively in international cartels. They also reached agreements with the international monopolies of other countries to divide up the world market. In the early twentieth century, American monopolies participated in international cartels set up in such industries as steel, electric power, maritime transportation, oil, tobacco, and zinc smelting. International monopolies assured the monopoly capitalist that he would receive high monopoly profits in the international market.

"The export of capital is a characteristic of modern capitalism when monopoly takes control."[39] The export of American capital increased rapidly after the early twentieth century. In 1914, for example, the total amount of capital exported from the United States reached $3.5 billion. Of course, right up to the eve of the First World War, American capital exports lagged far behind those of England, France, Germany, and other countries. Moreover, foreign investment in the United States itself came to about $6.7 billion, approximately double U.S. capital exports. This occurred because the United States had a vast domestic market capable of absorbing huge quantities of capital investment during the several decades it took to open up the West. American capital exports predominantly went to Mexico and Canada, and only then to Europe, East Asia, and Latin America. The United States exported capital not only to extract super profits from economically backward countries, but also to attempt to control these nations both economically and politically. For example, by 1912 to 1913, American monopoly capital held Mexico's vital economic arteries in its own hands. Using their investment position in the country, American monopolies controlled 78 percent of Mexico's mines, 72 percent of its smelting industry, 58 percent of its oil exploration, and 68 percent of its latex industry. Porfirio Diaz, the President of Mexico at that time, was a puppet whose strings were pulled by American monopoly capital.

The United States stepped up its aggressive and expansionist activities in both Latin America and the Asian-Pacific region during its transition to the stage of imperialism.

During the 1860s and 1870s, the United States repeatedly sent warships to attack the coastal cities of Korea. Beginning in 1882, it forced Korea to sign a series of unequal treaties that gave the United States the right to take timber from Korea's forests, to open mines and set up factories in that country, and to use its ports and coastal waters for navigation purposes. The United States also made every effort to grab important strategic points in the Pacific. In 1875, the United States forced Hawaii to sign a treaty that, practically speaking, made that island kingdom into America's dependency. The United States occupied Pearl Harbor in 1878 and Pago Pago in the Samoan Islands in 1887, and subsequently turned both into naval bases.

The United States convened the Pan-American Conference in 1889 under the slogan of "Pan-Americanism." It organized the Pan-American League to facilitate U.S. efforts in opening Latin America's door to expanded trade and to greater American interference.

Of course, the backward regions of the world had already been divided up by the major European capitalist states by the end of the nineteenth century when the United States had completed the settlement of the West and had turned to overseas colonial expansion. The United States was a step behind in carving out a colonial sphere for itself in the world. Because American imperialism could not tolerate its disadvantageous position regarding plunder of the colonies, it did everything it could to launch a war that would redivide the world once again. The United States made its first move against Spain—the weakest of the venerable colonial empires—when it launched the Spanish-America War in 1898. After defeating Spain militarily, the United States wrested the Philippines, Puerto Rico, and Guam away from Spanish hands. It severed Cuba from Spanish rule and turned it into an American protectorate. The United States also completed its annexation of Hawaii in 1898. Today Hawaii is the fiftieth state in the United States.

The Spanish-American War was only the initial stage of America's policy of large-scale aggression.

America did everything in its power to step up its aggression against China. By this time, however, Great Britain, France, Germany, Russia, and the other imperialist powers had already carved out their own spheres of influence in this country. In light of this fact, the United States put forth the "Open Door" policy in 1899, demanding an equal opportunity and an equal share of the profits. The "Open Door" notes aimed to facilitate not only American acquisition of rights and opportunities equivalent to those enjoyed by the other Powers, but also aimed to advance them by enabling the United States to use its own economic superiority in pursuing a policy of large-scale aggression against China.

American imperialism also put forward the policy of "Dollar Diplomacy" at the beginning of the twentieth century. This so-called "Dollar Diplomacy" was an open alliance between finance capital and the government. It synchronized the use of money with military and political measures to gain access to the economically underdeveloped countries. It sought to enslave these nations politically and economically and establish American hegemony over the world. American imperialism used a coordinated policy of "dollars" and "the big stick" to carry out further economic expansion and political and military aggression in both China and Latin America.

For example, the United States in 1900 participated in a joint military expedition (composed of troops from eight powers) against China, and intervened to suppress the Chinese people's Boxer Movement. As a result, it secured many rights and privileges in China, although they were granted under duress by the Qing dynasty government. In addition, the United States launched a financial offensive against China, opening branch offices of its banks and trusts there in the early twentieth century. In 1910, the United States linked up with Great Britain, France, and Germany to organize a four-power banking consortium. By granting a loan to the Qing government, it secured the right to build railroads in China. In addition, the United States did everything it could to control China's finances by granting or denying loans. Holding "dollars" in one hand and brandishing "the big stick" in the other, the United States also proceeded to carry out a series of aggressive, expansionist activities in Latin America. For example, in 1903 it instigated Panama's secession from Colombia, and used strong-arm tactics to purchase the Panama Canal isthmus. Not only did the United States build a canal in this location—with its great strategic significance—but also controlled it directly. This occupation has lasted even up to today. At present, the Panamanian people are waging a heroic struggle to demand the return of sovereignty over the Panama Canal Zone. This just struggle against American aggression is bound to be victorious. During the early twentieth century, the United States came to control the financial and economic lifelines of the Dominican Republic, Honduras, Haiti, and other countries by resorting to various methods such as armed intervention, grooming local puppets, purchasing stocks, and granting loans. American capital achieved supremacy throughout Central America and the Caribbean in this manner.

American colonial policy—when compared to that of the older, more established "brand name" colonial powers like England and France—developed its own unique characteristics. Comparatively speaking, America relied more extensively on clandestine forms of colonial aggression, and directly occupied fewer colonies. It exercised political and economic control over countries that were ostensibly independent in name, yet—in reality—had been turned into dependencies of the United States. The reason why the United States adopted this form of colonialism was determined by the particular historical conditions it encountered when it began to launch its own career of colonial aggression. The United States was a newcomer among the colonial powers. Some of the colonies it wanted to plunder had already been occupied by the other powers, while still others were being fought over by a number of other states. The United States used comparatively covert tactics of aggression because then it could deceive the people of these countries, and even use them against the more established, "brand name" colonialist powers. In this way it could create favorable opportunities for its own aggression. Another reason for American reliance on such tactics occurred because national liberation struggles were already growing in the colonies at the end of the nineteenth and the early twentieth centuries. Using the old type of colonial rule to establish and maintain an empire had now become far more difficult to accomplish. Relying on a more covert form of colonialism therefore was far more advantageous to the United States.

The United States did rely more extensively on economic expansionism and economic penetration in carrying out its aggression against colonies. However, this certainly did not mean—as the spokesmen for U.S. imperialism have contended—that the United States was a peaceful nation that never carried out military aggression. The first imperialist war on a global scale to redivide the colonies was the Spanish-American War of 1898. And this war was launched by the United States. Combining the use of "dollars" with that of "the big stick," the U.S. government would either appear in a peaceful stance to provide "aid," or would threaten others with war and then carry out military aggression. This represented the two-fisted counter-revolutionary strategy commonly used in America's aggression and expansion.

4. The United States Takes Advantage of the First World War to Make a Fortune

The Wartime Economic "Prosperity" and the Development of State Monopoly Capital

The First World War, launched in order to redivide the world among the imperialist countries, was a catastrophe in human history. However, this war that brought an unprecedented disaster for humanity nevertheless became a golden opportunity for the development of American imperialism. When the war began, America's ruling class calculated as to how best it could profit from the war and expand its own power. In the beginning, it cunningly adopted a policy of "neutrality," and sat on the mountainside to watch the tigers fight below. It also served as an "arsenal" for both sides involved in the war, and participated in a brisk munitions trade. The United States finally entered the war on the side of the Entente in April 1917. It did this in order to share in the spoils that would accrue to the victorious powers, and to defeat Germany—a country that was perceived as developing into America's most dangerous future competitor.

During the war, the enormous demand for military goods by the European belligerents and their diminished competitive strength in the world market created an excellent opportunity for the United States to expand its own industrial and agricultural production and commodity exports. Production in the American processing industry increased 32 percent during the First World War (1914–18).

However, the development of wartime industrial production was extremely lopsided. While munitions, automobiles, shipbuilding, metallurgy, chemicals, and other sectors related to military needs increased rapidly, production of daily necessities (textiles, leather, paper) and activity in the construction trades shrank considerably. Agricultural production, especially wheat, attained unprecedented growth. Wheat production in 1915 (one billion bushels, or 27.22 million tons) set a record, attaining a level higher than it would achieve at any time prior to the Second World War. Output in 1915 was a third higher than in 1913. The average annual amount of wheat exported (3.75 million tons) in the four years during the war was more than two-and-a-half times the average annual amount exported in the four years prior to the war.

As production boomed during World War I, the degree of concentration and monopolization greatly accelerated. In 1914, there were 3,819 large companies (each with an annual output value in excess of $1 million) in the processing industry. By 1919, however, this number had grown to 10,413 companies, each with an annual output value of $1 million. These companies accounted for 57 percent of all workers in the processing industry and 68 percent of the total output value of this sector.

In general, the war pushed the development of monopoly capitalism into state monopoly capitalism. The monopoly capitalists availed themselves of the opportunities presented during the war, and now directly came to use the power of the state to earn even higher monopoly profits. State monopoly capitalism appeared chiefly in these forms:

1. During the war, the government established a group of agencies, ostensibly to regulate the economy. These bureaus were all controlled by representatives of the monopolies and became convenient instruments for them to strengthen the monopoly corporations. For example, the War Industries Board, established in July 1917, was a central organization that controlled America's entire industry. It worked through various agencies to manage everything related to a) the allocation of raw materials, fuel, and labor power; b) the assignment of contracts for government procurement, and c) the setting of prices. This Board was headed by Bernard Baruch, a broker from the Morgan organization. Other responsible positions in this bureau were also held by Wall Street bosses and their representatives. They manipulated the wartime Bureau of Industry, acted like tyrants, and did everything they possibly could to increase the income of the monopolies.

2. Some companies were nationalized, and others previously bankrolled by the government were turned over to the monopolies. For example, the railroads were nationalized in 1917. The government then paid the state-owned railroad companies at their average annual prewar profit levels. The government spent close to $900 million in operating expenses to these companies during the period when they were nationalized. Such largesse enabled the railroad capitalists to enjoy a huge income.

3. Government measures—such as state procurement of goods, the granting of subsidies, and the making of loans—aided the monopolies. The revenues of the state treasury poured endlessly into the wallets of the capitalists through the conduit of military procurement. While this was going on, the monopoly capitalists could even use slogans such as "defense" and "national interest" as pretexts to intensify their exploitation of the working class.

Each form of state monopoly capitalism was a means to increase profits and to increase concentration in industry. The monopoly capitalists, assisted by the government, netted huge profits from the war. In general, corporate profits exceeded 25 percent during the war, and some went as high as 500 percent or even more. Americans had never enjoyed as opportune a moment as the First World War to make money. Millionaires emerged everywhere.

The condition of the working class, however, deteriorated further during the war. The monopoly capitalists frequently used the pretext of military necessity to lengthen the workday and to freeze wages. The government instituted military conscription and abolished the right to strike. It also quickly raised excise taxes and issued government bonds in order to underwrite its colossal military expenditures, and to raise the money that it lent to the other allies. In 1914, each American carried an average tax burden of $3.84. This burden, however, increased year by year during the war until it reached $51 by 1920. The government also issued five series of wartime bonds whose total value came to $21.4 billion. The heavy burden of excise taxes and national debt finally came to rest on the backs of the worker and farmer masses. During the war, real wages fell more than one-fourth. When he evaluated the "regulated" wartime economies of the capitalist countries, Lenin wrote:

> The results of the "regulated economies" in both the United States and Germany have been to create a type of *garrison camp* for the workers (and some of the farmers) and a *paradise* for the bankers and capitalists. The regulatory methods used by these countries "squeeze" the workers almost to the verge of starvation. By the same token, they guarantee (through covert, reactionary bureaucratic means) that the capitalist will receive profits *even higher* than the ones he enjoyed before the war.[40]

Intensified Overseas Expansionism during World War I

The American bourgeoisie made use of wartime conditions to step up its expansion in international markets and to rapidly increase its commodity exports. When the war ended, total international trade had shrunk to 60 percent of its prewar level. However, during the war, the total value of American exports had tripled, its imports had increased 80 percent, and its favorable balance of trade amounted to $11.6 billion. The United States further consolidated its superiority in the markets of Central America and the Caribbean region. It also grabbed the markets of South America and Canada, and strengthened its position in the markets of China and West Asia. Moreover, by supplying the belligerents with huge quantities of military goods, the United States compelled its original European competitors (including England) to become its economic dependents.

The United States rapidly expanded its merchant fleet in order to develop its foreign trade. During the war, the total tonnage of its merchant fleet increased tenfold (from 1.07 million tons to 11.08 million tons). Its fleet and naval strength were also substantially augmented. This laid the foundation of military strength for the United States to attempt to achieve world hegemony.

Because they had imported huge quanitites of goods and spent colossal sums on military expenditures, England, France, and the other major belligerents had little recourse but to pay the United States with large gold shipments and surrender some valuable foreign stock certificates. They even had to borrow money from the Americans. Not only did the United States take advantage of the war to recover more than $2 billion worth of stocks held by foreigners, but at the same time it rapidly increased its own exports of capital. In 1919, America's foreign investment reached $7 billion. It had also loaned about $10 billion to the Entente during the war. Some twenty countries fell into debt to the United States, and even the wealthiest—England—owed $4.4 billion. The United States went from a debtor to a creditor nation. It took into its own hands 40 percent (close to $4.5 billion) of the world's gold reserves, and strengthened its control over the capitalist world's finances. America's wartime export of capital for the most part was accomplished by government loans. This type of capital export conformed to the demands of the monopoly capitalists who wanted to extract every ounce of advantage. Just as Lenin said, "they skinned every cow twice."[41] The first "skinning" came from the interest the borrower paid on the loan. The second "skinning" came from the profits secured when the borrower used the loan to purchase American factory products. Government loans also facilitated American political and economic controls over debtor nations.

The United States greatly expanded its overseas strength during the course of the First World War. Prior to the war, the United States enjoyed a position of superiority in the Caribbean region. South America, however, was under England's powerful control, and the United States had not opened even a single bank there. By early 1921, though, the United States had already established about fifty bank branches throughout South America. Capital exports to all of Latin America also increased greatly, rising from $1.3 billion in 1913 to $2.4 billion in 1919. The United States accounted for more than half of the import and export trade of the twenty Latin American countries. The United States not only made great headway in controlling Latin America's economy, but also strengthened its political domination over these nations. As a result of the war, it became the most powerful ruler and the biggest exploiter of all of Latin America.

American capital also made further inroads into China during the war. Exports to China more than tripled in the period from 1913 to 1919, and investment increased dramatically. The United States made several loans (totalling $13 million at annual interest rates between 5 percent and 7 percent) to the Chinese government. It took advantage of this opportunity to grab not only the rights to build a 1,500 mile railroad in China, but also other rights and privileges. America's penetration of and aggression against China, however, ran into stiff competition from Japan. The United States and Japan subsequently reached a compromise agreement whereby both countries (in a ratio of seven to five) would float a $6 million bond issue to finance the construction of Chinese canals. In 1918, the American monopolies contacted England, France, and Japan to organize a new four-power banking consortium and contend for leadership in making loans to China.

The war fattened American imperialism, enhanced its power throughout the world, and boosted its ambition to achieve global supremacy. The Fourteen Points advocated by President Woodrow Wilson in 1918 represented such a program designed not only to strangle the revolutionary movement in Soviet Russia and throughout the world, but also to establish an American global hegemony. After the war ended, the United States became a center of finance capitalism's exploitative global activities and a core member of the world's counter-revolutionary forces.

"Getting rich quick" by taking advantage of the opportunities presented by the First World War left yet another extremely shameful, bloodstained chapter in the history of American capitalism's development. Lenin hit the nail on the head when he said:

> The results of four years of war now reveal a general law of capitalism as to how robbers divide up their booty: the richest and strongest grab the most; the weakest are themselves plundered, stepped on, squeezed, and strangled. . . . America's millionaires are almost the wealthiest and most secure in the world, considering their favorable geographical situation. They have made the biggest fortunes. They have turned every other country—even the wealthiest—into its debtor. They have plundered countless billions of dollars. . . . Every American dollar is stained. Each one is stained by the 'advantageous' military contracts that made fortunes for the rich and bankrupted the poor in every nation. Every American dollar is stained with blood. Each carries the blood that was shed by the ten million who died and the twenty million who were wounded in this war.[42]

5. The Collapse of the Relative Economic Stability of the 1920s and the Great Depression of the 1930s

The False "Prosperity" and Contradictions Inherent in the Relative Economic Stability of the 1920s

The American economic boom stimulated by World War I also yielded some serious contradictions. When the war came to an end, domestic and foreign purchases of military goods fell sharply. The transition from a wartime to a peacetime economy brought about a sudden decrease in production in many American industries. Industrial and mining production declined in 1919. However, Europe's urgent need in the immediate postwar period for industrial equipment and vehicles to heal the wounds of war provided American factories with new orders and temporarily moderated the severity of the crisis. Domestically, consumer demand that had been left unsatisfied during the war because of the lack of supplies also created a temporarily brisk market for consumer goods. Under such conditions, American industrial production experienced a new—albeit brief—upsurge that lasted from the latter half of 1919 up to March 1920. By 1920, the indices for the processing and mining industries both topped their highest prewar levels. The "boom" in American agriculture that had begun during the war continued until 1920. American exports set new records in 1919 and 1920. Exports of industrial and agricultural products—such as industrial goods, machinery, and wheat—increased even when compared to wartime levels.

However, the war had impoverished the people and created financial difficulties for the various European countries. It was impossible, therefore, to implement a large-scale economic recovery program at a moment's notice. People quickly used up the meager savings that they had put aside during the war because of the acute shortage of goods. America's industrial and agricultural capacity, which had expanded during the transition period, now quickly ran into this obstacle of a constricted world and domestic market. An economic crisis ensued. American exports began to fall in July 1920. When industrial production fell precipitously in July, the crisis quickly engulfed the entire national economy, and bottomed out only in March 1921. During the crisis, the index of industrial production fell 23 percent. Pig iron production dropped 55 percent, steel 53 percent, coal 28 percent, and cotton consumption 20 percent. The rate of unemployment reached 23.1 percent. More than five million workers were unemployed throughout the country. Agricultural prices also fell abruptly. Wholesale agricultural prices declined 41.2 percent between 1920 and 1921, and market prices for major agricultural products plunged even more than 60 percent or 70 percent. During this same period, the index for agricultural production declined 11.4 percent. The crisis bankrupted many small farms. American agriculture now entered a chronic crisis that would last for the entire decade of the 1920s.

The 1920–21 economic recession was the first global economic crisis to occur after capitalism entered the stage of its general crisis. The fact that the crisis occurred simultaneously in both the United States and the other major capitalist countries intensified its overall impact. In addition, the industrial crisis within America coincided with a domestic agricultural crisis, and that also caused it to be especially traumatic and far-reaching.

American workers—encouraged by the great October 1917 socialist revolution in Russia, and influenced by the proletarian revolutions in Western Europe—fought back bravely as they found themselves caught in this domestic economic turmoil. The working class movement reached a peak of activity in 1919. In order to improve their own economic conditions and oppose the government's armed intervention in Soviet Russia, the American working class staged more than 3,500 strikes this year. More than four million workers went out on strike. The American Communist party was also born at this high point in the workers' movement.

A new industrial "upsurge" appeared after the United States had weathered the economic crisis of 1921. The foundation for this "upsurge," however, had already been established during the First World War. The renovation of America's fixed capital assets during the war years had fallen far short of what was needed. For example, the capital required to renovate the railroads came to some several hundred million dollars. Housing construction and renovation also fell into a slump during the war years. This, however, eventually promoted the production of new machinery and equipment as well as the development of housing construction. Because the American bourgeoisie had made enormous profits during the war, they were now favorably placed—once the war was concluded—to promote the renovation of fixed capital assets and to expand production processes. The bourgeoisie now implemented a so-called policy of "rationalizing capitalism." They energetically developed new technologies (such as the automated assembly line) and achieved standardization in large-scale production. As a result, production capacity was greatly enhanced, and this subsequently facilitated a new upsurge in overall production. The United States also captured new foreign markets. In this sector, America took advantage of Europe's postwar lag in economic recovery as well as Western Europe's financial dependency on the United States. Domestically, the capitalists now permitted the workers to pay for cars, furniture, and other household durable goods on an installment payment plan. This method temporarily expanded the domestic market for consumer goods. All of these events created favorable conditions for the development of American capitalism. By 1929, American industrial production had eclipsed even the peak levels it had reached in the prewar and immediate postwar years. Steel and iron both surpassed their highest wartime production figures, reaching fifty-six million and forty-three million tons, respectively. The machine mannufacturing, automobile, and petroleum industries all expanded several times over, with auto production reaching 5,358,000 units and oil 137 million tons. American industry produced almost half (48.5 percent) of the industrial goods of the capitalist world.

At the same time, America's share of world trade rose from 11.1 percent to 14 percent, while England's fell from 15.1 percent to 13.2 percent. For the first time, the United States had taken the lead in trade conducted by the capitalist world. America now enjoyed an absolute dominance over the import and export trade of Canada and the twenty countries of Latin America, and far surpassed the trade carried on by England and Germany with these nations. America's export of capital also greatly increased. In 1919, American overseas capital investment came to $7 billion. By 1929, however, it reached $17.2 billion. This figure put the United States just slightly behind England, and second overall in the world. America's overseas capital investments invaded England's spheres of influence on a massive scale. In 1922, the United States replaced Britain as the foremost foreign investor in Canada. America's capital investment in Latin America reached $5.6 billion—close to the $5.9 billion figure invested by England. American capital also took advantage of Germany's postwar economic collapse to step in. For example, the United States opened up many subsidiaries in Germany. It seized stocks from numerous German companies, and it came to exercise control—in differing degrees—over German industries such as automobiles, petroleum, electrical goods, nonferrous metals, and banking. In order to resuscitate German imperialism's military and economic potential, American monopoly capital granted huge loans to Germany's largest banks and made vast investments in its industrial monopolies. By 1929, the United States accounted for 70 percent of long-term foreign investment in Germany. The significance of capital exports—as compared to the export of commodities—became even greater in the postwar period. In 1929, the income ($1.186 billion) derived from America's overseas investments was substantially greater than the net income ($241 million) derived from its foreign trade. By 1929, the United States held on its own more than half (or $5 billion) of the world's gold reserves (which totalled $9 billion). The center from which finance capital exploited the world had now moved from Europe to the United States.

The large monopolies increased their economic power after the American economy expanded both domestically and overseas. Their profits increased sharply. The share of capital held by the two hundred largest nonbanking corporations—as compared to all companies—increased from 33.3 percent in 1909 to 47.9 percent by 1929. The financial strength of the big banks also grew. While the total number of banks in the United States fell by 17.8 percent, the number of branch offices opened by the big banks multiplied sixfold in the period from 1921 to 1929. Corporate profits reached new heights in the 1920s. For example, they were more than 25 percent higher in 1928 than the peak levels they had reached during the war years (1916–17). The two hundred largest nonbanking corporations received more than 40 percent of the net income earned by all the other nonbanking companies. The ranks of the super-wealthy and idle rich increased dramatically. For example, forty thousand people in 1929 had annual incomes of more than $1 million. The capital assets of the eight large financial cliques were similarly astounding. The Rockefeller family fortune alone was worth more than $1 billion.

Generally speaking, American industry in the 1920s took off like a whirlwind after it had weathered the crisis of 1920–21. Capitalist speculation and a mania for making money became so rampant that it seemed like a force whose power could never be curbed. The American economy's temporary stability and high growth also stimulated a virtual torrent of bourgeois thinking. The American bourgeoisie and their house scholars made a huge racket. They argued that American capitalism had now entered a stage of "eternal prosperity," and that the "rationalization of capitalism" carried out by America's "new capitalism" would eliminate poverty and economic crisis. At that time President Herbert Hoover boasted that American capitalism would eradicate poverty, and that each worker—before too long—would have a chicken in every pot and a car in every garage. Opportunists of various kinds—including those labor bureaucrats and revisionists like Jay Lovestone, who had hidden themselves in the ranks of the Communist party (USA)—also became intoxicated by the "prosperity" hawked by the bourgeoisie. They also chimed in with their support, and sang the same old tune of "American exceptionalism." In order to sing the praises of American capitalism's "prosperity," they fabricated a spurious theory that the United States had somehow experienced a "second Industrial Revolution." They claimed that "it wasn't Karl Marx, but Henry Ford" who had pointed out to the workers the road to happiness. By doing so, they attempted to poison the beliefs of the working class and paralyze its militancy. At that time, the Communist International made a Marxist analysis of the contemporary political and economic situation in the United States. As early as 1925, it pointed out that the stability exhibited by capitalism in the 1920s was partial, temporary, and lacked substance. This temporary stability also concealed many serious contradictions. "Partial stability will produce a violent capitalist crisis, while an increasing crisis will also destroy that stability. This is a law of dialectics governing the development of capitalism in the present historical period."[43] Historical developments have completely verified this scientific prediction. The "prosperity" of the 1920s was merely a house of cards built on the refuse heap of World War I. An unprecedentedly severe crisis broke out in the United States in October 1929. Its stability and "prosperity" now completely collapsed.

The relative and unstable nature of American capitalism's prosperity in the 1920s had already revealed itself in a number of ways during that time.

First of all, not only were plants operating well below capacity, but high unemployment was also a common occurrence during the 1920s. Between 1921 and 1929, for example, major industries like coal mining, iron, steel, auto, and oil refining were running between 60 percent and 70 percent of capacity. This was particularly the case in 1929 when, at the peak of the industrial boom, all of America's processing industries were operating, on average, at only 73 percent of capacity. The rate of industrial growth began to slow down. For example, while the average annual rate of growth of industrial production was 4.8 percent in the period from 1901 to 1914, it fell to 4.3 percent during the years from 1921 to 1929. High unemployment frequently accompanied low usage of plant capacity. The reserve army of production became a standing army of the unemployed. According to American government statistics—which clearly have understated the real situation—average annual unemployment in the United States in the years 1921–29 ran at more than 2.2 million totally unemployed workers. The "rationalization of capitalism" that was promoted during this period substantially increased labor intensity, raised productivity, and brought about a huge increase in productive capacity. However, the "rationalization of capitalism" also forced many workers out of their jobs, increased unemployment, and led to a further decline in the overall purchasing power of society. This further aggravated the problem of a constricted market, and led inevitably to instability and a new economic crisis.

Second, during the 1920s, while industry sang its praises of American "prosperity," agriculture was mired in a chronic recession. One by one, the various European countries restored their agricultural production after the war. At the same time, however, the poverty of the working masses in the United States narrowed the potential market for agricultural goods. Supply exceeded demand, thereby forcing steep price reductions in agricultural commodities. As a result, agriculture remained stagnant for a long time. In addition to this, monopoly capital—in order to grow—used various methods to plunder agriculture. This caused the agricultural crisis to be even more protracted and more serious. Pressured by monopoly capital and the chronic agricultural crisis, a small number of large farmers began to use machinery in order to lower production costs and to strengthen their competitive edge. The utilization of tractors, agricultural machinery, and heavy trucks in American agriculture made great progress in the 1920s. For example, machine-powered tools constituted only 23.1 percent of agricultural implements in 1920, but 56.2 percent by 1930. One can say that the transition to mechanization began during the period of semi-mechanization prior to the war. However, only a few farmers used tractors. The vast majority of small and medium-sized farmers were in no position to make use of machinery. On the contrary, their circumstances even deteriorated due to the competition they faced from the wealthier farmers who possessed superior technology. Many small and medium-sized farmers subsequently went bankrupt. The chronic agricultural recession and the large number of farming bankruptcies profoundly revealed the partial nature—as well as shaky foundation—that underlay the appearance of capitalist stability.

Finally, the question as to who would control the markets of the world presented an irreconcilable contradiction for capitalism. After the First World War, the United States attempted to make use of its economic power to contend for world hegemony. It could not content itself with its control over the markets of Latin America, but made every effort to also penetrate into Asia, and especially China. Such ambitions created a sharp contradiction between the United States, on the one hand, and England and Japan on the other. As a result, Asia and the Pacific region became an important arena where the United States, England, and Japan each jockeyed for position. The contradiction between the United States and England was extremely sharp in their struggle for natural resources such as oil and rubber. This was particularly true with regard to oil. Access to petroleum posed a question that affected the lifelines of the great powers of the world. Whoever controlled the most oil would enjoy a position of superiority in all economic and military activities. The United States and England fought fierce overt and covert battles with each other in the major oil-producing areas of the world, such as the Middle East, Indonesia, and Venezuela. At the same time, the national economies of some colonial and semi-colonial countries (like China, India, Canada, and Argentina) also developed—to differing degrees—after the war. A global national liberation movement surged forward. The question of who would control the world market became even more acute. In 1927, Stalin clearly pointed out that this question of the world market carried within itself a profound contradiction. He said:

> The most far-reaching and acute crises of capitalism are produced precisely when increased production, trade expansion, technological progress, and an increase in productive capacity confronts a rather fixed world market, fixed spheres of influence in the world market, and fixed spheres of power among the various imperialist groups. Such crises breed new wars and threaten the existence of any stability.[44]

The Economic Crisis and the Great Depression of the 1930s

The temporary economic "boom" of the 1920s and the capitalists' illusion of having achieved "perpetual prosperity" stimulated wild commercial speculation and blind expansion of American industrial production. However, after the mid-1920s, three significant developments occurred. The large-scale renovation of America's domestic fixed capital and the boom in housing construction had now become a thing of the past. Second, the work of reviving the economies of the various European countries had either been completed or was nearing completion. Third, the ability of workers to buy on credit—a measure that temporarily expanded the domestic market for consumer goods—was also becoming increasingly ineffective. The crisis came to a turning point as the expanding forces of production encountered a domestic and foreign market that was shrinking day by day. By the middle of 1929, vast stockpiles of commodities were accumulating. The crisis, which spread rapidly, officially began on October 21, 1929 when stock prices fell sharply on the New York Stock Exchange.

This crisis was the most severe and prolonged in American history. The nation's industrial production fell 46.3 percent from its pre-Depression peak in 1929 to its Depression low point in 1932. When calculated on a monthly basis, the nation's industrial production fell 55.6 percent from its precrisis peak (reached in May 1929) to its nadir (which was reached in July 1932). Production at this point had fallen to the level attained in 1905–06. The production of capital goods also dropped especially sharply during the Depression because of the excess fixed industrial capital that was already in place in the 1920s. Machine tool construction fell 87 percent, pig iron 79.4 percent, steel 75.8 percent, automobiles 94.6 percent, and coal mining 40.9 percent. Declines in the shipbuilding and construction industries were also extremely severe. During the most difficult moments of the Depression, the automobile industry was operating at only 5 percent capacity and the steel industry at only 15 percent.

The crisis affected every industrial sector. Industrial production declined in three consecutive years. More than 130,000 companies in the United States went bankrupt during the Depression, and tens of millions of workers were forced out of their jobs and walked aimlessly on the streets. In 1933, unemployment hit 12.83 million people, or about one-fourth of the work force. The lengthy duration of the Depression forced the unemployed workers to face the rigors of cold and hunger, and many died of starvation. This was just as Marx had said: "Capital must depend on exploited labor to live. Just like the eminently barbaric slave owners, capital also must make its slaves accompany it to the grave, and at a time of crisis, must cause the deaths of large numbers of workers."[45]

The industrial crisis caused a further deterioration in the status of agriculture, which was already suffering from a chronic recession. Agricultural prices plummeted in the spring of 1930 because products could not find a market, and large quantities therefore had to be warehoused. Farm cash income in 1932 fell by 58 percent when compared to its level in 1929—and was even lower than that reached in 1914. Serious retrogressive features now appeared in agriculture: Horsedrawn implements replaced tractors because gasoline was too expensive. Manual labor replaced machinery because wages were so low. The use of chemical fertilizers fell dramatically.

Necessary replacements for worn-out farm machinery and implements were not being put into place. The quantity and quality of draft animals and livestock fell. Arable land deteriorated, and harvests diminished in size. As farmers generally became poorer, many simply went bankrupt. In order to resolve the crisis, the government and the big monopoly capitalists finally decided to destroy agricultural products on an organized, large-scale basis. Contemporary American newspapers published the following accounts. On December 4, 1932, the *New York Times* reported: "At today's grain prices, it is more advantageous for a family or a business office to use grain rather than charcoal as a fuel. Various schools in this state have already begun to use grain as a fuel." On August 24, 1933, the *New York Herald Tribune* reported: "The government plans to destroy 5 million hogs, and also to restrict the number of new-born piglets. The work of destroying the piglets has already begun."

On the one hand, there were tens of millions of workers who found themselves cold and hungry. Many were even dying of cold and starvation. On the other hand, a great deal of productive industrial capacity lay idle, and large quantities of agricultural products were being destroyed. This completely revealed the extent to which capitalist production had become unreasonable and decadent! In 1931, Stalin had criticized this, saying: "If an economic system doesn't know how to handle the 'excess' products that it has produced, and can only burn them up at a time when the masses everywhere are suffering from poverty, unemployment, hunger, and bankruptcy, then that kind of economic system has condemned itself to death."[46]

The crisis paralyzed the entire banking and credit systems. Foreign trade and capital exports suffered severe damage. The total value of imports and exports shrank about 70 percent during the Depression. If one eliminates the factor of price decreases, then imports fell by 34 percent and exports by 48 percent. There was a precipitous drop in the export of capital. While the value of stocks issued by the United States to foreign countries reached $1.3 billion in 1928, this amount had declined to $250 million in 1931 and stood at only $1.6 million in 1933. The export of capital, one of the foundations of imperialism, had virtually stopped. This point alone is sufficient to reveal how the Depression destabilized the entire capitalist system.

This economic crisis, which first erupted in 1929 in the United States, became a global economic crisis of unprecedented proportions. It engulfed every nation within the capitalist world—the industrial states as well as the agricultural nations, the imperialist countries as well as the colonies. The Depression caused industrial production throughout the entire capitalist world to drop 40 percent, in other words, to fall 10 percent below the 1913 level. During this same time period, however, production in the socialist Soviet Union flourished, and socialist construction made huge strides forward. Industrial production in the Soviet Union doubled between 1929 and 1933, and almost quadrupled when compared to 1913 levels. The high growth rate maintained by the Soviet economy completely revealed the incomparable superiority of the socialist system when compared to the capitalist one.

Not only did the monopolies artificially maintain high monopoly prices during the Depression, but they also received annual subsidies from the government that were worth several billions of dollars. As a result, they could still earn high profits. The heavy burden of the crisis was shifted onto the backs of the working people. Real wages for industrial workers during the Depression declined about 25 percent when compared to their levels achieved during the last half of the 1920s. That is, real wages declined to their 1900 level. Class contradictions intensified, and strikes became more numerous. The working class staged large-scale demonstrations throughout the country under the slogan of "We'll fight rather than starve." Farmers also fought back fiercely. They opposed the government's policy of maintaining high taxes, yet keeping its agricultural purchase prices low. They also boycotted the forced auction of farms. Hundreds of thousands of veterans—desperate to maintain their living standards—organized mass demonstrations that demanded higher pensions from the government. The Depression intensified the class contradictions within the United States to an unprecendented degree.

Roosevelt's New Deal

The American bourgeoisie became terrified when confronted with this kind of economic and political situation. It was precisely under these circumstances that Franklin D. Roosevelt assumed the presidency in March 1933. As soon as he took office, Roosevelt put into effect a so-called New Deal that would defuse the serious economic problems and imminent revolutionary crisis. He hurriedly pushed through a substantial amount of New Deal legislation, hoping thereby to use governmental measures to "regulate" the economy, rescue the United States from the Great Depression, and prevent the broad masses of workers and farmers from turning to revolutionary actions.

What was the essence of the so-called New Deal?

1. Roosevelt became President at the very moment when the credit crisis was at its most acute. Preventing a total collapse of the American financial and credit system became Roosevelt's top priority. The basic measures he undertook in this regard were the following: Roosevelt cleaned up the banks. He established governmental guarantees for bank deposits. He extended huge credits to the world of finance, and he devalued the dollar. The effort to clean up the banks was embodied in the Federal Emergency Relief Act, passed by Congress, which required all banks to temporarily halt all transactions involving deposits and withdrawals. The Treasury Department then "cleaned up" the banking system by reserving the right to approve each bank's resumption of activities. This method not only checked the run on banks, but also eliminated the smaller banks. Congress then passed the Federal Deposit Insurance Law whereby the federal government guaranteed bank deposits. This restored the confidence of depositors in the banks, and prevented any new wave of runs on the banks. At the same time, the government offered a huge $3 billion loan to the big banking monopoly capitalists, thereby strengthing their power.

This series of measures enabled the American banking system to achieve a certain degree of temporary stability. However, their greatest impact was to enhance the power of the big banks. Many small banks still went bankrupt. In fact, the total number of banks nationwide fell by one-fifth within a short period of time. The entire American banking and credit system became held by an ever smaller coterie of big monopoly oligarchs. Although the devaluation of the dollar and price inflation yielded some slight relief for debtors, the major beneficiaries were still the monopoly capitalists. They used inflation to lower the real wages of workers, to strengthen the competitive power of exports, and to increase profits.

2. The National Industrial Recovery Act (NIRA) mandated government "regulation" of industry. This law embodied three important elements: 1. The so-called "equal competition code" stipulated the scale of production, price levels, sales quotas, and the conditions of employment for workers in various sectors of industry. While nominally the purpose of this law was to "eliminate excess

production," in reality it accomplished an intensified cartelization process. Talk about equal competition was entirely fraudulent. Small and medium-sized companies could never compete successfully with the monopolies. Moreover, the monopoly capitalists controlled the right to implement and enforce the equal competition code. Their despotic behavior did accomplish the goal of industrial rationalization. It resulted in the further elimination of small and medium-sized companies, and led to unprecedented growth in the power of the monopolies. 2. The NIRA ran public works projects to increase employment and to raise the purchasing power of the masses. Between 1933 and 1937, the American government appropriated a total of $12 billion for this purpose. This also opened a new source of wealth for the monopolies involved in the supply of construction materials. However, the various public works projects absorbed only between 2 and 3.6 million workers annually. The remaining army of unemployed still numbered more than ten million. 3. In order to moderate the powerful militancy of the working class, the NIRA recognized—on paper—some basic rights of the workers (such as the right to participate freely in unions, the right to nominate and elect its own representatives, and the right of collective bargaining). It also provided a small amount of so-called welfare assistance for the starving unemployed workers. Roosevelt hoped to use these measures to ease the contradiction between the workers and the capitalists, and to blunt the fighting spirit of the workers. However, the extremely small amount of relief funds appropriated for the unemployed workers was totally inadequate when one considers that the army of unemployed reached ten million strong.

3. The Agricultural Adjustment Act used government bonuses and subsidies to reduce the amount of land under cultivation and to destroy crops. Its purpose was to diminish agricultural production, and thereby raise agricultural prices. Roosevelt hoped that this law would eliminate the serious consequences of the agricultural crisis and soften the militancy of the farmers. In 1933, the Roosevelt government signed several million contracts with farm owners in various states to reduce the area under cultivation. As a result, the area sown to wheat and cotton was reduced by more than 10 million acres. Corn acreage fell by almost nine million. The land left fallow was rented by the state on which it paid a fee to the farm owner. The government also paid the farmer a subsidy to compensate for his reduced production resulting from allowing his land to lie fallow. In 1934, this measure was expanded to apply to other agricultural products such as meat, milk, sugar, and yams. In order to eliminate the existing surpluses, the Roosevelt administration spent huge amounts of money to purchase various kinds of farm animals and agricultural products. After they had been bought by the government, these products were then destroyed. In the years 1933 and 1934, for example, the government destroyed 1.6 million boxcars full of grain, and slaughtered more than twenty-three million livestock, six million hogs, and five million sheep.

4. Passage of the Farm Mortgage Refinancing Act extended new credit opportunities to farmers. Its purpose was to avert the rash of bankruptcies that had

Index of Annual Industrial Production

1933	63.8
1934	69
1935	80
1936	95
1937	103.4
1938	81

occurred when farmers were unable to pay their mortgage obligations. The law enabled any farmer to refinance his mortgage with the Farm Credit Administration at a relatively low interest rate of 4.5 percent, provided that the debt incurred did not exceed 50 percent of the value of the farmland itself and 20 percent of the value of the building structures. This stipulation benefitted only the relatively wealthy farm owners. In reality the vast numbers of impoverished small farmers with heavy debts could never qualify for a government loan. In addition, those farm owners who did refinance their mortgages with the government merely exchanged one creditor for another. In other words, the state replaced private banks to become the farmers' main creditor. As a result, there was very little improvement in the farm situation in the first three years of the Farm Credit Act's implementation. Foreclosures still remained at alarming levels, reaching 600 thousand cases during this period, and involved approximately 10 percent of the nation's farms.

The purpose of Roosevelt's New Deal quite obviously was to solve the economic crisis and its consequences, to soften the revolutionary militancy of the people, and to consolidate the rule of monopoly capital over the workers. In a word, its purpose was to rescue the tottering system of American capitalism. The general method used to achieve this goal was to have the government intervene in all aspects of the economic life of the nation. In other words, it strengthened state monopoly capitalism.

When Roosevelt began to push ahead with his New Deal in early 1933, industry and agriculture had already weathered the worst part of the crisis and were on the road to recovery. Implementing the New Deal neither rescued the situation nor brought about an economic recovery. The New Deal's impact on alleviating the crisis was extremely slight. Only in the summer of 1933 did industrial production register a temporary increase. By autumn, however, production had fallen again and subsequently remained stagnant. A new crisis broke out once more in 1938. This was a special kind of recession that occurred under the conditions of the general crisis of capitalism. Not only did it last for four years, but moreover, it did not lead to a new industrial upsurge. For example, American industrial production in 1937 had just recovered to its 1929 level, but by 1938 had once again fallen by about 20 percent. The index of annual industrial production (with a base of one hundred in 1929) was as above. During this time period, companies frequently operated at less than capacity; the annual rate of plant utilization ranged between 50 percent and 75 percent of capacity. Renovation of fixed capital was very limited. The bourgeoisie were badly shaken by the Great Depression, and this had an even greater impact on new investment. The chronic agricultural crisis—coupled with the existence of a vast army of unemployed that frequently numbered around ten million—caused the domestic market to become abnormally constricted. All these factors undermined any real basis for a cyclical upsurge, and as a result, the American economy did not reach a new cyclical peak prior to the outbreak of a new crisis. This new recession hit with great force in 1938. During this crisis, industrial production dropped almost one-third, the processing industry was operating at two-thirds capacity, unemployment stood at 10.39 million, and the unemploymnet rate reached a high of 19 percent. The agricultural crisis once again intensified. Net agricultural income in 1938 was almost 20 percent lower than in 1937. The fraudulent propaganda claiming that the so-called New Deal was a "plan that guaranteed high production" and that America now enjoyed a "planned, crisis-free capitalism" was completely discredited in the face of the genuine severity of the crisis.

The New Deal was advantageous only to monopoly capital because it strengthened the ruling position of the monopolies. Monopoly capital earned its biggest profits ever during Roosevelt's tenure. For example, the after-tax profits of monopoly capital amounted to $3 billion in 1929, but increased to $6.5 billion in 1934. The degree of monopolization in various industrial sectors also became more pronounced. After the economy gradually revived, and monopoly capital's power had been consolidated and strengthened, the New Deal's historic mission had been completed. As a result, the Supreme Court declared (first in May 1935, and then in January 1936) as "unconstitutional"—and therefore null and void—two important New Deal laws. The first was the National Recovery Act, and the second was the Agricultural Adjustment Act. The prospects for a wartime prosperity had now become quite apparent on the eve of the Second World War. As a result, Roosevelt—a loyal representative of the capitalist system—realized that the time had now come to tear off his veil of reformism. He openly cut back or eliminated various welfare programs, prohibited strikes, and vigorously expanded the military to prepare for war.

America's Weakened Position in the International Economy

America's position in the international economy in the 1930s weakened substantially after suffering through two crises and a special type of depression. America's share of total industrial production in the capitalist world was 48.5 percent in 1929, but had fallen to 32.2 percent in 1938. This was not even as high as the 36 percent share enjoyed by the United States in 1913, prior to World War I. America's position in international trade also slipped. The pound bloc and the commonwealth preference system, both established during this period, boosted England's strength in the world market. At the same time, United States trade with the principal commonwealth countries (such as Australia, New Zealand, Canada, and South Africa) shrank dramatically. Germany also used its inexpensive commodities and system of "credit arrangements" to push aside the United States in the markets of Europe and Latin America. Although the United States achieved certain gains in Asia's markets, the growth rate of its trade there nevertheless fell far behind that of Japan and Germany. As a result of this kind of competition, America's share of the world's import-export trade declined. For example, during the period from 1929 to 1938, its share of imports fell from 12.2 to 8.1 percent and its share of exports went from 15.6 to 13.4 percent. Both retreated to their pre–World War I levels. Although the United States still maintained its primacy in global exports, England once again regained first place in total world trade.

During the 1930s, repayment of the huge war debts originally owed to the United States was no longer realistically feasible. It vanished into thin air. At the same time, not only did new capital exports from America fall off sharply because of the depression, but also vast quantities of its overseas investments were repatriated. As a result, American foreign investment fell to $11.4 billion in 1938, roughly a one-third reduction when compared to 1929. Of course, the profits still earned by American finance capital from its foreign investments between the two world wars remained staggering. American income from private foreign investment reached $13.9 billion during the years from 1920 to 1940, or $2.1 billion more than the total amount of new investment for the same period.

In the period between the two world wars, America's contradiction with England was the principal contradiction it faced—and had faced for a long time—within the imperialist camp itself. The United States consistently aided Germany and colluded with Japan in order to weaken England. It also attempted to use German and Japanese strength to weaken and destroy the socialist Soviet Union. However, when American interests became directly threatened—in other words, following the rapid expansion of the power of fascist Germany and Japan and the establishment of an aggressive German-Italian-Japanese axis—the Anglo-American contradiction receded to play a secondary role. Now the contradictions sharpened between the United States, on the one hand, and fascist Germany and Japan on the other. America's long-term policy of conniving with German and Japanese fascism was ultimately self-defeating. It only resulted in America ignominiously shooting itself in the foot.

6. The Abnormal "Prosperity" Enjoyed by the American Economy during the Second World War: The United States Becomes the World's Largest International Exploiter

On the eve of the Second World War, the American ruling class consistently pursued a reactionary policy of abetting aggression while adopting a wait-and-see attitude. While the United States passed a Neutrality Act in 1935 that prohibited the sale of military goods to belligerent states, it also secretly sold large quantities of strategic raw materials—and even weapons—to the German, Italian, and Japanese fascists. The United States also participated in the infamous "Munich agreement" which abetted Germany's annexation of Czechoslovakia. After the Second World War broke out in Europe, the United States government, pressured by its people, permitted the anti-fascist countries to purchase military goods in the United States on a "cash and carry" basis after November 4, 1939. Germany then declared its status as a neutral country to fraudulently purchase weaponry from the American monopolies. In reality, the United States supplied the belligerents on both sides with munitions and war material. Not only did this enable the American arms' merchants to make fabulous profits, but also stimulated a huge influx of gold into the United States from Europe's capitalist countries. After two or three years of fighting, the European combatants had virtually exhausted their gold and foreign currency reserves, and so could not continue to purchase weaponry in the United States without ready cash. Only after the American people resolutely demanded the provision of material aid to the anti-fascist countries did the U.S. Congress pass the Lend-Lease Act on March 11, 1941. On the basis of this legislation, the United States by the end of September 1945, had supplied various countries with $43.95 billion worth of munitions, equipment, food, raw materials, shipping costs, and labor services. In return, it received $7.34 billion worth of goods and services as compensation. Although the Lend-Lease Act objectively played a certain positive role in sustaining the war against the fascist powers, it also promoted America's global expansion. It enabled American monopolies to carve out vast and profitable markets for its commodities, and to earn a tidy fortune from participating in the war. The United States formally entered World War II on December 7, 1941 after Japan launched a surprise attack on Pearl Harbor.

Even prior to America's formal entry into the war, the U.S. government had already begun to "regulate" the economy, and had set up a group of "supervisory" agencies to accomplish that purpose. The Office of Production Management became the leading policy-making body for wartime military production. It was headed by the former President of General Motors, William S. Knudson. Many other specific agencies were established to serve underneath the Office of Production Management. However, all these bureaus—irrespective of their responsibility for specific economic sectors or fields—were in the hands of the monopoly capitalists or their trusted colleagues. The agencies that regulated the American economy during the Second World War were far bigger than those established during the First World War. They enjoyed unlimited power, and became effective tools for monopoly capital to make substantial fortunes.

The central problems facing America's wartime economy were a) how to generate the huge revenues required to fight the war and b) how to organize the production of military goods. America's wartime military expenditures totalled

$325 billion, or more than 80 percent of the national budget. However, only about 28 percent of this colossal military outlay was really used against the fascist countries. The other 72 percent became the profits of the monopolies, as well as a cash advance for preparing for a new war. The chief methods used by the American ruling class to raise the money needed for the war were to a) increase taxes, b) enlarge the national debt, and c) issue more paper money to induce inflation. Tax revenues, for example, were increased by the following measures. The government lowered the tax threshold, thereby expanding the number of people liable for taxes; it raised tax rates; and it imposed an excess profits tax. Total tax revenues collected between 1939 and 1945 came to $136.9 billion, of which 65.5 percent came from personal income taxes, indirect taxes, and other taxes paid by the workers. The excess profits tax levied on the bourgeoisie, however, generated only $28.4 billion in revenues. During the war, the government boosted sales of its bonds by almost sixfold, and by the end of 1945 had issued $278.1 billion of these notes. Banks and other corporations were the major purchasers of these government bonds. They bought approximately $200 billion of these securities, and earned between $3 and $5 billion annually in interest in the postwar period. Between 1939 and 1945, the amount of money in circulation increased from $6.5 billion to $26.7 billion. This occurred because the government issued more paper money. Currency inflation triggered a rise in prices. In the final analysis, all of these methods used to raise money to pay for the war shifted the burden of the Second World War onto the backs of the working people.

America's wartime military procurement took place on a colossal scale. By the end of 1945, the total value of military contracts as well as military goods and services paid for by the government came to $310.5 billion. During the last three years of the war, they constituted between 36 percent and 42 percent of GNP. Profits from military contracts fell mainly into the hands of the big monopoly capitalists. According to statistics, military purchases in the period from June 1940 to September 1944 amounted to $175 billion. Of this, 51 percent (or $89.5 billion) fell into the hands of the thirty-three largest corporations. The next largest 148 corporations received 24 percent (or $40.8 billion) of those contracts. The vast number of small companies earned peanuts.

During the war, the government funded the construction of more than two thousand factories in order to rapidly expand the production of military goods. A large majority, or two-thirds, of these government enterprises were "leased" free of charge to the monopolies to operate. Such an arrangement enabled the monopolies not only to avoid the risks involved in setting up factories that produced military goods, but also enabled them to earn a great deal of money by utilizing facilities for which they had paid nothing. After the war, the government simply sold off a large portion of these enterprises to the monopolies at a fraction of their original investment value.

The allocation of raw materials and labor power was also a major component of the federal government's "regulation" of the economy. Industries producing for the war effort were singled out for stringent surveillance.

Many factors promoted enormous growth in the American economy, and especially in that segment of its heavy industry that was tied to military production. Military contracts yielded fat profits. The Lend-Lease Act created a stable market for supplying other countries with military goods. And an American homeland far from the battlefields sustained no damage from the war. The index of industrial production (taking the years 1937 to 1939 as a base of one hundred) reached 227 by 1943, 223 in 1944, and 191 in 1945. The military-industrial complex enjoyed exceptional advantages, and, as a result, developed quite rapidly. In 1943, 66 percent of total industrial production was devoted to weaponry and munitions. American industry as a whole became a munitions factory which primarily manufactured lethal weapons.

American industrial production and capital concentration both grew during the war. For example, more than 500 thousand small-scale industrial enterprises and more than five hundred small commercial banks were forced to stop their operations as a result of decisions made by the wartime regulatory agencies. A wave of company mergers and takeovers swept over industry during the war. For example, large corporations with more than a thousand workers made up 0.4 percent of the total number of industrial enterprises and employed 39.7 percent of the industrial work force in 1939. By 1944, however, these large corporations constituted 1 percent of the total number of industrial enterprises and employed 52.8 percent of factory workers. The giant corporations among them—employing more than ten thousand workers—increased their share from 13.1 percent to 30.4 percent of the total number of industrial workers. People were also rather stunned by the speed in which capital was being concentrated. For example, the assets owned by large corporations, in other words, those valued at more than $50 million, constituted half of the total assets held by the entire processing industry in 1945. In 1937, large industrial and nonindustrial corporations, defined as those with assets of more than $1 billion, numbered thirty and their total assets came to $52.4 billion. By 1945, however, those numbers had increased to forty-five and their total assets reached $107.1 billion. American monpoly capital made stupendous profits during the war. Compared to the six years before the war, pretax corporate profits between 1940 and 1945 increased 4.4-fold and reached $116.8 billion. The profits made by those large corporations that had landed the fattest military contracts went up even faster. For example, the profits enjoyed in 1942 by each of the five largest corporations increased more than 100-fold when compared to the prewar period, and the profits of the next largest thirty-four corporations increased more than tenfold. The power of these financial cliques—such as the Rockefeller, Mellon, DuPont, and Cleveland groups—who enjoyed close ties to military industries, saw their fortunes skyrocket. However, the Kohn-Loeb and Boston financial groups—with their major spheres of power located in railroads and light industry—suffered a corresponding decline. The newly emerging First National City Bank and California financial groups rose to replace them.

During the war, industrial unemployment fell temporarily because of a dramatic expansion in the scale of production and a rapid rise in army recruitment. However, average annual unemployment between 1943 and 1945 still claimed a million people. The increase in industrial employment took place mainly in military production. For example, there were 2.8 million workers in military industries in 1939, a number which grew to 10.4 million by 1943. In the name of national defense, factory owners also forced workers to really exert themselves. Workers who took factory jobs in reality were forced into the equivalent of a military "boot camp." At the same time, commodity prices rose continually and supplies of consumer goods became extremely tight in wartime America. This occurred because of the lopsided expansion of military production and the massive export of materials. Government legislation regulating commodity prices also had no impact. Rationing of sugar, meat, oil, canned meat and milk, coal, shoes, coffee, and other goods began in 1942 and 1943. As the supply of daily necessities became short, a black market sprang up and flourished. Low-income, working class families could not afford the high prices charged on the black market. Lacking daily necessities, they suffered bitterly. The real income of industrial workers during the war was only about 90 percent of that in 1939. Almost two-thirds of working class families fell below the poverty line.

During the war, the global market for American agricultural products expanded suddenly. As a result, agriculture developed rapidly and broke free from the grip of the chronic depression in which it had been stuck for so long. The general index of agricultural production in 1945 was 20 percent higher than that in 1939. Net agricultural income increased about 2.5-fold and reached $15.6 billion. Farm mechanization and chemical fertilizer utilization expanded greatly because the war took so many millions of men away from the farms and left an acute shortage of agricultural labor power. For example, between 1940 and 1945, the number of tractors grew from 1,545,000 to 2,422,000; combines went from 230 thousand to 540 thousand; heavy-duty trucks increased from 1,047,000 to 1,490,000; and farms that used milking machines rose from 175 thousand to 365 thousand. The increase in the number of various farm machines in those five years was just about equivalent to the increases experienced in the prior ten-plus years, and even the prior thirty years. By 1945, 63 percent of all grain was being harvested by combines. Other farming operations also mainly used machinery. By this time, the United States had basically achieved the mechanization of its agriculture. Machinery had come to replace animal power on a widespread basis.

America's economic status in the capitalist world rose as the other capitalist powers impoverished their people and exhausted their resources in prosecuting the war. In 1945, the United States had claimed by itself 60 percent of the total industrial production of the capitalist world, almost one-third (or 32.5 percent) of the total amount of foreign trade, and three-fourths of total gold reserves. The

United States used the Lend-Lease Act to successfully enter the world market, especially those markets of the member nations of the British commonwealth. Wartime commodity exports, calculated by volume, almost tripled. The United States squeezed $13.5 billion from the people of various countries in export-import trade. American capital exports during the war also increased and reached $16.8 billion by 1945. The total amount of Britain's capital exports fell below that of the United States because England had either sold off, or lost, vast quantities of its foreign investment during the war. One of the consequences of the Second World War was that the United States not only took first place in industrial production and foreign trade in the capitalist world, but it also became the largest exporter of capital. As the biggest international exploiter, the United States not only exploited the colonial and semi-colonial countries of Asia, Africa, and Latin America, but even carried out a "jungle law" policy against its allies in Western Europe, North America, and the Pacific, making every effort to put them under its heel. Intoxicated by this wartime economic prosperity, the American bourgeoisie arrogantly announced that the twentieth century was "the American century." They were insufferably arrogant and bossy. The great leader Chairman Mao wisely pointed out in 1947 that "America's wartime prosperity is merely a temporary phenomenon. Its strength is superficial and transitory. The various irreconcilable domestic and foreign contradictions are like a volcano that daily threatens American imperialism. American imperialism is sitting on this volcano."[47] History has completely confirmed Chairman Mao's wise prediction. Five economic crises have already erupted in the United States in the more than twenty years since World War II. Dependent on war for its prosperity, the American economy is steadily declining—like a river flowing downstream. At the same time, American imperialism's foreign economic expansionism and political and military aggression have met with fierce resistance from the peoples of Asia, Africa, and Latin America. The struggles of the people of the world against American imperialism have grown day by day. They have dealt it serious blows, thereby hastening its decline.

4

France

France is one of the major countries of the contemporary capitalist world. It ranks first among the nations of Western Europe in terms of territory. Its GNP places it fourth, following behind the economies of the United States, Japan, and West Germany. French capitalism developed relatively early. Like England, it belongs among those widely known capitalist countries which enjoy a "brand name" reputation. Nevertheless, France also developed its own unique characteristics in its transition to capitalism and entry into its stage of imperialism.

1. The Decline of the French Feudal System during the Sixteenth through the Eighteenth Centuries, and the Initial Development of Capitalist Relations of Production

The Feudal Land System and Its Cruel Exploitation of the Peasantry

Throughout the Middle Ages, France remained one of the most entrenched feudal autocracies in Europe. Feudal relationships retained a dominant position in French society even up to the sixteenth through the eighteenth centuries. This was true even though France's autocratic system had begun to decline by this period, a commodity economy had greatly developed, and capitalist relations of production were just gradually beginning to emerge.

The economic base of French feudal society was the feudal land system. Prior to the bourgeois revolution of 1789, all the land in France was owned either by high-ranking or low-ranking feudal aristocrats. The aristocracy by itself held 60 percent of the land, and the monarchy and church each owned 20 percent. The landlords, however, never directly managed their estates—a phenomenon that was a unique characteristic of the French feudal land system. On the contrary, they divided their land into many small parcels, rented it to peasants to do the actual farming, and then cruelly exploited and oppressed them by imposing a land rent or *taille*.[1]

The feudal land system forced the peasantry to pay heavy rents to the feudal lords. Normally the rent was fixed at between one-third to one-half of the harvest. Rental payments in the form of corvee labor, payment in kind, or payment in money were used simultaneously and were relatively common in French villages at that time. Even though money rents had already gradually become the chief form of payment as a result of the steady development of a commodity economy, corvee labor and payment in kind did not altogether disappear. In addition to rent, the peasantry also bore other kinds of feudal obligations to the landlords. These feudal obligations can be roughly divided into three categories. The first comprised taxes, such as inheritance taxes, sales taxes, and judicial taxes. It also included corvee labor, such as building canals, roads, and houses for the landlords. The second category comprised special levies which peasants were forced to pay because the landlords monopolized essential tools of production and means of communication. Special levies on milling grain, making wine, baking bread, going through the city gates, and travelling on certain roads are examples of this second category. The third category comprised personal services that landlords forced peasants to provide in order to maintain their extravagant life style. For example, on summer evenings and nights, peasants often had to keep watch along the banks of ponds and lakes. They were required to splash the water to prevent frogs from croaking and thereby interrupting the sleep of the landlords. On New Year's Day or other festivals, peasants attended to the personal needs of landlords and also gave them presents. In addition, landlords enjoyed special rights on their manors, such as the right to go hunting, the right to go falconing, and the right to raise rabbits. Although the crops of the peasants were often trampled and damaged during the hunt, nothing could be done to stop these activities.

Chairman Mao pointed out that, in feudal society, "not only did the landlords, aristocrats, and royalty live by the rents exploited from the peasantry, but the governmental apparatus of the landlord class also forced the peasantry to pay taxes, provide corvee labor, and even support a vast cohort of bureaucrats and an army used mainly to suppress them."[2] In France, the peasantry was forced to pay a multitude of exorbitant taxes and levies to the feudal autocratic state. In general, these taxes fell into two categories. One category was direct taxes, such as the land tax, property tax, head tax, and military service tax. The other category comprised indirect taxes, such as a salt tax, liquor tax, and tobacco tax. These taxes increased year after year during the eighteenth century, and at times actually took half of a peasant's income. In addition, the church—an important instrument of social control that served the feudal monarchy—also extorted from the peasantry a tenth of its harvest. This was called the tithe.

Squeezed by heavy rents and taxes, the French peasantry confronted extraordinarily difficult conditions. When faced with a financial crisis, they frequently had to put up their land as collateral when borrowing money from loan sharks. Borrowing in this way would force them into a debt trap. If they were unable to clear their debt, their land would be seized. As a result, their only recourse was to approach the money-lender again and rent from him the land that previously had been their own. However, the peasant now suffered from the dual exploitation of both the landlord as well as the money-lender.

Such cruel forms of feudal exploitation not only impoverished the French peasantry, but also created chronic agricultural stagnation. Farm animals and agricultural tools were extremely scarce in the villages. The majority of peasants could rely only on their own labor power and on crude homemade tools to farm their land. The "three fields system," which required vast areas of land to lie fallow, was still widely practiced even up to the eve of the Great Revolution of 1789. Crop yields were quite low. In general, yields were only four to seven times greater than the quantity of seeds used in sowing.

As feudal exploitation intensified, class polarization in the villages also increased. In France, the expropriation of the peasantry was chiefly accomplished by forcing them to leave their land. This trend became especially evident during the latter half of the seventeenth century when the feudal aristocracy used the principle of the "tripartite system" to wantonly seize the common lands.[3] This action, of course, created many destitute farmers. Some of these poor peasants went to the cities to look for work. Others remained in the villages and became hired hands. The largest segment became beggars. Surprisingly enough, there were several tens of thousands of people in France in the 1760s who relied on begging to stay alive. For example, Paris, called the "city of prosperity," had a population of 600 thousand. Of these, approximately 20 percent were beggars. Contemporary documents record the following: "Paris simply is overrun with beggars. No matter where you stop, many beggars will suddenly appear from all directions and surround you. . . . They are all peasants, and can only run away to the city and beg because they have been forced to leave their villages" [source unknown].

Harsh feudal exploitation evoked strong opposition from the broad masses of peasants. During the sixteenth through the eighteenth centuries, the French peasantry staged many uprisings. Moreover, the scale of these rebellions became increasingly larger. By the eve of the bourgeois revolution of 1789, the struggle against feudalism in the various villages throughout the country had already assumed the proportions of a prairie fire. These struggles profoundly shook the foundations of the feudal system, and they propelled the entire society forward.

At the same time, capitalist relations of production also began to gradually emerge within the villages as a result of the development of a commodity economy. As handicraft factories with capitalistic features appeared here and there, contractors or brokers would also persuade peasants—eager to supplement their incomes—to undertake the production of handicraft goods in their own homes. The sight of wealthier farmers employing agricultural laborers also became more and more common. However, there were very few capitalist farms in France even up to the middle of the eighteenth century. The small farmer operating within a feudal system still remained quite prevalent.

Overseas Expansion and the Initial Development of a Capitalist Industry and Commerce under Aristocratic Rule

Although the village economy in the sixteenth through eighteenth centuries was comparatively backward, an urban-centered capitalist industry and commerce had developed very quickly and had attained a very high level. This was due to support from the state policy of mercantilism, to the stimulus of a foreign market, and to the demands of the feudal ruling class for an extravagant life-style.

France had already established a centralized, autocratic regime as early as the fifteenth century. Although this regime was a dictatorship of the feudal aristocracy, it did adopt a series of measures that promoted the development of industry and commerce. The government did this in order to increase the income of the monarchy and satisfy the material needs demanded by the ruling class. An expanded foreign market and a shift in oceanic trade routes that came with the Age of Discovery were also extremely advantageous to the development of capitalist industry and commerce in France. As a result, a factory-based handicraft industry and foreign trade had already attained rather high levels in France in the sixteenth century. At this time, the sprouts of a capitalist industry—the handicraft factory system—had already appeared in the silk, linen, woolen, carpet, lace, glassware, and metallurgy trades. Many of the products of these sectors became commodities intended for export. When these were added to the overseas sales of some agricultural products, they made France's foreign trade quite advanced, and placed it in a rather important niche in the national economy. Some of the great commercial cities of France, such as Marseilles and Lyons, had already gained a reputation throughout Europe at a very early date.

French capitalism made further progress at the beginning of the seventeenth century. At that time, the absolute monarchy energetically promoted a policy of mercantilism. It did so to strengthen its economic capability for foreign expansionism and to improve the state's financial situation. The policy of mercantilism was a product of the development of a commodity economy that emerged during the sixteenth to the eighteenth centuries. Its basic idea was to regard the size of the nation's gold and silver holdings as a measure of the country's wealth. As a result, mercantilists made every effort to increase a nation's favorable balance of trade, and to bring gold and silver into one's own country. French implementation of a mercantilist policy began with the reign of Henry IV (1594–1610). The government adopted many vigorous measures to encourage and foster the development of industry and commerce. Louis XIII (1610–60) continued to promote this policy until it reached its zenith during the reign of Louis XIV (1661–1715). At that time, the famous mercantilist Jean Baptiste Colbert served as France's Minister of Finance. He used the financial power of the state to create more than a hundred "royal handicraft factories" that enjoyed special rights. He also adopted further measures advantageous to the development of industry and commerce. He reduced the rate of taxation, eliminated some domestic tariffs, provided loans and subsidies to factory owners, reduced or annulled the tax burdens or military obligations for factory owners and artisans, raised funds to pay for the construction of roads and canals, and instituted protective tariffs.

France's handicraft industry made enormous progress as a result of the stimulus provided by the policy of mercantilism. Despite these advances, the dispersed form of the handicraft workshop remained the most important type of handicraft industry at the end of the seventeenth century. In general, handicraft producers performed their tasks in workshops that were geographically dispersed. For example, the Abberile Woolen Factory (located in the Department du Nord, a French administrative region which comprised the provinces of Hainault, Flanders, and Cambresis) was a typical example of this decentralized type of handicraft workshop. The scale of production in this factory was quite large. More than six thousand urban and rural handicraft laborers worked for this operation, yet some were located as much as eighty miles away from the factory itself. At this time, the number of centralized handicraft factories was very small, perhaps close to two hundred in total. Their scale of operation was also not very extensive. In general, they only employed ten or several tens of workers. The biggest centralized handicraft factories employed several hundred workers. These were the "royal handicraft factories" that enjoyed special privileges.

After 1700, the French workshop handicraft industry not only grew dramatically in terms of numbers, but also reached a sophisticated technological level. By the eve of the Great Revolution of 1789, for example, there were already 514 centralized handicraft factories, despite the fact that the decentralized form of the handicraft workshop was still predominant. Their scale of production had also greatly expanded. For example, the Loeb Heavy Woolen factory in Abberile employed 1,700 workers. The Anzin Coal Company even had upwards of four thousand workers. The rapid development of the workshop handicraft industry stimulated innovations in production technology. Some huge factories already began to use machinery and steam power. The technological level of French industry at that time was second to none among the countries of Western Europe. The technical virtuosity of French artisans—who enjoyed a respected reputation—was even well known abroad. Many products of the French handicraft industry—especially jewelry made from ivory as well as porcelain, carpets, lace, cosmetics, and elegant household goods—always sold well in either domestic or international markets. Europe's royalty, aristocracy, and middle classes all vied with each other to obtain such items.

Guided by the policy of mercantilism, France's absolute monarchy consistently emphasized the further development of its foreign trade after the seventeenth century. Moreover, it energetically advocated the acquisition of colonies and proceeded to step up its overseas expansionism. As a result, the French government actively implemented a policy of protective tariffs to prevent foreign goods from making inroads into the domestic market. On the other hand, it made enormous efforts to open up foreign markets and to encourage the export of its own commodities. The state spent huge sums to build a vast merchant marine and naval fleet. It also chartered many trading companies and conferred upon them special monopoly rights. The total amount of France's foreign trade increased fivefold in the years from 1716 to 1789. By the eve of the Great Revolution, total annual foreign trade had already reached approximately 1.1 billion *louis*.[4] This was second only to that of England, and put France in second place in international trade. At this time France's trading partners included Europe, the Americas, India, and West Asia. One-fourth of France's trade took place with its colonies. France mainly exported luxury goods and agricultural products. The main imports were raw materials (cotton, leather, timber) and special products from the colonies (spices, indigo, coffee, and cocoa). At the same time that French merchants were involved in commodity trade, they were also frequently engaged in the slave trade and piracy. They were not only businessmen, but also slave traders and pirates. And they used various methods to amass huge fortunes. They accumulated a vast amount of money capital that promoted the development of French capitalism.

Another important way in which mercantilism increased the wealth of the nation was by plundering the wealth of its colonies. Many French monarchs were extremely vicious colonial despots. Not only did Louis XIII set up a chain of colonial strongholds in Central America, South America, the Antilles, and the West Indies, but also directly participated after 1635 in the Thirty Years' War that ravaged Europe. He seized Alsace-Lorraine and expanded France's territory to the west bank of the Rhine River. The era of Louis XIV saw an even more frenzied period of foreign expansionism. In the years from 1667 to 1697, France took part in three wars, and occupied Canada, Louisiana, the rich islands of the West Indies, Madagascar, and portions of India. French colonialism reached its peak at the end of the seventeenth century. It was only after the eighteenth century that France's expansionist activities suffered setbacks and its colonial power became seriously attenuated. This was due to the sudden rise of England as a colonial power, the numerous defeats suffered by France in her fierce struggles with England over colonial hegemony, and France's expulsion from many important colonial bases in Canada and India by the British.

The conditions described above indicate that a capitalist economy in France had already grown to a certain extent by the sixteenth to the eighteenth centuries. Although the bourgeoisie did not yet exercise political power, its economic clout was already rather significant. At the same time, the number of industrial workers in France was also gradually increasing. On the eve of the

Great Revolution, the number of workers involved in handicraft production throughout the country had already reached nine million. They were the predecessors of the modern industrial proletariat. Politically, they had no power. Economically, they were extremely poor. In particular, the workers in the centralized handicraft factories faced the worst conditions. The work stretched from sixteen to eighteen hours per day. Their daily wage was only twenty to twenty-five *sou*, yet it cost four to five *sou* to buy a pound of bread.[5] The class consciousness of the industrial workers was gradually raised under the impact of this cruel exploitation and oppression, and they would often launch spontaneous rebellions.

The Bourgeois Revolution of 1789–94 and the Disintegration of the Feudal System

The development of a capitalist industry and commerce in France during the sixteenth to eighteenth centuries was partially due to the assistance it received from the monarchy. However, the purpose of the absolute monarchy in implementing a mercantilist policy and fostering industry and commerce was certainly not to promote the development of capitalism. On the contrary, it sought to open new financial resources for the ruling class to enjoy and to squander. Because the feudal system represented backward and reactionary relations of production, in the final analysis it served as a hindrance to social progress and a hindrance to the development of a capitalist economy. This can be seen in the following points:

1. The deep-rooted feudal land system tightly bound the peasantry to the land of the aristocracy. Ruthless feudal exploitation caused chronic stagnation and backwardness in agricultural production. The life of the peasantry was one of dire poverty. Because of this, two problems—the creation of a pool of free laborers, as well as a commodity market required for the development of capitalist production—could not be solved for a long time.

2. Under the rule of feudalism, the guild system imposed stringent regulations on the amount and quality of products and the number of workers. In addition, the autocratic government also rigorously controlled the activities of enterprises. Both sets of controls greatly shackled the development of production. In addition, the various regions within France had different weights and measures, different currencies, and different tariff systems. Customs houses were as numerous as trees in a forest. Travel was extremely inconvenient. Goods in transit were required to pay taxes each time they crossed a boundary line, forded a river, or passed through a village or small town. Naturally this limited the circulation of commodities. According to records, the price of Orleans liquor sold in Normandy went up twentyfold. Goods from China imported into France, however, only trebled or quadrupled in price. One can see from this example the

enormous difficulties faced by commercial transactions within France.

3. The rigid stratification of the feudal system and the special powers enjoyed by the ruling class were also a serious obstacle to the development of industry and commerce. All French citizens were divided into three Estates. The clergy comprised the First Estate, the aristocracy the Second. These two Estates were the ruling class, and the absolute monarch was its general representative. Even though the clergy and aristocracy constituted only 1 percent of France's population of twenty-six million, they nevertheless monopolized all the land, enjoyed exemption from taxes, held all the important posts, and enjoyed various kinds of special rights. They led a decadent, parasitic life of shameless debauchery. The broad masses of peasants, handicraft workers, and bourgeoisie comprised the Third Estate. They were the ruled class. Although the newly emerging bourgeoisie was powerful economically, it had no power politically. The sacred principle of France's feudal system could be summarized in this expression: "The clergy serve the monarchy with their robes, the aristocracy serve the monarchy with their swords, and the Third Estate serves the monarchy with its wealth" [source unknown]. This concretely reflected the different class status of the various Estates.

4. Feudal absolutism also severely impeded the development of a capitalist economy. In order to maintain these feudal rights, France's absolute monarchy established a huge military force and a bureaucracy replete with every possible ministry. These military personnel and government officials were supported by exorbitant taxes levied on the Third Estate. The aristocracy at the imperial court indulged in a life of even greater debauchery and dissipation, and spent money without restraint. Every year they would waste enormous sums of the state treasury to satisfy their search for pleasure. Added to this was their continuous initiation of wars of aggression. As a result, the citizens were left destitute, and the country faced difficulties. The financial condition of the state grew worse day by day, the tax burdens shouldered by the Third Estate became ever more onerous, and the working people sank deeper and deeper into misery.

The aforementioned conditions make clear that the feudal system in France had already become an obstacle impeding social progress and shackling the development of the forces of production. The crisis of the feudal system had already become increasingly evident as the class contradictions within France gradually intensified. By the end of the eighteenth century, conditions had become ripe for a bourgeois revolution. Finally, the French Revolution, an event of great historical significance, broke out in 1789.

The French Revolution was a violent struggle against feudalism. This revolution was a bourgeois democratic revolution led by the bourgeoisie and actively participated in by the broad masses of people. Only by relying on the great power of the peasantry and handicraft workers could the bourgeoisie triumph over the feudal system and achieve victory in the revolution. The revolution as a whole traversed a tortuous process which generally can be divided into the following three phases: The first phase lasted from July 1789 to February 1792. During this period, those who advocated a constitutional monarchy ruled France. The second phase lasted from August 1792 to May 1793 when the Girondist party exercised leadership. The third phase was the period of the Jacobin dictatorship. This lasted from June 1793 to July 1974.

In reality, the first two phases were a period of the dictatorship of the bourgeoisie. Those in power were finance capitalists and liberal aristocrats. They had countless ties to the forces of feudalism, and basically did not desire to carry out thoroughgoing changes. Only under the powerful pressure of revolutionary circumstances did they carry out a series of anti-feudal measures. For example, even though the famous decree of August 4, 1789 proclaimed "the elimination of all feudal rights," in reality it did not truly release the peasantry from its feudal chains. Only some secondary feudal rights, such as the special rights of the feudal lords to hunt, and raise rabbits, were freely surrendered. The most important rights—such as the right to rental payments or levies on goods—could be rescinded only if the peasant followed a stipulated procedure that offered compensation to the aristocrat. Although the tithe was nominally abolished, each citizen was still required "to use other means to provide for the expenses of the church and the livelihood of its priests" [source unknown].

The anti-feudal measures actively promoted by the big bourgeoisie were merely directly advantageous to the development of that self-same big bourgeoisie. Not long after the revolution, they eliminated tariff barriers within the country, abolished the guild system, established a unified system of weights, measures, and currency throughout France, and proclaimed the unlimited freedom of industrial and commercial activities. In addition, they also passed the Declaration of the Rights of Man which established sacred and inviolable rights in private property. Moreover, they set down in legal form the bourgeois concepts of "liberty, equality, and fraternity."

The big bourgeoisie was especially hostile to the workers' movement. In order to suppress the resistance of the workers, they passed the outrageously reactionary Le Chapelier Law.[6] In this manner, "the French bourgeoisie, at the very beginning of the revolutionary upheaval, had the audacity to snatch away the right of association just secured by the working class."[7]

The land question faced by the French peasantry was not solved either during the period of the dictatorship of the big bourgeoisie. This was because the big bourgeoisie did not truly consider the basic interests of the peasantry. Although they abolished the feudal system of land ownership and destroyed the feudal lords' monopoly rights over land, the purpose of France's wealthy bourgeoisie was merely to make land into a commodity, an object of free investment, and a convenient commodity for the development of capitalism. What they feared even more was that the system of private ownership would be restricted. They did not want to use revolutionary methods that would enable the peasantry to obtain land without paying for it. As a result, when they sold the lands owned by the aristocracy and the estates held by the church, the wealthy bourgeoisie set extremely stringent conditions. For example, the price of the land was set very high, the period of payment was to be quite short, and the land parcels had to be very substantial in size. Obviously the broad masses of poor peasants lacked the strength to carry such a burden. As a result, large areas of land fell into the hands of the bourgeoisie and rich peasantry.

The radical faction of the bourgeoisie, basing itself on an alliance formed between the peasantry and the urban poor, held political power during the third phase of the revolution—the period of the Jacobin dictatorship. Lenin pointed out that "the Jacobin party of 1793 was the representative of the eighteenth century's most revolutionary classes, i.e. the urban and rural poor."[8] During the period when they exercised political power, the Jacobins adopted a series of revolutionary measures that not only were anti-feudal, but that also gained the support and assistance of the masses of people.

The Jacobins, in a comparatively thorough way, solved the land question of the peasantry. According to the regulations stipulated by three laws regarding landed property, the common lands that had originally been taken by the aristocracy were to be distributed to the peasantry on a per capita basis. In areas where there was no common land to distribute, each household was given one *arpent* of land.[9] Land confiscated from either the royal family, the Church, or from aristocrats who had fled abroad was divided into small parcels and sold to the peasantry. Payments for this land were spread out over twenty years, and no interest was charged. The various other feudal rights were also abrogated entirely without compensation. As a result, a broad stratum of small farmers emerged in France.

The Jacobins also adopted numerous economic policies advantageous to the urban poor. For example, they advocated a comprehensive program of social security. They declared that those engaged in hoarding, cornering, speculation, and profiteering would be treated as criminals; they set maximum price limits for grain and various kinds of daily necessities; and they prohibited black marketeering. They even went so far as to pass a resolution permitting the baking of only one kind of bread (the "bread of equality") in order to change the gap in living standards between the rich and poor.

The measures that the Jacobin dictatorship carried out reflected its character of revolutionary democracy. However, because the Jacobins did, after all, represent the interests of the bourgeoisie, it was therefore inevitable that they carried the limitations of the bourgeoisie. For example, the Jacobins emphasized in particular "the sacred and inviolable right of private property" in the constitution that they enacted during their dictatorship. Regarding the land question, not only did the Jacobins not confiscate all the land of the feudal lords, but they did not distribute that land to the peasants without first requiring them to compensate its previous owners. On the important question of how to handle the workers, the Jacobins actually passed a law that only fixed maximum wages, but did not set a minimum floor. And the Jacobins continued to implement the reactionary Le Chapelier Law.

To summarize, the great French Revolution was an even more thoroughgoing and more profound bourgeois revolution than the English revolution of the seventeenth century and the American War of Independence of the eighteenth century. It used revolutionary methods to overthrow entrenched feudal rule. It used democratic forms to solve the land question of the peasantry. It thereby created advantageous conditions for the development of French capitalism. Moreover, it also gave impetus to the anti-feudal struggles in other European countries, and promoted the national liberation movement in Latin America. Therefore, the French Revolution has been of extremely great significance in world history. As Lenin has pointed out: "This great revolution gave to its own class, to that bourgeois class which it served, many things. Throughout the entire 19th century, it provided a civilized and cultured period for all humanity. All this transpired under the imprint of the French Revolution."[10] Chairman Mao also pointed out (when he analyzed the specific characteristics of the Chinese revolution) that "the bourgeois revolutions in Europe and America, but especially in France, were comparatively thoroughgoing, particularly during their revolutionary phases."[11]

2. The Rapid Development of the Economy after the Bourgeois Revolution and the Establishment of the Capitalist System

The Persistence of a Small-Peasant Economy and Its Influence on the Development of a Capitalist Economy

The bourgeois revolution in France shattered the feudal land system and brought about profound changes in the economic relations within the village. The establishment of a widespread and pervasive system of small landholdings then emerged after many peasants obtained land. The persistence of this small-peasant economy has subsequently been an important characteristic of the French national economy.

However, under the conditions of capitalism, the small peasantry could not free themselves from a miserable fate. Marx pointed out: "The landed property of the aristocracy had already been replaced by the capital of the bourgeoisie . . . during the 19th century. The small parcels of land owned by the peasantry now only enable the capitalists to extract profits, interest, and rent. They are a pretext that permits the tillers of the soil to earn their own wages as they themselves please."[12] After the revolution, the shackles of capitalism replaced the shackles of feudalism. Not only did the French peasantry suffer cruel exploitation at the hands of industrial and merchant capitalists, but they also had to pay exorbitant taxes to the bourgeois state. Even when poverty stricken and at the end of their rope, they had to endure exorbitantly high rates on the loans that they had borrowed from loan sharks. Marx cited a vast quantity of documentary evidence when he offered the following trenchant comment about the oppressed conditions faced by the French peasantry in this period. "In 1840, for example, the total value of agricultural production came to 5.237 billion francs. After deducting the costs of farming and that portion consumed by the peasantry, the net agricultural income came to 1.665 billion francs. Interest payments on real estate mortgages took 550 million francs, taxes totalled 350 million francs. Notary fees, stamp taxes, and mortgage taxes amounted to 107 million francs. Legal costs were 100 million francs. What was finally left over amounted to only 558 million francs, or an average per capita income that didn't even come to twenty-five francs" [source unknown]. One can see from this how destitute the French peasant really was.

The poverty-stricken French peasant could not avoid the road to bankruptcy. Engels emphatically pointed out that "their plight was absolutely hopeless when capitalism ruled, and their efforts to protect their system of small landownership were absolutely fruitless."[13] Prior to the middle of the nineteenth century, tens of thousands of small peasant households fell into the ranks of the propertyless virtually every year. Even more were on the brink of bankruptcy, stuck in a precarious situation.

However, despite the extremely dire poverty of the peasantry, not only was the small peasant economy in France not destroyed, but continued to exist on a widespread basis for a long time. An important reason for this situation was that abnormally high interest rates on loans were prevalent in French villages. This delayed the process of separating the small peasant farmer from his land. For example, a poor peasant might borrow money from a loan shark and put up the land as collateral. The farmer did this initially in order to preserve and protect his ownership of his small plot of land. However, once the peasant had fallen into the trap set by the money-lending capitalist, he was invariably pressured to "not only hand over rent and the profit from his occupation, but also *all his net profit* to the capitalist, even to the point of turning over *a portion of his own wages* to the capitalist."[14] Therefore, the venal loan sharks preferred to have peasants (those who had already gone bankrupt and could not repay their debts) still remain on the land so that they could continue to suck their blood. This was what enabled the system of small landholding in France to be preserved for a long period of time. In addition, owing to a steady increase in population, agricultural land was also gradually divided up into even smaller parcels. As a result, many new, small peasant households came into existence. Therefore, a small peasant economy in France not only maintained an absolute dominance over agriculture right up to the latter half of the nineteenth century, but even grew. In 1862, for example, there were 2.44 million small peasant households that owned between one and ten hectares of land in France. By 1882, this had increased to 2.60 million. In addition, there were still 2.20 million of the smallest peasant households who did not even own one hectare.

The long-term and widespread existence of a small peasant economy severely hampered the development of a capitalist economy in France. First of all, it firmly tied the broad peasantry to their small parcels of land and restricted the formation of a pool of free labor. In particular, French peasants could not raise many children because of the extreme poverty of village life. The rate of increase of the French population was much slower than that of any other European nation, and thereby created a widespread shortage of labor power in industry and agriculture. Next, the impoverished small farmer lacked the power to purchase many commodities. These people were basically self-supporting, and directly produced a great portion of the goods for their own consumption. Therefore, the French domestic market was extremely limited, and the development of a commodity economy and a capitalist industry was greatly affected. Finally, the small peasant economy was quite feeble. Peasants lacked the necessary farm animals and farm tools. If it was difficult for them to purchase costly agricultural tools and implements, how much more difficult was it for them to undertake large-scale soil improvements or water conservancy works? It was just as Marx had pointed out: ". . . the small land parcels did not permit any division of labor during the tilling season, nor the application of any science, and as a result there was no development of any kind whatsoever."[15] This kind of situation not only created a stagnant and backward agriculture, but also eliminated the necessary preconditions for industrial development.

An important trend after the Revolution of 1789 was the growth of capitalist relations of production in agriculture—a trend which also co-existed with the widespread existence of a small peasant economy. As the village economy became polarized and fragmented, a small number of the well-to-do peasants now began to buy up land from those farmers who had gone bankrupt. These wealthier peasants now set up capitalist farms. On the other hand, the bourgeoisie, who had seized large tracts of land during the revolution, and that segment of the aristocracy which had retained its manors, also gradually turned to capitalist management. By 1862, there were already 150 thousand capitalist farms throughout France. They occupied 40 percent of the arable land and employed more than 900 thousand agricultural workers.

Capitalist farms could utilize machinery and chemical fertilizer, and by adopting new farming techniques and methods, enormously raised the level of productive forces in agriculture. Moreover, the revolution had made a shambles of feudal relations, and this was invariably advantageous to the development of production. Therefore agricultural output saw a dramatic increase after the revolution. The total value of agricultural output in France went from three billion francs in 1812 to 7.5 billion francs in 1870, in other words, an increase of two-and-a-half times. If one takes into consideration the fact that the price of agricultural goods declined in this period, then the real increase in output was even greater. This was unprecedented in French history. Of course, the rate of increase in agricultural production was still much slower than that of industry. In 1812, the total output value of French agriculture was 50 percent higher than that of industry. However, by the end of the 1860s, it was only 62.5 percent of the total output value of industry.

The Rapid Development of Industrial Production and France's Basic Completion of Its Industrial Revolution

The bourgeois revolution in France swept away feudal obstacles and, in the period after the revolution and prior to the 1870s, brought about an enormous growth in capitalist industrial production. Two specific consequences of this were the basic completion of France's industrial revolution and the final establishment of a capitalist system.

This period of French industrial development can be divided into three stages: The first stage lasted from 1795 to 1815, in other words, after the bourgeois revolution until the end of the Napoleanic dictatorship. In this stage, France laid the initial foundation for its modern industry. The postrevolution Napoleonic regime initially represented the interests of the financial bourgeoisie and the industrial and commercial bourgeoisie. In order to assist the development of domestic industry and commerce, it established a policy of stringent protective tariffs. To productive industries, the regime gave out substantial contracts for goods as well as subsidies and grants-in-aid. In addition, it promoted competitions for awards, established a system of patent rights, and organized international fairs. The Napoleonic regime also created the Bank of France, established the Ministry of Industry and Commerce, and enacted the Napoleonic Code (the purpose of which was to strengthen the bourgeois right of private ownership of property). Napoleon also launched a series of wars of aggression in order to extend French economic power abroad and control the entire European market. Napoleon defeated Holland, Italy, Austria, and the German states in succession and occupied half of Europe. Not only did France plunder a vast amount of wealth from these defeated countries, but it also secured a huge market. At this time, France and England became locked in a fierce struggle to decide who would dominate the world. In 1806, Napoleon announced that he would implement what he called the Continental System, which strictly prohibited the maintenance of any economic relationship between Continental Europe and England. Its purpose was to strangle England economically.

The aforementioned policies greatly stimulated the development of French industry. In the period from 1789 to 1815, pig iron production more than doubled, and woolen knitwear output quadrupled. The utilization of machinery in industry increased dramatically, and there even appeared some large-scale businesses. For example, the Richard-Lenoir Textile Mill employed 12,822 workers in 1810; this factory even owned its own cotton fields. The wealth accumulated in the hands of the bourgeoisie also expanded rapidly at this time. As a result, the conditions for the further development of capitalist industry became more mature, thereby laying the initial groundwork for France's industrial revolution.

However, it must also be recognized that certain policies of the Napoleonic government played a definitely destructive role in the development of the French national economy. This was especially true during the latter years of Napoleon's rule when continuous warfare created difficulties for the nation's finances and brought about shortages of goods as well as price inflation. The wartime draft saw three million men in the prime of life enter the army, of which approximately one million died on the battlefield. As a result, in some villages there were almost no adult males, and the lack of labor power became an extremely serious liability. In addition, Napoleon's Continental System created self-imposed difficulties for France. Many industrial sectors found themselves in a predicament because they were cut off from their traditional sources of raw materials. Foreign trade also dropped precipitously. All these factors influenced the course of the French industrial revolution, and even speeded up the collapse of the Napoleonic regime itself. Generally speaking, even though the development of French industrial production during the period of Napoleon's rule was very rapid, it was in fact quite slow and even backward when compared to England's growth and accomplishments in this field. At the time, the extent of machine utilization in France was still quite limited. France, generally speaking, was still at the handicraft production stage.

The second stage of France's industrial revolution took place between 1815 and 1848, that is, during the Bourbon and Orleans dynasties. At this time the domestic and internationl political situation was comparatively stable, and the wounds suffered during the war had gradually healed. In order to speed up the development of industry, France hired many skilled technicians from abroad and imported a large amount of machinery from England. This significantly raised the technical level of domestic industry. As a result, an industrial revolution now developed on a massive scale throughout France.

The most important sector of French industry was textiles, and it was also the earliest to use machinery on an extensive scale. By the end of the 1840s, there were already 566 cotton textile mills located throughout France, with a combined total of 116,000 spinning machines and 3.5 million spindles. The silk industry could claim ninety thousand machines, and the woolen sector was also beginning to use shearing and spinning machines. Once its textile production had grown dramatically and it had taken over first place in its overall composition of exports, France became England's principal competitor in this field. Production also rapidly increased in the metallurgical and mining industries because of the renovation of existing machinery and the spread of new technology.

Pig iron production went from 110,000 tons in 1818 to four million tons in 1848. Coal production went from 880,000 tons in 1815 to four million tons in 1848. However, France was not self-sufficient in its coal supply, and therefore had to import one-third of its annual consumption. The extremely rapid increase in the utilization of steam engines reflected the large-scale development of an industrial revolution in this period. In 1820, France had only thirty-nine steam engines; by 1848, it had 5,212 steam engines with a combined total of sixty-five thousand horsepower. The French machine-manufacturing industry had initially been established in the 1820s and 1830s, when it began to manufacture machines and steam engines. The rapid development of industrial production also brought forth developments in communications and transportation. In 1831, France began to construct its first railroad line, which was thirty-nine miles long. By 1848, however, the total amount of railroad mileage came to 1,931. However, because French steel production was insufficient to meet domestic demand, costly rails had to be imported from England. The tariff on a single rail, for example, came to 275 francs per ton. Railroad construction therefore could not continue on an even more extensive scale.

The third stage of France's industrial revolution occurred during the period of the Second Empire, in other words, from 1848 to 1870. During this stage, France's industrial revolution was essentially completed because its temporary domestic stability created the conditions that were advantageous to a new upsurge in industry. Marx pointed out that "under its rule (i.e., that of the Second Empire), bourgeois society avoided various kinds of political entanglements and achieved a high level of development that it had never even imagined. Industry and commerce had expanded to their greatest extent; finance capital fraudulently celebrated its joy at criss-crossing the world."[16]

The exceptionally rapid growth of heavy industry was a special characteristic of French industrial development in the 1850s and 1860s. In the space of twenty years, coal and iron production both doubled, reaching 13.46 million tons and 1.38 million tons, respectively. Steel output increased eightfold, although in absolute terms the amount was quite small. Only some 100 thousand tons of steel were produced, almost all of which was used to manufacture swords and weapons. Steel production still could not meet the needs of other sectors of the economy. Railroad construction demonstrated another special characteristic of France's industrial development in this period. By 1870, the construction of the major trunk lines of France's railroad system had already been largely completed. For example, total railroad track now reached 17,924 kilometers. However, what merits our attention is the fact that by 1857, a majority of France's railroads had already become concentrated in the hands of six large companies. Large-scale railroad construction resulted from the industrial revolution, and it served to promote the development of French industry.

The development of light industry also proceeded at a relatively high tempo owing to the further use of new technologies. Machine production had already replaced work done by hand in the textile industry and other important sectors of the economy. The utilization of steam power had also become far more common. The French national economy experienced a period of unprecedented growth throughout the 1850s and 1860s. GNP doubled, and the total output value of industrial production trebled, reaching twelve billion francs. With this achievement, France's own industrial revolution was basically completed, and the capitalist system was finally securely established.

Nevertheless, it must be pointed out that some important flaws still existed in French industry at this time. These deficiencies also forcefully explain the uneven character of capitalist economic development. First of all, even though heavy industry had grown significantly, light industry retained an important position in the overall economy, especially in those sectors that produced high-class luxury goods, valuable household articles, and sophisticated fashions. For example, the annual output value for the entire mining and metal processing industries came to only 565 million francs at this time. However, the output value of apparel and luxury goods came to 1.5 billion francs. Moreover, even though many large companies (defined as employing more than a thousand workers) had emerged in French industry, small enterprises still constituted the greatest proportion of all business operations. Of all French enterprises 75 percent were small companies with fewer than ten employees. Close to 60 percent of all workers were employed in these small industries. Also, a number of handicraft factories still existed; these handicraft factories averaged only 1.7 workers. In addition, French industrial growth was quite slow, especially when compared to that of the other capitalist countries. Although French industrial production ranked second in the world in the early 1860s, it was still far behind that of top-ranked England. Because its growth rate could not match that of the newly emerging United States and Germany, by the end of the 1860s France was eclipsed by both powers and slipped to fourth place.

As France's industrial production grew, and as the bourgeoisie made huge fortunes from this growth, the condition of the working class continuously deteriorated, and the class struggle became ever sharper. After the Revolution of 1789, the Napoleonic regime used various kinds of reactionary measures to deal with the workers. Although wages improved slightly (increasing by approximately 15 percent from 1800 to 1810), a longer workday and abominable work conditions pushed workers into a bitter existence. During the Restoration, the exploitation suffered by the French working class became more intense. The workday reached fourteen to sixteen hours per day, labor intensity greatly increased, commodity prices soared, yet wages fell significantly. The condition of the working class continued to deteriorate in the 1830s. During the eighteen years of rule of Louis-Philippe, real wages declined 15 to 20 percent. The economic boom times of the 1850s and 1860s accentuated the glaring contrast of the great fortunes made by the bourgeoisie and the increasing poverty of the working people. The average wage for a worker increased nominally 8 to 10 percent, yet the cost of food and rent increased by 50 percent. The income level of the great majority of workers made it difficult for them to maintain even the lowest living standards. They were living in a constant state of hunger and cold. The bourgeoisie, however, lived intemperately and enjoyed every luxury, all assiduously squeezed from the workers. It was just as Marx pointed out: "The misery of the masses stood out in sharp relief to the shameless display of extravagant and dissipated luxury."[17]

The class struggle within France became more acute day by day as industrial capitalism grew and as the proletariat became increasingly impoverished. As early as the beginning of the nineteenth century, French workers began to form their own organizations and often fought spontaneously against the bourgeoisie to secure their own economic interests. Of course, they were still not very politically mature, and the development of capitalism was also in its initial stage. In particular, large-scale, modern industry had not yet been established. These historical conditions led to the development of the theory of utopian socialism, which was advocated by such representative figures as Saint-Simon (1760–1825) and Fourier (1772–1837). The continued growth of France's industrial revolution brought about the gradual maturation of the French working class, and led them toward the political arena. The 1831 uprising of the silk workers of Lyons particularly symbolized the fact that the French workers' movement had entered a new stage. From that moment on, "the class struggle between the proletariat and the bourgeoisie . . . came to occupy first place in the history of Europe's most advanced country."[18] The Paris uprising of 1832 was followed by a second uprising in Lyons in 1834. Strikes had become increasingly prevalent by the 1840s, and the French proletariat completely revealed its enormous strength during the Revolution of 1848. By the Second Empire—and especially after French workers participated in the meetings of the First International held in September 1864—the powerful workers' movement became even more vigorous, and finally brought about the crisis of the Second Empire.

The Growth of Money-Lending Capitalism and the Expansion of French Capitalism Overseas

French money-lending capitalism was already quite advanced as early as the feudal period. It grew even more under the new social and economic conditions that prevailed after the Revolution of 1789, and became an important characteristic of French capitalism as a whole.

French money-lending capitalism (or "loan shark" capitalism) was extremely diverse in its range of activities. It permeated almost every nook and cranny of the national economy. Among its various activities, the most important were to enslave in debt the vast community of small producers; to invest in the national debt; to extend loans to domestic and overseas enterprises; and to be involved in various kinds of speculative activities. The socioeconomic changes brought about by France's bourgeois revolution of 1789 created numerous advantageous conditions for money-lending capital. First of all, the creation of a widespread system of land ownership by small farmers, and the pervasive existence of medium and small-sized enterprises throughout industry provided a huge target of exploitation for money-lending capital. In particular, the poverty-stricken and backward small-peasant farming economy served as fertile soil, enabling this type of money-lending capitalism to flourish even more luxuriantly. Second, the political situation in France experienced great volatility and change within the space of little more than half a century. The state treasury often found itself in a predicament, and constantly needed to borrow funds from money-lending capitalists in order to maintain required levels of state expenditures and cover any emerging deficits. Finally, beginning in the nineteenth century (which coincided with the rapid growth of capitalism throughout Europe as a whole), France was also moving forward with its own industrial revolution, and therefore had a pressing need for vast amounts of capital. Conditions such as these stimulated the development of French money-lending capitalism.

Because of the continuous warfare that occurred during the Napoleonic period, normal economic activity in France frequently suffered damage, and profit margins became very unstable. As a result, those with money took advantage of the financial difficulties of the government to engage in massive speculation on the debt, and they earned rich profits in this activity. At this time, the newly created Bank of France and the credit system that had been revived by the Napoleonic government also played a very great energizing role. After the restoration of the Bourbon dynasty, economic activity became rather brisk owing to the domestic recovery from damages sustained during the war. Money capital turned to the exchanges to speculate in stocks and industrial and commercial enterprises. A large number of banks, exchanges, and bogus joint-stock companies were established. By 1830, the total value of negotiable securities had increased to 4.85 billion francs from 1.5 billion in 1815. However, because the banks and exchanges were primarily a speculative arena for finance capitalists to play with various crises, the true credit available to industry and commerce at this time was not very substantial. The period of the Orleans monarchy presented an outstanding and unprecedented opportunity for the growth of the credit market because political power had been taken over by France's financial cliques, and government finances were in dire straits. Deficits were piling up, and Paris floated new bond issues every few years to cover the shortfall. The finance capitalists took advantage of these most favorable circumstances to lend money to the government. In the process, they greatly increased their own economic clout. It was just as Marx had pointed out, "The reason the government is running a budget deficit, after all, is because such an arrangement is directly in accord with the interests of those groups within the bourgeoisie who run the Chamber of Deputies and pass its legislation. The national budget deficit is the object of their speculative activities and a principal source of their wealth."[19]

By the end of the July Monarchy, for example, France's national debt had climbed to 5.5 billion francs. Finally, France's investment capitalists took advantage of the nation's unprecedented economic boom of the 1850s and 1860s. Like fishing in turbulent waters, they cleverly and ingeniously manipulated the banks and the stock exchange to greatly enrich themselves. Never before had their speculation been so rampant. Never before had they pocketed such surprisingly high profits. The Pereire brothers, Isaac and Jacob Emile, were good examples of the typical French plutocrat. In 1852, Isaac Pereire founded the Credit Mobilier, capitalized at only twelve million francs. By 1885, the capitalization of the Credit Mobilier had risen to sixty million francs. Pereire then floated a bond issue worth 62.5 million francs, while simultaneously making loans valued at 112.8 million. Pereire finally declared bankruptcy in 1867 after the collapse of his speculative schemes.

Generally speaking, French investment capital grew far more rapidly than did industrial capital during this period. In 1869, for example, Paris alone could claim thirty-three billion francs of negotiable securities, or four times the total output value of French industry as a whole. French banks and the Bourse, however, did not confine their lending and speculative activities to France itself, but loaned vast sums to other countries, thereby turning France into a net creditor nation. By 1869, for example, total French capital exports came to ten billion francs, and ranked second internationally only to England's efforts. Finally, the high interest rates—characteristically charged by French capitalism—became even more accentuated during the period of France's transition to imperialism, and even became the distinguishing mark of French imperialism as a whole. This fully confirmed Lenin's famous conclusion: "French capitalism began its growth as a small-scale money-lending operation, and ended as a large-scale money-lending capitalism."[20]

In addition to the export of capital, French capitalism also aggressively promoted the export of its commodities as an important means of expansionism. As France's industrial revolution matured, its total foreign trade increased from 621 million francs in 1815 to 1.859 billion francs in 1850. A change also occurred in the composition of that foreign trade. For example, raw materials grew to assume 78 percent of all French imports, while manufactured goods constituted 70 percent of all French exports—even though there had been no change in the government's overall policy of protectionism. It was not until the Second Empire that the government altered its policy on free trade, and then did so only because of domestic industrial expansion and increased competition from abroad. Beginning in 1860, the French government signed in succession a number of trade agreements with countries like England, Belgium, Germany, Italy, Sweden, Norway, Holland, Austria-Hungary, and Portugal. These agreements stimulated extremely rapid growth in France's foreign trade sector, which totalled 5.969 billion francs in 1870.

As the capitalist economy grew, France also intensified the plunder of its colonies. The many wars of conquest that Napoleon had launched in the early nineteenth century greatly expanded France's territory. After the collapse of the First Empire, France once again returned to its 1790 borders. By the 1830s, France had recovered its strength, and now began to accelerate the plunder of its colonies. In 1830, for example, France occupied Algeria. After that, it took over the Ivory Coast in 1843, and Guinea in 1843. French colonial expansionism reached its peak during the 1850s when the government launched a series of wars of aggression in Asia, Africa, and the Americas. Between 1854 and 1860, for example, France took part in many aggressive actions directed against China, and plundered that country of vast amounts of treasure. In 1858, France provoked a war in Indochina. It occupied Saigon between 1859 and 1861, conquered Cochin China in 1862, and made Cambodia into its protectorate in 1863. The French government sent an expeditionary army against Syria in 1860, and militarily intervened in Mexico between 1862 and 1867. France also extended its aggressive power into Egypt after the Suez Canal had been completed in 1869. France's colonial possessions grew enormously after these expansionist activities took place. In 1820, for example, France's colonies comprised only twenty thousand square kilometers in area, with a population numbering 400 thousand. By 1860, however, its colonies accounted for 200 thousand square kilometers with a population of 3.4 million people. By 1876, France's colonies reached 900 thousand square kilometers with a population of six million. During this period, France was second only to England as a colonial power.

3. The Formation of Monopoly Capitalism

The Impact of the Franco-Prussian War on the French Economy: The Social and Economic Policies of the Paris Commune and Their Great Significance

The development of French capitalism entered a new historical period beginning in the 1870s. Moveover, the Franco-Prussian War, which broke out in 1870 also had an extremely important influence on the socioeconomic transformation of France in this period.

The Franco-Prussian War was the result of many years of contention between the ruling classes of Prussia and France, each of whom wanted to exercise hegemony over Europe. France launched this war for three reasons: 1. It wanted to expand into the Rhine River basin to thwart any potential unification of Germany. 2. It intended to use this opportunity to plunder the wealth of other European nations. 3. It hoped to secure French hegemony over the European continent. Not only did Prussia count on the war to achieve the military unification of Germany, but it also desired to occupy the Alsace-Lorraine region of

France and eventually achieve Prussian hegemony over the European continent. It was France that initially declared war on Prussia on July 19, 1870, thereby instigating this war. However, the outcome of the conflict not only failed to achieve the goals of Napoleon III, but rather resulted in the collapse of his Second Empire. This crushing defeat was the inevitable result of the intensifying political and economic crises in France in the 1860s. It was just as Marx had pointed out: "France's disaster in 1870 is an event unparalleled in recent world history. It reveals that the France of the bureaucrats, the France of Louis Napoleon, the France of the ruling class and its parasitic state, is nothing but a rotting corpse."[21]

The Franco-Prussian War put an end to the prosperity that had prevailed in France after the resolution of its 1857 economic crisis. It brought about a sharp reduction in industrial production, a violent drop in imports and exports, exhausted its treasury, and caused serious damage to the national economy. During the war, many plants were forced to close, causing a severe shortage of consumer goods and a subsequent price inflation. Colossal military expenses (in excess of fifteen billion francs) only intensified the financial crisis. When the convertibility of paper currency was halted, the financial markets were immediately thrown into great turmoil. After the war, France paid an indemnity of five billion francs and ceded the important industrial and mining regions of Alsace and Lorraine to Germany. This brought numerous and intractable difficulties for the French economy in subsequent decades. The Franco-Prussian War, therefore, is an important turning point in the economic history of France.

France established its Third Republic after the Second Empire had collapsed in the wake of defeat in the Franco-Prussian War. However, political power was usurped by the bourgeoisie. The newly established Government of National Defense was in reality a government of national betrayal. It made every effort to place the heavy burden of the war on the backs of the working people, and it actively colluded with the Prussian government, and planned to use the military strength of the invaders to help it disperse the armed detachments of the workers. As a result, class contradictions in France became increasingly acute, and the conditions for a violent class conflict ripened and matured. When the reactionary Thiers government forced the workers into a decisive military showdown, the working class of Paris used revolutionary violence to overthrow the rule of the bourgeoisie and to seize political power on March 18, 1871. Moreover, the workers created a new type of state—the dictatorship of the proletariat—after smashing the old state machinery. This was what constituted the historically famous revolutionary event known as the Paris Commune.

The establishment of the Paris Commune was a great revolutionary event, an event of earthshaking, epochal importance. It was the first proletarian revolution in the history of mankind, as well as the first attempt to establish a dictatorship of the proletariat. At the very beginning, the new governing authority was in the hands of the National Guard's Central Committee, a group elected by the workers of Paris themselves. From its inception, it vigorously adopted measures to improve, in a significant fashion, the living conditions of the working people. For example, it banned the sale of goods that had been sold to pawn shops. Pawnshop articles valued at less than fifteen francs had to be returned to their original owners. It postponed the payment of housing rents and prohibited evictions, and it appropriated a million francs to assist the destitute.

Governmental power passed into the hands of the Commune Committee on March 26, after a formal general election. Marx pointed out: "The Paris Commune was a large-scale effort at frugality and thrift. Not only did the Commune begin its work with political reforms, but it also carried out economic reforms."[22] Within a very short time, the commune issued a series of important resolutions and decrees. The most important of these, from a social and economic aspect, were the following: First, the Commune instituted a relatively reasonable wage scale for government officials. Based on the principle that "under the new social system, there should be neither overpaid and underworked officials nor excessively high salaries," the Commune abolished the system of high compensation. It stipulated that "the highest annual salary, without exception, for military officers and municipal government officials would be 6,000 francs" (in other words, equivalent to the wages of a skilled worker). In addition, "the daily salary for members of the Commune Committee would be 15 francs." "Those holding other jobs could not draw salaries from that employment."[23]

Second, the Commune actively worked to improve the living conditions and working conditions of the workers. For example, the commune raised workers' wages. It prohibited employers from embezzling workers' wages or deducting any fines or penalties from those wages. It stipulated that all wages must be turned over to the worker. It abolished the "employment centers" that acted as intermediate exploiters, and instead established legitimate offices where workers could register for employment. It prohibited bakeries from adding night shifts. And the Commune even went so far as to discuss the issue of limiting the workday to eight hours.

Third, the Commune carried out a certain degree of supervision and expropriation of capitalist enterprises. For example, it established a special committee to supervise the railroads and the production of military necessities. It confiscated the enterprises of those capitalists who had run away and turned them over to workers' cooperatives to manage, and it also drafted a plan to set up a workers' cooperative society that would be involved in the production of goods.

Fourth, the Paris Commune aggressively attacked the controlling power of the church and its special economic privileges. For example, it proclaimed the separation of church and state, abolished the state budget for religion, and nationalized church property.

Fifth, the Commune took into full consideration the economic interests of the urban poor and other workers, and helped them to solve their many difficulties. For example, it closed the loan shark agencies created by the money-lenders and returned the collateral held by them, without compensation, to their original owners. It reduced housing rents and reassigned to other people the homes of those landlords who had run away. It established welfare agencies to provide comfort and financial assistance to the disabled as well as to the family dependents of those serving in the military. The commune put a ceiling on the price of bread and guaranteed the supply of daily necessities.

Sixth, the Commune paid attention to the basic interests of the farmers. It explicitly proclaimed a policy of "land to the tiller," and made definite efforts to secure the participation of the broad masses of farmers in the revolution.

The above-mentioned economic measures undertaken by the Paris Commune fully confirm Marx's following comment. The Paris Commune was "in reality a government of the working class, and was the product of a class struggle between the producing class and the owning class. The Paris Commune had finally found the political form which could enable the workers to liberate themselves economically."[24] Because the Commune survived for only seventy-two days, there was not much time to implement these measures. Some policies could not be carried out at all. However, their profound and lasting significance will never be expunged. The Paris Commune was "the greatest example of the largest proletarian movement of the nineteenth century."[25] The heroic workers of Paris sacrificed their blood and their lives in exchange for the extremely valuable and profound lessons gained in the proletarian revolution. Although the Paris Commune was defeated, nevertheless, just as was pointed out by Marx, "the heroic March 18th movement was the dawn of a great social revolution that forever liberated man from class society."[26] It dramatically proved that the capitalist system was heading into a decline. After this, the world proletarian revolution entered a new historical period, and capitalism also began its transition to its highest and final stage.

The Relatively Slow Development of the French Economy at the End of the Nineteenth and the Beginning of the Twentieth Centuries

French capitalism entered its transition to imperialism beginning in the 1870s. The entire national economy now underwent a profound transformation. This transformation, first of all, was inseparable from the development of production. French industrial production almost doubled (it increased 94 percent) in the last thirty years of the nineteenth century. The development of heavy industry was particularly rapid: Both coal and iron production more than doubled, and the amount of steel produced went up sixteenfold. New industries such as aluminum, plastics, and nonferrous metals all made some initial progress. Although light industry was comparatively slow in its development, it also made some appreciable gains. For example, the amount of cotton consumed in the textile industry increased to

1,599,000 quintals in 1900 from 937,000 quintals in 1869. (One quintal is equivalent to one hundred kilograms.) The level of mechanization was greatly enhanced in all sectors of industry.

French industrial development accelerated even more in the twentieth century. Even though the development of heavy industry led the way in this period, some of the new industrial sectors made rather large gains too. In 1913, French automobile production reached forty-five thousand units and aluminum production climbed to 13,500 tons, both second only to U.S. production levels. French production of chemicals and man-made fibers ranked third in the world. Because of the very rapid development of heavy industry, the metallurgical industry had already replaced textiles in playing the decisive role in the national economy. However, despite all this, light industry had not yet entirely relinquished its important niche. Cotton consumption still increased to 2,713,000 quintals in 1913. French fashions, cosmetics, silks, and wines, as before, were important exports that enjoyed a ready market throughout the world. In addition, the communications and transportation sectors also expanded in conjunction with the development of commerce and industry. By the eve of the First World War, France had 42,826 kilometers of railroads and boasted 1,038,000 tons of ocean-going shipping.

It must be pointed out that despite the rather significant gains made by French industry in this period, it was clearly very backward when compared to the new capitalist countries like the United States and Germany. While French industrial production went up 2.9-fold in the period from 1870 to 1913, Germany's increased 4.6 times and the United States 8.1 times. As a result, France's share of the world's industrial production went from 10 percent in 1870 to 7 percent in 1913. Moreover, small and medium-sized companies still made up the great bulk of enterprises operating throughout French industry. Light industry still remained important. By the end of the nineteenth century, there were 3.3 million industrial workers in France, but only 1.11 million worked in large enterprises that employed upwards of one hundred workers. If differentiating according to the sector of industry, then the total number of workers in five light industries—such as food, textiles, services, leather, and household goods—comprised 49.9 percent of the total number. Moreover, right up to the eve of the First World War, there were still fewer Frenchmen working in industry than in agriculture. France was basically still a country where both agriculture and industry remained equally vital.

There were a number of important reasons that brought about the relatively slow development of French industry in this period. The first was the impact of the Franco-Prussian War, a topic which has already been discussed above. The second was the lack of coal and iron resources necessary for heavy industry. French coal deposits were very limited, the coal available for coking purposes even scarcer, and, as a result, coal self-sufficiency became a chronic problem. Even though iron ore was relatively abundant, it contained an excessive amount of phosphorus and therefore was unsuitable for use. As a result, both raw materials and fuel had to be imported, resulting in relatively high costs. Third, investment capitalism in France was rather advanced. Because large amounts of capital flowed abroad to seek out even higher profits, what remained for domestic enterprises was quite scant. As a result, France's own industries complained of a shortage of investment capital. Fourth, the small farmer economy which was predominant in agriculture brought about a constricted domestic market and an insufficient supply of mobile labor power. As a result, the slow development of agricultural production also limited industrial production. Fifth, the widespread and long-term existence of small and medium-sized enterprises throughout industry also played a very large and adverse role, hampering France's rapid development.

At the end of the nineteenth and the beginning of the twentieth centuries, French agricultural production—like that of industry—grew much more slowly than that in other countries. At this time, the most important characteristic of French agriculture was the continued absolute predominance of the small farmer economy. Of course, as a result of many bankruptcies and the dissolution of small farms, land had become more concentrated in fewer and fewer hands. Capitalist farms now rapidly increased in number. By 1911, the number of hired workers in agriculture already reached two million. The utilization of machinery and chemical fertilizer, as well as the degree of agricultural specialization, reached new levels on the capitalist farms. However, the size of French farms, in general, was comparatively small. On the average, they did not exceed twenty-five acres in size. At the same time, farms in the United States averaged 138 acres, in England sixty-three acres, and in Germany 33.5 acres.

During this same period, grain output in France also increased to a certain extent, although the size of that growth was modest. For example, the output of wheat—that very important crop—increased from 74.2 million quintals in 1870 to merely 87.9 million quintals in 1913. Some specialized crops—such as grapes, vegetables, and flowers (commodities that had great economic significance for France)—even showed a decline in production. The reason why French agricultural production did not grow rapidly was mainly because of the widely dispersed management of land and the relatively slow development of industry. At the same time, it was also affected by the chronic agricultural crisis that confronted the capitalist world at the end of the nineteenth century. Therefore the yield per unit of land was not very high, despite the fact that the land was fertile and the weather favorable in France. At this time, France ranked between eleventh and seventeenth in world output of several important crops.

The relatively slow development of industrial and agricultural production was also reflected in foreign trade. The increase in the total amount of France's foreign trade in this period was minuscule. Particularly critical was the growing trade deficit because imports greatly exceeded the expansion of exports. Only because France was a typical creditor nation could it use the income generated from its huge foreign investments to remedy this shortfall. Only because of this factor did France not experience an overall adverse balance in international payments.

The Formation of Monopoly Capitalism: The Money-Lending Characteristic of French Imperialism

Like other capitalist countries at the turn of the twentieth century, France also underwent a process that led to the further concentration of production and of capital. Monopolies were created on this basis, and France's transition to the stage of imperialism began.

Concentrated production and the emergence of monopolies began first in French heavy industry, and in particular in metallurgy, mining, and machine manufacturing. Because these sectors of the economy consistently received substantial support from the government in the aftermath of the Franco-Prussian War, and because they also made comprehensive use of new technical inventions (such as the Thomas steel-smelting process and other innovations), their output also increased comparatively rapidly, and the process of concentration and monopoly also began to appear earlier than in other economic sectors. For example, 80 percent of France's mineral production in 1914 was concentrated in the Briey basin, and one-third of that amount came from four large mines. (The total number of mines came to thirty-nine.) In 1906, the number of workers employed in large enterprises (defined as those that had upwards of one hundred employees) comprised the following percentages of all workers employed in these industries: 97.2 percent in metallurgy, 98.5 percent in coal mining, 57.1 percent in chemicals, and 50 percent in metal working. The monopolies in these industries were de Wendel, Schneider, Marlene Aumugul, Dehn Anchinn, Kuhlmann, Saint-Gobain, and some ten others.

The degree of concentration achieved in light industry was less than that in heavy industry. However, beginning at the end of the nineteenth century, light industry also began its transition from concentration to monopoly. By 1906, large enterprises in the textile industry already employed 52 percent of all workers in this industry; in papermaking and plastics, the proportion reached 55 percent. The Flax Company was the largest monopoly in light industry, and it controlled approximately 90 percent of linen production in France. The most common organizational form of a monopoly corporation in France was the syndicate.

Lenin pointed out that monopolies "first divide up the domestic market. Then, to differing degrees, they take control over the entire nation's production and put it into their own hands. However, under the conditions of a capitalist system, the domestic market is inextricably linked to the foreign market."[27] Monopolies inevitably had to expand their operations abroad. While engaged in fierce struggles with each other, they also concluded international agreements among themselves to divide up the world market, and thereby created international monopolies. For example, during this time period, French monopoly capital participated in the 1901 establishment of the international zinc syndicate, the setting up of an international steel rail cartel in 1904, the 1908 creation of an international glass bottle syndicate, and a series of other international monopolies. By the beginning of the twentieth century, French monopoly capital exercised complete control over France's economy. French capitalism now entered its transition to the stage of imperialism.

The development of French monopoly capitalism, as described above, was basically the same as that experienced by the entire capitalist world. However, because the timing of France's transition to imperialism came relatively late, and because its industrial development was comparatively slow, the degree of its concentration lagged far behind that of the United States, Germany, and the other capitalist states. In addition, the development of monopolies in the various sectors of the economy was extremely uneven. For example, concentration was not very apparent in the production of luxury goods and fashions—the so-called "special products of Paris"—which in large measure were still the preserve of small and medium-sized enterprises. Even though the production of cotton and linen had already come under the control of monopolies in the textile industry at quite an early date, the silk industry remained extremely dispersed and its technology quite backward.

What merits our attention is the fact that the process of concentration of French banking capital resembled neither the slow pace of industrial development nor its comparative backwardness. For some time, France was a country that possessed large amounts of money capital. Banks wielded great clout as early as the first half of the nineteenth century. They gathered into their own hands—by various channels—the money and savings which had been accumulated over a long period by various strata of society. Beginning in the 1870s, the floating of substantial bond issues by the government, the increase in industrial production, and the inflation caused by commercial speculation further stimulated the development of bank credit operations. Many new, large banks were created in this period, and they played a crucial role in the economic and political life of the country. France had a combined total of 266 banks in 1908, with branches and sub-branches located everywhere. The most famous of these were the Credit Bank of Lyon, the National Discount Office, and the Company-General. They were called "the three great banks," and they held 70 percent of the deposits of the entire country. As bank capital grew in leaps and bounds, it gradually merged with industrial capital, thereby establishing the omnipotent control of finance capital. In France, the most powerful groups of finance capital were organized by the two hundred wealthiest families.

The advanced state of French bank credit operations illustrates the fact that French capitalism had already amassed a vast amount of "surplus capital" in the process of its growth. Lenin pointed out: "Capitalism will be capitalism. Surplus capital will not be used domestically to raise the living standards of the people, because then it might lower the profits sought by the capitalist. On the contrary, that surplus capital will be exported to the backward countries to seek higher returns."[28] This type of situation was extremely prominent in England, France, and the other widely recognized capitalist nations. The total amount of French capital exports came to ten billion francs in 1869, increased to thirty billion francs in 1900, and then zoomed upward to sixty billion francs in 1914. This vastly exceeded the total amount of France's domestic capital investment for the same time period. France was second only to England as the largest exporter of capital. However, while England's export of capital was closely linked to its vast colonial possessions, "France's situation was different. Its foreign investment went chiefly to Europe, and principally to Russia, which received not less than 10 billion francs. The majority of the capital was in the form of loans, and not investment in industrial ventures."[29] There are two reasons why French capital exports mainly took the form of loan capital. First, loaning capital not only secured the most profitable return, but also reduced risks. The other reason was that France was not as competitive as some other countries. It had numerous weaknesses, and its economic development was relatively slow and backward. Politically and militarily, it also faced a strong adversary in Germany which glared at her like a tiger about to devour its prey. As a result, France was compelled to use capital exports as an important political instrument in its foreign policy considerations.

Although the export of large quantities of capital can, to a certain degree, bring about stagnation in a country, it also brought many economic advantages to France. One of these advantages was income from interest which completely made up for the huge trade deficit, thereby guaranteeing a surplus in France's international balance of payments. This played a very large stabilizing role in the French national economy, even enabling France to "reap windfall profits by relying on the income from bonds earning high interest. This occurred despite France's stagnating population growth, lethargic commerce and industry, and slumping trade exports."[30] Of course, what this also did was to create a French imperialism whose decadent and parasitic character was quite prominent and deeply ingrained. For example, on the eve of the First World War, the stratum of coupon-clippers in France reached two million people. When their family dependents are calculated in, the total number exceeded five million people. This group, amazingly enough, constituted more than one-eighth of the entire population. This situation completely reflected the special characteristics of French monopoly capitalism. Therefore, Lenin pointed out that "French and British imperialism are different. The French are more appropriately called money-lending imperialists."[31]

4. The First World War Weakens and Damages the French Economy

The First World War broke out in 1914. This conflict occurred under the conditions of intensified unequal development of capitalism and the unprecedented sharpening of contradictions among the imperialist countries. France was one of the main actors in this war. Its war aims were to defeat an increasingly powerful Germany, to regain Alsace and Lorraine, to seize the Saar mining area and Germany's colonies, and finally to restore its position of hegemony over the European continent. To counter Germany and its allies, France made long-term preparations prior to the war. It signed treaties with Russia, England, and other countries, and created the Entente bloc.

Not only was France an important battlefield throughout the whole course of the war, but ten of its northeastern provinces were occupied by German troops not long after the beginning of the conflict. As a result, the French national economy suffered serious damage. The bourgeois government adopted a series of measures to manage and control the economy. Its purpose was to extricate itself from a difficult economic situation, to remedy the damages sustained in the loss of the industrial areas of the northeast, to meet the needs of the military, and to guarantee the wartime profits of monopoly capital.

First of all, the state concentrated all its energy in actively fostering industrial production for the military. In addition to completely guaranteeing the supply of capital, raw materials, and labor power, the government also allocated large sums of money to build and expand many military plants. This brought about the unprecedented growth of a military-industrial complex. Consumer industries were repeatedly cut back. For example, cotton consumption during the war fell by almost half.

Second, the state also gave special assistance to those sectors of the economy which were vital to the prosecution of the war but which confronted severe difficulties. Let us take the electric power industry as an example. Coal-fired plants that generated electricity were greatly restricted in their operations because France lacked adequate coal production. As a result, the government invested heavily in hydroelectric plants during the war, hoping to maintain the supply of electrical energy. Other examples existed in the French chemical and pharmaceutical industries. In the past they had depended on Germany but now they basically achieved self-sufficiency as a result of government support.

Third, the government stepped up the utilization of new technology and equipment in industry. It actively promoted the mechanization and standardization of production, and it vigorously developed mass production in order to solve the wartime difficulties engendered by shortages of industrial products and insufficient labor power.

Finally, the government imposed comprehensive controls over the entire national economy. All activities pertaining to industrial or agricultural production were directly managed by the state. For example, the supply of raw materials, the allocation of labor power, and the distribution of products were all handled by the state. In addition, the government imposed a system of rationing for daily necessities.

As a result of adopting the measures mentioned above, the government shifted the French national economy entirely onto a war-footing, and also enabled state monopoly capitalism to grow further. Despite these efforts, the damage sustained by the French national economy during the war was extremely severe. Statistics indicate that France's material losses during the entire wartime period came to 200 billion francs. Human losses were approximately 1,365,000 men.

With the exception of very few sectors, French wartime industrial production dropped sharply. This was because all the areas occupied by the German army had originally been industrial and mining centers, and their products occupied a very large proportion of the total production of French industry. For example, these areas produced 94 percent of the copper, 81 percent of the pig iron, 63 percent of the steel, 74 percent of the coal, 81 percent of the woolen knitwear, and 76 percent of the granulated sugar. The vitality of industry was undermined after the loss of these products and, even though the government made great efforts in other geographical regions, it was impossible to attain previous levels of production at a moment's notice. In addition, the wartime general mobilization put 7,935,000 men into military service; this was approximately more than half of all the able-bodied men in France. Because the military draft took these people principally from the productive sectors of the economy, it created a serious labor shortage. One must add to this list of problems the appearance of severe shortages of raw materials, fuel, and foodstuffs. As a result, industrial production suffered life-threatening blows, especially during the first two years of the war when production fell most dramatically. Even though there was a modest rise beginning in 1916, production only reached 57 percent of the prewar level by 1919, or immediately after the end of the war.

Agricultural production also suffered heavy damage. The northeastern region occupied by the German army also happened to be the area where French agricultural levels were comparatively high. These areas produced 20.4 percent of the total amount of wheat in France, 11.7 percent of potatoes, and 49.5 percent of sugarbeets. In the unoccupied areas, the military conscription of 3,586,000 agricultural workers made agricultural production, which was already feeling pinched for labor power, even more difficult to maintain. A dramatic decrease in the total number of livestock during the war also caused huge problems in tilling the soil and in transportation. As a result, agricultural production fell precipitously. For example, the amount of wheat produced went from 86.9 million quintals in 1913 to 36.6 million quintals in 1917, creating an extremely severe food crisis in France during the war.

Foreign trade also gradually deteriorated as industrial and agricultural production declined. Even though the total amount of France's foreign trade in the period of 1914 to 1918 went from 11.2 billion francs to twenty-seven billion francs, the serious nature of its trade crisis is reflected by the following two factors. First, this increase was created by a runaway inflation. The wholesale price index (one hundred in 1913) went from 102 to 339 between 1914 and 1918. Second, while the amount of imports went from 6.4 billion francs to 22.3 billion francs (as a result of the import of vast quantities of military goods and foodstuffs), the total amount of exports actually decreased, going from 4.8 billion francs to 4.7 billion francs. As a consequence, France's wartime trade deficit expanded substantially, and came to more than sixty billion francs for a five-year span. This forced France—which earlier had been celebrated as a creditor nation—to repeatedly borrow from abroad, and in particular, to approach the United States. By the end of the war, France owed a total of $4 billion to the United States, and became America's debtor.

The colossal wartime military expenditures and the decline in production and trade brought about a gradual deterioration in the state's financial condition. To make up for such deficits, the French government did everything it could to raise taxes and levies, to print more money, and to issue more bonds. It shifted the heavy burdens of the war onto the backs of the vast number of working people. Between 1914 and 1918, the amount of money in circulation in France went from 7.325 billion francs to 27.536 billion francs, and the amount of bonds floated went from 700 million francs to 21.9 billion francs. At the same time, commodity prices rose severalfold. For example, the price of one quintal of wheat was twenty-four francs in 1913, but by 1917, the official price set by the government had already reached seventy-five francs. The black market price for wheat was simply out of sight.

The imperialist war brought deep misery to the working people of France. The wartime inflation and the steady rise in commodity prices greatly depressed workers' real wages. The average wage of the French worker in 1918 was only about one-third that of 1914. The so-called "rationing system" implemented by the government during the war in reality forced cutbacks in the daily necessities of the workers. Therefore the living conditions of the working class deteriorated to an abysmally low level. The farmers also confronted a difficult situation. The war hastened the bankruptcy of many small farmers and the fragmentation of their small holdings. It forced many to abandon their farms, and turned them into destitute and homeless vagabonds. On the other hand, the French monopoly bourgeoisie enjoyed various special privileges in the production and marketing of goods as a result of the protection extended to the economy by the government. The floating of huge bond issues also enabled the monopoly bourgeoisie to earn huge commissions and interest payments. The war, in truth, was a wonderful opportunity for them to make huge fortunes. The profits squeezed out by the monopoly oligarchs, especially in the military-industrial complex, were simply shocking. For example, the Grome-Roane Company, which manufactured military vehicles, repaid the entire investment of its stockholders during the first year of the war. In addition to that, the company still made approximately ten million francs in pure profit. Under these conditions, class contradictions became even sharper. The French working class with its glorious revolutionary tradition continuously launched fierce attacks against monopoly capital. The French workers' movement developed vigorously throughout the entire period of the First World War.

5. The Turbulent French Economy between the Two World Wars, and the Enhanced Role of Monopoly Capital

The Recovery and Development of the National Economy in the 1920s

The First World War caused enormous damage to the national economy of France. However, because the Entente won the war, France partially achieved its predatory goals. In addition, a vanquished Germany was temporarily incapacitated as France's adversary. Both these factors created favorable conditions for the postwar economic recovery and development of France.

First of all, France regained Alsace-Lorraine. It also acquired administrative rights over the Saar coal-producing region. Both acquisitions enabled it to expand production in metallurgy, mining, chemicals, textiles, and numerous other industrial sectors. The chronic problem of shortages of raw materials and fuels was also basically solved. Next, Germany's payment of huge war reparations provided the necessary capital to revive and rebuild the postwar French economy. France was the biggest recipient of war reparations. Up to July 1931, it received a total of 8,151 billion gold marks of the 20,678 billion Germany paid to the victorious nations. At the beginning, these reparations were also principally paid in goods whose values were set at extremely low prices. In addition, France also seized—from the hands of Germany—control over Togo, the Cameroons, Syria, Lebanon, and other colonies. It expanded its colonial sphere of operations, and increased the sources of its overseas plunder. Finally, the large-scale work of reviving and rebuilding the regions that had suffered wartime damage stimulated the replacement or renovation of large quantities of fixed capital. It increased the demand for machinery, raw materials, and consumer goods, and resulted in an expanded domestic market and a dynamic national economy.

Industrial production in postwar France achieved large gains under the stimulus of such factors. If the index of total industrial production in France in 1919 stands at 57.9 (with 1913 as one hundred), then by 1924 it had already increased to 109. By 1930, it had even reached 140. The pace of this growth was much faster than that of the United States, England, or any other country. Moreover, the industrial upsurge in this period mainly occurred in heavy industry. The automobile, aircraft, chemical, plastic, and other new sectors were the most prominent industries to participate in this economic boom. For example, the number of cars produced in 1920 was only forty thousand, but by 1929 had shot up to 254,000. Other sectors, such as machine manufacturing, metallurgy, construction, and mining, also made comparatively large gains. As a result, France's portion of world industrial production increased from 5 percent in 1920 to 8 percent in 1930. France's industrial population first exceeded its agricultural population in 1926. Of those employed in industry, 47.9 percent were employed in heavy industry. By the end of the 1920s, that portion exceeded 50 percent. These statistics concretely reflect the enormous transformation of the French national economy. By this time, France had developed into a country where industry took precedence over agriculture.

However, agriculture in the 1920s did not have access to the same advantageous conditions that were enjoyed by industry. As a result, the general tendency in agriculture was one of stagnation. Basically it was stuck in a chronic crisis. Except for exceptional years like 1924, the total amount of agricultural production was consistently below that of prewar levels. Wheat—an important grain—never reached prewar levels. The chronic stagnation in agricultural production greatly speeded up the process that led to the eventual bankruptcy of the small farmer. The total number of farm families in France fell from 5.505 million in 1908 to 3.966 million in 1929. Of the more than one million farm households that had gone bankrupt in the competitive agricultural sector, the vast majority were small farmers. As a result, land ownership in the villages became increasingly concentrated in fewer and fewer hands. This trend promoted the development of an agrarian capitalism. New capitalist farms in France greatly increased in number during this period.

France's foreign trade faced yet another kind of quandry in the 1920s. French imports and exports greatly exceeded their prewar levels because of the comparatively rapid development of industry in this period and the simultaneous weakening of its previously vigorous adversary—Germany—in world markets. Nevertheless, the rate of growth of France's foreign trade was still quite slow when compared to that of the United States and Japan. As a result, France's overall rank in world trade fell. In addition, huge trade deficits occurred every year, with the exception of the years between 1924 and 1927.

Prior to the war, France's trade deficit had always been rectified by the income derived from capital exports. However, as a result of the First World War, France lost almost half of the 60 billion francs that it had originally invested overseas. France made great efforts in the postwar period to step up the export of capital, hoping to regain its former status. However, overseas capital investment by 1929 still came to only sixty percent of the prewar level. Because its income from this source was so greatly reduced, France could no longer maintain a favorable balance in its international payments. In addition, there were two major changes in French capital exports after the war. First, there was a substantial increase in capital exports earmarked for manufacturing rather than for bond issues. Second, investment increasingly flowed to the colonies. However, generally speaking, French imperialism still retained its distinctive character as money-lending imperialism.

The Economic Crisis of the 1930s

Throughout the 1930s, France found herself in a seriously deteriorating situation, and changes began to appear in its social and economic development that were completely unlike those of the 1920s. The economic decline in this period was mainly brought about by an economic crisis. An unprecedentedly severe Great Depression broke out in 1929 in the capitalist world. Although this crisis began in France later than in the other capitalist countries, it became especially protracted. The Great Depression in France originated in 1930 with the bankruptcy of the Shell Bank. This bank had close ties with all the major monopolies, and the announcement of its bankruptcy immediately sounded the alarm that the economic crisis had arrived. The other industrial and commerical enterprises were drawn very quickly into the huge whirlpool of the Depression.

The impact of this crisis on France—as with the other capitalist countries—was unprecedented. It cut short the economic prosperity of the 1920s and brought about a severe decline in industrial production. The general index of French industrial production fell 36.2 percent when calculated from its highest point prior to the Depression to when it bottomed out after 1929. The greatest extent of decline was in heavy industry, where some sectors fell between 40 and 50 percent. Cutbacks in light industry were not as severe. However, because light industry had not made much progress during the 1920s and, like the textile industry, still had not recovered to its prewar level, its circumstances were even more dire. In general, this crisis set French industrial production back almost twenty years; that is, it fell back to its 1911 level. France's share of the industrial production of the postwar capitalist world—a share which had just risen—now dropped once again to 5.1 percent.

During the Depression, the industrial crisis became closely intertwined with the ongoing crisis in agriculture. On the one hand, the industrial depression brought about even more painful changes to an agricultural sector already plagued by chronic stagnation. Conversley, the agricultural crisis intensified and prolonged the industrial crisis. Both were caught in a vicious cycle. The agricultural depression was most severe between 1932 and 1935. At that time, agricultural products were piling up like mountains, while—paradoxically—the bottom was falling out of its prices. For example, the price of one quintal of wheat in France in 1930 fluctuated between 150 and 165 francs. Its price, however, fell to below eighty francs in 1935, and even then could find no buyers. The extent of the drop in prices for agricultural products was, in general, far greater than that experienced by industrial goods. This was because the industrial and commerical monopolies always forced down agricultural prices as far as possible while raising the prices of industrial goods as much as they could, thereby creating an enormous "price scissors" differential. Of course, the real victims of this were the broad masses of small farmers and agricultural workers. The owners of large farms and the wealthy peasants had modern technology and equipment and used hired labor. The cost of their products was much lower than that of the small farmers, and that enabled them to earn rather large profits even during the agricultural depression.

The economic crisis greatly intensified the struggle among the great powers to seize their share of the market. This had a significant impact on France's foreign trade. France found itself in an even more unfavorable position in the world market because its industrial base was rather feeble compared to the newly emerging capitalist states. For example, France's auto exports fell by more than half under the impact of auto exports from England, Belgium, and Luxemburg. And French auto exports were chased out of the market by fierce American competition. The deterioration of France's foreign trade in this period was revealed not only in a decline in absolute numbers but was also reflected in the change in the position of French trade. France's share of total world trade fell to 5.1 percent in 1937 from 6.4 percent in 1929. Moreover, because French exports fell more than imports, the trade deficit correspondingly increased and the income from foreign investments decreased. Therefore, France's unfavorable international balance of payments problem continually expanded.

Generally speaking, the Great Depression in France exhibited the following unique characteristics: First, the Depression began one year later than it did in the other countries. The main reason was that France was involved in large-scale recovery and construction work after the war, and these activities reached their zenith only in 1930. Second, the duration of the crisis was particularly long. Only in 1936 was there a slight recovery. However, following a second economic crisis which enveloped the capitalist world, France once again fell into the depths of an economic crisis in the latter half of 1937. Third, the impact of the Depression on France was also much more severe, on average, than on the other major capitalist countries. As a result, France's share of the capitalist world's industrial production and foreign trade fell.

Monopoly Capital Strengthens Its Controlling Position: Domestic Class Contradictions Intensify

Monopoly capitalism in France developed further in the period between the two world wars. The concentration of production and of capital now speeded up when compared to this same process in France prior to the First World War. The power of a small number of large enterprises grew constantly. Both politically as well as economically, the control of finance capital became ever more pervasive and ever more penetrating. Just as Lenin pointed out, "now that monopolies have been formed and manipulate billions in capital assets, they absolutely cannot avoid penetrating into every nook and cranny of society, nor can they be indifferent to the political system or any of its particular 'details.' "[32]

The strengthening of monopoly capital in postwar France was, above all, inseparable from the economic growth of this period. In particular, the economic boom of the 1920s vigorously promoted the process of concentration in the various sectors of the economy. In the metallurgical industry in the 1920s, for example, the ten largest companies accounted for 75 percent of total production in that field. In the electric industry, 60 percent of production was in the hands of one large corporation. In the automobile industry, the three largest companies controlled 75 percent of total production. The trend to greater concentration also became gradually stronger in light industry. This was especially evident in the field of banking capital where the process of concentration remained, as before, very rapid. The big banks further strengthened their own monopoly status by establishing additional branches and sub-branches, by controlling local banks, by subsidizing industrial and commerical enterprises, by organizing bank cartels, by engaging in private mergers and the mutual exchange of stocks, and by other methods. For example, the National Credit Bank (which appeared in the 1920s) was a product of the combined investment of many large banks. To take another example, the three biggest savings banks (the Credit Bank of Lyon, the National Discount Office, and the Company-General) expanded the number of their branches from 1,700 in 1913 to 3,300 in 1930. Examples of the close interpenetration between bank capital and industrial capital are too numerous to mention individually.

To a very large extent, the growing strength of French monopoly capital in this period came from the support it received from the political power of the state. One of the most commonly used methods of French monopoly capital in the early postwar period was to obtain huge amounts of "compensation" from the government on the pretext of having suffered losses during the war. These so-called "losses" were always shamelessly exaggerated by the monopolies. For example, the Longueville Metallurgical Company had assets worth only fourteen million francs in 1914, yet it actually demanded 438 million francs from the government as "compensation" for "losses." This type of gouging went so far that the Mary Company (whose main operations were not in the areas occupied by the Germans) even demanded 109 million francs in "compensation" for its "losses." Despite the unreasonable basis for these requests, the French government still complied with each and every one of the demands of the companies concerned. During the Depression of the 1930s, the monopolies not only escaped harm, but became even more powerful as a result of continuous government subsidies, purchase orders, and awards. During the Depression, state monopoly capital also grew substantially. For example, the number of companies that were nationalized increased greatly. This was an important measure adopted by the bourgeois government to shield the oligarchs of the monopolies from the impact of the Depression and to guarantee their high monopoly profits. Such a situation completely illustrates the fact that finance capital in France was already enjoying absolute control. As a result, they were able to use the governmental organizations under their control to brazenly plunder the national treasury.

Domestic class contradictions also became increasingly acute as a result of the further development of monopoly capital. Between the two world wars, workers' real wages declined even more as a result of increased taxes and rising commodity prices than they had previously. Workers' real wages even declined 9 percent during the industrial boom years of 1921–26. The conditions for

French workers deteriorated even more during the Great Depression. Falling production and plant closures created more and more unemployment. For example, unemployment in France reached more than half a million people in 1935. And half of the total number of industrial workers were really part-time employees. The wages of those still employed were cut back, but the workday was extended from twelve to fifteen hours. In the villages, the income of farmers once again fell because of the imposition of additional taxes, a decline in prices for agricultural products, and a broadening of the "price scissors" differential. Farmers' lives became extremely difficult.

Intensified class contradictions pushed forward the development of the workers' movement. The French proletariat once again launched a powerful revolutionary upsurge after the war. This was especially true after the birth of the French Communist party in 1921 when the workers' movement entered a new era. In the 1920s, French workers not only struggled to improve living and working conditions, to increase wages, to achieve an eight-hour workday, and to expand the power of their unions, but they also raised militant slogans that called for restricting the control of finance capital, demanded the reversion of large corporations, banks, and railroads to state ownership, and asked for support for the revolution in the Soviet Union. The intensified attack on the working people carried out by the monopoly bourgeoisie during the Depression of the early 1930s aroused even more powerful resistance from the broad masses. A mammoth workers' movement, just like a huge prairie fire, burned fiercely throughout the length and breadth of France.

The frightened French ruling class hurriedly sought to find counter-measures to resolve this situation. They tried hard to openly establish a fascist dictatorship within France in order to save themselves from their doom. In February 1934, the highest ruling group of French monopoly capital—the "two hundred families"—conspired to carry out a fascist coup d'état. This attempt, however, was frustrated because of the energetic counterattack of the workers and farmers. After this, the French proletariat and the French Communist party actively led the masses from various social strata in organizing a People's Front movement. This movement was opposed to fascism and the outbreak of a new war, and sought to secure democratic rights and improvement in the living conditions of the working people. In terms of economics, the People's Front demanded that the government: 1. regulate the Bank of France, 2. nationalize the military-industrial complex, 3. reform the tax system so that the big capitalists would have to pay taxes, and 4. establish a forty-hour work week without reduced wages. These four items basically reflected the demands of the masses of people.

Under pressure from its rank-and-file membership, and in order to confuse the masses, the leadership of the right wing of the French Socialist party temporarily made an alliance with the French Communist party and participated in the People's Front. Relying on the strength of the People's Front, Socialist party leaders like Leon Blum, Camille Chautemps, and Edouard Daladier served as

France's Prime Ministers between 1936 and 1938. In the beginning, they hypocritically implemented some of the demands of the People's Front. However, before too long, they tore off their masks and turned around to attack the mass movement of the people. Not only did they rescind some of the reforms which had already been partially implemented, but they also increased taxes, lengthened the working day, and even devalued the franc three times (which caused an inflationary price spiral). At the end of 1938, the Daladier government went so far as to carry out the brutal suppression of an anti-government general strike. In September 1939, it prohibited the French Communist party from carrying out any activities, and arrested many people throughout France. As soon as the sky was covered with dark clouds, the forces of reaction became extremely active. The monopoly bourgeoisie and their running dogs counted on this development so that they could stamp out the rising revolutionary movement. However, just as Chairman Mao has pointed out, "their various efforts to suppress the revolutionary people have, in the final analysis, only served to make that people's revolution more widespread and intense."[33] The struggle of the French proletariat against the rule of monopoly capital did not subside even up to the outbreak of the Second World War.

6. The Serious Damage Sustained by the French Economy during the Second World War and the Intensification of Class and National Contradictions

The French Economy Languishes under the Military Occupation of Fascist Germany

The Second World War broke out in full force in September 1939. France and its ally England immediately threw themselves into this imperialist war to redivide the world once again. France's war aims were: 1. to attempt to extricate itself from the continously deepening political and economic crisis domestically, 2. to weaken Germany's power, and 3. to consolidate and strengthen the rule of monopoly capital. However, France also entertained the vain hope of using Germany's fascist military power to destroy the socialist Soviet Union. As a result, France's ruling groups prior to the outbreak of the war not only did not take energetic measures to forestall the increasing threat of war from German fascism, but even went as far as to harm the sovereign rights of its allies. France openly collaborated with Hitler and vigorously abetted the aggressive arrogance of fascism. Even after the war broke out, the French government still continued to pursue its policy of conniving with the aggressors, and consistently failed to order its troops into battle. As a result, France's ruling groups pursued a self-destructive policy, like lifting a rock only to drop it on their own feet. Within a very short period of time, France was quickly occupied by German troops. In

June 1940, the Pétain government signed a humiliating armistice with the German fascists. France had now completely lost its independence, and its entire economy turned onto the road of war, serving the aggressive activities of German fascism.

Strictly speaking, not all of French territory was occupied by Germany prior to Fall 1942. At that time, the fascist troops directly occupied only about two-thirds of the entire country. The occupied areas included Paris as well as France's most important industrial regions in the north and in the east. The unoccupied region of the South of France was under the administration of the puppet government of the traitor Petain. However, the so-called unoccupied region of France was also likewise under the absolute control of German fascism. There was no real difference between it and the occupied areas. Moreover, by the end of 1942, not even this formal difference existed after Hitler's army directly occupied this region. As a result, it can be said that all of France was enslaved and plundered by German fascism during the entire period of the war. The damage and losses suffered by the French economy also cannot begin to approximate those suffered during the First World War.

During the Occupation, the Hitler gang of bandits not only looted France of vast quantities of gold reserves, foreign exchange, precious art objects, locomotives, ships, food, raw materials, and machinery, and deported large number of workers to Germany to work there as slave laborers, but they even imposed a huge "occupation fee" in France. Initially, this occupation fee was set at 400 million francs daily, but beginning in 1942, it went up to 500 million francs. In addition, France was also required to pay one billion francs every month to fascist Italy.

Industrial production in wartime France was in a state of utter paralysis and disintegration under the extreme devastation caused by the occupying forces. At the time, the only industries that could continue to survive were basically those sectors that served the needs of the German military. Moreover, industry as a whole was put under strict controls. Generally speaking, industrial leaders lacked even the power to invest in the renovation of plant and equipment. The occupation forces also used various kinds of compulsory methods to force many French companies to merge directly with German monopolies. This created even greater disorganization and fragmentation of France's industrial network. As a result, industrial production dropped precipitously. The general index of industrial production in 1941 stood at only 65 percent of that of 1938. It subsequently deteriorated year by year, and by 1944 had fallen to only 40 percent of the 1938 level. It must also be pointed out that 1938 was a Depression year in France, and production then was quite low. If production levels in 1944 didn't actually approach even half those achieved in 1938, then one can see the dire straits to which industrial production in wartime France had really sunk!

The status of agriculture during the Occupation was largely similar to that of industry. The main difficulties faced by agriculture were insufficient labor power and great shortages of tools and fertilizer. The size of harvests fell substantially as a result. According to 1943 statistics, the total value of France's entire agricultural production declined 40 percent compared to that of 1938. The deteriorating status of agriculture caused severe food shortages, and the working people of the entire country faced hunger and starvation for a prolonged period.

The decline in industrial and agricultural production had a severe impact on foreign trade. French imports in 1943 had decreased 69.7 percent compared to 1938 (and if one factors in the element of inflation, the real decline was more than 75 percent). Because of the frenzied plunder carried out by the Germans, exports fell merely 19.3 percent. While the vast majority of French exports during the war were shipped to Germany, the German occupation forces provided France with hardly anything of value.

In general, the entire French national economy suffered severe damage during the Second World War. According to incomplete statistics, the losses sustained by the French economy totalled a stupendous 4.893 trillion francs (calculated in 1945 prices). As a result, all of France looked like a disaster area, with scenes of devastation and poverty that met the eye wherever one looked. Irrespective of city or countryside, the picture was one of unrelieved desolation.

The Treasonable Activities of the Monopoly Bourgeoisie and the Anti-fascist Struggles of the People

Prior to the Second World War, France's monopoly bourgeoisie continuously enjoyed extremely close ties with Germany's financial oligarchy. After the outbreak of the war, the monopolies of both countries did not sever their contacts with each other even though military actions had already commenced between the two states. The monopolies still collaborated with each other and continued to maintain so-called "industrial ties." Even after June 1940, when France signed an armistice agreement after its defeat, France's monopoly bourgeoisie did not hesitate to sell out the interests of the French nation. It took further steps to barter away to German fascism whatever honor it still retained. They did this so that they could continue to do business as usual, in other words, collect high monopoly profits. In May 1941, the oligarchs of France's automobile monopolies were the first to slavishly express their wish to be of service, and concluded an "Agreement for Close Cooperation" with fascist Germany and Italy. After that, the monopoly capitalists of the metallurgical, electrical, chemical, textile, tanning, timber, and other industrial sectors vied with each other to be the first to sign various formal "joint venture agreements" with their German counterparts. Without a sense of shame, they willingly served as vassals of the enemy so that they could gain some advantage and reap windfall profits from the war.

During the occupation, the oligarchy that headed France's monopolies mobilized a total of 80 percent of France's industrial corporations to produce goods purchased by fascist Germany. According to statistics, Germany in the several years of its occupation used the great majority of almost 800 billion francs (this was approximately equivalent to the total amount of the "occupation fee" that it skimmed off from France) to pay for the goods that it had ordered. The French monopolies not only supplied Germany with the everyday products that it needed, but they also directly supplied the fascist military with more than 5 percent of its aircraft, 12 percent of its aircraft engines, more than 20 percent of its trucks, more than 10 percent of its locomotives, and large amounts of lethal weaponry, including chemical weapons and tanks. According to materials made public at the postwar Nüremburg International Court, the value of the automobiles, aircraft, ships, and material goods that France by itself produced for Hitler's fascist forces during the war was not less than 203 billion francs.

Because the French monopoly bourgeoisie spared no pains to offer their services to fascist military aggression, they also reaped astounding profits from these efforts. During the war, the rate of profit for some large enterprises and big corporations ran as high as 200 to 400 percent. Some enterprises still continued to do business as usual and made vast sums of money even though they had been forced to merge with German monopolies. For example, the oligarchs of the large "Metallurgy Committee" monopoly still received twenty billion francs in compensation even though their Lorraine Steel Company had been turned over to a German concern. Moreover, after the conclusion of the Second World War, when France had once again regained Lorraine, they bought back this company at an extremely low price.

During the period of the fascist occupation, France's monopoly bourgeoisie also made every effort to have the traitorous Vichy government (headed by Petain) adopt a series of measures to help them get rich. For example, the Vichy government set up a unified, specialized administrative branch—the Organization Committee—that increased managerial controls over raw materials, fuels, and other products in order to meet the military needs of the German fascists. This committee in reality was a nationwide organization of the big monopolies. France's "two hundred families" all sent their own representatives to participate on this committee. They used this committee to mutually feather their own individual nests and to share the loot, thereby greatly enhancing the power of monopoly capital. Even the fascist occupation forces made use of this committee to extend their control over all of France's economic activities, in order to make it serve their war of aggression even better.

While the monopoly capitalists were making huge fortunes from the war, the French working people were slipping into greater poverty. During the war, large numbers of the young and able-bodied were forcibly sent to Germany to work as slave laborers. Many died as a result of the cruel mental and physical conditions there. By the end of the war, approximately three million French workers still remained alive in Germany. Because they suffered a dual form of exploitation and oppression (oppressed by both the German occupation forces and their own country's monopoly capitalists), the living and working conditions of those workers still left behind in France became absolutely terrible. Labor intensity in factories and mines increased continuously, and the workweek was extended to more than sixty or seventy hours. Wages were frozen for a long time, but commodity prices continued to rise. Real wages for French workers in 1943 were only 60 percent of those of 1938. During the war, a system of rationing was implemented that fixed the quantity of goods available to each person. (In reality, this system of rationing only applied to the working people. The wealthy basically were not restricted by this arrangement at all.) However, the quantity of goods within the system of rationing was still not enough by half to maintain the most basic needs of the citizenry. For example, the daily food ration for each person amounted to only one hundred to 350 grams of coarse bread. Even the highest ration of 350 grams was subsequently reduced to 250 grams, and then once again to 200 grams. Moreover, goods whose supply was guaranteed under the rationing system were often not available for purchase for some several months at a time. Of course, various commodities were always available on the black market. However, because their prices in general were ten to twenty times higher than those of goods that were retained within the system of rationing, how could the broad masses of working people afford to buy them?! The situation of the small farmers in the villages was also similarly difficult. They were forced to hand over to the Occupation authorities all the agricultural goods that they had produced, but did so at very low prices. Afterwards they could once again buy back—at higher prices—a very small amount of grain.

The traitorous puppet government actively cooperated with the German Occupation Army not only in matters such as this, but also in setting up a terrorist, fascist dictatorship within France. All the political rights of the broad masses of citizens were flagrantly torn away. The various democratic organizations, without exception, were suppressed by force. Patriots and revolutionaries suffered cruel persecution. More than 600 thousand people were sent to prison or to concentration camps. They suffered inhuman treatment, and lived out their days in the shadow of death.

The bloodstained rule of the clique of French traitors and of the German fascists aroused strong resistance from the broad masses. The revolutionary people of France forgot neither class hatred nor national hatred. They heroically organized a massive Resistance movement from the very first day that the fascist armies set foot on French soil. Under the leadership of the French Communist party, the broad masses of workers and peasants organized revolutionary armed forces, set up an anti-fascist national front, and fought an unyielding war with the German aggressors and their running dogs, the Vichyites. Two hundred-fifty thousand fighters served in the Resistance in 1941. Not only did they carry weapons and fight bloody battles with the enemy, but they also organized workers' and shopkeepers' strikes in various places throughout France. They rescued French workers who were being shipped to Germany, undertook sniping operations against officials of the reactionary government as well as the officers and troops of Hitler's army, and destroyed communication lines. At the same time, General Charles de Gaulle—who had fled abroad—organized a Free French movement in London that was both anti-fascist and supportive of French independence. The French revolutionary armed forces liberated Paris in August 1944. By September of that year, all of France was basically liberated.

However, the fruits of victory paid for with the blood of the French people were very quickly seized by the big bourgeoisie. At that time, the leadership of the French Communist party (the largest political party within France, and enjoying substantial influence among the masses of the people) erroneously implemented a right opportunist line. They entertained the wishful notion of using parliamentary means to alter the policies of the bourgeoisie and the capitalist system. In order to gain high posts, with handsome salaries to match, the leadership group of the French Communist party disgracefully made compromises with the big bourgeoisie, turned over their weapons, and abandoned armed struggle. Within three years, they were driven out from the government by the forces of reaction, and immediately suffered cruel suppression. This historic error of the French Communist party must serve as a serious warning for the world's proletariat and revolutionary people.

5

Germany

Germany has been a late arrival to the cohort of major capitalist countries. Prior to the middle of the nineteenth century, Germany's economic development lagged substantially behind that of England, France, and the other advanced capitalist states. However, its rapid industrial growth during the latter half of the nineteenth century eventually enabled Germany to catch up with—and then even surpass—both France and England. As a result, Germany became Europe's leading industrial power. After entering its stage of monopoly capitalism, German imperialism vainly attempted to achieve world domination. Its aggressive character was thoroughly exposed when it became the chief instigator of two world wars. During those two wars, state monopoly capitalism in Germany grew to the highest levels ever achieved in the capitalist world at that time. However, even such concentrated power could not save Germany from its ultimate fate of defeat and destruction.

1. The Slow Development of the Economy Prior to the Eighteenth Century and the Emergence of Handicraft Workshops

The Decline of the Economy in the Sixteenth and Seventeenth Centuries

The German economy temporarily enjoyed a period of prosperity during the fourteenth and fifteenth centuries. During this time, Germany's urban, guild-dominated handicraft industries—such as weaving, mining, weapons manufacture, engraving, and printing—became famous throughout Europe. Because the trade routes from the Mediterranean to the North Sea and the Baltic Sea passed through Germany, commercial activities flourished and business became brisk in many German cities. In particular, the cities of the Hanseatic League[1] (located in northern Germany) enjoyed an even greater period of prosperity when they controlled Northern Europe's trade. A thriving industry and commerce also brought simultaneous progress in agriculture. Even the venerable system of corvee labor became obsolete and started to gradually crumble when the peasants in Germany's villages began to pay their rents in money or in kind. By the end of the fifteenth and the early sixteenth centuries, the sprouts of capitalism were already appearing in Germany's weaving and mining industries.

However, during the transition from feudalism to capitalism that took place during the sixteenth and seventeenth centuries, the German economy gradually declined and even stagnated. Ironically, this occurred just at the time when capitalist handicraft industries in the advanced nations of Western Europe were beginning to make substantial progress.

The important geographic discoveries that were made at the end of the fifteenth century were an external factor that contributed to Germany's economic decline. Once the great discoveries had been made, the trade routes of Western Europe shifted from the Mediterranean to the Atlantic Ocean, and no longer passed through Germany. Holland and England emerged to become the principal focal points for the new commercial routes, while the various German cities lost their hold over European trade and suffered a disastrous decline. In addition, both Sweden and Holland—though at different times—seized those German ports that enjoyed access to the North Sea and the Baltic Sea after the Thirty Years' War (1618–48). This turned Germany into a landlocked country and further separated it from the new trading centers of the Western World. Such adverse conditions as these led to the decline of the Hanseatic League and to the gradual weakening of German industry and commerce as a whole.

"External factors are the conditions for change, but internal factors are the basis for change."[2] The decline of the German economy in this period was principally due to the development of internal contradictions within German society. These internal contradictions stemmed from the feudal system: it was reactionary in nature and had actually become stronger over time rather than weaker. More specifically, the revival of serfdom in Germany, the strengthening of its guild system, and the further fragmentation of its feudal political system exemplified the reinvigorated nature of German feudalism. Let us examine the reasons behind each case.

The great German Peasant War (1524–25) was cruelly suppressed in the 1520s. After it had been put down—and especially after the Thirty Years' War (1618–48)—the system of serfdom was once again resuscitated in Germany. The landed aristocracy, in a tyrannical and brazen manner, plundered and enslaved the peasantry once again. As Engels wrote regarding mid-seventeenth-century German village conditions, "(s)erfdom today has become a universal system. A free peasant is just as scarce as a white crow."[3] This was particularly true in northeastern Germany where the peasantry had completely turned into serf-like farmhands, owning only a thatched cottage and a small vegetable plot. The chains of corvee labor were once again fastened on the bodies of the serfs and their wives and children. The revival of the feudal system of serfdom caused a significant deterioration in the already unfavorable situation which confronted the peasantry. The peasants' motivation for work dropped, and this seriously hampered the effort to raise the level of the forces of production in agriculture. It also had an adverse impact on the further development of industry and commerce. Engels pointed out that "the revival of serfdom throughout Germany was one of the factors that hindered the development of its industry in the seventeenth and eighteenth centuries."[4]

A guild system had become thoroughly entrenched in Germany ever since the Middle Ages. The guilds' tendency to protect their vested interests—by restricting membership and monopolizing certain jobs—even intensified once the economic situation deteriorated after the sixteenth century. They increasingly harrassed nonguild handicraft workers. And the disputes that flared up between the various guilds regarding the scope of their respective activities also grew more and more fierce. The forces of an increasingly obstinate traditional guild system shackled the progress of industrial and commercial activity in Germany's cities, and stunted the growth of the newly rising bourgeoisie.

Germany's feudal political fragmentation became even more accentuated when these traditional forces of political decentralization raised their heads in the context of the urban and rural economy. Of course, political fragmentation existed in Germany since the Middle Ages. However, after the Thirty Years' War, the Holy Roman Empire (which nominally ruled Germany) was carved up further into 360 tiny self-governing states. At that time, countless internal tariffs were imposed within Germany due to the proliferation of dukedoms and principalities and the general condition of political fragmentation. A wide variety of commercial laws and regulations, as well as systems of weights and measures, were also in effect. The large number of different currencies then in circulation throughout Germany created an extremely chaotic economic situation. More than six thousand different kinds of currency—give or take a few—were in use in the various German states. All these factors severely hampered the development of a commodity economy and capitalism. At the same time, the endless disputes and wrangles among the dukes and princes of the various states—even their collusion with foreign powers—embroiled Germany in chronic warfare. This constant political instability caused even greater and more continuous damage to Germany's productive forces, thereby undermining its economic vitality.

German industry and commerce declined precipitously after the sixteenth century as a result of the various developments mentioned above. For example, six thousand weavers had been employed in the handicraft industry in the southern German city of Augsburg at the beginning of the sixteenth century. By the seventeenth century, however, only five hundred remained at their jobs. The production of woven cotton in other German cities also fell by 90 percent. The situation in mining and metallurgy was even bleaker. German commerce also lost the independence and prosperity that it had once enjoyed, and now became merely a brokerage for Dutch, English, and French merchant capital.

The Initial Development of Handicraft Workshops in the Eighteenth Century

Germany's commodity economy gradually revived at the end of the seventeenth century. Capitalist handicraft workshops now appeared, and had—by the eighteenth century—achieved a certain degree of growth. Industrial activity in the villages was the first to accelerate. In order to pay the increasingly higher taxes and rents demanded by their aristocratic landlords, the poor German peasants—serfs, in reality—had to sell the products from their sideline household handicraft occupations in order to supplement their incomes. Merchant-capitalists now took advantage of the economic predicament confronting these serf-like peasants, and they made use of the favorable conditions that existed in the countryside because the power of the urban-based guilds did not extend that far. Merchant-capitalists now began to purchase, at low prices, the products the peasants made in their sideline household handicraft industries. Eventually they forced the peasants to work directly for them. Merchant-capitalists allocated raw materials to the peasants and paid them meager wages. In return, the peasants produced such items as yarn, lace, and woolen and hemp fabrics. These merchant-capitalists gradually organized group after group of these scattered handicraft workshops that were under their control. The dyeing of the fabrics and the final touch-up work were done at a centralized handicraft workshop that had been built by the merchant-capitalist. The more prosperous merchant-capitalists gradually forced even the local handicraft guilds to work for them. As a result, many urban handicraft workers eventually became financially dependent on these merchant-capitalists.

At the turn of the eighteenth century, tens of thousands of Protestants from both the French and Spanish-ruled Netherlands—and from Czechoslovakia, Switzerland, and other countries—emigrated in waves to the urban areas of eastern Germany. They fled because they suffered religious persecution in their native lands at the hands of Catholics. The vast majority of these Protestants, however, were skilled handicraft workers and merchants. They carried with them not only capital and advanced technology, but also their accumulated experience in organizing handicraft workshops. The influx of these Protestant immigrants now accelerated the development of a workshop handicraft industry in Germany's cities.

The rise of Prussia (a militaristic, feudal kingdom that arose in 1701) also stimulated the development of a German workshop handicraft industry. During the latter half of the eighteenth century, the King of Prussia, Frederick the II, energetically promoted policies intended to assist industry and commerce. He did this in order to create a strong economic and financial base that could support a powerful, aggressive military force. The government provided subsidies to these newborn industrial and commercial ventures, granted them preferential tax treatment, set up a system of protective tariffs that would shield them from foreign competition, and compelled itinerant peasants to work in such handicraft workshops.

This was how Germany's handicraft workshop industries gradually developed. In the front ranks of this growth were the metallurgical, metalworking, textile, glass, and porcelain industries of the Rhine River region, and the silver and copper mining, metalworking, and textile industries of Saxony. By 1786, a total of 165,000 people were employed in Germany's workshop handicraft industries. Their total annual output value came to ninety-one million marks. The city of Berlin accounted for ten thousand of those workers and eighteen million marks of that output.

However, it must also be pointed out that the growth of a workshop handicraft industry in Germany during the eighteenth century was still rather limited in scope. In this period, the workers in the handicraft workshops were still either semi-serfs or guild handicraftsmen. They had not yet become employees in the pure sense of the term. The merchant brokers continued to rely on various methods of feudal exploitation. While they were indeed merchants as well as employers, these merchant brokers were not yet industrial capitalists. The handicraft workshops basically still remained a scattered and fragmented form of production relying on the exploitation of vast numbers of household handicraft workers as its foundation. Right up to the end of the eighteenth century, capitalist relations of production developed extremely slowly and very tentatively in Germany. The existence of feudalism in Germany's urban and rural areas, and the lack of national unity served as serious impediments to rapid growth. Germany was still in the initial phase of a capitalist workshop handicraft industry just at the moment when England was lauching its own industrial revolution.

2. The Disintegration of Feudalism and the Establishment of Capitalism

The Extensive Growth of a Workshop Handicraft Industry during the First Half of the Nineteenth Century, and the Beginnings of Germany's Industrial Revolution

A bourgeois revolution broke out in France in 1789. "The French Revolution struck the confused world of this so-called Germany like a thunderbolt. Its impact was enormous."[5] Peasant uprisings against feudalism quickly engulfed every region of Germany—beginning in Alsace—from 1789 to 1793. Workers' assistants in the handicraft industries in many German cities also participated in a series of demonstrations and strikes, and rose up to oppose their cruel exploitation. Although these uprisings did not succeed, they nevertheless shook the foundations of serfdom as well as the guild system in Germany.

In 1792, the French army defeated a joint Austrian-Prussian invading force, and took advantage of its victory to occupy the left bank of Germany's Rhine River basin. Napoleon on several subsequent occasions militarily defeated the forces of the various German dukes and princes, and eventually extended his control to include all of Germany. Napoleon's military victories dealt a further blow to the feudal system in Germany. On the left bank of the Rhine River basin, the French occupation army carried out a series of bourgeois reforms. It abolished the feudal rights of the aristocracy; lifted from the peasantry its obligation to perform corvee labor or pay rent to the landlords; it confiscated and sold the lands that belonged to the church and to the criminals; declared "freedom for industrial activities" in the cities and abolished guild restrictions; and put into effect a new bourgeois civil code. Influenced by these kinds of developments, some regions on the right bank of the Rhine River were also compelled to implement similar reforms, though to a different extent. In order to facilitate his own rule, Napoleon also forced the numerous small German principalities to merge with each other, thereby ameliorating Germany's abnormally fragmented political situation. These changes created an advantageous environment for the development of German capitalism. Other steps also promoted the development of German industry. For example, Napoleon's policy of sealing off the Continent from England, Prussia's imposition of protective tariffs after the defeat of Napoleon, and the importation of English machinery into Germany after England announced in 1825 that it would lift its ban on the export of such machinery were all helpful measures in this regard.

Germany's workshop handicraft industry grew extensively in the first three decades of the nineteenth century. The utilization of machinery also increased. The mining, metallurgical, and metalworking industries were principally concentrated on the left bank of the Rhine River; advanced cotton and hemp-weaving industries arose in Saxony and Silesia. The first water-powered spinning Jenny was installed in 1783 in Elberfeld. By 1814, Saxony by itself already accounted for more than 270,000 mechanized spindles. By 1831, there were more than one thousand mechanized cotton textile looms in operation throughout Germany.

The establishment of a German tariff league (or *Zollverein*) gave a powerful impetus to the further development of German industry, and brought about a genuine revolution in industry. After the Napoleonic wars, some thirty-eight states still existed within the boundaries of Germany; feudal political fragmentation continued to hamper the formation of a domestic market and the development of industry and commerce. When political unification could not be achieved, the question of tariff unification rose to the top of the agenda. The impetus which came from Prussia's newly risen bourgeoisie finally resulted in the organization of a German customs union in 1834. This alliance brought together eighteen major states. They accounted for three-fourths of Germany's population and two-thirds of its territory at that time. The most important provisions of the *Zollverein* (or customs union) demanded the following: a) the abolition of internal tariffs, and the simultaneous creation of a duty-free trade market by the various members of the alliance; and b) the establishment of a uniform tariff system and uniform tariff rates on foreign imports. The establishment of the *Zollverein* was an important step in Germany's progress in economic and political unification.

Germany began its industrial revolution during the 1830s. The earliest to become an advanced sector was the textile industry—just as in England and France. Cotton spinning and weaving led the way, and developed rapidly on the foundations of a factory system. There were already 313 spinning factories and 750 thousand mechanized textile looms among the various states of the *Zollverein* in 1846. Chemnitz in Saxony was the center of the cotton spinning and weaving industry, and was already at that time called "Germany's Manchester." Mining and metallurgy also made considerable progress, and were centered in the Ruhr and Saar regions along the Rhine River. The annual coal production of this region exceeded three million tons during the decade of the 1840s. Pig iron output came to approximately 200 thousand tons. The first steamship appeared on the Rhine in 1824. In 1835, the first railway—though only eight kilometers long—was opened to traffic between Nuremburg and Fürth. The first steamship companies were established soon afterwards. By 1848, Germany's railway network had reached 2,500 kilometers in length.

However, even by the end of the 1830s, Germany's industrial revolution had not yet passed its initial stage. The handicraft workshops and small handicraft industries still dominated industry; the output share that came from factory production was not large. Germany's own machine manufacturing industry was still basically nonexistent. The vast majority of its machinery was imported. Except for coal mining and railroad mileage, German industrial levels were clearly inferior to those of France, and lagged considerably behind those of England. Germany was still an agricultural nation where more than 70 percent of its people were engaged in farming.

The Bourgeois Revolution of 1848

The various social contradictions within Germany in the 1840s were extremely complicated and sharp. Many exactions pressed down heavily on the backs of the semi-serf peasants: the rights of the feudal lords, ransom money, death taxes, a use tax on livestock, taxes on medical treatment, protection money, a 10 percent tax on slaughtering animals, a tax on the right to make declarations, a tax on beekeeping, rental fees for candles, a tax on the use of adjoining land, fees for affixing a seal, the tithe for the church, rent, inheritance taxes, and so forth—what Marx called "this vast heap of medieval obligations and taxes, this vast heap of moldy, putrid trash left over from antiquity."[6] The vast peasantry was permeated with hatred for the system of serfdom, and continuously rebelled against feudalism. Factory workers and handicraft workers faced a poverty-stricken, inhuman existence under the dual oppression of both feudalism and capitalism.

Engels penned these words about the workers in Elberfeld: The transport workers were "totally demoralized people, with no fixed abode or definite employment, who crawl out of their refuges, haystacks, stables, etc., at dawn, if they have not spent the night on a dungheap or on a staircase." Factory laborers continuously "work in low rooms where people breathe more coal fumes and dust than oxygen—and in the majority of cases beginning already at the age of six." "The weavers, who have individual looms in their homes, sit bent over them from morning till night, and dessicate their spinal marrow in front of a hot stove." Some who had become alcoholics had previously been healthy craftsmen, "but three years of such a life suffice to ruin them physically and mentally: three out of five die from consumption, and it is all due to drinking spirits."[7] These shocking vignettes of Elberfeld epitomized the miserable life faced by the vast numbers of German workers at that time. Driven beyond endurance, Silesian weavers rebelled in 1844. Several thousand weavers sang battle songs like "Bloody Judgment," demolished the home of the factory owner as well as the factory buildings, burned the merchants' ledgers, and fought bravely against the capitalists and the reactionary troops sent to suppress the uprising. The Silesian weavers' uprising indicated that workers were already beginning to become conscious of their own class interests. It symbolized the fact that the working class had stepped on to the stage of history and had become a powerful political force. The young German bourgeoisie also challenged the rule of the landed aristocracy. They demanded national unification, the abolition of feudalism, and recognition of their right to share national political power. Germany had become a volcano that was about to experience a huge eruption.

Poor harvests in 1845 and 1846, coupled with an economic crisis in 1847, further intensified the distress and hostility of the masses of people. Revolution was imminent. The February 1848 revolution in Paris also exerted an influence on the German people. It was under these circumstances that a bourgeois revolution finally broke out in Germany in 1848. The citizens of Berlin launched an armed uprising on March 18, 1848. After a tenacious battle that lasted eighteen hours, the King of Prussia begged for mercy and asked to surrender. At the same time, uprisings also broke out in the various German principalities, and the masses of people everywhere achieved victory. Vast numbers of peasants attacked the castles of the landed aristocracy. They burned the contracts that they had originally signed to buy out their feudal obligations to the aristocracy. Then they forced the feudal aristocrats to guarantee that they would not subsequently reimpose taxes. The feudal aristocracy was compelled to turn over political power to the bourgeiosie under these conditions. However, the German bourgeoisie—weak and long dependent on the feudal aristocracy—was especially fearful of the massive revolutionary strength of the proletariat. As a result, as soon as they achieved political power, they quickly collaborated with the feudal aristocracy and betrayed the revolution. The feudal aristocracy staged a comeback in July 1849.

The defeat of this bourgeois revolution was proclaimed when the feudal military forces of Wittenburg dissolved the bourgeois Frankfurt Assembly.

Germany's 1848 revolution was a classic example of an incomplete bourgeois revolution. Marx pointed out that: "the German Revolution of 1848 was merely a *caricature of the French Revolution* of 1789." "It was truly a tempest in a teapot."[8] The German Revolution of 1848 left many things undone: for example, it did not resolve the basic task of national unification, and it was unable to destroy the feudal system at a single stroke like the French revolution accomplished in 1789. However, the German ruling class, frightened by the revolution, felt compelled to implement certain social reforms. This caused further damage to the feudal system, and as a result, to a certain degree cleared the path for the development of German capitalism.

The "Prussian Model" of Capitalist Agricultural Development

The development of capitalism in German agriculture in the nineteenth century became a representative type which Lenin characterized as the "Prussian Model." By the early 1870s, this type of developmental model had achieved a decisive victory in the majority of Germany's villages.

Under pressure from France's bourgeois revolution and from Napoleon's control of Germany in the early nineteenth century, Prussia's Prime Ministers Stein and Hardenburg—who represented the interests of the landed aristocracy—first put into effect the October Decrees (1807), and then instituted the Readjustment Decrees (1811) in order to "reform" the system of feudal serfdom. However, these reforms did not tamper with any aspect of the system of landownership dominated by the Junkers—Prussia's landed aristocracy. Stein simply made a verbal announcement that the peasantry's personal dependency on the landlord class was abolished as of that moment. Hardenburg stipulated that if a peasant wished to free himself from his feudal obligations, then that peasant could either pay a huge "buy-out fee" to the landlord, or hand over—without any compensation—a piece of land equivalent in value to that buy-out fee. This "fee," in general, amounted to anywhere from one-third to one-half of the value of the land. The Prussian government subsequently enacted legislation that restricted even this practice: only prosperous peasants could qualify to buy out their feudal obligations. Germany's bourgeois revolution of 1848 substantially speeded up the pace of the agricultural reforms. The Prussian government enacted a new Readjustment Law in March 1850. Although it protected (just like previous legislation had done) the system of landownership enjoyed by the Junkers, it did stipulate that those ancillary feudal obligations owed by the peasantry would be abolished without any required compensation. In addition, it permitted all peasants, not just prosperous ones, to buy out their major feudal obligations (such as various kinds of compulsory corvee labor and land rents)—but at a high price (equivalent to a sum of money eighteen times the annual rent paid in cash). At the same time, the government also set up a land bank that specialized in handling the payment of such redemption monies. After this, the process of buying out one's feudal obligations greatly accelerated. The number of peasant households who bought back their feudal obligations every year in Prussia increased ninefold during the decade from 1850 to 1860 as compared to the period from 1816 to 1848. By 1865, approximately 1.5 million peasant households had completed the formalities involved in redeeming their feudal obligations. The redemption process in the other German principalities also moved forward rapidly.

This type of "buy-out" in reality "was a kind of tribute tax shouldered in the development of society. It was a kind of tribute tax paid by the serfs to the big landlords."[9] The buy-out process, which took half a century, enabled the Junker landlord class to pocket a vast sum of ransom money. For example, in Prussia alone, this amount came to between 900 million and one billion marks. It also enabled the Junkers to seize even more land. As a result, small peasant households (which accounted for 71.4 percent of the total number of German farming households) owned merely 9 percent of the total amount of arable land by the early 1860s. However, the Junkers and rich peasants (who accounted for 28.6 percent of the total number of agricultural households) owned 91 percent of the total amount of arable land. With even more money and even more land now at their disposal, the Junker landlords gradually transformed their own estates by using bourgeois management methods. They utilized more and more machinery and fertilizer; they intensified the squeeze on the farm workers in order to raise labor productivity; and they actively expanded the scope of capitalist management. However, the farm workers on the Junker estates still retained their semi-serf status. Economically, they were subject to the dual exploitation of both capitalism and feudalism. Politically, they had no rights to speak of. Forming a labor association or boycotting field work was strictly prohibited. Moreover, there was the ever-present danger that they could be imprisoned at any time by the landlords.

The existence of vast numbers of semi-serf farm workers hampered the widespread application of new technology in agriculture, and also hampered any rapid increase in the forces of production in agriculture. Their frightful poverty was also disadvantageous to the expansion of a domestic market and the development of a national economy. The course of capitalist development in the villages—in fact the development of the entire economy—was consequently much slower in Germany during the middle of the nineteenth century than it was in the United States. However, the retention of many feudal remnants in Germany concurrently strengthened the ruling status of the Junker landlord class domestically. Their interests gradually became identical with those of the bourgeoisie. The constricted nature of the domestic market, coupled with Junker greed in expanding their landed estates, brought both sides into close collaboration on political and economic issues. Both groups exerted every effort to capture foreign markets and territory, and turned Germany into a militaristic country of an exceptionally aggressive character.

As the above comments illustrate, "the Prussian Model" of capitalist agricultural development in Germany embodied the following unique characteristics. First, it was achieved on the basis of a series of top-down "agricultural reforms" carried out by the landed aristocracy. Second, the large estates (run by landlords and farmed by serfs) were eventually transformed into Junker-bourgeois farms as a result of a lengthy process of development. On the one hand, the Junker landlords gradually became bourgeoisified. On the other hand, the vast number of semi-serf peasants became destitute farmers and hired hands. Third, because the system of landownership of the Junkers was left intact, "capitalism for a long time retained semi-feudal traits."[10] As a result, the process of capitalist development slowed down, and the social and political rule of the Junkers became consolidated. Therefore, the "Prussian Model" was a path of reform that was not only suited to the development of capitalism, but also preserved the remnants of feudalism to the greatest extent possible. Just as Lenin pointed out, it was this developmental model that enabled "the landlord economy based on the system of serfdom to gradually transform itself into a Junker-type bourgeois economy. At the same time, this process also led to the emergence of a small group of 'wealthy farmers' who, within a few decades, subjected the peasantry to the cruelest forms of expropriation and oppression."[11]

However, when compared with the system of feudal serfdom, the "Prussian Model" of capitalist agrarian development still represented a step forward. To a certain degree it promoted the development of German agriculture. As the management of Junker farms continuously improved, the planting of crops and animal husbandry both expanded, and industries devoted to the processing of agricultural products began to flourish. By the middle of the nineteenth century, the German potato and beet harvests ranked first in the world. The number of horses, cattle, sheep, and pigs also increased, doubling and even quadrupling in size. Prussian liquor distilled from potatoes was sold abroad, and became Prussia's representative on the world market. The Junkers made a fortune in beer brewing. They gradually became industrial capitalists, and strengthened their own political and economic status in Germany, and even in Prussia itself.

The Rapid Growth and Economic Boom during Germany's Industrial Revolution of the 1850s and 1860s

Germany's industrial revolution went through three stages, with its initial stage taking place in the 1830s and 1840s. The second stage occurred in the 1850s and 1860s after the bourgeois revolution of 1848. This was a stage of decisive importance when industry boomed and when large-scale factories and the capitalist system were established throughout Germany. The third stage took place after the creation of the German Reich in 1871. The industrial revolution then entered its final period.

The new situation that emerged after Germany's bourgeois revolution of 1848 prepared favorable conditions for the industrial upsurge of the 1850s and 1860s. The victory of the "Prussian agricultural model" and the disintegration of the system of serfdom created the prerequisites for industrial development. A portion of the vast amount of "buy-out" money was turned into industrial capital; large numbers of impoverished peasants entered factories and mines as mobile labor power; and the constantly increasing needs of the Junker farms (which had expanded their own operations) opened up a market for industrial goods. The urban guild system gradually weakened and was abolished in 1869, facilitating the rise of large-scale factories. At the same time, the *Zollverein* was expanded in 1852 to embrace all of Germany. In 1863, the various German principalities unified their trade laws, their laws on negotiable bills, and their systems of weights and measures. These steps further reduced the unfavorable impact caused by Germany's internal political divisions, promoted the unification of a domestic market, and facilitated the development of a capitalist industry and commerce.

Under conditions such as these, the sudden rise of a militaristic Prussia directly stimulated an upsurge in German industry, and especially in heavy industry. Guided by Bismarck's reactionary policy of "blood and iron," the Prussian government in these decades made every effort to unify Germany by force and to seek hegemony over Europe as a whole. Preparing for war, the government stepped up the construction of railroad lines and purchased vast quantities of military goods. Railroad construction, stimulated by Prussia, now surged forward throughout Germany. The railway boom created an enormous and concurrent demand for coal, rails, locomotives, and rolling stock, thereby energetically promoting the expansion of coal mining, metallurgy, machine manufacturing, and other sectors of heavy industry. It also triggered a mania for creating new companies. Marx wrote the following on the contemporary situation in 1859: "All the rage at the moment is to try to make a fortune, to look to the future, to open new mines, to build new factories, to construct new railroads, and especially to invest in joint-stock companies and to speculate in stocks."[12] Several tens of banks opened for business one after the other, and joint-stock companies rose up like bamboo shoots after a spring rain. In Prussia alone some 295 joint-stock companies—with a total capitalization reaching 2.4 billion marks—were established in the short period of twenty years. Capital floating throughout German society was gathered together in large quantities and invested in production. At the same time, foreign capital from Holland, Belgium, England, France, and other countries also poured in a steady stream into the Rhine River region where rich profits were to be made. The difficulties that stemmed from Germany's insufficient primitive capital accumulation were overcome. Its industrial revolution surged forward swiftly.

Coal production in Germany went from 6.7 million tons to thirty-four million tons in the years 1850 to 1870, or a 5.1-fold increase; pig iron production went from 210 thousand tons to 1.39 million tons, a 6.6-fold increase; steel production went from 5,900 tons to 170,000 tons, an almost twenty-nine-fold increase; cotton consumption more than quadrupled, going from eighteen thousand tons to eighty-one thousand tons. The use of steam engines gradually became more common, and railroad transportation also became increasingly advanced. During this same period of time, steam power in Germany went from 260 thousand horsepower to 2.48 million horsepower, an increase of approximately nine times. Railroad mileage more than tripled, increasing from six thousand kilometers to 18,876 kilometers. Rail freight increased 28.1-fold. As Engels pointed out, Germany after the 1848 revolution "achieved more in twenty years than in the previous century."[13] Generally speaking, German industrial production in these twenty years approximately tripled.

Germany's own machine manufacturing industry was established during this period of time. If during the early 1850s Germany sought equipment and technical assistance from English companies to build its own railroads, then by the late 1860s, German capitalists had now already committed themselves to building railroads as far away as Russia and Romania. At this time, the rate of growth of the production of the means of production surpassed that of the production of consumer goods. The swift development of heavy industry was the cornerstone for Germany's industrial upsurge of the 1850s and 1860s, and became an important characteristic of Germany's industrial revolution. Germany elbowed its way into the ranks of the advanced capitalist states because it relatively quickly put the focus of its industrial development on heavy industry. As a result, it rapidly overcame its backward situation. Germany's share of total world industrial production stood at 13.2 percent in 1870, which exceeded that of France but was still considerably small when compared to England and the United States. At this time, the industrial revolution in the advanced areas of Germany had already been basically completed. However, large-scale capitalist industry could not achieve a dominant position throughout all of Germany because Germany was still not unified and the economic development of its various regions was extremely uneven.

The various contradictions inherent in the capitalist system were also clearly revealed in Germany following the development of large-scale industry. Two economic crises erupted in 1857 and 1866 after the crisis of 1847. To varying degrees, these crises struck at the textile industry, the metallurgical industry, and foreign trade, and they caused repeated setbacks to the progress achieved in industrial development. Class contradictions in Germany also became increasingly sharp. The vast numbers of destitute farmhands and small farmers who had bought out their feudal obligations still had to cope with many feudal remnants which, like poisonous snakes, continued to be tightly fastened around their bodies. At the same time a new form of exploitation, capitalism, opened its bloody mouth, intending to gobble them up. The situation facing industrial workers was also extremely arduous. In the 1860s, masses of textile spinners were packed into tiny, damp, and unventilated factory workshops all day long, working fifteen hours from morning until evening. There was no time set aside for eating meals. The best that workers could do was to hang a white pail containing food (like potatoes) around their necks. When the machinery unexpectedly broke down or the yarn snapped, the workers would quickly grab a bite to eat. Working under conditions like this year in and year out left the faces of the workers pale and sallow, atrophied their muscles, and ruined their health. Coal miners in Saxony were required to work underground for twelve hours at a stretch, yet their average daily wage came to only a little more than one mark. And they frequently suffered from the threat of being dismissed or being laid off. Generally speaking, the wages of German factory workers were especialy low, being one-fourth to four-fifths that of the wages of American, English, or French workers. As the contradictions between the great mass of German factory workers and the bourgeoisie sharpened day after day, so also did strikes become more frequent. Unions also gradually appeared in the 1860s and grew in strength.

Since the 1840s, Germany was a country facing many social contradictions. Economically, the fetters of feudal relations remained a serious impediment, while at the same time, exploitation from capitalism was rapidly expanding. Politically, an aristocratic landlord class held control. Its contradictions with the broad mass of working people were extremely sharp, and its contradictions with the bourgeoisie were also growing. The tasks of a bourgeois revolution urgently needed resolution since German unification had not yet been realized. At the same time, a German proletariat had already appeared. The German proletariat learned from the already rather advanced experiences, class consciousness, and militancy of the working classes of England, France, and other countries to become a serious threat to the feudal aristocracy and the bourgeoisie. All of these factors caused Germany to become the focal point of the various contradictions of contemporary European society. This social development raised the need for working out a solution to the theory and tactics of a proletarian revolution. The tradition of German classical philosophy—as well as a historical environment where the German working class had carried forward its struggles under mature conditions—were two additional factors that were particularly advantageous to the resolution of this task. As a result, Germany became the home of Marxism.

3. The Creation of Germany's "Junker Bourgeois" Reich

Industrial and Agricultural Development after the Franco-Prussian War

A militaristic Prussian government launched a series of wars in the middle of the nineteenth century with the aim of unifying Germany by force. After defeating Denmark in 1864 and Austria-Hungary in 1866, Prussia attacked France in 1870. In the end, Prussia was victorious and compelled the French government to agree to the humiliating Treaty of Frankfurt. Several new conditions appeared after this war which vigorously promoted the further development of German capitalism and, in addition, accelerated Germany's transition to monopoly capitalism.

Prussia achieved the unification of Germany after defeating France. On January 18, 1871, the King of Prussia, William I, established a centralized German Reich and ended Germany's chronic feudal political fragmentation.[14] The principal controls over military affairs, foreign policy, legislation, and economics—powers that had previously belonged to the various principalities—were now centralized in the hands of the imperial government. The Reich government not only unified the currency system throughout the country, but also standardized the system of managing and operating Germany's transportation and communications networks. It instituted a protective tariff in 1879. All these measures accelerated the creation of a unified domestic market, enhanced the competitive strength of German capital, and cleared away the obstacles on the road of advance for large-scale capitalist industry.

By the terms of the Treaty of Frankfurt, Germany not only took all of Alsace and part of Lorraine from France, but also extorted a huge indemnity of five billion gold francs. Alsace and Lorraine were advanced industrial and mining areas. Their acquisition not only expanded Germany's cotton textile industry by more than half, but also provided Germany's steel and chemical industries with rich iron ore resources and sylvite deposits. The indemnity of several billion francs was used for industrial construction and increased military expenditures, and set off a new flurry of creating companies. There were far more railroads, factories, and mines constructed in the four years after the Franco-Prussian War than had been built in the previous twenty-five. Stalin pointed out: "Germany accelerated its own industrialization as a result of its victory in the war against France in the 1870s. At that time Germany extorted an indemnity of five billion francs from the French people, and invested this money into its own industry."[15] Germany's road to industrialization represented a striking example of how "one country used military force against another in order to extort an indemnity."[16]

Victory in the Franco-Prussian War not only boosted Germany's status within Europe to an unprecedented degree, but also whetted the appetite of the Junkers and Germany's bourgeoisie. These late-arriving German robbers were infatuated with seizing foreign markets and colonies and striving to achieve domination over the world. As a result, they did everything they could to expand Germany's preparations for war. Government military expenditures rose steeply to pay for the huge armaments and naval buildup. At the same time, the government accelerated railroad construction to facilitate the mobility of its military forces. German military expenditures in the period from 1879 to 1914 increased almost fivefold. Between 1871 and 1914, the total amount of Germany's steamship tonnage increased from eighty-two thousand tons to 5.1 million tons. Its railroad network expanded from twenty-one thousand to sixty-two thousand kilometers. During this process, Germany's many industrial sectors—especially those in heavy industry—received more and more contracts for goods, and grew with unprecedented speed.

From the 1870s right up to the eve of the First World War, German industry advanced in leaps and bounds. This was due not only to the various kinds of changes brought about by the Franco-Prussian War, but also to the continued utilization of the newest technological achievements from other countries as well as the energetic efforts to keep the level of industrial wages low. During this period of time, Germany's industrial production increased 5.7-fold. When we speak of the speed of that industrial development, we can say that Germany's far exceeded that of France and England, yet was slower than that of Japan and the United States.

German heavy industry grew even more rapidly during these years. The important role once played by light industry had now been assigned to heavy industry. Between 1870 and 1913, for example, Germany's production of the means of production increased 7.5-fold while the production of consumer goods increased only 3.4-fold. Coal production went from thirty-four million tons to 277.3 million tons; the amount of pig iron produced went from 1.39 million tons to 19.31 million tons; steel increased from 170 thousand tons to 18.33 million tons. These increases were 8.2-fold, 13.9-fold, and 108-fold, respectively. The rapid growth of mining and metallurgy played an enormous role in the entire range of industrial development.

Beginning in the 1890s, Germany's machine-building industry developed at an unprecedented speed. The electrical machinery and shipbuilding industries both achieved prominent successes. The output value of electrical machinery went from seventy-eight million to 368 million marks in the period 1895–1910. Germany did not possess any large-scale shipbuilding industry prior to 1896, yet was producing an average of approximately 305 thousand tons annually from 1899 to 1913. The production of comparatively precise instruments—such as tool-making lathes and so on—also grew continuously during the same time period. New industries (like chemicals and electrical goods) developed even more rapidly. On the eve of the twentieth century, Germany's production of basic chemical products (like acids, alkalis, etc.) ranked first in the world. Its dyes, medicines, and photographic chemicals were also world renowned. "The electrical industry is the sector most capable of representing the newest technological achievements of late nineteenth, early twentieth century capitalism. It is the most advanced in the United States and Germany, the two most advanced and newest capitalist countries."[17] In the twenty-two years between 1891 and 1913, the total output value of Germany's electrical industry went up twenty-nine times. As power plants that produced electricity increased in number and an electric power grid expanded throughout Germany, the use of electric power also gradually increased in areas like street lighting, streetcar transportation, telecommunications, and industrial production. The electrification of industry was rapidly achieved.

Germany completed its industrial revolution by the end of the 1870s and the early 1880s. By the early twentieth century, capitalist industrialization had also been achieved in Germany. In 1895, Germany's industrial workers and their family dependents numbered 35 million, or 67 percent of Germany's total population. Taking the total number of industrial workers in the whole country as the baseline, the proportion of those engaged in heavy industry increased from 35.1 percent to 54.5 percent in the time period from 1895 to 1913. On the eve of the First World War, Germany had already established a rather complete industrial system based on the most advanced technology, and had become a capitalist industrial power with heavy industry as its leading sector.

The high speed of its industrial development further elevated Germany's status within the capitalist world. By the early twentieth century, German industry—after completing its transition to monopoly capitalism—had left England behind. In 1913, Germany's share of total world industrial production stood at 15.7 percent, second only to the United States. Germany's rocket-like economic development and the rapidity with which it overtook England (that venerable capitalist country) revealed an intensification of the uneven economic development of the various capitalist countries in the era of imperialism.

As industry developed rapidly, Germany's agriculture also grew to a certain extent. During this period of time, Germany's annual output of various grains increased between 60 percent and 93 percent, depending on the grain involved. The number of heads of cattle and horses increased by approximately one-third, while the number of pigs more than tripled. However, an increase in the overall level of productive forces in German agriculture came rather slowly due to various kinds of usurious practices maintained by capitalism, and by the vestiges of feudalism left behind in both city and countryside. These feudal vestiges hindering agrarian development included the Junkers' colossal waste of land and capital, in other words, their construction of sumptuous villas, and their maintenance of not only vast enclosed tracts for hunting, but also scenic wooded areas for sightseeing. On the eve of the First World War, one-third of the wheat needed in Germany, half of the oils and fats, a majority of its meat and fish, all of its cotton and natural rubber, and many other kinds of raw materials had to be imported in order to satisfy domestic needs. The relatively backward condition of German agriculture, compared with that of industry, became increasingly worse. It could not satisfy by a wide margin the growing needs of industry and the urban areas for both raw materials as well as foodstuffs.

Economic crises also increased in both severity and frequency after Germany's transition to monopoly capitalism. Five industrial crises erupted one after the other within less than half a century. The massive industrial construction and speculative frenzy that followed the Franco-Prussian War led to the violent crisis of 1873. The general index of German industrial production fell 6.1 percent during the crisis. Moreover, the duration of the economic slump was rather long. Only in 1876 did industrial production revive to reach its predepression peaks. The chronic agricultural crisis that beset the world in the latter half of the nineteenth century also had an adverse impact on the German economy. The two industrial crises of 1882 and 1890 were intertwined with this agricultural crisis, thereby making the depression in industry both more severe and more protracted. The crisis of 1900 hit industries like steel, cotton textiles, and sugar refining—but to varying degrees of severity. Not too many years had passed when yet another serious industrial crisis broke out in 1907. This crisis was even more acute; it brought about a 6.5 percent decline in production throughout industry. Steel and shipbuilding were hit particularly hard. By 1913, the signs of a new crisis were once again appearing. However, the course of the depression was cut short when the First World War broke out. These crises revealed that capitalist relations of production were increasingly becoming shackles on the further development of the forces of production.

Increased Concentration in Industrial Production, and the Development of Monopoly Capital

The process whereby industrial production became more concentrated in Germany proceeded very rapidly, and accompanied the swift development of industry after the 1870s. As soon as new industries—such as electrical products, and chemicals—sprang up, they were organized on the basis of the latest technology as large-scale, joint-stock companies. The smaller enterprises, which often found themselves at a competitive disadvantage, suffered especially severe blows during the periodic economic crises. Many of these smaller companies went bankrupt and collapsed, or were taken over by the big corporations. The government's policy of setting up protective tariffs basically benefitted only the large enterprises. Such a policy further strengthened the power of these big corporations, and promoted the concentration of production. According to statistics, the 2.97 million small companies (those employing fewer than five workers) that accounted for 91 percent of all German enterprises used only 7 percent of the total amount of steam power and electrical power consumed in Germany. However, some thirty thousand large enterprises (employing more than fifty workers) that accounted for 0.9 percent of the total number of enterprises used more than three-fourths of the steam power and electrical energy available. Finally, the 586 largest corporations (those employing more than 1,000 workers) used approximately one-third of the total amount of steam and electrical energy. This was exactly as Lenin pointed out: in Germany "several tens of thousands of the largest corporations have everything while the many millions of small companies have nothing."[18] At this time Germany far exceeded both England and France in the category of concentrated industrial production, and was second only to the United States in this area.

The Growth of Cartels in Germany

Year	Number of Cartels
1870	6
1879	14
1890	210
1905	385
1911	550–600

Monopolies rapidly coalesced and developed on the basis of this concentrated production. The increase in the number of German cartels can be seen from the above table. These cartels were scattered extensively throughout such industries as coal mining, metallurgy, electricity, chemicals, textiles, leather, brick and tile, ceramics, and foodstuffs. By the end of the nineteenth century, the cartel had become the most common form of monopoly organization in Germany. The emergence of the cartel was itself determined by the special characteristics of Germany's social and economic conditions at this time. The most important of these characteristics were the following. First, Germany was still thoroughly saturated with the vestiges of feudalism, and the wages of its workers were extremely low. Consequently, the purchasing power of the people was also quite low, and resulted in an extremely constricted domestic market. Second, the vast foreign markets had already been seized much earlier by England, France, and the other "veteran" capitalist states. Germany, a latecomer, found itself in an extremely disadvantageous position in this competition. These two points made the issue of a market for its goods all the more acute for Germany. Third, the abolition of the guild system as well as the beginnings of an industrial revolution both came rather late in Germany. As a result, many comparatively tiny companies coexisted within the same industry with a small number of advanced enterprises, yet possessed vastly different levels of technology. Under such conditions, the pressing need of Germany's industrial corporations was to conclude agreements among themselves that would divide up the market as well as fix prices, in other words, establishing cartel agreements. Moreover, the cartel—as a form of monopoly organization—was exactly appropriate because it had just the advantage of relative flexibility, yet provided the easiest way of organizing within one structure a comparatively large number of enterprises with vastly dissimilar technological endowments. As a result, cartels became prevalent throughout Germany.

As the cartels grew rapidly and their foundations became more firmly established, an even more advanced form of monopoly organization gradually emerged. Beginning in the twentieth century, the majority of Germany's cartels gradually acquired the character of syndicates. A small number of huge syndicates, trusts, and *konzerns* (or concerns) appeared in some major industries. Some industrial sectors eventually came under the control of one or two monopolies. Prior to the First World War, the Rhenish-Westphalian Coal Syndicate concentrated in its own hands more than 90 percent of the coal produced in that region—and more than half of the coal produced in all of Germany. An alliance of steel and iron companies monopolized 98 percent of the steel and iron produced in all of Germany. Each of the chemical, electrical, and merchant marine sectors were controlled by two monopoly groups. In the chemical industry, one group was composed of the Meister, Lucius, and Bruning Company along with the Kalle Company AG; the other group was composed of the Badische Anilin und Sodafabrik and the Friedrich Bayer Company. The electrical industry was controlled by the Allgemeine Elektrizitats-Gesellschaft (AEG) and the Siemens-Schuckert group. In the merchant marine sector, a majority of the steamers was concentrated in the hands of either the Hamburg-America Line or the North German Lloyd. The firm of Alfred Krupp (established in 1811) held the commanding heights in the armaments industry. Krupp produced coal, metallurgical products, machinery, and armaments—all in one huge concern. It employed eighty thousand workers in 1913.

This speedy concentration of industry brought about a similarly swift concentration in banking, a process accomplished primarily through two channels: mergers and associations. For example, the Deutsche Bank swallowed up thirty-two banks, in succession, between 1873 and 1906; by the eve of the First World War, it was associated (in varying degrees) with eighty-seven other banks, and controlled capital amounting to between two and three billion marks. It became one of the most capital-rich banking groups in contemporary Europe. In 1909, the nine largest banks in Berlin, headed by the Deutsche Bank, held a total of 11.3 billion marks in capital, and accounted for 83 percent of the total capitalization of all German banks. Branches of these large banks could be found all over Germany. They concentrated in their hands the vast majority of the entire nation's savings deposits, and became absolute rulers of the German banking world.

Germany's industrial monopoly capital and its bank monopoly capital grew increasingly close together in the process of this development. German banks principally took the form of comprehensive banks; in other words, not only did they offer discounts on promissory notes and made loans, but they also concurrently handled investments and provided other services. The big banks exerted a decisive impact on industry when they permitted companies to overdraw on their accounts, when they granted long term loans, when they issued shares in certain companies, and when they themselves participated in the purchase of such stock. Moreover, Germany was comparatively short of idle capital, and its industrial firms were relatively deficient in funds. Not only were these industrial enterprises largely the creation of big firms, but they were also dependent on the active participation of the big banks. As a result, the level of mutual dependency between German industry and the banks was extremely high, and the ties between the bank monopolies and industrial monopolies appeared particularly close and direct. In fact, the union of the two represented a typical example of the formation of finance capital. A whole series of important German industries and industrial monopoly groups arose precisely because of the support and active organizational efforts of the big Berlin banks. For example, the Deutsche-Luxembourg Mining and Iron Smelting Company was created in 1879 through the efforts of the Darmstadt Bank. In 1893, the big Berlin banks actively assisted in the establishment of the Rhenish-Westphalian Coal Mining Syndicate, and the reconstitution of this syndicate in 1903 came as a result of the pressure exerted by the Discount Company. The Schaaffhausen Bank had its hands in the metallurgy industry. The Gauss Company, Essen's largest smelting concern, expanded with its assistance. In 1904, it purchased a large number of shares in the Phoenix Company, then forced this same company to merge with the Steel Alliance. In the electrical industry, the first joint-stock company—the German Edison Practical Electricity Company (which changed its name in 1887 to the General Electric Company, or "AEG" in German)—was established in 1883. By 1896, the number of joint-stock companies in this industry had increased to thirty-nine. However, in 1910 they were merged into two huge monopoly groups: the General Electric Company (AEG) and the Siemens-Halske-Schuckert Company. All of these mergers came as a result of the work of the big Berlin banks. The Deutsche Bank was involved everywhere with a variety of creative ventures. Who would have expected that, in the period 1897–1910, it would be able to raise more than 7.3 billion marks by selling stocks in various companies? Bank monopoly capital made a fortune by getting involved in such activities. The profits earned by German banking houses through the sale of negotiable industrial securities exceeded one billion marks in the period 1891–1900. At the same time, industrial monopoly capital also purchased stocks in banks and engaged in other types of activities that brought about a close association between the two.

As bank capital and industrial capital enhanced their mutual ties, so too did the personal links grow stronger between the two. In 1908, the managers and trustees of the six largest Berlin banks served as bank representatives on the boards of 751 industrial, communications, insurance, and commercial companies. On the other side, fifty-one of the biggest industrial capitalists in 1910 served on the boards of directors of these same six large banks.

In the development of its monopoly capital, just as in the concentration of its industrial production, Germany eclipsed England and France and ran neck and neck with the United States. By the early twentieth century, the monopolies had already become the basis of the entire economic life of Germany.

The Creation of the "Junker-Bourgeois" Reich and Its Special Characteristics

Germany underwent its transition to monopoly capitalism at the end of the nineteenth and early twentieth centuries, and as a result became an imperialist country.

Lenin pointed out that: German imperialism was "a Junker-bourgeois imperialism."[19] This characteristic differentiated German imperialism from that of the

the other imperialist countries. Its form was not accidental because Germany's unification and its entry into the stage of monopoly capitalism were both achieved under the leadership of the Junker landlord class. The Junkers, with their deeply ingrained tradition of militarism, constituted the leading force within imperialist Germany's ruling political circles, and always preserved the strong remnant forces of feudalism within the country. Some three hundred oligarchs of finance capital controlled the lifelines of the national economy, and they, acting in collusion with the Junkers, constituted the leading personnel in Germany's ruling groups. Consistently up to the end of the First World War, Germany was a country under the joint dictatorship of the Junker landlords and the monopoly bourgeoisie. It was a warlord, Junker, bourgeois imperialist country.

A "Junker, bourgeois imperialist" Germany possessed the following specific characteristics: First, a very small handful of Junker landlords and monopoly plutocrats instituted an extremely savage, warlord-like rule within Germany, and imposed the cruel exploitation of both capitalism and feudalism on its people. Second, the fanatical expansionism of Junker militarism was combined with the boundless greed of monopoly capital to infuse German imperialism with an especially aggressive character and to make it carry out a frenzied policy of foreign expansionism. Third, infatuated with achieving world hegemony, the German imperialists actively prepared for war, and thereby stimulated the growth of state monopoly capitalism at a relatively early date.

During Germany's transition to monopoly capitalism, the Junker landlords and monopoly capitalists intensified their efforts at suppressing and exploiting Germany's working people, and especially its industrial working class. Although the wages of German factory workers had historically been quite low, their average real wages fell once again by more than 10 percent in the period 1885–1914. The policy of arms expansion and war preparation added to the heavy burdens of the broad masses of workers and peasants. Not only did the monopoly bourgeoisie use coordinated lockouts, dismissals, and other despicable methods to suppress the workers and restrict their union activities, but they openly utilized the army, the police, and the judiciary to constantly and violently suppress strikes. In 1878, the reactionary Bismarck government promulgated the notorious "extraordinary decrees," outlawed the Social Democratic party, and, one after the other, forcibly dissolved several hundred workers' organizations. As the suppression increased, the resistance and militancy of the working class also became more intense. Beginning in Westphalia and winding its way through Saxony to Silesia, a strike involving more than 100 thousand mine workers took place in Germany in 1880. No matter whether it was "the German Kaiser Wilhelm or Bismarck, each had to bow his head in front of the vast army of some several hundred thousand striking workers."[20] The reactionary government was finally forced to rescind the "extraordinary decrees" in 1890. Germany's Social Democratic party was tempered in this struggle, and its ranks became even more invigorated. Contrary to the wishes of the reactionary ruling class, the number of voters supporting the Social Democrats in the Diet elections more than tripled between 1877 and 1890. Despite having faced eleven years of an illegal existence as well as criminal sanctions, the Social Democratic party had become Germany's strongest political party. However, the forces of opportunism in the German workers' movement grew after the death of Engels. With Eduard Bernstein as their representative, the well-known "brand name" revisionists of the Second International emerged to fit the needs of monopoly capital. They noisily advocated the erroneous theory of "evolutionary socialism," propagated the notion of a peaceful transition to socialism via a parliamentary path, furiously opposed the class struggle of the proletariat, and vainly attempted to destroy the proletarian revolution and the dictatorship of the proletariat. They usurped the leading positions in the Social Democratic party and caused serious damage to the revolutionary struggles of the German proletariat.

As domestic class contradictions sharpened, and as the scramble for markets greatly intensified, the German government began to battle the other well-known, "brand name" imperialist states for what it called its own "place in the sun." Trying to divert the attention of its own people, imperialist Germany's Junker bourgeoisie now made strenuous efforts to expand militarily and economically, and actively threw themselves into a struggle to redivide the world. In the period 1870–1913, Germany's foreign trade increased five-fold, and its export of capital grew by several tens of times. After the Sino-Japanese War (1894–95), Germany invested in China's banks, railroads, and mines. Germany then savagely plundered the Chinese people of their wealth by granting loans to the Qing dynasty government that imposed various kinds of slavish economic and political conditions. At the same time, German monopoly capital also actively participated in various kinds of international monopoly groups. German participation in such international cartels rose from forty in 1897 to one hundred in 1919.

In the early 1880s, Germany began to follow in the footsteps of England and France, and took the path of plundering colonial possessions. During the earliest phase, the spearhead of Germany's aggression was pointed at the coastal areas of Africa. It also invaded the Irian Islands (New Guinea) in the Pacific Ocean. By the 1890s, German imperialism raised its demands. Now it sought to establish its own colonial empire and wanted to achieve global domination. It began a frantic campaign of aggression against China, and continued to expand its power into other parts of Asia. Germany seized China's Jiaozhou Bay in 1897. By coercing the Chinese government into granting special rights in railroad construction and mining operations, Germany was able to turn all of Shandong province into its own sphere of influence. Germany also served as the "point man" in suppressing China's Boxer Movement in 1900. At that time it participated in the notorious "joint army of eight nations" along with the other imperialist robbers. Germany not only left a huge debt in blood to the Chinese people, but also extorted a substantial indemnity from the Chinese government. Although its colonial empire was much smaller when compared to that of England and France, Germany's overseas possesions (on the eve of the First World War) still came to 2.9 million square kilometers, containing a population of 12.3 million people.

Dominated by its greedy desire to redivide the world, the German Junker-bourgeois policy of military expansionism and war preparations marched forward step by step until it stood at the forefront of the imperialists' ranks. At the end of the 1870s, Germany's annual military expenditures came to approximately 400 million marks. However, by 1913—the eve of the First World War—those expenditures had climbed to 2.1 billion marks. Germany's state monopoly capitalism began to develop prior to World War I and flourished in an environment of military expansion and war preparations. The state, in a systematic way, offered very lucrative contracts for military goods to various monopolies. The state set high tariffs and granted export subsidies that helped the monopolies sell their products abroad. The government even used special laws to enhance the power of the monopolies. There were other examples. Another aspect was the German government's implementation of a policy of nationalization. Based on the demands of its military strategy, the German government on the eve of the First World War owned forty-four of the largest mines, twelve of the biggest steel companies, 24 percent of the electrical power plants, and 20 percent of Germany's salt production. More than 80 percent of the railroad network was government-run. This kind of nationalization of industry in imperialist Germany in reality resembled a narrow passageway where the state and the monopolies were both close to each other and intermingled with each other. The boards of directors of such nationalized companies were usually dominated by representatives of the largest trusts and concerns. Moreover, in some sectors there were some companies that were jointly run by the state and by private individuals, such as the Rhenish-Westphalian Electric Company. Lenin wrote about this: Germany "in many respects, namely in technology, production, and politics, is second to the United States. But it is superior to the United States in respect to the organizational character of its finance capitalism and in its change from monopoly capitalism to state monopoly capitalism."[21] State monopoly capitalism in Germany made substantial progress during the First World War.

4. The Development of State Monopoly Capitalism during the First World War (1914–18), and the Collapse of the German Reich

The Rapid Development of State Monopoly Capitalism during the War

The First World War was a war fought by the imperialist powers to redivide the world and to contend for world hegemony. Imperial Germany was the chief criminal in launching that war. The Great War began on August 1, 1914 when

Germany, using as a pretext the assassination of the Archduke of Austria-Hungary, declared war on Russia and France.

After war broke out, the Allies imposed a tight blockade on Germany, and Germany's economy—dependent on imports for its raw materials and foodstuffs—encountered serious difficulties. The rapid movement of military supplies and the drafting of large numbers of workers intensified the disruption of the economy. Under these circumstances, the German state vigorously implemented a wartime policy of government "regulation" of the economy, thereby promoting the development of state monopoly capitalism. The government's motivation for these actions proceeded from the viewpoint of continuing its war of aggression as well as guaranteeing extremely high profits for the monopoly bourgeoisie.

Lenin pointed out that: "in order to mobilize the strength of the people for a predatory war, Germany was forced to create *a central organization* that would represent the interests of the likes of some several hundred financial magnates or aristocrats to direct the entire economic life of sixty-six million people."[22] In August 1914, the German government first established a Wartime Industrial Committee and then created a Wartime Raw Materials Bureau; both were directly controlled by monopoly capitalists. The Wartime Industrial Committee shouldered the responsibility for reaching decisions on government purchases of goods and for administering production needed by the military. The several credit banks set up under its authority issued war bonds and extended loans to various munitions companies. The fifty-nine "Quartermaster Companies" established under the Wartime Raw Materials Bureau specialized in administering and distributing raw materials to various industries. Vital raw materials and loans were always provided on a priority basis to the monopolies, and as a result, the vast majority of medium and small-sized companies, one after the other, were forced to stop work or even compelled to go out of business. In July 1915, the German government enacted additional legislation that compelled the cartelization of industry, and stipulated that the political authorities of the confederated states had the right to force any company to join a monopoly group. The enforcement of this law led to the speedy recovery of the Rhenish-Westphalian Coal Syndicate, which had been on the brink of collapse. It brought cartels into industries (such as the shoe industry) which previously had had none. Finally, it brought outside industries into those sectors of the economy (such as metallurgy, chemicals, and shipbuilding) that had already been cartelized, and amalgamated them into cartels. All these developments greatly enhanced the power of the monopolies.

As the war turned into a stalemate and the German army suffered repeated defeats on the battlefield, the German government announced the Hindenburg Program to augment mobilization efforts. This program carried the following stipulations: All male citizens between the ages of seventeen and sixty were required to enter military service. Those workers retained in their factories were not permitted to change their place of employment on their own volition. Factories were required to meet those needs generated by the war and to produce goods required by the military. Workers in those factories that were closed because they could not manufacture goods needed by the armed forces were either shifted to other plants or sent to the front lines as soldiers. In reality, this reactionary program was similar to a court verdict: it condemned the German working people to a sentence of hard labor. At the same time it strangled many medium and small-sized companies. In 1916 alone, 95 percent of Germany's cotton weaving plants were forced out of business.

The German government also established an Imperial Grain Bureau and Imperial Clothing Bureau during the war, and instituted strict controls over the supply and distribution of food, clothing, fuel, and other daily necessities. Once a system of rationing went into effect, rationed goods became increasingly scarce, and the living standards of the working people were reduced to the lowest possible level. However, the rich and powerful continued to live well—just as they had before the war—because luxury goods and gourmet delicacies remained outside the system of rationing.

The cost of the war was colossal. Germany's military expenses for the duration of the war, calculated on the basis of constant 1914 prices, were approximately eighty billion marks, equivalent to more than 40 percent of the national income of this period. Under such economically depressed circumstances, the German government used reactionary methods (such as forcing its citizens to buy government bonds, increasing taxes, permitting inflation, and plundering occupied territories) in order to shift the heavy burden of war-related expenditures onto the backs of the working people both within Germany and outside it. Between 1914 and 1918, the German government floated nine bond issues, one after the other, totalling sixty-two billion marks. At the same time, the German invaders ruthlessly plundered the areas they occupied. One category alone—that of goods and materials—came to six billion marks.

The protracted imperialist war caused the German economy to deteriorate further, and industrial and agricultural production both suffered great damage. Military production developed in a lopsided fashion, based as it was on sacrificing civilian industry. As the supply of raw materials dwindled and labor productivity constantly fell, industrial production as a whole deteriorated. While German military production increased 10 percent in the time span 1913–18, production in civilian industry shrank 59 percent, and industrial production as a whole fell 43 percent. German agriculture, faced with insufficient manpower and hampered by shortages of livestock, machinery, fertilizer, and fodder, also experienced a serious decline.

The Intensification of the Class Struggle and the Revolution of 1918

Lenin pointed out: Wartime Germany's " 'regulated economic life' resulted in creating a military boot camp for the industrial workers (and a portion of the farmers) and the establishment of a paradise for the bankers and capitalists."[23] The German monopoly bourgeoisie reaped windfall profits from the war. For example, the wartime profits of the Krupps munitions concern came to at least 800 million marks, or equivalent to the total profits earned by this company in the twenty years of peace prior to 1914. The wealth of the Krupps company increased fourfold during the First World War.

On the other hand, Germany's working people suffered great hardships during the war as state monopoly capitalism developed and the economic situation deteriorated. Millions upon millions of industrial workers and farmers were drafted into the military, and many gave their lives on the battlefield in vain. Those workers that remained in the factories and fields passed their days like "slaves condemned to military hard labor." After the prewar labor laws limiting the exploitation of women and children workers were abolished, the workday for adult male industrial workers was extended to twelve hours. Exorbitant taxes, runaway inflation, and frantic black market speculation all resulted in halving the average real wages of a worker when compared to those he received prior to the war. Between 1914 and 1918, more than 6.3 million Germans perished as a result of military combat, starvation, poverty, and disease. Aggressive by nature, the imperialists left a huge debt in blood to the German people.

The war led to revolution. As Germany's domestic class contradictions grew more acute, the mood of the working people became increasingly revolutionary. The victory of the Great October Socialist Revolution in Russia, combined with the rout of German imperialism on its Eastern and Western fronts, speeded up the outbreak of the revolution. Responding to appeals made by groups of proletarian revolutionaries, sailors at Kiel fired the first shot in November 1918. Within a few days, armed uprisings throughout Germany were successful, and workers' and soldiers' soviets were established in many large cities. The semi-feudal monarchy was overthrown, and the German Reich collapsed. However, the reactionary leadership of the Social Democratic Party became involved in new forms of treachery, and proceeded to sell out this revolution. From the very beginnings of the global conflict, they had taken the standpoint of chauvinism in supporting this imperialist war. In January 1919, political power was transferred from the soviets to the Diet, and the joint dictatorship of the monopoly bourgeoisie and the Junker landlords was restored. However, there was a significant difference between this and the status quo ante. The leading role politically in Germany's Weimar Republic was no longer played by the Junkers, but rather by the monopoly bourgeoisie. With the defeat of the 1918 revolution, the German proletariat was unable to accomplish its historic mission of achieving a socialist revolution. However, this revolution struck heavy blows against Germany's capitalist system. The German people achieved certian bourgeois democratic rights during the revolution. The revolution tempered Germany's working class, and advanced the workers' movement in Germany and in Europe. And at the same time, the German Communist party was born in the midst of this revolutionary struggle.

5. The Development of State Monopoly Capitalism between the Two World Wars

Economic Chaos in the Immediate Postwar Period

Germany was defeated in World War I. The Allies then forced Germany to accept the Versailles Peace Treaty on June 28, 1919. The purposes of this peace treaty were as follows: to plunder and enslave the German people; to keep Germany down and prevent it from once again becoming a competitor with the victorious powers; and to make Germany into an outpost of opposition to socialist Russia.

The peace treaty carried the following stipulations. Alsace and Lorraine were ceded back to France, while Poznan went to Poland. Other regions were incorporated into Belgium, Denmark, and Lithuania. As a result, Germany lost one-eighth of its territory, one-twelfth of its population, a majority of its iron ore and zinc deposits, one-third of its coal and steel production, and one-seventh of its arable land. The Versailles peace treaty also expropriated all of Germany's colonies and all its overseas investments, and these in turn were divided up and confiscated by the victorious powers.

Under the terms of the Versailles "peace treaty," the Allies severely limited Germany's military capability. They also stationed their own troops on the left bank of the Rhine River. They directly managed Germany's tax revenues, customs houses, railroads, rivers, harbors, and other public agencies. The peace treaty even forced Germany to deliver to the Allies vast amounts of goods (for example, various kinds of rolling stock, ships, agricultural machinery, and even cows) as compensation and as reparations. The Paris Conference of January 1921 fixed the amount of Germany's indemnity at 226 billion gold marks. This figure was subsequently changed to 132 billion gold marks at the London Conference of April 1921. Germany at this time lacked the wherewithal to pay such a stupendous amount of money. The shadow of the reparations issue shrouded the entire country. Lenin pointed this out about the Versailles peace treaty: "It was an appalling, predatory peace treaty. It made slaves out of tens of millions of people, including among them the most civilized."[24] However, the Versailles peace treaty left untouched the ruling power of either monopoly capital or the Junker landlords in Germany. On the contrary, it left an escape route for the revival of German militarism in order to make use of it when necessary to suppress the German people and to oppose socialist Russia.

The German economy in the immediate postwar period became quite volatile due to the loss of territory and the payment of reparations. German industrial production in 1919 fell by a huge margin, and stood at only one-third that of the prewar level. That is to say, the German economy had regressed to the level it had reached in 1888. Industrial and agricultural production, led first by heavy industry, began a modest revival in the three years after 1919. However, the

German government's delay in paying reparations, then its refusal to pay anything at all, brought about the reparations crisis of 1923. France and Belgium took advantage of this favorable opportunity and militarily occupied the Ruhr, the region where German heavy industry was most heavily concentrated. This action dealt a deadly blow to a German economy which had just taken a turn for the better, and created an unprecedentedly chaotic situation. In this same year, German industrial production once again fell dramatically. At its worst, only one-seventh of all industrial enterprises managed—with the greatest effort—to be fully operative. Millions of unemployed tramped through the streets, reserves of commodities were nil, and circulating capital was in extremely short supply. The system of bank credit was on the verge of disintegration, the gold reserves in the national treasury were nearly exhausted, and the government's budget deficit was alarming. Germany's government was forced to turn for assistance to the printing press, and frantically printed paper money night and day. As a result, commodity prices increased many times over within a single day, and a runaway inflation reached astronomical proportions. For example, the price of beef on Berlin's central market: at the beginning of February 1923, one pound of beef cost 3,400 marks; on October 29, the cost had risen to fifty-six billion marks; and on November 5, the price had escalated to 280 billion marks. By the end of 1923, the amount of paper currency in circulation had increased to more than 1.8 trillion times that of the prewar level. Banknotes in reality had become worthless scraps of paper. Business was virtually at a standstill, and barter came into vogue.

The oligarchs of monopoly capital took advantage of this economic chaos to fish in troubled waters. They stole huge sums from the state treasury, jacked up commodity prices while simultaneously cutting workers' wages, and seized small and medium-sized companies. Their wealth rapidly expanded as a result of these activities, and a group of giant, speculative monopolies emerged. The Hugo Stinnes concern exemplified this trend. However, the masses of rank-and-file industrial workers and farmers were the ones who suffered the hardships of unemployment and the cruel inflation. In 1923, the income of the entire industrial working class shrank by several billions of gold marks. This situation, where the people were left without a means of livelihood, brought about a new wave of revolutionary struggle. In the fall of 1923, Germany's working class staged a mammoth, nationwide strike, and demanded that the government stabilize the mark, guarantee the supply of food, and increase wages. As the conflict developed, the working class went even further in raising slogans that called for the overthrow of the reactionary Cuno government and the establishment of a worker's government. The sparks from this civil war soon engulfed all of Germany after the Cuno government was forced to resign. Saxony, Thuringia and other places created workers' governments. A well-known armed uprising broke out in Hamburg. The revolutionary struggle had crested. However, Germany's ruling class—energetically supported by the traitorous actions of the Social Democratic party, as well as receiving assistance from foreign capital

—once again cruelly suppressed the revolution. The militancy of the people ebbed once more.

Economic Revival and Growth during the Period of Relative Stability

Germany's economy began to revive and even entered a period of relative post-war stability in 1924. It was during this period that German industrial production reached and then surpassed prewar levels. The Dawes Plan and the capitalistic Industrial Rationalization Movement both played important roles in this process.

In 1923, the Allies hurriedly drew up the so-called Dawes Plan (engineered by the United States) in order to prevent the collapse of bourgeois Germany and forestall any German efforts to renege on paying either their indemnity or other war debts. The important provisions of the Dawes Plan were as follows. Assisted by loans monitored by the Allies, Germany would implement monetary reforms aimed at stabilizing its currency. The amount of indemnity to be paid in the five-year period from 1924–25 to 1928–29 was further reduced, yet stipulated more specifically. The one billion marks due at the beginning of this period would be progressively increased to 2.5 billion marks at the end of this time period. As Germany accepted the terms of this indemnity plan, both France and Belgium withdrew their troops from the Ruhr. The Dawes Plan was yet another plan to enslave the German people and was a continuation of the Versailles peace treaty. It paved the way for foreign capital to penetrate Germany on a massive scale. At the same time, it flashed a green light to German monopoly capital to revive its military and economic potential.

At the end of 1923, the German government carried out monetary reforms (according to the stipulations of the Dawes Plan), and stabilized its currency. However, this stability was achieved at the cost of reparations payments paid for by the blood and sweat of the German people. As the French and Belgian occupation forces left the Ruhr, German monopoly capital once again came to control this important base of heavy industry. A vast river of foreign capital, principally from the United States, also flowed into Germany. Altogether Germany obtained 32.6 billion marks in foreign loans and investments between 1924 and 1930, and this solved the difficulties caused by the extreme shortage of capital. At the same time, Germany also received vast amounts of equipment and technical assistance from the United States. Under these conditions, Germany's bourgeoisie launched an extensive Industrial Rationalization Movement. Plants and equipment were renovated throughout all of Germany. Companies with obsolete plants were gradually eliminated when they could no longer meet the competition. The Ford System and standardized production became fashionable. However, the average workweek for a worker climbed to fifty-five hours, and labor intensity was much higher than before; although real wages still remained below prewar levels.

By 1927, German industry, generally speaking, had regained its prewar levels. This achievement was based on intensified exploitation of the broad masses of workers that resulted in higher labor productivity. Heavy industry developed much more rapidly than light industry because of the massive renovation of fixed capital and because Germany's ruling class energetically revived the potential of its military-industrial complex. Growth in those industrial sectors related to the military—like petroleum, automobiles, machine manufacturing, and aluminum smelting—was the most rapid.

German agriculture made a distinct recovery during this period of relative stability. However, the area sown for major agricultural crops (excluding potatoes) as well as the amount harvested still remained lower than prewar levels due to the adverse impact of territorial losses. The number of heads of livestock also did not reach prewar levels. This phenomenon—where agriculture remained backward compared to that of industry—became increasingly acute. Also, Germany had to import annually several million tons of food grains and vast quantities of industrial raw materials. At this time, Germany's foreign trade recovered and even surpassed prewar levels. It recaptured and strengthened its traditional status in Europe's markets, and opened new ones in Latin America and other regions.

Production and capital became further concentrated during this process of economic recovery. German monopoly capital experienced new growth and acquired new power. More and more trusts were established. During the 1920s, the colossal Farben Chemical and Industrial Trust and the Steel Trust were organized. They became two massive pillars capable of supporting a revived German military-industrial complex, with all its latent potential. The strong tendency to create trusts, as well as the state's policy of using coercion to create cartels, promoted the further growth of cartels and syndicates. For example, the number of cartels in Germany increased from one thousand to 2,100 between 1922 and 1930. In this area, Germany continued to maintain its world leadership. German state monopoly capital in the 1920s was enormous in all its various aspects. The total amount of capital belonging to state-owned enterprises came to several tens of billions of marks. The state owned almost all the railroads, a majority of the electric power and aluminum smelting capacity, two-fifths of the production of salt and lead, and portions of the coal, iron, and machine-manufacturing sectors. By the 1920s, Germany had even eclipsed the United States in the degree of monopolization that characterized some industrial sectors. The profits of Germany's monopoly bourgeoisie also rose continuously; the profits of its large corporations increased 62 percent between 1925–26 and 1928–29.

In this era of relative stability, the German monopoly groups once again extended their talons throughout the world. Their foreign investments totaled ten billion marks. They actively participated in a majority of the international monopolies. Moreover, Germany either held an important niche or played a leading role in many international cartels—such as in steel, rails, gunpowder, electric light bulbs, nitrogen, and rayon. German and American capitalists collaborated with each other on an unprecedented basis during this same period. Not only did various large American financial cliques assist German monopoly capital in financial matters, but they also made cartel agreements advantageous to the latter. They shipped a stream of strategic goods and material to Germany, and thereby hastened the revival of German militarism.

One thing should be pointed out. The recovery and development of the German economy in this period of relative stability also contained some serious contradictions and inherent weaknesses impossible to surmount. The heavy burden of reparations and the intensified exploitation of the workers caused the domestic market to become relatively more attenuated. Germany found itself at a disadvantage in international competition due to the controls placed over it by the victorious powers. The national economy depended extensively on foreign capital, especially from the United States. The production of the means of production expanded in a lopsided and blind manner, and the unequal development of various sectors of the economy became increasingly acute. At the same time, speculation became more frenzied. All of these factors determined the developmental trajectory of the German economy, especially its extremely volatile character. Beginning in 1927, numerous symptoms indicating an economic crisis (such as a decline in the production of consumer goods, and a fall in the rate of growth in all areas of production) appeared sequentially in Germany. Just as the wind that sweeps through the tower heralds a rising storm in the mountains, a new and severe crisis was approaching over the horizon.

The Economic Depression of 1929–33 and Hitler's Fascist Seizure of Power

In June 1929, the Allies proposed a new reparations plan (the Young Plan) to deal with a German economy that found itself stuck in a multifaceted crisis. The Young Plan contained the following important components: It ended the Allies' direct economic and financial control over Germany. It continued to provide a substantial loan of $1.3 billion U.S. dollars to Germany. The Allies withdrew their occupation forces from the Rhine River region. And the Young Plan reassessed the total amount of Germany's reparations and rescheduled its payments. For example, it reduced the total indemnity to 113.9 billion marks and offered a payment schedule that would require fifty-nine years to complete. It is obvious that this plan was a reflection of international imperialism's fear of an economic crisis and fear of a revolution in Germany. It was also a product of the further collaboration between German monopoly capital and the countries—most prominently American imperialism—that had won the First World War. Its purpose was to shore up the rule of monopoly capital in Germany and continue to plunder the broad masses of the German people. In reality, the Young Plan opened the road to Germany's termination of its reparation payments. After it had appealed to America's President Herbert Hoover to grant it a deferment on any future payment of reparations, Germany stopped those payments altogether in 1929. However, objective laws cannot be altered. Contrary to the wishes of the ruling classes of the United States, Germany, and various other countries, the Young Plan and the termination of reparations payments could neither slow down any further deterioration of the German economy nor stop the onset of an economic depression.

The most acute, the most profound, and the most prolonged economic crisis in German history broke out at the end of 1929, and occurred under the impact of a worldwide economic crisis (especially the economic depression which broke out in the United States). During the Depression, industrial production declined sharply. The fall in the production of the means of production was particularly dramatic, and resembled a river plunging down a steep spillway. Between 1929 and 1932, for example, coal production fell 32.7 percent, pig iron 70.3 percent, and steel 64.9 percent. The output value of the machine manufacturing industry declined 62.1 percent, automobile production fell 64.2 percent, and electric power slipped 23.4 percent. Ship construction fell 83.6 percent in terms of tonnage, and the amount of cotton consumed declined by 21.4 percent (taking 1933 as the low point). In general, industrial production as a whole fell 40.6 percent when one compares the highest pre-Depression statistics with the lowest point reached during the Depression. Included in this statistic is the 53 percent decline in the production of the means of production and a 25.3 percent fall in the production of consumer goods. These statistics represented a retrogression to levels achieved at the end of the nineteenth century and the beginning of the twentieth. Several hundred thousand small and medium-sized companies went bankrupt during the Depression era. Even some large concerns were on the brink of collapse. For example, the Steel Trust was forced into a reorganization, and the cotton textile industry's Duerbach concern had to declare bankruptcy. Only one-third of plant capacity was being utilized during the worst moments of the Depression. Unemployment peaked between six and eight million people, a figure which was close to half of all industrial workers in Germany, and was the highest of any European country.

A severe monetary crisis—influenced by the industrial depression—also broke out in Germany in July 1931. The collapse of the Darmstadt Bank served as the fuse that set off the explosion, and the large Berlin banks found themselves engulfed in a raging firestorm. The gold reserves in the treasury were sharply cut by 80 percent, and the entire system of credit was on the verge of total collapse. The German government frantically rode to the scene and tried to save the large banks. The government provided them with deposits in excess of one billion marks, and even purchased about 70 percent of the bank stocks held by Germany's private citizens. A crisis in agriculture appeared somewhat later. This occurred because the German government beginning in 1930 had already increased (by severalfold) the tariffs it imposed on agricultural imports, and had also restricted the sale of foreign agricultural products in Germany. In 1933, agricultural prices went through the roof. In 1934, on the other hand, agricultural production fell through the floor. Many small farmers went bankrupt, and even competed with each other to sell their land. The number of tenant farmers increased rapidly, farm indebtedness rose continuously, and farm income as a whole fell 30 percent.

Germany's foreign trade suffered a precipitous drop as a result of the blows it received from the global economic depression. Between 1929 and 1935, the total amount of German exports was reduced by 69.1 percent and that of imports by 70.8 percent.

During the Depression, Germany's bourgeois government adopted various kinds of reactionary policies to shift—in a thousand and one different ways—the heavy burden of the crisis onto the backs of the working people. On the one hand, the government actively supported the monopolies and the Junker landlord class. It gave them more than ten billion marks in subsidies and loans; it increased the level of state purchases; and it speeded up the practice of forced cartelization. On the other hand, the government increased by several billion marks the amount of taxes levied on the working people. At the same time it imposed massive cutbacks in the relief benefits enjoyed by the unemployed, and reduced the wages and salaries of the employed. As a result, the real income of industrial workers was reduced, on average, by one-third during the Depression era. That is, it stood at only 64 percent of its prewar level.

A serious consequence of the Depression was that it once again aggravated Germany's domestic class struggle. A new wave of strikes began between 1930 and 1932. Each year, several hundreds of thousands of workers in different locations staged many hundreds of strikes. The vast army of unemployed also actively participated in some militant actions. The mass movement reached a new peak in January 1933 when the working people of Berlin staged three massive demonstrations, one after the other. The position of Germany's ruling class was in immediate jeopardy. In this tense situation—and relying on support from the ringleaders of the Social Democratic party—Paul Hindenburg, the President of Germany, impatiently handed over governmental power on January 30, 1933 to Adolf Hitler, the leader of the thoroughly reactionary fascist thugs and the loyal running dog of monopoly capital. Beginning with this day, Germany opened the darkest page in its history—the period of its fascist dictatorship. The rise to power of fascism in Germany, however, was not a measure of the strength of the bourgeoisie. On the contrary, as Stalin pointed out, "it must be seen as an indication of the weakness of the bourgeoisie. It must be regarded as an indication that the bourgeoisie no longer could use the old methods of the parliamentary system and bourgeois democracy to achieve their control, but rather were compelled to adopt administrative means of terror in their domestic policy. It must be regarded as an indication that the bourgeoisie also could not find a way out from their present predicament on the basis of a peaceful foreign policy, but rather were compelled to adopt a policy of war."[25] The usurpation of political power by the Hitler elements was a reflection of the unprecedented severity of the general crisis of capitalism in Germany.

The Militarization of the Economy under a Fascist Dictatorship: The Development of State Monopoly Capitalism

The Hitler elements used deceit and force to usurp political power. Before they came into office, they hoisted the flag of "national socialism," made many promises, used sweet words to hoodwink the masses, and poisoned and bewitched their minds. However, even though a crow may stick on some peacock feathers, it is, after all, still a crow. After their seizure of power, the fascists immediately discarded their disguises and revealed their own savage faces. When we speak of fascism's class character, it is exactly as Dimitrov pointed out in his report to the Seventh Congress of the Communist International: Hitler's fascist regime was "an openly terroristic dictatorship based on the most reactionary, most chauvinistic, and most imperialistic elements of finance capital" [source unknown].

After Hitler and his coterie assumed office, they immediately began to reorganize the national economy along the lines desired by the monopoly bourgeoisie. They used the principle of state monopoly capitalism to militarize the economy and surmount the serious consequences of the economic crisis. Moreover, they prepared to launch another war of aggression to redivide the world once again.

Having absorbed the reactionary lessons learned by German imperialism during the First World War, the fascist government now created a complete array of economic regulatory agencies whose mission would be to regulate the entire national economy in a comprehensive way. A General Committee for the German Economy was set up in July 1933 under the Third Reich's Ministry of Economics. It was the economic headquarters, directly controlled by the oligopolists, that made the necessary preparations for waging a war. It was responsible for directing the nation's economic policy and formulating the relevant laws and decrees. Two vast, overlapping systems intended to regulate the nation's economy were established in 1934. They were based on the "Regulations Regarding the Organic Structure of the German Economy," and took as their foundation the major established business federations as well as various monopoly organizations. One regulatory system was organized by industrial sectors and comprised economic groups arranged in four tiers. The other regulatory system was organized according to geographical regions, with a provincial economic bureau and municipal and local branches. The people who headed these two systems at their various levels were either monopoly capitalists or their trusted colleagues. In conjunction with the intensified war preparations included in the "Four Year Plan," a Supreme Organization to Administer the Four Year Plan (headed by Hermann Goring) was also created in 1936. This "Supreme Organization" coexisted on an equal footing with the previously mentioned regulatory agencies. However, they eventually became embroiled in power struggles with each other because their responsibilities overlapped. This created myriad economic problems.

By intervening and regulating the economy, the Hitler government rapidly pushed the German economy onto the track of militarization. Within a six-and-a-half year period of preparing for war (from 1933 to Fall 1939), German military expenditures reached ninety billion marks. This was equivalent to three-fifths of the total national budget during that period, or one-fourth of the entire national income. This colossal expenditure of money to prepare for war was more than triple the total amount of reparations Germany paid after the First World War. The fascist government shifted the burden of these military expenditures onto the backs of the German people by raising taxes, enlarging the national debt, and permitting inflation. German taxes increased by sixty billion marks in these years, and the national debt and the amount of currency in circulation more than tripled. Although Hitler repeatedly said that he would "save the German people from the shackles of the Versailles peace treaty," facts completely exposed his "promises" as fraudulent and shameful!

In the process of militarizing the economy, the regulatory agencies of the fascist state systematically provided the raw materials, labor power, capital, equipment, and other priority supplies to those sectors involved with the production of military necessities. As a result, heavy industry—and, in particular, the munitions industry—rapidly expanded. The uneven development of various industrial sectors became even more pronounced. Between 1933 and 1939, for example, the production of the means of consumption increased only 43 percent. The production of the means of production increased 3.1 times. However, military-related production expanded 12.5-fold. The rate of German industrial growth during this period exceeded that of the United States, England, and France. Germany also produced far more goods in absolute terms than did either England or France. In 1939, German military production was more than triple that of the United States and England combined. Huge military contracts yielded startling profits for the monopolies. For example, in the period 1932–33 to 1938–39, the total value of military contracts obtained from the government by the Krupp Company increased from 9.3 million marks to 145 million marks, or almost a sixteenfold increase. At the same time, its net profit rose from 6.5 million marks to 122 million marks, or close to a nineteenfold increase.

The Hitler government also adopted a series of extremely reactionary measures intended to strengthen the position of Germany's monopoly bourgeoisie. These measures included the following: First, the government incited an extremely chauvinistic movement to "keep the Jews in line." It robbed Germany's Jews of capital worth several billions of marks, and forced them to turn over this capital to "Aryan" financial cliques and the arch-criminals of the Nazi party. Second, the government energetically promoted forced cartelization, coercing many small and medium-sized companies outside established channels to merge with the monopolies. Third, the implementation of the "Law to Reform Joint-Stock Companies" led to the bankruptcy of a majority of Germany's small companies. Fourth, the government forced several hundred thousand handicraft enterprises and retail shops to close, all on the pretext of "putting in order" the handicraft industry as well as small commercial operations. As a result, the various monopoly groups came to control 85 percent of the total amount of Germany's share capital, while the multitude of small business proprietors went bankrupt. Before the Hitler elements came into power, they repeatedly made "guarantees" to the medium-sized and petty bourgeoisie: "We will confiscate the property of big business and rent it cheaply to those who own small industries and commercial operations." This is what became of these "promises" in reality!

But this was not the whole story. As it was expanding the role of state monopoly capital, the fascist government also turned over—under very favorable conditions—a portion of state-owned property to private monopoly groups. Between 1932 and 1939, the portion of state-owned share capital rose from 13.2 percent to 17 percent of the total amount of Germany's share capital. As soon as the economy revived from the Depression, the fascist government immediately sold its state-owned assets to private concerns. The government gradually began to return the stocks (that it had previously purchased at preferential prices from the large Berlin banks and the large industrial and shipping companies during the economic crisis) to those same private monopoly capital groups. However, in dealing with the industrial working class, the Hitler elements quickly changed their tune once they seized political power. After their seizure of power, they openly advocated the reactionary slogan of "guns rather than butter," and forced the broad masses of industrial workers to tighten their belts and "sacrifice." Average real wages for industrial workers consistently remained at the pitiful level of the Depression decade. Taxes and other levies were as numerous as the hair on an ox, and took one-fourth of the wages of a worker's meager income. As a result, the real income of almost half of Germany's industrial workers was even lower than in 1932 when the economic Depression had reached its nadir.

The vast number of farmers in Germany also suffered from oppression and pillage under the rule of fascism. The Reich Foodgrains Bureau and its several tens of thousands of subordinate organizations tightly controlled the entire economic life of the farmers. Hitler's pals quietly reneged on their outrageous claims that they would "confiscate and redistribute land, and abolish rent." These were lies that they had put before the farmers in the past. On the contrary, they brazenly put into effect in Germany's villages the Farmland Inheritance Law, and energetically cultivated the reactionary class of wealthy farmers. As a result, the Junker landlords and rich farmers—all in the very short period of six years prior to the Second World War—seized several million hectares of land that belonged to farmers. This caused the ranks of the destitute tenant farmers to increase by more than one million households.

At the same time, the Hitler government also loyally implemented the will of monopoly capital by energetically promoting a policy of economic expansionism and military plunder abroad. Through "bilateral trade agreements," it put into effect a "system of clear transfers" that was disadvantageous to various southeastern European countries. This system of "clear transfers" used barter rather than money to settle accounts. The German government systematically plundered these countries' strategic raw materials (such as petroleum, nonferrous metals, bauxite, and lumber) and agricultural products, while expanding the export of commodities to these nations. Between 1932 and 1938, for example, Germany's share of the foreign trade of Bulgaria, Greece, Hungary, Rumania, and Yugoslavia increased between one-third to fourfold, depending on the country. As a result, some of the nations of southeastern Europe became—to different degrees—dependencies of Hitler's Germany, supplying it with agricultural raw materials or serving as a market for the sale of German commodities. In addition, the German monopolies vigorously pushed their way into many Latin American countries and other regions, enslaving and exploiting the people there. By the eve of the Second World War, Germany's capital investment in Latin America already amounted to one billion U.S. dollars, half of which was invested in Argentina. German capital had a significant influence in many Latin American countries' industries, such as in metallurgy (and especially the extraction of nonferrous metals), petroleum, electricity, saltpeter mining, telecommunications, banking, and shipping. In the area of trade, fascist Germany also intensified its efforts to enter the markets of Latin America, putting itself into contention with the United States and England. Between 1929 and 1938, the share held by the United States and England of the import and export trade of the twenty nations of Latin America clearly fell. On the other hand, Germany's share of Latin American imports rose from 10.6 percent to 17.8 percent, and its share of Latin American exports rose from 8.1 percent to 10.3 percent. In conjunction with its foreign economic expansionism, fascist Germany also carried out a savage policy of political and military expansion against foreign countries. In 1936, Germany intervened militarily in the Spanish Civil War. In 1938, it occupied Austria and then Czechoslovakia's Sudentenland. At the same time, Hitler's Germany openly formed an alliance with fascist Italy and Japan, and became the axis of reaction of the contemporary world.

The ties between Germany's monopoly bourgeoisie and the fascist political system were enormously strengthened by the comprehensive development of state monopoly capital. On the one hand, the chieftains of the monopolies, people like Thyssen, Vogel, Bosche, Schacht, Siemens, Krupp, Dietrich, and their trusted colleagues, held numerous governmental positions in the various administrative branches of the fascist regime. In particular, they served as responsible officials in agencies that regulated the military economy. On the other hand, some several hundred Nazi chieftains like Hitler, Goring, Goebbels, and Himmler owned various kinds of property and became new billionaires and millionaires. When we speak of this "alliance of individuals" between the bourgeoisie and the political power of the state, then we can say that Hitler's Germany not only created a record unprecedented in German history, but also a record in the contemporary capitalist world.

Hitler's bloody fascist dictatorship caused Germany's class contradictions to sharpen to an unprecedented degree. An anti-fascist People's Front—a German People's Front—was formed in Berlin in late 1936 under the leadership of the German Communist party. Despite facing unusually adverse conditions, the broad masses of Germany's working people—rallying around the People's Front—still resolutely participated in various forms of resistance against the terroristic rule of fascism and in opposition to the war preparations and foreign aggression of the Hitler government.

6. The High Degree of Development of a Militarized State Monopoly Capitalism during the Second World War, and Its Eventual Collapse

Government "Regulation" of a Militarized Economy, and the Unrestricted Plunder of the Occupied Territories

The sudden rise of fascist Germany and its intense effort to gain world hegemony aggravated to an unprecedented extent the contradictions between German imperialism on the one hand and the imperialists of England, France, and other countries on the other. It also accelerated the full-scale outbreak of a Second World War. On the eve of the war, the ruling classes of England, France, and various other nations had adopted a "noninterference policy" toward the aggressive activities of the Hitler gang of bandits. They vainly attempted to instigate fascist Germany to attack the socialist Soviet Union. They hoped their noninterference would yield benefits, just as if they were "sitting on a mountain top to watch the tigers fight." However, exactly as Chairman Mao predicted in October 1938, "[t]hey picked up a rock only to drop it on their own feet. This was the inevitable result of Chamberlain's policy."[26] On September 1, 1939, the Hitler gangsters brazenly attacked and invaded Poland. The flames of war finally burned the hands of the English and French imperialists, and the first shots of the Second World War in Europe were exchanged.

When we speak of the various imperialists involved, we can say that the Second World War was an unjust war to redivide the world. By the first half of 1941, the Hitler gang already occupied ten European countries, including France. They controlled vast areas with a population close to 300 million people and territory reaching five million square kilometers. On June 22, 1941, the German fascists, once again acting in a treacherous manner, launched a blitzkrieg attack against the Soviet Union, and temporarily occupied large areas of the western part of the Soviet Union.

Germany's militarized state monopoly capitalism achieved unprecedented growth during the war. In degree as well as in scope, we can say that Germany's militarized state monopoly capitalism far surpassed the level it had reached in Germany itself during World War I, and also exceeded the scale attained by any other capitalist country in World War II.

After this vast conflict broke out, the organizational apparatus of the fascist state that regulated the economy became even more complex. Two organizations contended with each other to gain control over the wartime economy: The first was the General Office of the Economy that operated under the Supreme Command of the Ministry of Defense; the other was the Military Preparedness Committee of the Ministry of Munitions. As the newer and the more established regulatory agencies tried to elbow each other out of the way, they created a great deal of confusion. The Hitler government, however, made use of these myriad regulatory agencies, and—proceeding from the standpoint of the requirements of an aggressive "total war"—adopted a series of reactionary measures to raise the revenue to pay for the expenses of war. It also stringently controlled and regulated the wartime economy, fanatically expanded production needed by the military, and did its utmost to strengthen the ruling status of the tycoons of monopoly capital.

Among those capitalist countries that were belligerents in the war, Germany's wartime military spending was second only to that of the United States, and amounted to 622 billion marks spent over six years. It consumed 92 percent of state expenditures, and exceeded by 15 percent the national income of Germany proper (according to 1937 boundaries) during that period. In order to make good on such alarming wartime expenditures, the fascist government levied exorbitant taxes domestically and frenetically plundered the occupied territories. During the war, total tax revenues in Germany reached 182.7 billion marks; the national debt increased 342.2 billion marks; and the amount of currency in circulation increased more than six times. According to incomplete statistics, the plunder from occupied territories was at least more than 200 billion marks.

The Hitler government stringently regulated industrial raw materials and labor power. It based its decisions on the general principle of giving priority to the production of military goods. Within Germany itself, the government did all it could to expand the production of raw materials, especially the production of synthetics and fuels. It strictly controlled the allocation of raw materials, supplied them to the monopolies on a priority basis, and constantly lowered the consumption ceilings set on raw materials. As the various monopoly groups fought with each other to secure access to strategic raw materials, they now became massively involved in illegal purchases, cornered the market for speculation, and even adulterated goods and materials. As a result, supplies of raw materials became increasingly difficult to obtain, while waste became more prevalent. With regard to labor power, the fascist government channeled several million housewives, handicraftsmen, small shopkeepers, vendors, students, and workers in civilian industry into factories producing military goods. This was done in order to compensate for the labor shortage caused by the military conscription of large numbers of skilled workers. In order to make up for serious shortages of industrial raw materials and labor power, the German fascists also systematically and with the utmost zeal plundered the occupied territories of their raw materials. They forcibly shipped to Germany as slave laborers more than ten million prisoners taken on the front lines or citizens taken from the occupied territories. Of these, half died from inhuman physical and mental suffering.

The crimes involved in German fascism's plunder of the occupied territories really are too numerous to be recounted. However, they did include the following: The confiscation of all the military equipment that had outfitted several hundred modernized divisions; the seizure of several million vehicles of various sorts and sizes; the appropriation of more than 1.5 billion U.S. dollars in gold and foreign exchange; the plunder of vast quantities of finished industrial products and agricultural goods. To take merely one category as an example, grain from the occupied territories supplied between one-seventh and one-fifth of Germany's wartime needs. The newer and older financial cliques in Germany both took over as their own private property the great majority of the large factories, mines, and banks of the various occupied nations. A large number of German landlords and wealthy farmers poured into Czechoslovakia, Poland, and other countries. They forcibly seized the property of the farmers there and set up their own estates. Nazi officials and soldiers were even more rapacious. They looted wherever they went, and continuously shipped "war trophies" back to Germany. The list goes on and on. All these criminal activities were merely a part of the sanguinary content of Hitler's "New European Order."

The power of the magnates of German monopoly capital grew further as a result of wartime regulation of the economy and the frenzied plunder of the occupied territories. During the war, these tycoons came to hold even more government positions and came to exercise an even more pervasive power over the economy. Under their pressure, two thousand lower-level cartels were forced to merge with other large monopoly groups. During the war, the number of the largest corporations with assets over fifty million marks increased from sixty-three to 108, and the total amount of their capital doubled. The assets and the deposits of several of the large Berlin banks doubled and quadrupled, respectively. State monopoly capital also expanded. Its share of the nation's total capital increased to one-third. A group of new, fascist financial magnates arose to stand side by side with the powerful old financial cliques. The rise of a concern headed by Hermann Goring (the number two leader in fascist Germany) was a notable example. This was a new concern that arose in the 1930s by plundering the property of the Jews and by robbing the state treasury. Its financial strength increased very rapidly as a result of its massive plunder of the metallurgical industries of Austria, Czechoslovakia, Poland, and other countries. In 1941, its capital amounted to 2.5 billion marks, and by 1943, had risen to six billion marks. By then it had become one of the largest concerns in Germany as well as in Europe.

The Lopsided Growth of the Militarized Economy and Its Collapse

Industry in fascist Germany grew to a certain extent during the war as a result of the intensified exploitation of domestic human and material resources and the shameless plunder of occupied territories. Industrial production as a whole increased 19 percent between 1938 and 1943. While the production of the means of production increased 63 percent, the production of consumer goods, on the contrary, shrank almost 10 percent. The unequal development of these two major segments of industry became an unprecedentedly serious problem. The consumer goods industry shrank further in 1944, while the production of the means of production stagnated.

Fascist Germany's military industry expanded in an extremely lopsided manner. The total number of workers in Germany's military industry in 1939 came to 2.1 million, and by 1944 had rapidly increased to six million. On the whole, German military production expanded 6.3-fold in the period from 1938 to 1944. At the same time, the German invaders also manufactured vast quantities of armaments in the occupied areas of Europe. These were supplied to German army units who were either stationed within the local areas or allocated to those units serving on the Eastern front. By the end of 1941, the six countries of France, Belgium, Holland, Denmark, Norway, and Poland by themselves had supplied to Germany weapons and munitions whose total value came to 12.8 billion marks.

During the war, the expansion of German industry (with military industry as the backbone) was sustained by the granting of 700 billion marks worth of government contracts for military goods and was maintained by the plunder of the natural resources of the occupied territories. Generally speaking, those sectors of heavy industry that served military production experienced some growth. However, their difficulties also mounted year by year. For example, the annual amount of coal production in Germany during the war consistently fluctuated around 400 million tons. Then stagnation set in. Pig iron and steel production even dipped below their prewar levels. Even though the quantity of electricity generated increased, the power industry had almost no reserve capacity by the end of the war. Blackouts became more frequent year after year. In general, very little of the machinery and equipment in use in industry was replaced. The widespread employment of the old, the weak, and of foreign slave labor to perform arduous work brought about an obvious decline in labor productivity. Germany's industrial base weakened year by year.

During the war, Germany's agriculture also steadily deteriorated, having to confront a situation of serious shortages in manpower and material resources and a huge influx of foreign slave laborers, war prisoners, and ordinary citizens. Grain production fell below prewar levels, and was incapable of satisfying demand. The efficiency of the transportation industry fell more and more, and fuel shortages brought large numbers of vehicles to a standstill. Foreign trade came to a halt; moreover, the favorable balance of trade that existed prior to the war turned into an unfavorable one.

Once Hitler's aggressive military forces began to suffer defeats and the war entered Germany itself, the fragile nature of the militarized, fascist economy became thoroughly exposed. As soon as the sources of its foreign plunder were cut off, Germany's stockpiles of raw materials gradually became exhausted. Supplies were totally insufficient to meet demand, a problem that grew with each passing day. Replenishing manpower ran into huge difficulties. Transportation was in an even bigger mess. As a result, German industrial production plunged straight down, beginning in the fall of 1944. For example, if the index in 1938 were set at one hundred points, then the index of the production of the means of production had declined to between thirty and forty-five points in 1945, and the index of the production of consumer goods had dropped between eighteen and twenty-eight points. The economy already lacked the ability to support the Nazi war machine.

Imperialism's war of aggression and the lopsided growth of a fascist, militarized state monopoly capitalism brought an unparalleled disaster to the German people. The war of aggression claimed the lives of seven million Germans, of whom five million fell on the battlefield. Millions and millions of military slave laborers suffered great physical and mental hardships at the hands of the Hitler gang while working in German factories and villages. The broad masses of workers struggled for their very existence, and lived just on the brink of starvation and death. The material and cultural wealth of Germany also suffered unprecedented destruction in the chaotic flames of war. The sole beneficiary was Germany's monopoly bourgeoisie whose hands were stained with blood. From wartime military contracts they earned at least seventy to eighty billion marks in profit.

Chairman Mao has pointed out that "all reactionaries are paper tigers." "Wasn't Hitler regarded as invincible? However, history has proved that he was a paper tiger."[27] The objective logic of historical development confirms this. Supported by and cooperating with the anti-fascist struggle of the entire world—and led by the great Marxist-Leninist, Stalin—the Red Army of the Soviet Union liberated Berlin in April 1945. Hitler, the chieftain of German fascism, committed suicide in order to evade punishment. On May 8, 1945, fascist Germany surrendered unconditionally. History had condemned fascist Germany's militarized state monopoly capitalism to suffer a complete collapse.

6 Japan

Japan has been the most recent addition to the ranks of the major capitalist countries. In fact, it was only as recently as the Meiji Restoration of 1868 that Japan emerged from its feudal system and stepped across the threshold into the world of capitalism. This was quite late when compared to the historical development of the advanced nations of Europe and America which, by this time, were already on the eve of their own transition to monopoly capitalism. However, Japan grew very rapidly after becoming a capitalist nation, and within half a century, leaped ahead to join the ranks of the capitalist powers. It quickly matured into an imperialist country, but one that was still heavily imbued with militaristic and feudal characteristics. Japanese imperialism flourished by waging wars of aggression and by plundering its colonial possessions. As a result, the history of the rise of Japanese imperialism is also a history of Japanese militarism's aggression against China and Korea. Finally, the history of Japan over the past century reveals a fundamental axiom: Any country which hopes to develop its economy on the basis of war, aggression, and militarism will ultimately meet its inevitable historical fate of total collapse.

1. The Disintegration of the Feudal System and the Meiji Restoration (1868)

Land Relationships during the Latter Period of Feudalism and the System of Exploitation in Japan

Although Japan's entry into modern capitalist society began with the Meiji Restoration, embryonic capitalist relations had already appeared more than a hundred years before within the womb of its feudal society. During the 265 years prior to the Meiji Restoration, Japan was ruled by the Tokugawa clan. This period (from 1603 to 1867) has been called the Tokugawa Era, and it was during this time that Japan's feudal order disintegrated and when the sprouts of Japanese capitalism first appeared.

Marx pointed out that "Japan had a purely feudalistic system of land ownership as well as an advanced, small farm economy."[1] These words best summarize the basic characteristics of Japan's feudal system. They also incisively point out the reason why capitalist relations of production appeared comparatively late in Japan. During the Tokugawa era, all land was owned by the feudal lords. Feudal manors were divided into four categories: those that belonged to the military government (the *bakufu*, or "tent government") of the Tokugawa clan; those that belonged to the feudal lords (or *daimyō*); those that belonged to the emperor and the aristocracy; and those that belonged to the Buddhist temples and Shinto shrines. The leader of the Tokugawa clan was called the generalissimo (or *shōgun*), and the organizational structure by which he ruled was called the *bakufu*. Not only was the *shōgun* the supreme ruler of Japan, but he was also the biggest landlord, owning more than 26 percent of all the cultivated land. The *bakufu* controlled more than 260 vassal states (or *han*) throughout the entire nation. The direct rulers of each vassal state were called feudal lords (or *daimyō*). As a group, they owned 70 percent of the remaining land. The emperor and his court officials (the *kuge*) were powerless under the *bakufu* system. They did not participate in the political decision-making process, although their families did own vast tracts of land. The temples and shrines served as the spiritual prop of the feudal class. They also directly owned large quantities of land.

The *shōgun* and *daimyō* maintained large bands of vassals (known as *kashin)* who served as an armed force capable of suppressing the peasantry. They were a very large group, numbering 400 thousand men by the middle of the nineteenth century. In general, the warriors owned no land, but lived on stipends derived from the domains of the *shōgun* and *daimyō*. However, they did enjoy special privileges such as exemption from taxes, and the right of summary execution of commoners. The organizational structure and system of feudal landownership was like a pyramid. It began at the top with the *shōgun*, then proceeded downwards to include the *daimyō*, and finally extended to the ranks of the *samurai*. It resembled a large mountain that weighed heavily on the backs of the people.

Japan's feudal lords did not organize their rural economy along manorial principles, but rather turned their land over to the peasants who then operated a small-scale and fragmented farm economy. As a result, Japan developed what Marx referred to as an "advanced, small farm economy." The peasantry, which constituted 80 percent of the population, never owned any land during the entire Tokugawa period. They served as hereditary tenants on the domains of the feudal lords, and each peasant household farmed approximately two *chō* of land (one *chō* being equivalent to .99 hectare). The feudal lords cruelly exploited the peasantry. Because economic exploitation and political control were directly interlinked, the rent and the taxes paid by the peasants were combined into one lump sum called the annual rice tribute, or *nengumai*. The amount taken from the peasantry ranged from 40 percent to 80 percent of the annual harvest. In addition to this, peasants had to pay taxes for such actions as crossing a bridge, taking a boat, cutting grass, gathering firewood, going fishing or hunting, preparing salt. They were also required to perform a certain amount of corvee labor annually for their overlord. There were two principles guiding the feudal lords' exploitation of the peasantry. The first was: "Don't let them die, but don't let them live." The second was: "Peasants are like sesame seeds. The more they are squeezed, the more oil they produce." Japan's feudal rulers imposed a system of collective responsibility on every five households in order to intensify their suppression and exploitation of the peasantry. In addition, legislation explicitly stipulated that "peasants can wear only clothing made of hemp and cotton," "they cannot eat too much rice," "they cannot purchase or drink sake or tea," "they cannot smoke," and "they cannot build a house that is inappropriate to their social status." Peasants lacked even the right to use their own names.

Japan's feudal ruling class also instituted a rigid system of social classification in order to maintain the feudal system of political power and exploitation. Citizens were divided into four categories: warriors, peasants, handicraftsmen, and merchants. In addition to these groups were the so-called *semmin* (or outcasts), also named *eta* or nonpersons. These pariahs could live only in specially designated ghettos, could not marry anyone from the so-called "four categories of people considered as human," and could work only as executioners, prison guards, night watchmen, or butchers. Their social status was inherited from generation to generation, and could never be altered.

The reason that the Tokugawa *bakufu* could maintain this comprehensive system of feudal control was that it was tied to a foreign policy of national seclusion (or *sakoku*). At the end of the sixteenth and the early seventeenth centuries, wave after wave of Portuguese, Spanish, Dutch, and English missionaries and merchants came to Japan. They kidnapped Japanese citizens and sold them elsewhere as slaves. They engaged in predatory trade practices, preached the Christian faith, and even sold guns and cannons to the *daimyō* of various fiefdoms in southern Japan. All of these activities constituted a threat to the feudalistic rule of the Tokugawa family, and as a result, they declared a policy of national seclusion for Japan in 1638. Except for Dutch merchants who were permitted to carry on a limited trade at Dejima in Nagasaki harbor, all other merchants and missionaries were expelled. Japanese citizens were also prohibited from emigrating.

The Development of a Commodity Economy Linking the Countryside with Japan's Cities and the Growth of Capitalist Relations of Production

Even though the Tokugawa *bakufu* did everything possible to maintain and strengthen the feudal system, it could not, however, alter the objective laws governing the inevitable disintegration of the feudal system and the inevitable birth of capitalist relations of production. A period of relative peace emerged once the Tokugawa family had established a regime that unified the country. To enhance their revenues, both the *bakufu* and the *han* governments temporarily paid more attention to agricultural production, rewarding those who opened new lands in wilderness areas. As a result, agricultural production made definite progress prior to the eighteenth century. Cultivated land increased dramatically. For example, land under cultivation in 1598 amounted to 1.5 million *chō*, but had increased to 2.9 million *chō* by 1716–35. The feudal authorities' somewhat lax enforcement of the restrictions placed on what could be grown on the "newly opened fields" had positive benefits. It enabled the peasants to cultivate not only mulberry trees (for sericulture and for making paper)[2] but also to grow tea plants, lacquer trees, indigo, hemp, cotton, sugar cane, and tobacco as cash crops. The steady expansion of such economic crops promoted the development of a commercialized agriculture as well as a household handicraft industry in Japan.

Faced by the onslaught of a commodity economy, impoverished peasants and handicraft workers left the villages in droves. They migrated to the cities to seek a new life, causing a steady increase in the urban population. While these events were occurring, the *bakufu* and *han daimyō*—in order to satisfy their ostentatious life-style as well as meet their financial obligations—had to sell the annual rice tax and other items they had robbed from the peasantry. An additional factor stimulated even more the development of communications and trade among and between the various regions of Japan, and promoted the growth of an urban economy: This was the "alternate residence" (or *sankin kōtai*) system which had been instituted by the Tokugawa *bakufu* to control the feudal lords of the various fiefdoms.[3] By the middle of the eighteenth century, the population of Edo—where the Tokugawa *bakufu* was located—had already topped 800 thousand. (Tōkyō is the present name for Edo. Edo was renamed Tōkyō in 1868.) The population of Ōsaka was around 400 thousand, and that of Kōyto, the residence of the emperor, was around 350 thousand. In addition to these three well-known cities, many castle towns (where the *han daimyō* resided) had populations ranging from thirty to fifty thousand people.

The cities were both the centers of the handicraft industry and of trade. It was here—packed in like sardines and controlled by the guilds—that many handicraftsmen (who had originally come from the villages) produced cloth, household utensils, metal goods, pottery, the swords carried by the warriors, and more than a hundred other kinds of handicraft goods. Day by day the urban merchant class grew in strength. In the cities, the prominent merchants established rich and powerful grain warehouses, wholesale businesses, consignment stores, and banking houses. They purchased, stored, and sold the annual rice taxes and rice stipends that had been sold to them by the feudal lords, the warriors, and the peasantry. Many *daimyō* who had fallen into financial difficulties sought loans from these wealthy merchants, frequently offering them one or two years' worth of rice taxes as collateral, or even turning over their right to collect the annual rice tax. By the latter half of the Tokugawa era, such merchants had become a powerful force. Prosperous merchant houses (or *dai-shōnin*)—like the Mitsui family of Edo and the Kōnoike family of Ōsaka—now began to emerge. The rise of commercial capital played an enormous role in corroding and disintegrating Japan's natural economy, its hierarchical social system, and the entire apparatus of its feudal political regime.

Even more critical were the dual trends of intensified feudal exploitation and commercialization of the annual rice tax. Both accelerated the impoverishment of the peasantry and its social fragmentation. Although it was strictly forbidden to buy or sell land, poor peasants had little recourse but to offer their plots (which had been in the family for generations) as collateral or as security to merchants or wealthy peasants. In this way, peasants could borrow money to pay for the grain that would sustain their lives. By the eve of the Meiji Restoration (1868), one-third of Japan's peasant households had already lost their land, a process that created large numbers of destitute people bereft of any future hopes. The merchants and wealthy peasants then seized the land that had been put up as collateral by the poor peasantry when they were unable to meet their mortgage payments. Although they were not the *de jure* owners of such land, the merchants and wealthier peasants in reality exerted controlling rights over it. As a result, they became a landlord class: the newly risen exploiters of the villages. The appearance and growth of this emerging landlord class symbolized the disintegration of the feudal system of landholding.

As their economic situation deteriorated, household handicraft production increasingly became a supplementary occupation of the peasantry. This development opened up new vistas for the activities of the merchants who had been hamstrung in the urban areas by suppression from the feudal lords and by restrictions imposed by the guilds. After the eighteenth century, commercial moneylenders tightened their grip on the peasantry. Initially they would purchase peasant handicrafts at very low prices, sell them on distant markets, and make enormous profits in the process. Then they provided the peasants in advance with the raw materials and tools required for production, thereby turning them into bona fide wage laborers who sold their labor power. This kind of capitalistic household handicraft industry (or decentralized handicraft workshop system) became quite common in the development of silk and cotton weaving, as well as in the manufacture of pottery, wooden furniture, and lacquer ware. By the latter half of the eighteenth century, some peasants and their sons and daughters had entirely disengaged themselves from agricultural pursuits and had become absorbed into the workshops or mills organized by the merchants. Here they produced standardized products according to a division of labor. In effect, a centralized, capitalistic handicraft workshop system had emerged. These kinds of workshops were apparent in industries like silk weaving, dyeing, papermaking, iron smelting, and brewing. However, because of the rigid control exercised by the forces of feudalism, Japan's handicraft workshop industries grew very slowly and were quite feeble. Not only did the handicraft workshops lack the support of mercantilist policies that were enjoyed by their counterparts in Western Europe, but they also lacked access to the primitive capital accumulation looted from the colonies by Western European governments. There were only some four hundred-plus handicraft workshops in all of Japan prior to the Meiji Restoration, and most were feudalistic in character.

The Crisis of the Feudal System and the Collapse of the Tokugawa **Bakufu**

The great leader Chairman Mao pointed out: "The landlords' cruel economic exploitation and political suppression of the peasantry led to numerous peasant uprisings that opposed the rule of the landlord class." "The class struggles of the peasantry, peasant uprisings, and peasant wars have been the only genuine motive forces in the development of history."[4] As commodity relationships became more commercialized, the life-style of the feudal lords also became increasingly extravagant, and their exactions from the peasantry became more and more extensive. For example, after the beginning of the eighteenth century, the *bakufu* and the various fiefs constantly increased the rates on the annual rice tax, raising them from about 50 percent of the harvest to 60 percent, then 70 percent, and finally even up to 80 percent and 90 percent. Often the annual rice tax would be collected one and even two years in advance. Exorbitant taxes were as numerous as the hairs on an ox. For example, there was a tax on the number of rooms in a house, a tax on the number of daughters in a family, a tax on newborn infants, and so on ad infinitum. Both the *bakufu* and the *han* governments also resorted to other measures in order to replenish their increasingly depleted treasuries. Such measures included constant enlargement of the scope of the commercial monopolies these governments controlled, and the frequent debasing of their currencies by altering their metallic content. Such policies plundered the peasantry and left them without a livelihood. Many peasants could do little but abandon farming and flood into the cities to look for alternative work. These developments brought about a steady decline in agricultural population as well as annual increases in farmland lain to waste. Agricultural production began to decline dramatically after the beginning of the eighteenth century. Famine, infanticide, and the sale of young women into prostitution became common sights in the villages. The population almost stopped growing. However, the more severe the oppression, the greater the resistance. Many destitute peasants rebelled when confronted with the prospect of starvation. Poverty triggered increasingly more frequent uprisings; 1,163 peasant rebellions have been recorded during the period of Tokugawa rule. Many took place during the eighteenth century, but their incidence accelerated especially after 1800 when 505 occurred between the years 1801 and 1867. For example, the famous Tempō Uprising of 1837—led by Heihachirō Ōshio—

linked a rural-based peasant rebellion to an uprising by the urban poor who were protesting the high commodity prices charged by the merchants. Centered in Ōsaka, the rebellion eventually spread throughout Japan. Such peasant uprisings dealt serious blows to the feudal rule of the *bakufu* and the *han.*

Opposition to the Tokugawa *bakufu* came not only from the ranks of the peasantry, handicraftsmen, and merchants. It even emerged from within the ranks of the ruling class, where sharp contradictions had grown more acute with each passing day. The financial situation of the *bakufu* and *han* governments had steadily deteriorated under the impact of a slumping agricultural sector. For example, during 1834–36, the *bakufu*'s annual average financial deficit reached 590 thousand *ryō* of gold, and exceeded 700 thousand *ryō* between 1854 and 1856. Many *daimyō* were also deeply in debt, and were therefore less and less able to pay stipends to their samurai vassals, who often slid into poverty. As a result, warriors from various ranks began to voice their increasing dissatisfaction with the rule of the *bakufu* and the *han* governments. They vented their feelings in the expression: "Although we give our last measure of loyalty to our lords, those retainers happy to serve are few and far between." Some warriors pursued alternative occupations—such as making writing brushes, umbrellas, rainwear, toys, and carvings—in order to support themselves. Some disregarded "dignity" and "face" and threw in their lot with the wealthy merchants, either adopting merchant sons, marrying relatives to merchant daughters, or selling titles to warrior status. Still others ran off to Europe and the United States to study science and culture, and returned to Japan as intellectuals propagating Western ideas. Some became landless, itinerant samurai (or *rōnin*) because they were unable to find an official post. The *baku-han* regime and the system of ranks and hierarchy that served it began to disintegrate under these circumstances. Not only did the warriors increasingly become the spokesmen for the merchants and the emerging bourgeoisie, but they also turned into opponents of *baku-han* rule.

Just as Japan's feudal system was on the verge of collapse, the Western capitalist powers, searching for overseas markets, burst in. The United States was the first country to use force to "open" Japan's "door." In 1853 and 1854, the U.S. government sent warships commanded by Commodore Matthew Perry to threaten Japanese ports. As a result, Japan was forced in 1854 to conclude the Treaty of Kanagawa. The Japanese government agreed to open the ports of Shimoda and Hakodate to trade and to permit an American consul to reside at Shimoda. In 1858, the United States once again intimidated Japan into signing a new unequal treaty. This United States–Japan Treaty of Amity and Commerce (or *Ansei* Treaty) stipulated that Americans enjoyed the right of extraterritoriality in Japan; that American goods could be shipped freely into Japan; that import tariffs could not exceed 5 percent; and that foreign currencies could circulate freely in Japan. After America took the "first slice" from Japan, England, Russia, Holland, and France followed suit and also imposed similar treaties. These treaties pushed Japan to the brink of semi-colonial status. The European powers then used the special privileges that they had secured to dump cheap commodities in Japan that had been produced by their large-scale industries. They also used their special privileges to purchase raw silk, copper, oil, tea, and aquatic products at very low prices from the Japanese. In the eight years from 1860 to 1867, Japan's exports increased 3.5-fold, yet its imports rose fourteenfold. On the one hand, these developments dealt a blow to Japan's workshop handicraft industries. On the other hand, they accelerated the disintegration of the feudal economy. At the same time, foreign merchants took advantage of the gap between Japan's domestic rate of exchange between gold and silver (one to five) and the world market rate (one to fifteen). These merchants made huge profits by importing silver into Japan and exporting large amounts of gold. This seriously damaged Japan's monetary system and financial foundation, and intensified Japan's domestic class and economic contradictions.

A dynamic movement to "expel the barbarians and overthrow the *bakufu*" arose in Japan at the beginning of the 1860s. The peasantry was the main force participating in this struggle. In the fourteen years between 1854 and 1867, more than 131 peasant uprisings took place. However, the scattered and backward nature of the peasantry prevented it from articulating a clear-cut, anti-feudal program and from becoming the leading force of the revolution. Japan at this time was at the early stages of an emerging and developing capitalistic workshop handicraft industry. Neither a bourgeoisie nor a proletariat had yet emerged as an independent political force. The newly risen landlords and commercial moneylenders had become powerful economically, and consequently began to raise concurrent demands for reforms. However, they were also intimately tied politically and economically to the feudal class and the *baku-han* system, and so were not the leading force to oppose feudalism. The leadership of the "expel the barbarians, overthrow the *bakufu*" movement thus fell into the hands of lower ranking samurai, especially those from the powerful Western *fiefdoms* of Satsuma, Chōshū, Tosa, and Hizen. These lower ranking samurai were well-informed and possessed comparatively high political and organizational skills. At the same time, they also confronted a deteriorating economic situation. Representative figures were Takamori Saigō, Toshimichi Ōkubo, Kōin Kido, and Hirobumi Itō. Associated with them were a small number of court officials (ranging from the emperor to other members of the aristocracy) such as Tomomi Iwakura. They took advantage of the people's revolutionary demands and the dissatisfaction of some *han daimyō* with *bakufu* rule to launch a coup d'état on January 3, 1868. Assisted by the vast financial strength of the great merchants of Ōsaka and Kyōto, they raised slogans such as "revere the emperor, expel the barbarians" and "return political power to the imperial family." They finally overthrew the rule of the *bakufu* and established a new imperial political system after a civil war that lasted only a few months. The fifteen-year-old Emperor Mutsuhito was now installed as head of state, the country was named "Dai Nippon," and the era became known as Meiji (or "enlightened rule").

The Meiji Restoration (1868): A Bourgeois Reform Movement that Compromised with the Feudal Ruling Class

The Meiji political system was a regime that represented the interests of the landlord and bourgeois classes. After its establishment, this regime hoped not only to maintain the vested interests of the feudal ruling class, but also wanted to use the power of the state to accelerate the development of capitalistic production in order to prevent Japan from becoming a colony of the Western powers. For this reason, the Meiji government—pressured by powerful peasant uprisings—carried out social, political, and economic reforms in the decade immediately after its establishment. Its slogans were "create a wealthy country and a powerful army" (*fukoku kyōhei*) and "boost production and invigorate industry" (*shokusan kōgyō*). This was the essence of the Meiji Restoration.

The Meiji Restoration was a bourgeois reform movement that compromised with the feudal ruling class. Although broad in scope, its main aspects can be summarized in the following points. First, the Meiji government abolished the old fiefs, established new prefectures, and set up a unified, nationwide political system. In 1869, for example, the various *han* returned both their land and household registers to the central government. In 1871, the names of the old *han* domains were dropped and a new system of prefectures—controlled by officials appointed by the central authorities—was set up. These measures established a system of centralized political power. Concurrently, the customs stations and currencies of the various *han* were eliminated. This put Japan's financial house in order and unified its currency. Such reforms greatly accelerated the formation and development of a Japanese nation and a unified market. However, the personnel staffing the administrative, military, and police positions at various levels of the government were former samurai, aristocrats, and *han* officials. These were the people who constituted the social foundation of the regime that eventually instituted militaristic rule domestically and launched wars of aggression abroad.

Second, the Meiji Restoration abolished social ranks as well as guild organizations. Between 1869 and 1871, for example, the government step by step abolished titles such as *daimyō* (feudal lord), *kuge* (court aristocrat), and *bushi* (warrior) and did away with the entire caste system of rank and status. Then, it declared that "the four categories of people are equal." The government also abolished the handicraft guilds and the merchants' associations, and permitted citizens the freedom of residence, movement, and choice of occupation. All these steps were advantageous to the development of capitalism. However, in order to maintain the vested interests of the feudal classes, the people were still put into three categories politically: an aristocracy (composed of former *daimyō* and *kuge*), a gentry (composed of former *bushi*), and common citizens. Economically, the government continued to provide "hereditary stipends" to the aristocracy and gentry. Finally, the government enacted legislation in 1876 that substituted payment in bonds for the payment of stipends. Bonds worth 175 million yen were issued to more than 310 thousand recipients. The upper stratum of the aristocracy and gentry then used these funds to invest in banks, railroads, and other companies. Others bought real estate and became new landlords with substantial assets. Though they had now joined the ranks of the bourgeoisie, they still retained their feudal titles.

Third, the Meiji-period government regarded the social systems of Europe and the United States as models. Government leaders studied European and American culture, imported European and American science and technology, and created the conditions for the development of a capitalist economy. In order to accomplish these goals, the state relied on a land tax exploited from the peasantry (as well as loans secured from abroad) to purchase foreign technology and equipment, build railroads, and establish model factories run by government officials. The government also sent public officials, technicians, and workers to Europe and the United States to absorb new information and new technologies. It hired foreign technical experts, organized industrial exhibitions, opened technical schools, and granted a variety of subsidies and bonuses to guide and promote the development of private capitalism. However, Shinto and militarist ideologies that encouraged worship of the Japanese emperor, the "Japanese spirit," and "the way of the warrior" (or *bushido*) were also played up and promoted by the Japanese government at the very same time that it was copying and learning from the cultural and educational systems of Europe and the United States.

Fourth, the Meiji government instituted land reforms and fostered a landlord class. However, it did not act on this issue immediately. After its establishment the imperial government gave absolutely no thought initially to either grappling with or resolving the land question. It was only after being pressured by peasant rebellions that the Meiji government began in 1872 to carry out land reforms. By recognizing the right of private ownership of land—and by acknowledging the principle that those who actually cultivated the land were its owners—the government in effect abolished the system of land ownership traditionally enjoyed by the old feudal lords. This satisfied the demand for land among a segment of the peasantry. However, the real power over 1.3 million *chō* of land (constituting nearly one-third of Japan's cultivated area) had already—prior to the land reforms—passed into the hands of commercial money-lenders and wealthy peasants, either in the form of collateral for loans, or as security that had been pawned. As a result, the land reform expropriated the poorer peasants and transformed one-third of the nation's peasant households into tenants. It fostered the growth of a new landlord class that served as a pillar of support of the imperial government in the village community. In 1873, the government enacted legislation that reformed the land tax code. The new legislation eliminated the plethora of previously existing levies, and instituted a single, unified, and nationwide land tax. The new land tax was pegged at the assessed value of a parcel of land. The tax rate was set at 3 percent of this "legally determined land price," had to be paid in currency, and was the responsibility of the owner of the property.[5] The reform of the land tax code benefitted the landlords but not the peasants. The Meiji government and the big landlords used the mechanism of the land tax and land rents to amass a vast amount of capital. These funds, plundered from the peasantry, became the principal source of Japan's primitive capital accumulation. In fact, up until 1885, more than 80 percent of the state's tax revenues were derived from the land tax.

To summarize, the Meiji Restoration embodied two aspects. On the one hand, it swept away some of the obstacles of feudalism and accelerated the process of primitive capital accumulation, thereby creating favorable conditions for Japan's development into a strong capitalist power. On the other hand, however, the Meiji Restoration retained much of the entrenched, reactionary, and backward forces of feudalism and militarism that had pervaded Japanese politics and economics. This laid the foundation for Japan's subsequent development into a militaristic and feudalistic imperialism.

2. Japan's Industrial Revolution and the Establishment of Capitalism

The Initial Development of Large-scale Capitalist Industry Promoted by the Government during the 1870s and 1880s

The establishment of the Meiji political system did not mean that Japan had eliminated the unequal treaties that it had been forced to sign with the United States and the major powers of Europe. Japan remained enslaved to foreign countries and lived under the constant threat of being conquered and turned into a colony. Confronting such circumstances, the Meiji government intervened extensively in the economy in order to accelerate the development of capitalism, enhance Japan's military capability, and prevent it from being taken over by the West. The government threw itself wholeheartedly into economic work. It established state-owned factories, granted special privileges to private capital, and promoted an industrial revolution throughout Japan. As a result, Japanese capitalism from its very inception bore the striking characteristics of state capitalism.

Japan's industrial revolution was a top-down revolution. Its first modern, large-scale industries were, in fact, set up by the government. After they were built, the Meiji regime then took over those feudalistic enterprises that were previously run by the *shōgun* and the *daimyō*. It reorganized and transformed these operations with technologies and equipment imported from the West. In addition, the government built and managed a large number of state-owned factories. These factories can be grouped into four major categories:

1. Military factories such as arsenals, munitions plants, and shipyards. These constituted the backbone of state-owned industry.

2. Transportation and communications operations. The government emphasized these sectors not only because of their crucial military significance, but also because they were an important factor in the development of capitalism. For example, the government began construction of a Tōkyō-Yokohama railroad in 1872. By 1894, the government-owned railway net stretched 929 kilometers.

3. Mines. The state managed more than ten mines that extracted gold, silver, copper, and coal. Their purpose was to increase the state's access to natural resources and supplies of gold and silver.

4. Cotton and silk-weaving factories. These sectors were major components of the handicraft industry during the period of feudalism. The government then built a number of model plants in these industries in order to induce private entrepreneurs to adopt the Western factory system and its advanced technology.

After the regime had established a number of these industries (an achievement that rested on the blood and sweat squeezed out of the peasants and workers by the state), the government announced in 1880 that it would sell these very same state-owned enterprises (except for those related to military production) to private individuals. The purpose of this sale was to reduce the state's financial responsibilities and burdens, as well as encourage and foster the development of private capitalism. As a result, the great majority of these enterprises were sold at very low prices to prominent "government-affiliated merchants," in other words, those wealthy merchants with close connections to the government (or "*seisho*"). For example, Mitsui obtained the Miike Coal Mine, the Shinmachi Yarn Spinning Factory, and the Fukuoka Silk Reeling Factory. Mitsubishi acquired the Nagasaki Shipyards, the Kobe Shipyards, the Takashima Coal Mine, the Sado Gold Mine, and the Ikuno Silver Mine. Companies were frequently sold at prices between one-third and one-half of their capitalized value. Some wealthy "government-affiliated merchants" then quickly sold such recent acquisitions to pocket even heftier profits.

In addition to selling off its factories at low prices, the government also granted entrepreneurs special privileges, subsidies, loans, gifts, and other inducements in order to foster the growth of private capitalism. For example, the Mitsui family (which operated commercial ventures and old-style banks in Edo, Ōsaka, Kyōto, Nagasaki, and other places during the *bakumatsu* period, i.e., from the 1830s to 1868) had provided substantial financial support to the new government during the Meiji Restoration and afterward. As a result, it secured a government-sponsored monopoly over the right to issue "Mitsui money" and to directly manage the income, expenditures, and currency transactions of the national treasury. It was on this foundation that the Mitsui family in 1876 created the Mitsui Bank as well as the Mitsui General Trading Company (Mitsui Bussan), with the latter enjoying a monopoly position over Japan's foreign trade. Another example was Yatarō Iwasaki, who managed a merchant house in the fiefdom of Tosa during the latter period of the *bakufu*. When the fiefs were abolished, Iwasaki assumed a portion of the *han's* liabilities and assets. The government gave him several ships which had originally belonged to this fiefdom, and with these as his basic assets, Iwasaki founded the Mitsubishi Steamship Company. Mitsubishi helped the government transport troops in 1874 when Japan became involved in some aggressive activities against Taiwan. At this time, the government gave to Mitsubishi—without demanding any compensation—an additional thirteen ships. Mitsubishi also gave the government a hand in 1877 during the war to suppress the samurai uprising in the old fiefdom of Satsuma in southwest Japan, and helped it to suppress a peasant uprising that demanded a reduction in the land rent. Mitsubishi received an annual subsidy of 250 thousand yen from the government at this time, and used it to purchase eighteen additional ships. In the process it became a great *zaibatsu* (or financial and industrial combine) monopolizing maritime trade.

By the beginning of the 1880s, some of the major reforms of the Meiji Restoration had already been completed. The political situation was stable. Moreover, the monetary reforms of 1880–85 (which stabilized the currency) created the conditions for large-scale imports of foreign technology, and for promoting private investment in industry. As a result, around 1885 Japan's industrial revolution entered a new stage of rapid growth. A huge wave of industrial ventures—promoted, guided, and nurtured by the government—swept over Japan. In the ten years between 1884 and 1893, the capitalization of industrial enterprises increased 15.5 times, that of trading companies 13.1 times, and that of commercial companies 4.3 times. By the eve of the Sino-Japanese War in 1893, there were already 3,019 factories in Japan, each of which employed more than ten workers. Six hundred seventy-five of these factories relied on machine power. Total employees in industry numbered 380 thousand. Japan's industrial revolution expanded to all major productive sectors. Like all the other capitalist countries, private investment in Japan's industrial revolution was centered on the cotton textile industry. Between 1887 and 1890, investment in cotton textiles constituted almost 40 percent of total investment in all sectors combined. In 1882, for example, Eiichi Shibusawa (pooling his own capital along with that of some aristocrats and wealthy merchants) founded Japan's first modern, large-scale textile plant—the Ōsaka Spinning Mill. Many large textile spinning companies were subsequently established. In the period between 1887 and 1893, the number of cotton spindles increased from 84,428 to 475,158. Cotton yarn production went from 1,213,000 *guan* (with one *guan* being equivalent to 3.75 kg.) to 10,667,000 *guan*. These statistics represented sixfold and ninefold increases, respectively, within a seven-year period. As a result, the cotton textile industry took on a new look. After 1885 the weaving industry also initiated its own technological revolution. Large companies were established in this sector one after the other.

However, from its very inception Japanese capitalism lacked a stable foundation. The primary source of capital for industry was the land tax and land rents paid by the peasantry. Payments for imported machinery relied chiefly on raw silk exports. The market for industrial products was mainly the peasantry, who constituted 70 percent of Japan's population. However, productivity and living standards in the countryside were extremely low because agriculture was stuck in the rut of a semi-feudal, small-farm economy, and because of the exploitation of the peasantry who suffered from the extremely high land rents. At the same time, the cruel exploitation of Japan's industrial working class caused an even greater contraction in its domestic market capacity. The majority of Japan's industrial workers were women who had migrated from the villages. Their working conditions were extremely bleak, and their wages very low. For example, according to 1890 statistics, an experienced worker in military-related industries earned only 2.4 *jiao* daily. A male worker in a silk factory made 1.5 *jiao* daily, while a woman worker earned between 0.9 and 1.2 *jiao*. However, one *jiao* at that time could only buy three *jin* (with one *jin* being equivalent to half a kilogram) of husked rice. The industrial bourgeoisie's exploitation of its factory workers was frequently feudalistic in character. For example, a master-apprentice system[6] and an "eating place" system[7] pervaded occupations such as civil engineering, mining, and fishing. A contract system[8] and a dormitory system[9] were prevalent in the textile industry. A hierarchical step system within each job category—and a system of penalties that included fines, reduced pay, and reduced food allowances—were both common in all factories. All these arrangements were manifestations of feudal relationships and of a patriarchal system that had now been shifted over into the realm of capitalist exploitation. All of these feudal procedures caused the rapid emergence of a sharp contradiction between the constricted domestic market and a rapidly developing large-scale industry. In addition, the continued existence of the unequal treaties that Japan had been forced to sign with the Western countries flooded this constricted domestic market with even more foreign commodities. Consequently, Japanese industrial growth—and foremost in its textile sector—very quickly encountered difficulties. A crisis of overproduction broke out in 1890. The price of yarn plummeted, sales stagnated, and production had to be cut back for three months.

Japan's War of Aggression against China in 1894–95 and Its Impact on Japan's Industrial Revolution

Japan's Meiji Restoration resolved neither the problem of securing adequate land for the peasantry nor the problem of expelling foreign power from Japanese territory. As Japanese capitalism developed and as the land rent became more exploitative, the contradictions between the working class and the bourgeoisie, between the peasantry and the landlords, and between Japan's national bourgeoisie and foreign capitalism grew increasingly more salient. A worker-peasant movement developed as a result. Confronted by these conditions, the absolutist Meiji regime adopted dual tactics. On the one hand, it steadily intensified its suppression of domestic opposition. On the other hand, it made plans to carry out aggression against foreign countries, seize foreign markets and colonies, and use these activities to divert the attention of the people, and thereby alleviate Japan's domestic contradictions. As a result, Japanese militarism, counseled by American advisers, launched aggressive operations as early as 1874 against China's province of Taiwan. It also occupied the Liu Qiu (or Ryūkyū) archipelago (whose name was changed to Okinawa in 1879). The Japanese government used a pretext (that Liu Qiu immigrants in Taiwan were being oppressed by the natives) to initiate these activities. After 1875, Japan also began an incremental campaign of aggression against Korea. After the 1890 textile crisis, Japan's bourgeoisie began to openly raise demands for expansion into China and Korea. In January 1891, the Alliance of Textile Manufacturers presented to the Minister of Agriculture and Commerce a "Petition to Abolish Customs Duties on Cotton Textile Exports." It read, in part, as follows: "The urgent obligation of this industry is to seek increased exports for our nation's cotton textiles, . . . and the countries which constitute the target of our exports are principally China and Korea" [source unknown]. However, China and Korea by that time had fallen into the spheres of influence of the Western powers, and they were already flooded with British textiles. It was difficult for Japan, a country whose industrial strength was still quite feeble, to attempt to use competitive methods to gain access to the Chinese and Korean markets. As a result, Japan's absolutist regime (representing the interests of the landlords and bourgeoisie) relied on two favorable conditions—its close proximity to China and the existence of contradictions among the various imperialist powers—to launch a large-scale war of aggression against China. This was the Sino-Japanese War which began on August 1, 1894.

Hoping to strike a blow against Russian influence in Korea and China, England and the United States (both openly and covertly) supported Japan in this endeavor, thereby inflating the arrogance of the Japanese aggressors. In addition, the corruption and incompetence of the Chinese government enabled the Japanese aggressors to secure a victory that was beyond even their own expectations. In April 1895, the Japanese forced the Qing dynasty to sign the Treaty of Shimonoseki, a treaty that deprived China of many of its rights and was an insult to the nation as a whole. Under the terms of this treaty, Japan secured the following special rights and privileges:

1. China was forced to recognize Korea's "independence" as well as Japan's domination of the Korean market.

2. Japan incorporated China's Taiwan province and the Penghu Islands into its empire.

3. Japan received an indemnity of 230 million ounces of silver.[10]

4. Japan forced China to open its cities of Shashi, Chongqing, Suzhou, and Hangzhou to trade. China also recognized the right of Japanese citizens to establish manufacturing industries in Chinese ports.

This war served as a turning point for Japan. It had now changed from an oppressed country into an oppressor. The war also represented a turning point in Japan's industrial revolution. Its economy now entered a new stage.

First of all, Japan's acquisition of a dominant position in the markets of Korea and Taiwan—coupled with its expansion into the mainland China market as a whole—enabled it to enlarge its exports by two-and-a-half times in the period from 1895 to 1905. About half of its total exports (except for raw silk) went to China, and almost all of its cotton yarn was shipped to either China or Korea. This stimulated Japan's industrial growth, and especially the extremely rapid development of its textile sector.

Second, the war also substantially accelerated the development of Japan's heavy industries (those which focused on military production) as well as its communications and trade sectors. For example, the government's wartime military expenditure of 245 milllion yen went for the most part to military-related industries. After the war, the government once again proposed a new plan for expanding its military forces. Direct military spending consistently took 40 percent of the national budget. More than 90 percent of the indemnity secured from China went to pay for expanding Japan's military forces. All of this paved the way for major growth in steel, shipbuilding, coal, and railroads. The creation of the Yawata Iron and Steel Company in 1897 was an important symbol of this growth. Most of the iron ore that this facility used came from China's Daye Iron Mine, located in Hubei province.

Next, Japan's acquisition of a huge indemnity enabled it to shift in 1897 from the silver standard to the gold standard. This proved to be healthy for Japan's domestic system of credit, promoting the speedy development of its banking sector. It also tied Japan's financial markets very closely to those in Europe and the United States, thereby enhancing Japan's overseas competitiveness.

Finally, Japan's victory over China—that vast and venerable country—elevated Japan's international status. Victory enabled Japan to gradually eliminate the unequal treaties which the foreign powers had previously imposed. It also dissipated the danger of Japan becoming a Western colony or semi-colony.

Japan's industrial, communications, trade, banking, and commercial sectors all made startling gains in the ten years (1894–1904) after the beginning of the Sino-Japanese War. The number of companies in these sectors increased 3.1-fold, rising from 2,844 to 8,895 during this decade. Their capitalization went from 245 million yen to 931 million yen, or a 3.8-fold increase. Factories employing more than ten workers went from 3,019 in 1893 to 8,274 in 1903. Factories using machine power increased from 675 to 3,741. And the number of factory workers rose to 484 thousand from 380 thousand. By this time, all major sectors of modern industry had been established, and had grown to dominate the production of handicrafts and the handicraft factory system. Japan's industrial revolution had achieved a major victory.

The Characteristics of Japanese Capitalism's Development

We can see the following prominent characteristics in the development of Japanese capitalism.

First, a large-scale Japanese capitalist industry developed under the massive assistance and zealous protection of an absolutist political system. As a consequence, Japanese industrial growth was not only quite rapid, but also quickly developed close links to the government and enjoyed special considerations and protection from that source. A small number of capitalist businesses (such as Mitsui, Mitsubishi, Suimitomo, Yasuda, Furukawa, Kuhara, Fujita, and Shibusawa) emerged with special rights to play a dominant role in the economy. Mitsui and Mitsubishi were the largest of these companies. Using the Mitsui bank, the Mitsui family gained control over industries such as textiles, papermaking, electricity, coal, and other sectors. Mitsubishi achieved dominance over maritime trade, shipbuilding, mining, railroads, and other industries through its control of the Mitsubishi Bank. It was precisely for this reason that Japan's modern industry and banking were extremely centralized right from the very beginning of their existence. By the end of 1901, for example, Japan's eight largest banks held 51 percent of the total deposits of the entire Association of Japanese Banks, which had more than 170 members. In 1903, the eight largest companies in the textile field controlled 49 percent of the capital of the fifty-one companies that participated in the Association of Textile Manufacturers. By the early 1880s, cartels began to appear in several industries such as papermaking, cotton spinning, and hemp weaving. As a result, two processes in Japan, the development of capitalism and its transition to monopoly capitalism, became largely identical.

Second, Japan's capitalist industry developed by relying on imported foreign technology. On the one hand, this enabled the Japanese to establish, relatively quickly, a modern, large-scale industry based on a not-very-advanced, native handicraft factory system. On the other hand, it also created a fragile foundation for Japanese industry, as well as a significant Japanese dependency on foreign countries. Prior to the Russo-Japanese War, Japan essentially lacked an indigenous, independent machine-manufacturing sector. Heavy industry was also quite limited. Textile production overwhelmingly dominated Japanese industry. In 1900, for example, the textile sector accounted for 73 percent of Japan's factories, 46 percent of its horsepower, and 67 percent of all industrial employees.

Third, state capitalism and the military-industrial complex in Japan became especially advanced. This occurred because Japanese capitalism developed a) under the impetus of state capital and b) within the context of the government's prosecution of overseas wars of aggression. Even though the first group of state-owned factories had been sold at very low prices to private capitalists, the overall status of state-owned industry—which focused on military production—

remained quite strong. Victory in the Sino-Japanese War boosted the arrogance of Japanese militarism. However, the Japanese militarists were unable to obtain China's Liaodong Peninsula (a piece of land they considered a "juicy morsel") after the conclusion of the war. Using this failure as a pretext, the Japanese government put forward a reactionary plan for military expansion, pledging never to forget this bitter incident by "sleeping on brushwood and drinking bile." By 1898, the total amount of capital that the government had invested in state-owned enterprises—such as army plants, naval installations, railroads, post offices, telegraph and telephone operations, and steel facilities—came to 148,400,000 yen. This represented about half of the capital then invested in Japan's privately owned factories, mines, and transportation networks. The development of state capitalism, which focused on the military-industrial complex laid the economic foundation for Japan's transition to militarism.

Finally, Japanese capitalism developed on the foundation of a semi-feudal agriculture. Not only did this cause Japan's working class to suffer the cruelest and most acute forms of oppression and exploitation, but it also created some unique characteristics that distinguished the development of Japanese capitalism from that of the other major capitalist countries. The first was the serious lack of coordination between industry and agriculture. Because Japan's developing industries could not find adequate raw materials or markets domestically, they encouraged even more intensified forms of expansionism and aggressiveness on the part of Japanese capitalism. Second, the existence of a vast, hidden surplus population in the villages (created by the semi-feudal ruling system there) brought a plentiful and cheap supply of labor power to industry. A capitalist could still turn a tidy profit even if he used handicraft labor and backward facilities. As a result, Japan's large-scale capitalist industry coexisted for a long time with a backward, family-based handicraft sector. Even by the early twentieth century, some sectors—such as silk manufacturing, cloth dyeing, ceramics, glassmaking, and production of matches—still remained at the stage of the handicraft workshop. Third, the backwardness of the villages left Japan short in the area of primitive capital accumulation. Industrial capital was heavily dependent on bank capital. The banks also charged high interest rates. As a result, banking capital consistently enjoyed an absolute superiority over industrial capital. By 1902, for example, the assets of industrial capital did not come to even half those of banking capital.

The Controls Imposed by Semi-feudal Relationships in Japan's Villages and Their Impact on Agricultural Backwardness

The land reforms carried out after the Meiji Restoration not only abolished the rights of landownership enjoyed by the feudal ruling class, but also established in their place the rights of private ownership—which now included the farmer who tilled his own plot. To a certain degree, these changes readjusted the old relations of production and promoted the development of the forces of production in agriculture. Certain improvements in agricultural technology also took place under the impetus of large-scale industry. As a consequence, the area of land under cultivation, total agricultural production, and production per unit of land all expanded. Let us take rice paddy as an example. When we compare the average of the three years between 1878 and 1880 with the average of the ten years between 1891 and 1900, we can see that the area of sown paddy went from 2.28 million hectares to 2.76 million hectares, the total amount of rice produced increased from 3.95 million tons to 5.79 million tons, and the amount produced per hectare went from 1.7 tons to 2.1 tons. Sericulture and tea cultivation, stimulated by export demands, also made comparatively significant progress. Silkworm cocoons (used to make raw silk) and tea leaves were Japan's principal sources of foreign exchange, and occupied an important niche in Japan's export trade.

However, the development of Japanese agriculture became increasingly uneven. The production of hemp, indigo, sugar cane, and soybeans (which were extensively cultivated in the past) now fell off dramatically. Cotton production, which had achieved rather substantial progress for a period of time, almost completely vanished by 1900. Food grain production also fell far short of satisfying domestic needs. As a result, imports increased with each passing day. Let us once again look at rice paddy, the principal crop with the most extensive cultivation in Japan, as an example. An average of 370 thousand hectoliters of rice (with one hectoliter being equivalent to 180 kilograms) was exported annually between 1885 and 1889. However, Japan had to import 2.74 million hectoliters of rice annually between 1900 and 1904. Even the great bulk of wheat and unrefined sugar had to be imported. According to my calculations, 70 percent (or 17.33 million people) of Japan's work force in 1900 was employed in either agriculture, forestry, or aquaculture. If such a huge population engaged in agricultural production could not supply Japan's basic food requirements, then it was even less capable of supplying the agricultural raw materials required for industrial use. Every bit of cotton had to be imported. All this resulted from the controls imposed by semi-feudal relationships in the villages.

As mentioned previously, the Meiji Restoration land reform policy (of determining land ownership rights on the basis of who actually controlled the land) deprived one-third of all peasant households of their plots and made them into tenant farmers. Even after the reforms, many peasants who farmed their own land fell into bankruptcy and became tenant farmers because of the heavy burden of the high land tax, the steady expansion of a commercialized agriculture, and the intensified exploitation from commercial money-lenders. For example, while only 30.3 percent of all cultivated land was farmed by tenants in 1872, this figure had climbed to 40 percent in 1892 and 44.5 percent in 1903. The lands lost by the peasantry became concentrated in the hands of landlords. By the early twentieth century, the fifty thousand biggest landlords in Japan (constituting less than

1 percent of all farm households) owned one-fourth of all the cultivated land.

A decline in the percentage of ownership by individual peasants and the concurrent increased concentration of land ownership in the hands of landlords did not bring about the development of large-scale, capitalist farming as had occurred in England, the United States, and other countries. On the contrary, it brought about an expanded number of semi-feudal tenant farmers who ran small farms. This is to say that very few of the landlords and commercial money-lenders who had foreclosed on the land of bankrupt peasants made use of hired agricultural labor to establish capitalist farms. On the contrary, they generally divided the land into small parcels, rented them out to impoverished peasants, and then sat back and enjoyed the proceeds of the rent payments. As a result, not only did the number of farm tenant households constantly increase, but management over the land became more and more fragmented. During the Tokugawa period, for example, each household tilled on the average two *chō* (or 4.9 acres) of land. By 1886, however, each household cultivated only eight *fan*, three *mu*, and two *bu* (one *chō* was equivalent to ten *fan*; one *fan* equaled ten *mu*; and one *mu* equaled thirty *bu*). This did not approach even half of the land available to each household during the Tokugawa era. To explain this unusual phenomenon, Japan's landlord and bourgeois scholars have frequently pointed to the existence of natural conditions—"overpopulation and scarce land" or "irrigated paddy fields require the fragmentation of landholding"—as causes. These, however, are fallacies that apologize for the feudal land system. The crux of the matter lay in the support and protection that was given the landlord class by Japan's absolutist regime. Land rents in Japan usually claimed between 50 percent and 60 percent of the total harvest. Such high land rents made it more profitable to rent out scattered parcels than to concentrate them as capitalist farms. At the same time, Japanese landlords preferred to invest the capital they had accumulated from their rental income in banking, industry, and commerce. This occurred because primitive capital accumulation was inadequate in Japan, and because bank interest rates and industrial profits were both very high. As a result, Japanese landlords became super-parasites, enjoying income from both land rents and stock dividends, yet devoting nothing to agricultural management. In addition, the overall level of Japanese industry remained quite low despite its comparatively rapid development. This was particularly true in textiles, a major industrial sector, which mostly employed women and children as workers. As a result, those peasants who had lost their land could not be completely absorbed by industry. This created a large, hidden surplus population with little alternative but to rent and till tiny plots of land, be gouged by high rents, and live from hand to mouth.

Landlord-tenant relationships in Japan were feudal relationships. Landlords appropriated the entire surplus production of their tenants (and even some products essential to the work process) by charging sky-high rents. In addition, they relied on the political authorities and the force of tradition to impose a system of control on the tenant farmers that went beyond the sphere of economics. Commercialized farming already constituted between 40 percent and 60 percent of agricultural production at this time. Tenant farmers were exploited by both capitalism and commercial capital when their products entered the domain of commodity circulation. Some tenant farmers also worked concurrently as casual laborers in order to make ends meet, thereby becoming semi-proletarians. All these developments reflected the side of capitalist exploitation suffered by the tenant farming economy. The rule of semi-feudal relationships in the villages was one of the sources of Japan's agricultural backwardness, as well as of the distorted development of its entire economy.

3. The Emergence of Japanese Monopoly Capital and Its Distinctive Militaristic and Feudal Character

The Russo-Japanese War (1904–05) and the Rapid Development of Heavy Industry

While the Sino-Japanese War of 1894–95 stimulated the development of Japan's industrial revolution and the establishment of capitalism there, it was the Russo-Japanese War that played an extremely important role in hastening its transition to monopoly capitalism. Japan made China and Korea the targets of its aggression in both wars.

Japan's war against Russia and its further aggression against China were the result of the growing intensification of its domestic and political contradictions. As Japan's industrial revolution accelerated, the lives of its workers and peasants deteriorated, and a worker-peasant movement grew in strength. In 1889, Japan's autocratic regime promulgated one of the world's most reactionary constitutions. It vested supreme power in the emperor and the military commanders, and instituted a militaristic rule over the people. This made the people even more angry and aroused greater resistance on their part. As these class contradictions were becoming more acute, Japan's economic contradictions were also intensifying. The economic boom that began with the Sino-Japanese War had not been sustained for very long when a crisis hit the textile industry in 1897 and 1898. The first comprehensive economic crisis in Japan's history broke out subsequently in 1900. This crisis was tied in with a global economic crisis which Japan had not recovered from even by early 1904. Under these circumstances, Japan's newly emergent landlord and bourgeois classes decided to participate in the imperialist powers' wars to divide and redivide the world. Japan now put forth its "mainland policy" in a vain attempt to impose Japanese rule over all of Asia. Czarist Russia was Japan's initial opponent. After a long period of preparation, Japanese militarism in February 1904 began its attack—without a declaration of war—on Russian military forces stationed both in China (at Luda) and in Korea. Japan's intention was a) to expel czarist power from Korea and from China's northeastern provinces, b) annex Korea, and c) become the sole ruler over China's Northeast.

Lenin pointed out that "Japan . . . required the assistance of other countries. Neither financially nor militarily did it have the capacity for independent action."[11] In 1902, England concluded a treaty with Japan that established an Anglo-Japanese military alliance. Britain had a dual purpose in making this agreement. First, it hoped to use Japan to strike at Russia. Second, it wanted to consolidate its own vested interests in China and throughout Asia. The United States also supported Japan, hoping that Japan and Russia would injure each other in any confrontation, and thereby smooth the way for America's own expansion into East Asia. Japan spent 1.7 billion yen on the war, of which 800 million came from loans granted by England and the United States. Japan defeated czarist Russia by relying on the military power it had developed over a long period of time, and by counting on the vast support of the United States and England. Japan and Russia—these two imperialistic gangsters—then completely disregarded China's territorial sovereignty, fighting their battles wherever they wished on Chinese soil. Both powers brought the disasters of war to the Chinese people. After the war was concluded, they once again ignored the opposition of the Chinese people when they cavalierly divided up China's territory. According to the Treaty of Portsmouth (1905), Japan forced Russia a) to cede the southern half of Sakhalin Island, b) to recognize Japan's *de jure* right to control Korea, and c) to give Japan the Russian leases on Luxun, Dalian, and the southern portion of China's East Central Railway (stretching from Changchun to Luxun).

Japan's victory over Russia played an important role in stabilizing and strengthening the political structure of Japanese militarism. Victory also enhanced Japan's international status, released Japan from its domestic economic crisis, and stimulated an industrial boom. The war, which claimed the lives of 560 thousand Japanese and created a nationwide famine, also enabled the bourgeoisie to make a fortune. They accumulated a vast amount of capital by taking advantage of the wartime inflation, the skyrocketing prices of valuable securities, and government procurement of military goods. They also relied on Japan's expansionism and plunder of China and Korea to enlarge their sources of raw materials and markets to an unprecedented degree. As a consequence, a rapid upsurge in new business ventures once again took place in Japan in the postwar period. For example, in the space of just over two years (from the latter half of 1905 to 1907), investment in either newly established or expanded enterprises totalled 674,770,000 yen, or approximately triple the total amount invested in the previous decade. Although this boom was cut short by the economic crisis of 1907, the war's role in stimulating the economy had not yet been entirely exhausted. In the decade from 1904 to 1914, Japanese industrial production increased two and a half times. The number of factories employing more than ten employees more than doubled, increasing from 8,274 to 17,062. Factories that utilized machine power increased 2.7-fold, going from 3,741 to 10,334 in number. Machine-generated horsepower increased tenfold, going from 100 thousand horsepower to one million. The number of factory workers grew 2.2-fold, going from 484 thousand to 1,086,000.

Japanese industrial development during this period exhibited one distinctive characteristic. Based on the raw materials it had seized from China and Korea, the Japanese chemical and heavy industries (including sectors such as electricity, coal, steel, machine manufacturing, and shipbuilding) made the most substantial gains and grew faster than light industry. Japan's industrial revolution was now in transition from a textile-centered, light industry to a steel-centered, heavy industry. For example, more than ten large companies emerged in the steel industry. Pig iron production more than quadrupled in the decade from 1904 to 1914, increasing from sixty-eight thousand tons to 302 thousand tons. Rolled steel output expanded almost fivefold, going from sixty thousand tons to 283 thousand tons. The rate of self-sufficiency in steel was greatly increased. Because of its military importance, the machine-manufacturing industry—especially the machine tool building industry—became the most favored recipient of government assistance. By 1910, Japan possessed its own independent machine-building industry. While Japan's chemical industry had basically not amounted to anything in the past, it created many new companies—focused primarily on fertilizer production—in the postwar period. However, light industry still retained its dominance within Japanese industry up until the First World War. For example, textile production in 1914 accounted for 43.7 percent of total industrial output value. Even taken collectively, the metals industry, machine-manufacturing, electric power, natural gas production, and chemicals produced only 24.2 percent of total industrial output value.

In foreign trade, Japan achieved substantial growth after expanding into the markets of Korea and northeast China. This occurred after Japan successfully revised its treaties with the Western powers in 1911, and after the government concluded new commercial treaties with various nations that guaranteed Japan's right to set its own tariff rates. Between 1904 and 1914, for example, the total value of Japanese exports went from 319,260,000 yen to 591,100,000 yen, and the total value of imports increased from 371,300,000 yen to 595,740,000 yen. However, Japanese foreign trade frequently ran a deficit because it depended on foreign supplies of raw materials and machinery.

The Emergence and Special Characteristics of Japanese Monopoly Capital

Both during and after the Russo-Japanese War, Japan's industrial production and the tempo of its capital concentration greatly accelerated. This followed the rapid development of its heavy industry and stronger government support for its big capitalists. In particular, the crisis of 1907–08 brought about the bankruptcy of many banks and industrial enterprises that had been set up during the war on a purely speculative basis. This crisis speeded up production and the concentration of capital. As a result, the Russo-Japanese War represents a dividing line, a decisive stage in which Japan entered the transition from a freely competitive capitalism to that characterized by monopoly.

By 1914, large corporations employing more than five hundred workers constituted only 0.7 percent of the total number of industrial enterprises, yet employed 25.7 percent of all factory workers. Large corporations with a capital value in excess of five million yen represented only 0.37 percent of the total number of companies, yet controlled 38.5 percent of total corporate capital. The concentration of capital in banking was even more striking. In 1914, for example, five major banks (Mitsui, Mitsubishi, Sumitomo, Yasuda, and Daiichi Kangyo) controlled 22.5 percent of the total deposits and 18.4 percent of the total loans held by all of Japan's 2,153 banks.

Based on this increasing concentration of production and capital, cartels began to appear in the 1880s in sectors such as textiles, papermaking, and hemp weaving. By the early twentieth century, these cartels had expanded further and increased their strength to the point where some even became trusts. While this was occurring, monopolies (like cartels, syndicates, trusts, and concerns) were emerging one after the other in all the other major industrial sectors. For example, cartels appeared in industries like silk reeling (1905), chemicals (1907), and flour milling (1914). The sugar (1908), machinery (1909), petroleum (1910), and coal industries either set up syndicate-like mechanisms with joint marketing arrangements or concluded agreements with each other regarding production and sales. The Yawata Iron and Steel Company held an absolute monopoly within the steel industry. In 1913, for example, it held a 73 percent monopoly over pig iron production and 84 percent over steel production. By 1913, monopolies in various sectors of the economy already controlled about 75 percent of the total capital of Japan's industrial and commercial enterprises. Most prominent among Japan's monopolies were the large financial and industrial combines known as the *zaibatsu*—concerns like Mitsui, Mitsubishi, Sumitomo, Yasuda, Kawasaki, Yamaguchi, Asano, ōkura, Furukawa, and Katakura. The first four among these were called the "four great *zaibatsu*" and, in effect, ruled Japan. Not only did these four major *zaibatsu* control the lifeblood of the national economy, but they also colluded with the political oligarchs (called the *genrō*), the bureaucrats, and the military leaders. They pulled the strings behind the political parties and directly influenced the government. For example, the *genrō,* Kaoru Inoue, who worked with Mitsui to arrange the merger and creation of the Mitsui General Trading Company, served as Mitsui's chief adviser. Jotairo Yamamoto and Kaku Mori, influential politicians who were members of the Seiyūkai political party (or Friends of Constitutional Government party), had close ties with Mitsui. Ōkuma Shigenobu, the Secretary-General of the Kaishintō political party (or Constitutional Reform party) and Katō Takaaki (the son-in-law of the President of Mitsubishi, Yataro Iwasaki), the Secretary-General of the Kenseikai political party (or Constitutional Association), also closely collaborated with Mitsubishi. They were the most consistently active political leaders in Japan at the end of the nineteenth century. They served either as prime ministers or important cabinet ministers, and acted as representatives of the *zaibatsu.*

Compared to its European and American counterparts, Japanese monopoly capital exhibited the following striking characteristics in terms of form and substance: First, Japan's big finance capitalists were organized into powerful cliques within the economy. They also had a long history. Many, in fact, had emerged as commercial tycoons during the feudal era. For example, the founding fathers of Mitsui (Takatoshi Mitsui), Mitsubishi (Yataro Iwasaki), Sumitomo (Masatomo Sumitomo), and Yasuda (Zenjiro Yasuda) had all served as managers of either powerful wholesaling establishments, banking houses, or mines during the latter years (1853–68) of the Tokugawa *bakufu.* These individuals colluded with the government during the Meiji Restoration to form large-scale "government-business enterprises," or "*seisho.*" They subsequently received substantial governmental assistance and became capitalists who enjoyed special privileges. However, even after they had developed into modern monopoly capitalists—or finance capitalists—they still retained the traits characteristic of commercial money-lenders by charging outrageously high interest rates. In short, they carried the heavy imprint of feudalism. *Zaibatsu* management generally made use of special stock holding arrangements that centered on a family-based holding company. This family holding company then controlled other subordinate and collateral companies, which collectively appeared as a family-owned combine. In general, the stocks of the *zaibatsu* corporations were closely held, and sold only to a small number of people with intimate ties to the family that owned the company. An extremely rigid system of "patriarchal" centralization was quite common throughout the *zaibatsu.* The highest authority never resided with a board of directors elected by stockholders, but rather belonged to family conferences attended by the principal members of the family and their relatives. In some cases, this authority was exercised by only one person. In 1900, Mitsui actually put in place a "family constitution" to consolidate its family's control over the business. This charter formulated strict regulations governing all aspects of the company's operations. Its full text contained ten chapters and ran to more than one hundred clauses.

Second, although Japan's major *zaibatsu* combines each had their own focus of operations, they did not, in general, confine their activities to specific sectors but rather penetrated into all areas of industry, finance, commerce, and transportation. Each *zaibatsu* formed a comprehensive monopoly that integrated everything from the extraction and import of raw materials to their processing, transportation, and sale. In short, the *zaibatsu* adopted the organizational form of a combine. For example, the Mitsui Holding Company (Unlimited), founded in 1909, established a colossal network that controlled more than two hundred large companies throughout the Japanese economy.[12] It directly controlled companies involved in commercial ventures, mines, and warehouses, yet also owned a series of large collateral enterprises in coal mining, papermaking, textiles, and electrical goods. Mitsubishi, Limited (a part of the Mitsubishi *zaibatsu* system) was also reorganized, first in 1908, and then in 1911, into a huge combine.[13] This combine directly owned companies in mining, shipbuilding, transportation, banking, and real estate. It also owned subsidiary enterprises in shipping, sugar refining, chemicals, textiles, and other sectors. In 1912, Sumitomo spun off its bank from its main headquarters, and then reorganized itself into a huge concern that operated companies in banking, trade, textiles, machine manufacturing, coal mining, forestry, electrical power, insurance, and trusts. In the same year, Yasuda also set up a family holding company, or "*nozensha*," that began to run insurance, textile, construction, and railroad companies.

Third, state monopoly capitalism also grew to a certain degree. This was strikingly evident in the continuous expansion of the state-owned economy that centered on military-related industries. For example, the government in 1906 owned only sixty-six factories producing military equipment. By 1914, however, that number had expanded to 842. This nationalized military-industrial complex consistently played the central role in heavy industry. The government also nationalized the principal railroads in 1906, aiming to promote its dual policies of foreign aggression and support for domestic monopoly capitalism. By linking together the Korean railways with the South Manchuria Railway Company (located in northeast China), the Japanese government created a railroad network capable of serving its military aggression against China. When it nationalized the railroads, the government bought the assets of thirty-two private railroad companies (including Mitsui and Mitsubishi) for the colossal sum of triple their original capitalization. Moreover, it issued these companies government bonds earning 5 percent interest, creating yet another opportunity for the monopoly capitalists to reap windfall profits. In order to pave the way for its monopoly capitalists to plunder the colonies, the Japanese government in 1906 established the South Manchuria Railway Company (located in northeastern China) and the Tōyō Colonial Development Company (located in Korea) in 1908. These became centers for pillaging the Chinese and Korean peoples. In addition, the government also created three state-owned banks: the Bank of Japan, the Yokohama Specie Bank, and the Industrial Bank of Japan. In 1910, the government—working in conjunction with thirteen *zaibatsu* banks—organized a banking syndicate which became an instrument for monopoly capital to control the nation's monetary and financial matters.

The Roots of Japanese Imperialism's Extremely Aggressive and Militaristic Character: Japan's Colonial Plunder of China and Korea

The great leader Chairman Mao has pointed out that Japan "is an imperialist country with a militaristic, feudal character."[14] This penetrating judgment summarizes the basic features of Japanese imperialism: it developed on an economic and social foundation deeply imbued with the residual forces of feudalism, and flourished by relying on an overstimulated military economy, wars of aggression, and the plunder of colonies.

Lenin also pointed out that "both Japan and Russia possessed a monopoly over the military. Both occupied extremely advantageous positions, either possessing vast territories or enjoying the geographic proximity to easily plunder other peoples, such as the Chinese. This partially supplemented and partially substituted for the newest and most modern monopolies of finance capital."[15] Japan and czarist Russia were the only imperialist countries that were also China's neighbors. These two imperialist states (newly risen, yet economically backward) frantically contended with each other to partition China militarily during the late nineteenth and early twentieth centuries. They became imperialist powers imbued with an extremely aggressive, militaristic, and feudalistic character.

The Japanese imperialists and their slavish scholars justified Japan's military aggression as resulting from "overpopulation" and "crowded living conditions." They said this in order to create a pretext for Japan's aggression against other countries, conceal its criminal acts during this aggression, and numb the revolutionary spirit of the people. Chairman Mao pointed out that "the imperialistic character of Japan's society and economy produced Japan's imperialistic war. Its war is retrogressive and barbaric."[16] The source of the aggressive and militaristic character of Japanese imperialism—like that of other imperialist powers—was rooted in the imperialistic nature of its society and economy. Japan's particularly virulent form of military aggressiveness was also due to the fact that it was an imperialist country with a militaristic and feudal system of autocracy. And, when speaking of Japan's political institutions, it should be mentioned that its emperor system was a most reactionary, autocratic system of governing. This regime deprived the masses of people of their most rudimentary political rights. The impotent Diet was merely a fig leaf that concealed the reality of absolute rule. The political oligarchs (or *genrō*) and members of the military cliques (or *gunbatsu*)—individuals who came from samurai families skilled at warfare—held a special place in this government and exercised supreme power. The highest policy-making body in the regime was the council of the *genrō*. It was an advisory group whose membership was drawn from the various military cliques, and who reported directly to the emperor and enjoyed a status equivalent to that of the cabinet. It carried the greatest voice in determining national policy, directly commanded the armed forces, and controlled Japan's military-industrial complex. In speaking of Japan's economic institutions, we must differentiate between its large-scale, capitalist industry and its semi-feudal, backward agriculture. This dichotomy created unusually sharp class and economic contradictions within the country. Because Japan's industrial workers and farmers lived in dire poverty, the home market was extremely limited in size. As a result, reliance on foreign trade grew greater and greater. In the early twentieth century, 30 percent of Japan's industrial products had to be sold on the foreign market. Between 80 percent and 100 percent of the iron ore, petroleum, cotton, wool, rubber, and agricultural goods consumed by its industries depended on foreign supplies. Japan was also engaged in a sharp conflict with the imperialistic powers over securing sources of raw materials and markets for its own products. It was under such circumstances that Japan's financial cliques—whose real economic strength put them at a disadvantage vis-à-vis the other great powers—found it convenient to act in collusion with the military cliques—whose military power, on the other hand, was quite real. Both groups now utilized Japan's advantageous geographical situation to plunder its neighbors. They energetically promoted a policy of military aggression, seeking thereby to attenuate Japan's numerous domestic contradictions.

In the aftermath of its two wars with China and Russia, Japan took by force foreign territories (including Taiwan, Korea, and the Southern Kuriles) that were equivalent in area to 76 percent of Japan itself. In addition, Japan obtained special privileges as well as leased territories in China, and became a "*newly risen* imperialist Great Power."[17] Japanese imperialism dramatically revealed its militaristic and feudal character by most brutally and barbarically controlling and plundering its colonies.

China's province of Taiwan was the first colony seized by Japan. Here, Japan established a system of control enforced by its military and police contingents headed by a Governor-General appointed from either the army or navy general staff. As a supplement to this police control, Japan also fastened two terroristic systems on the population: the *baojia* system and the *lianzuo* system. (The *baojia* system was a system of mutual surveillance and collective responsibility. Every ten households on Taiwan were grouped together into a *jia*, and every ten *jia* were grouped into a *bao*. Each person was held liable for any criminal activities perpetrated by any other member of the *baojia* group.) Between 1899 and 1906, Japan constructed a railroad network that crisscrossed Taiwan. Japan launched this project in order to consolidate its rule over Taiwan, increase its plunder of that colony's resources, and turn the island province into a military base for aggression against the Chinese mainland and the nations of Southeast Asia. Between 1910 and 1914, Japan relied on this railroad system to transport its troops as they carried out barbaric, large-scale massacres of the native Taiwanese people. In addition, the Japanese appropriated for themselves 97 percent of Taiwan's forests and open areas. A portion of these lands became government property, owned by the Governor-General; the other portion was sold to Japanese businessmen who enjoyed special privileges. Once military force had created an opportunity and laid a foundation, Japan's *zaibatsu* (led by Mitsui) quickly followed to take full advantage. Initially, the *zaibatsu* were active in commercial ventures, and came to monopolize Taiwan's trade in granulated sugar, husked rice, tea, and other products. They were also the sole vendors of other important goods such as opium, salt, camphor, and cigarettes. Subsequently, the Taiwan

Sugar Company (founded in 1900 by Mitsui and other capitalists who enjoyed special rights) made use of the semi-slave labor of the Taiwan people to plant sugarcane and operate a sugar refining industry. In this way they turned Taiwan into a source of raw materials for Japan's sugar processing industry. In 1911, for example, Japan's sugar imports from Taiwan accounted for two-thirds of the total value of commodities that Taiwan exported to Japan.

Japan was able to expel both Chinese and Russian influence from Korea as a result of its victories in the Sino-Japanese and Russo-Japanese Wars. Japan then forced Korea in November 1905 to accept the Korean-Japanese Convention of 1905, a "security treaty" that gave it control over Korea's foreign relations. Finally, in August 1910, Japan announced the signing of a Treaty of Annexation, thereby extinguishing Korea's independence. In order to suppress any resistance that might emanate from the Korean people, Japan stationed two army groups there in the period immediately after annexation. The Japanese government then built 16,214 police stations, staffed them with 22,000 military policemen and 200 thousand auxiliaries, and turned Korea into a human hell totally devoid of justice. Lenin commented as follows: "The Japanese there combined all the methods and all the most up-to-date techniques of the czars with purely Asiatic corporal punishments and unprecedented brutality."[18] In 1906, the Japanese government declared that it would nationalize the farmlands, wastelands, forests, and post road stations that had formerly belonged to Korea's imperial family. The government then established the Tōyō Colonial Development Company in 1908 which bought and sold farmland in Korea, solicited Japanese citizens to resettle there, and plundered the country of its natural resources. Once it had confiscated all the publicly owned land, Japan then began to rob the farmers of their privately held land. This was initiated in 1914 under the guise of an official "land survey." As a result, many Korean farmers were forced to leave their family plots, resettle on Japanese-owned properties, and were eventually compelled to grow rice and cotton for Japan. Within the brief period of four years (1912–15), Japanese rice imports from Korea increased 4.5 times. During the same time period, more than 90 percent of Korea's iron, coal, mica, tungsten, zinc, and other important mineral resources fell into the hands of the Japanese. In 1911, the Japanese government built a bridge across the Yalu River as well as a railroad from Dandong to Shenyang in order to make Korea a base for its aggression against China.

After the Russo-Japanese War, Japan began to brazenly expand into China's northeastern provinces. Not only did it secure the Liaodong Peninsula as a leased territory that would come under the rule of a Japanese Governor-General, but it also used its controlling rights over the South Manchuria Railway to extend its aggressive power throughout all of northeastern China. The four pillars that supported Japan's aggression and plunder of China's northeast were 1. the Kwantung Army in the military sphere, 2. the Japanese Consulate in foreign affairs, 3. the Kwantung General Office in administrative matters, and 4. the

South Manchuria Railway Company in the economy. When the South Manchuria Railroad Company (which served as the nerve center for Japan's economic plunder of the northeast) was established in 1906, it was capitalized at 200 million yen by the Japanese government. The government then purchased half of the company's planned stock offering of one million shares, with the remaining half million shares sold to the public. Because the prospects for the company's profitability were very good, the finance capitalists vied with one another to purchase these stocks, and so the total amount bid was 1,079 times the face value of the securities. This company completely monopolized the transportation, coal mining, electrical power, shipping, and warehousing industries in northeast China—as well as monopolizing all subsidiary operations of the railroad. It subsequently developed into an all-inclusive "empire" under the name of the South Manchuria Railway Company.

Japan lacked capital; however, it was forced to export what little it did have in order a) to ensure control over its colonies and b) to ensure foreign markets for its commodities and sources of raw materials and food for itself. By 1914, the total amount of Japanese investment in China was 800 million yen. In Korea that investment was around 300 million. At the same time, the amount of capital imported into Japan by England and the United States reached 1.78 billion yen. While enslaving other countries, Japan itself could not escape being exploited by European and American finance capital. This truly revealed the essence of Japanese imperialism: outwardly strong but inwardly weak.

4. The Economic Boom during the First World War, and the Great Advances Made by Finance Capital

Overseas Expansion during World War I and the Economic Boom

The Russo-Japanese War created an economic boom in Japan that was, however, cut short by a crisis in 1907. Except for the period from 1910 to 1912 when there was a turn for the better, the entire economy simply collapsed after 1907. The downturn was so severe that the ruling class cried out in alarm: "This economic depression is unprecedented. We simply cannot find a way to extricate ourselves from this misfortune by relying only on our own strength" [source unknown]. Just when this impasse had been reached, the First World War—an imperialist war to redivide the world—broke out in July 1914. Japan's ruling class was deliriously happy and welcomed this event as a "heaven-sent opportunity of the Taisho era" [source unknown]. On August 23, 1914, Japan declared war on Germany, using as a pretext its obligation "to scrupulously abide by the friendship inherent in the Anglo-Japanese alliance."[19] On September 2, 1914, Japan announced that it would enter the war on the side of the Entente powers headed by England and France. However, Japan's participation in the war was a fraud.

What was real was its effort to seize this opportunity to carry out aggression against Germany. Japan now sent its warships into the Chinese port of Longkou on the Shandong Peninsula. Japan then occupied Jiaozhou Bay, Qingdao, Jinan, and all of Germany's possessions in the Pacific Ocean. As if this were not enough, the Japanese government also presented China with Twenty-one Demands in January 1915, and used its military forces stationed in northeast China and in Shandong province as leverage. These demands, had they been accepted, would have ended China's independence. The savage face of Japanese imperialism was completely exposed.

Taking advantage of the opportunities that presented themselves when the Western countries were fully involved in World War I, Japanese imperialism also carried out a policy of large-scale economic expansionism into the vast regions of Africa and Asia while it was simultaneously pursuing its policy of military expansionism in East Asia. During World War I, Japan's foreign trade experienced unprecedented growth as a result of a continuous flow of orders for large quantities of military supplies from England, Russia, and other countries. Japanese imports and exports, for example, increased more than fourfold between 1914 and 1919. Its trade surplus reached 1.33 billion yen. In one fell swoop, Japan had turned from a country that had chronically suffered trade deficits prior to World War I into a nation that now enjoyed a substantial surplus. Japan was also becoming a leading actor on the stage of international shipping. Japanese vessels now became actively involved in the Mediterranean, the Atlantic, and even the oceans around North and South America. This occurred when much of the shipping registered with the wartime combatants was either destroyed or rendered useless by naval blockades. During the war, Japan's income from its merchant marine amounted to 1.89 billion yen, the result of a brisk market in shipping, the imposition of exorbitant transportation fees, and sharply increased maritime insurance charges. By 1919, Japan (which had been a debtor nation before the war) had now become—in one leap—a creditor, with 500 million yen out on loan and with cash reserves of 2.15 billion yen tucked away in its banks.

Stimulated by Japan's overseas military aggression and by its economic expansionism, Japanese industrial production completely revived. Beginning in 1915, and especially in 1916, an unprecedented wave of speculation hit Japan. This involved both the creation of new companies as well as the expansion of existing facilities. Total investment in business ventures increased from 2.5 billion yen to more than forty billion yen; the number of factories grew from 17,062 to 43,949; and the number of factory workers increased from 1.09 million to 1.52 million. During the same time period, total industrial output value increased almost five-fold, going from 1.34 billion yen to 6.54 billion yen. In general, real industrial production (after adjusting for inflation) doubled.

Japanese industrial development during the First World War was characterized by the following prominent features. Although every industrial sector made rather significant gains, heavy industry developed more rapidly than light industry. Within heavy industry itself, shipbuilding and machine manufacturing grew most quickly. Shipbuilding, for example, expanded 7.6-fold. Machine manufacturing grew 6.5-fold. These two sectors directly stimulated the development of the steel industry. Steel production went from 400 thousand tons in 1914 to 813 thousand tons in 1919. Pig iron production increased from 300 thousand tons to 613 thousand tons during the same time span. Japan's degree of self-sufficiency in both products increased from 48 percent to 73 percent and from 34 percent to 48 percent, respectively. The chemical industry also became one of the fastest growing sectors during the war.

Japan pushed its way into the ranks of the industrialized, capitalist countries by relying on the First World War to alter the relative proportions contributed by industry and agriculture to its national economy. For example, agriculture (including aquaculture) accounted for 50.5 percent of the total output value of industry and agriculture in 1914. By 1919, however, its share had slipped to 38.9 percent. Conversely, the output value of industrial and mining ventures increased form 49.5 percent to 61.1 percent. Of course, the level of Japanese industry was still rather low when compared to the advanced countries of Europe and America. By 1920, Japanese industrial production accounted for only 2 percent of the total production of the capitalist world, and even that small share was dominated by light industry.

Japan's Intensified Plunder of China and Korea

Chairman Mao pointed out: "The First World War provided the opportunity for Japanese imperialism to act as the sole ruler of China for a certain period of time."[20] One of the most important reasons for Japan's wartime economic prosperity was its military aggression and economic expansion into China. Prior to the Great War, Japan's aggressive forces were basically targeted on Taiwan, China's northeastern provinces, or Inner Mongolia. However, during World War I, Japanese imperialism's aggressive claws now began to stretch out to threaten all of China. As soon as the war began, Japan seized Germany's leased territory in Shandong province, and also took over German railroad rights in that province. Then it presented Twenty-one Demands, grouped in five categories, to the Chinese government of Shikai Yuan. The most important demands were the following: 1. Germany's special rights in Shandong province would be transferred to Japan. Japan also demanded the right to construct railroads there as well as gain additional special privileges. 2. Japan wanted to extend the time period (to ninety-nine years) for its leases on Luxun and Dalian and its special rights over the South Manchuria Railway and the Dandong-Shenyang Railroad. In addition, it demanded that the eastern part of Inner Mongolia and southern Manchuria become Japanese colonies. 3. Japan demanded the right to jointly run the Hanyehping Coal and Iron Company, and to control the factories and mines in the Changjiang (Yangtze) River basin. 4. Japan demanded that the Chinese government make a public announcement that Beijing would never cede any of its coastal ports, bays, or offshore islands to any other country. 5. China was asked to employ Japanese advisers in its military and financial operations. Police departments and military factories were to be jointly run by Chinese and Japanese personnel. The construction of railroads and ports was to be turned over to Japan. Because of strong opposition from the Chinese people, these gangster-like demands were not realized in their entirety. However, Japan was able to secure some of them after Shikai Yuan signed a treaty in May 1915 regarding Shandong province and "Manchuria." In addition, Japan and China concluded the Nishihara loan agreements between 1917 and 1918. Under these agreements, Japan loaned 145 million yen to China. The annual interest rate of 8 percent charged by the Japanese was so high that it caused surprise and brought denunciations from various parts of the world.

Japanese imperialism now turned China into its largest commodity market, biggest supplier of raw materials, and most important investment location in the aftermath of the military and economic aggression it had carried out during the First World War. Between 1913 and 1918, Japan's share of China's foreign trade jumped from 18.9 percent to 38.6 percent. Its share of China's imports increased dramatically from 20.9 percent to 43.5 percent, and exceeded the combined total enjoyed by England and the United States. In order to plunder China's mineral resources, squeeze its cheap labor, and strangle its national industry, Japan also expanded its investments in China and established companies throughout the nation. In 1913, there were approximately ten thousand Japanese citizens residing in China. By 1919, this number had increased to 240 thousand. During this same time period, Japanese investment in China grew from 1.4 billion yen to 3.45 billion yen. More than one hundred Sino-Japanese "joint ventures" now operated in all sectors of the economy, including manufacturing, mining, communications, transportation, agriculture, forestry, real estate, commerce, and banking.

During the Great War, rapid increases in Japan's urban population and in the size of its armed forces created correspondingly greater demands on Japan's food supplies. Japanese domestic rice production—stimulated by continuously rising prices—grew to a certain degree. However, because domestic supplies fell far short of satisfying the demand, Japan intensified its plunder of Korea's agriculture. Japan's colonial authorities took the large tracts of land that they had seized from Korean farmers and sold those tracts to the Japanese bourgeoisie and landlords at low prices. The Japanese authorities then forced Korea's farmers to grow rice for export to Japan. For example, Japan exported 525 thousand hectoliters (*dan*) of rice from Korea in 1912. By 1915, that amount reached 2,333,000 hectoliters. When it created the Korean Mining Company in 1915, Japanese imperialism also intensified its plunder of Korea's mineral resources and increased its access to strategic raw materials useful in war. There were altogether 1,900 companies in Korea in 1919 producing a total annual output value of 260 million yen. Of these, almost one thousand (with a total annual output value of 240 million yen) belonged to Japanese citizens.

Finance Capital Flourishes While Japan's Working People Become More Impoverished

Lenin pointed out that "imperialist wars have greatly speeded up and intensified the transition of monopoly capitalism into state monopoly capitalism. The state has become ever more closely bonded to the most powerful alliances of capitalists, and its appalling oppression of the working masses has become even more shocking."[21] In order to meet the needs of its war of aggression, the Japanese government during the First World War took steps to enhance the role of state monopoly capitalism. It constantly raised taxes and fleeced the people. Government wartime revenues, for example, went up 2.5-fold. And, the government also enacted legislation regarding awards, subsidies, and regulatory practices which subsidized finance capital and fostered the development of a military- industrial complex.

The extremely rapid wartime development of industry—especially heavy industry—that resulted from government subsidies greatly enhanced the concentration of production and the accumulation of capital. In various sectors of industry as well as in banking, finance capital systematically gained the upper hand. Let us take a few specific representative sectors as examples. In the textile industry, seven major companies held dominant positions prior to the war. During the war, four of these companies merged. As a result, five major companies (Kanebo, Tōyō, Dai Nippon, Fuji Gas, and Nisshin—all controlled by either Mitsui or Mitsubishi) emerged to dominate the industry. The steel industry—except that segment that had already been nationalized—belonged to the large *zaibatsu* companies like Mitsui, Mitsubishi, Asano, ōkawa, and Sumitomo. Shipbuilding involved only three companies: Kawasaki, Mitsubishi, and the Ōsaka Iron Works. These three firms accounted for 60 percent to 70 percent of the work force, capital, and productive capacity of the entire industry. In banking, the capital assets of the twenty largest *zaibatsu* and national banks constituted one-third of all bank capital assets and about one-half of all savings deposits. As a result of the war, every *zaibatsu* conglomerate vastly expanded its capital holdings. Beginning in 1917, for example, the Mitsubishi *zaibatsu* reorganized (one by one) its shipbuilding, papermaking, trading, mining, and iron manufacturing companies. These had previously operated as joint capital ventures, but were now run solely with Mitsubishi money. The capital assets of the Mitsubishi Bank subsequently grew from ten million to fifty million yen. In 1918, the Mitsui *zaibatsu* increased the capitalization of the Mitsui General Trading Company by 100 million yen and the Mitsui Holding Company by 300 million yen. Then, in 1919, it also added 100 million yen to the capital assets of the Mitsui Bank. During the war, the rate of profit enjoyed by the *zaibatsu* corporations generally ranged between 50 percent and 70 percent.

In order to adapt to the rapidly expanding foreign market after World War I broke out, the *zaibatsu* began to offer higher wages as bait to entice their industrial employees to work additional shifts and to work at night. As a result, both the workweek as well as labor intensity increased. However, because the price of necessities grew faster than workers' income, real wages in 1919 fell by 32 percent compared to 1914. Statistics indicate that, by the end of the war, a family needed an annual income of two thousand yen to maintain an average life-style. However, the income of 98 percent of all industrial workers fell below this level. In fact, 92.3 percent of all industrial workers actually had an annual income below five hundred yen. An upsurge in grain prices also brought absolutely no relief to the poverty-stricken farmers. On the contrary, it only stimulated an increase in land rents and frantic speculation in grain. Those who suffered were tenant farmers and part-time farmers who relied on the sale of household handicrafts to supplement their income.

Facing a steadily deteriorating life during the war, the masses of workers and farmers intensified their struggles against the monopoly capitalists and landlords. Prior to 1916, approximately one hundred strikes—demanding either increased wages or improved working conditions—took place annually. The victory of the October Revolution in Russia added impetus to the worker and farmer movement in Japan. Because the number of strikes reached 398 in 1917, or about five times the number of the previous year, 1917 has been called "the boom year in industrial strikes." The number of strikes increased once again in 1918, reaching 417. The Rice Riots (which broke out in August and September of 1918) were an unprecedentedly massive uprising by the Japanese people who were fighting for their very right to exist. The Rice Riots became an epoch-making event in the history of Japan's worker and farmer movement. They began as an uprising of fishermen and transport workers from Toyama prefecture who had been provoked into action by commercial speculators forcing up the price of rice. The Rice Riots quickly engulfed two-thirds of Japan, involved almost ten million participants, and lasted one month. Rice stores, pawn shops, companies, business enterprises, and police stations all became targets of the uprising. The angry people sought to destroy these structures and burn them down. The Rice Riots dealt a severe blow to the rule of Japan's bourgeoisie and landlords.

5. A Crisis Envelops the Japanese Economy in the 1920s

The False Prosperity of the Postwar Period, and the Crisis of 1920–21

Japanese imperialism could be regarded as an upstart during the First World War. By the postwar period, however, it had earned its credentials, and now joined the victorious Allies as one of the five major world powers. This qualification enabled Japan to participate in the Versailles Peace Conference and share in the loot. Disregarding the fierce opposition of the Chinese people, Japan now took over all the rights that defeated Germany had previously enjoyed in China's Shandong province. It also seized all the Pacific islands that had once belonged to Germany, and turned them into nominally mandated territories. However, pressured by European and American imperialism at the 1922 Washington Conference, Japan was compelled to retract a large portion of the Twenty-one Demands it had previously made on China, and also had to withdraw its troops from Shandong province. Its naval strength was curbed and kept inferior to that of England and the United States.[22] After the First World War, and especially after the victory of the October Revolution in Russia, the entire capitalist system entered a period of general crisis. All the contradictions inherent in imperialism became unprecedentedly sharp. Japan's political and economic situation became turbulent, and its crisis all-encompassing.

Japan's economy—which had flourished as a result of the war—carried within itself some acute contradictions. As soon as the Great War ended in November 1918, commodity prices zoomed, stock prices fell steadily, production began to sag, business bankruptcies increased, and unemployment grew dramatically. Japan's favorable trade balance also turned negative. Just as these signs of an economic crisis were appearing, revolutionary struggles (which opposed Japanese imperialism) also broke out and surged forward, not only within Japan, but also outside. A tidal wave of strikes and work slowdowns hit Japan in the aftermath of the Rice Riots. Unions were organized everywhere, and a national labor federation—the Japan Federation of Labor, or Sōdōmei—was born. A mass demonstration that involved half a million participants took place in Korea on March 1, 1919. Its leaders issued a declaration of Korean independence and launched a powerful nationalist movement against Japan. The anti-imperialist, anti-feudal May Fourth Movement also arose in China in 1919. This movement opposed Japanese imperialism's aggression, and its revolutionary calls to "Eliminate the Twenty-one Demands," "Recover Qingdao or Die," and "Boycott Japanese Goods" reverberated throughout China. Japanese imperialism found itself surrounded—both domestically and on the international scene—by the revolutionary people.

A false prosperity temporarily appeared in Japan after April and May of 1919, and lasted for some months until the end of the year. During the latter half of 1919, investment in new construction and plant expansion reached 500 million yen on a monthly basis, or double the highest amount for the same period in the previous wartime year. However, this prosperity lacked any foundation. It appeared only because the Japanese economy was so closely linked to a thriving American economy that now imported large quantities of raw silk, texiles, ships, and other commodities from Japan. In addition, England, France, Germany, and the other countries that had been exhausted by the war had still not recovered. Not only were they unable to return quickly to their markets in Asia, but they even needed to import from Japan some civilian industrial goods that they lacked during World War I. All these factors temporarily opened a comparatively vast international market for Japan. Blinded by their greed, Japan's monopoly bourgeoisie seized this timely opportunity to engage in yet another extensive wave of reckless creation of new business enterprises. This frenzied speculation and indiscriminate establishment of new corporations intensified the contradictions in Japan's economy. Before too long, commodities flooded not only the domestic markets of both Europe and the United States, but also inundated the markets of Asia. Those factors which had propped up Japan's economic prosperity now vanished. Japan's trade deficit began to increase after January 1920. Led by declines in the price of raw silk, commodity prices as a whole began to drop sharply. Stock prices on the Tōkyō Stock Exchange plummeted on March 5, 1920, leading to a run on banks and causing many financial institutions throughout Japan to suspend operations. When an economic crisis broke out in the United States, England, and other countries in June and July of 1920, Japan once again suffered a serious blow. Its impact intensified Japan's own crisis, and caused it to spread.

The 1920–21 crisis resolved the contradiction that existed between the unprecedented boom in production in wartime Japan and the entirely inadequate domestic capability of sustaining that growth. Total industrial output value declined 19.9 percent during the crisis. Total output value in mining fell even further, plunging 48 percent. Of plant capacity, 40 percent to 50 percent lay idle in various sectors. Prices of various industrial products fell between 55 percent and 82 percent. Such a severe crisis was also linked to a rapid deterioration in Japan's export trade. Exports, for example, fell 40.3 percent during the period of the crisis, and the decline in exports of manufactured goods reached 45.6 percent. This sharp contraction in exports and slump in shipping caused Japan's international payments deficit to reach 351,250,000 yen during the years 1920–22, and its foreign currency reserves to fall from 1.3 billion yen to 600 million yen.

Although Japanese agriculture was characterized by small-scale farming operating within a semi-feudal system, it had also become linked to a capitalist system of reproduction as a result of the development of commercialized agriculture. Moreover, silkworm cocoons—an important agricultural product—were the raw materials that eventually yielded the raw silk that was sold in large quantities on the international market. As a result, when Japanese industry became depressed, agriculture also suffered a serious impact. During this crisis, for example, the price of silk cocoons and various other agricultural products fell by approximately half. Many farmers went bankrupt when this crisis hit. Farm households in Japan, for example, fell by thirty-five thousand during the two years 1921–22. Although more than twenty thousand of these households were either tenant farmers or poor peasants, many others were also wealthy farmers who had owned more than two *chōbu* of land (one *chōbu* being equivalent to .99 hectare) and who had prospered during the war.

To stop this crisis, the Japanese government (by the end of May 1920) had disbursed more than 300 million yen in emergency bailout funds to various banks, stock exchanges, and syndicates—as well as to cotton spinning mills, sugar mills, steel factories, and other business enterprises. This brought about some improvement in a rapidly deteriorating situation, although it was only after the spring of 1921 that the decline in industrial production was finally arrested. However, the economy remained sluggish until 1923.

Japan's economy—which had not yet emerged from its depressed condition—suffered yet another crisis when the Great Kanto Earthquake hit the Tōkyō area on September 1, 1923.[23] The earthquake destroyed a great portion of Tōkyō and Yokohama, and brought chaos to the economy. Although the earthquake was a huge disaster for the masses of people, it also created a golden opportunity for the bourgeoisie to raise commodity prices. While all this was happening, the Japanese government undertook various relief measures to alleviate the crisis brought about by the earthquake. Only in 1924, after the government had extended substantial loans to those capitalists who had sustained damage, did the economy gradually extricate itself from its stagnation.

Fed up with the miseries inflicted by the war and the economic crisis, and encouraged by the example of Russia's October Revolution, Japan's working class began to initiate some heroic struggles during these crisis years. For example, twenty-four thousand workers staged a strike at the Yawata Iron and Steel Company in 1920. In 1921, twenty-eight thousand workers struck at the Kawasaki Shipyards, Mitsubishi's Kobe Shipyards, and the Mitsubishi Electrical Machinery Plant. These strikes led to violent confrontations with the police. Moreover, the striking workers issued a manifesto demanding that workers manage the factories. These actions revealed the mighty organizational strength of the working class. During the same time period, the Japanese Communist party, led by Sen Katayama and others, was founded in July 1922. Its creation was based on the already rapid dissemination of socialist thought. Directed by the Communist International, the Japanese Communist party put forward a correct militant program that advocated the destruction of the emperor system and the liberation of the Japanese working class and the Japanese people. In addition, it achieved a very great victory when it led the people in a struggle against "the three detestable laws."[24] The Japanese government was eventually forced to rescind its reactionary laws banning "extremist social movements."

Finance Capital Intensifies Its Control during the Period of Relative Stability

Two years of sluggish economic performance followed in the aftermath of the 1920–21 depression. Only beginning in 1924 did the economy enter a period of relative stability and slow progress. However, this growth was sustained for a scant three years when, in 1927, the economy once again fell into turmoil and entered a new crisis. During the entire decade of the 1920s, the only sectors of Japanese industry that experienced comparatively substantial gains were those—such as steel, electric power, chemicals, and machinery—that served military production and that received special protection from the government. Other industries—such as textiles and coal—remained stagnant. Some—like shipbuilding—even declined steadily. The average annual growth rate for Japanese industrial production in the period 1921–29 was only 3 percent—compared to 9.4 percent for France, 7.1 percent for Germany, and 4.3 percent for the United States. In fact, it was higher only than the 1.7 percent growth rate sustained by that venerable, yet decaying, empire, England. The relative nature of Japan's economic stability was dramatically revealed in its stagnant foreign trade. While the total value of exports in 1924 came to 1.807 billion yen, the highest level achieved in 1929 peaked at only 2.149 billion yen. The decade of the 1920s was a period of intense conflict as the capitalist world competed for markets. Japan's foreign trade was dependent on three links. The first link involved the export of raw silk to the United States in return for cotton and machinery. The second link constituted the export of cotton textiles to Britain's colonies in exchange for coal, iron, and other raw materials used in heavy industry. The third link involved the export of various kinds of light and heavy industrial goods to China in return for food and raw materials. In the 1920s, Japan faced growing competition from—and reduced exports to—the United States, England, and other countries. Tōkyō also confronted a disadvantageous situation because the local national industries of China, India, and other nations had grown considerably during World War I. As a result, Japan's productive forces—rather weak in comparison with those of the United States, England, and other countries—experienced serious difficulties in trying to expand abroad. Between 1920 and 1929, for example, Japan's trade deficit reached 3.3 billion yen. Not only did this wipe out the vast reserves Japan had accumulated during the First World War, but it also necessitated borrowing from foreign sources and running up a foreign debt. Between 1923 and 1927, for example, Japan's foreign debt reached 910 million yen. In 1924, Japan borrowed $150 million from the United States at an annual interest rate of 6.5 percent—a rate so high that the agreement was ridiculed within Japan as "the loan that brought national humiliation."

The relative nature of Japan's economic stability was also revealed in the agricultural stagnation which gripped this country during the entire decade of the 1920s. Except for 1927, the annual production of rice fell below 1919 levels. This was a result of a) the continued existence of semi-feudal controls in the villages and b) the effort to gradually shift Japan's agricultural base to its colonies. For example, the amount of grain that Japan plundered from Korea and China's province of Taiwan averaged about 1.74 million hectoliters annually between 1912 and 1916. Between 1927 and 1931, however, that annual average had climbed to 8.47 million hectoliters. Large quantities of cheap grain imported from the colonies brought about a steady decline in grain prices within Japan and caused agriculture to slump into a chronic depression.

In the postwar decade of economic crisis, the *zaibatsu* went on an unconstrained binge of acquisitions. They now took full advantage of the opportunities that presented themselves when many small and medium-sized business enterprises went bankrupt. During the period of relative stability, the *zaibatsu* energetically promoted a policy of "industrial rationalization," and thereby promoted the trend within industry toward the establishment of cartels and trusts. As a result, Japan's finance capitalists strengthened their grip over the economy, even though the economy itself had not grown substantially in the postwar period. While there were only seven comparatively important cartels operating in Japan prior to the war, that number had increased to thirty-one (operating in more than twenty sectors of the economy) by 1929. By 1927–28, monopoly capital controlled the following major industrial sectors in Japan:

1. The steel industry. In 1925, the privately owned steel companies organized a Steel Producers' Federation. In 1926, the state-run and privately owned companies jointly established a cartel on pig iron production. Eventually only twenty-two large corporations—out of an original number of 187 steel companies—were finally left after the process of mergers and acquisitions had run its course. Except for the government-run Yawata Steel and Iron Company, all these twenty-two corporations were controlled by a small number of *zaibatsu* like Mitsui, Mitsubishi, Asano, Ōsaka, Yasuda, and Sumitomo.

2. The copper industry. Four *zaibatsu*, Furukawa, Kuhara, Mitsubishi, and Fujita, organized a cartel on copper production in 1921 and set up a "Wednesday Meeting Club." Sumitomo subsequently joined the cartel. By 1927, these five big *zaibatsu* monopolized 95 percent of copper production.

3. The coal industry. The Federation of Coal Producers, established in 1921, monopolized 90 percent of coal production. By 1927, nineteen large corporations, part of the Mitsui, Mitsubishi, Kaijima, Furukawa, Yasukawa, and Asano *zaibatsu* systems, monopolized 62 percent of Japan's coal production.

4. The six big companies in the textile field, Kanebō, Tōyō, Dai Nippon, Fuji Gas, Ōsaka Godo, and Nisshin, controlled not only 53 percent of the spindles of the fifty-nine companies that constituted the Textile Federation, but also owned 50 percent of the capital assets of the cartel. The Kanebo Company, controlled by Mitsui, played the central role in the Federation.

5. Out of nearly two hundred firms in the field of paper manufacturing, only three large companies, Fuji, Prince, and Karafuto, controlled 85 percent of all production.

6. Of the fifteen companies involved in the sugar industry, three, Dai Nippon (which belonged to the Fujita *zaibatsu*), Meiji (which belonged to Mitsubishi), and Taiwan (which belonged to Mitsui), monopolized 62 percent of all production.

7. The flour industry was completely monopolized by two firms: Mitsui's Nippon Flour Milling Company and Mitsubishi's Nisshin Flour Milling Company.

As the financial cliques made substantial gains within the economy, their power in the realm of politics also became more significant. After the war, two major bourgeois political parties, the Seiyūkai (or Friends of Constitutional Government party) and the Kenseikai (or Constitutional Association), which later became the Minseitō, served as the political representatives of the Mitsui and Mitsubishi *zaibatsu*. They took turns in putting together the cabinets that ran the government, and imposed reactionary controls over the Japanese people.

From the Financial Crisis of 1927 to the Great Depression of 1929

The financial crisis which broke out in March 1927 not only ended Japan's temporary postwar economic stability, but also initiated a new era of even greater economic turmoil and crisis. Confronted by the increasing impoverishment of the masses of workers and farmers—as well as a steady deterioration in its position in foreign markets—Japan's postwar industry now relied mainly on bank loans and governmental assistance to sustain itself. While this brought about unprecedented growth in bank lending operations, it also caused a huge increase in bad debts, thereby gradually eroding the trustworthiness of the banks involved. This contradiction, building steadily in intensity, was like a time bomb. It finally exploded at a January 1927 conference that debated the issue of how the banks were going to resolve the problem of the notes that they had issued after the 1923 earthquake. As depositers began a run on banks, Tokyo's capital-rich Watanabe Bank and the Akasaka Savings Bank were forced to suspend business on March 15, 1927. Other banks either increased their level of deposits, declared a holiday, or simply collapsed. A wave of trouble engulfed Japan's banking community. To solve the problem, Giichi Tanaka (the Secretary-General of the Seiyūkai who served as Japan's Prime Minister during the period of this crisis) allocated 500 million yen in emergency relief to the big banks, such as Mitsui and Mitsubishi. And he aggressively printed huge quantities of paper money. For example, 1.1 billion yen in paper currency were issued on April 20, 1927. On April 21, 2.7 billion yen were released, a one-and-a-half-fold increase over the previous day. Even measures such as these were insufficient to stop the growing run on banks, and the government was left with no alternative but to announce on April 22, 1927 that all banking operations would be halted for three weeks. The financial crisis eased only after the government overhauled the banking system and only after it allocated another 700 million yen as a bailout for the banks.

Unable to stay in business, many small and medium-sized local banks went bankrupt during this financial crisis. As a result, fewer loans were now available to those small and medium-sized enterprises and local industries that had previously enjoyed close ties to the local banks. Lack of funding became an increasingly severe problem. Production stoppages and business bankruptcies increased in 1927 in sectors like cotton textiles, flour, cement, chemical fertilizers, and papermaking.

Just as the Japanese economy was entering a period of great turbulence, the capitalist world also fell into an unprecedentedly serious economic crisis. This development began in October 1929 when stock prices on the American stock exchange collapsed. The crisis spread very quickly to Japan because its market was so closely linked to that of the United States. This crisis also struck Japan much harder than did the recession of 1920–21. The Japanese economy, moreover, was inseparable from foreign trade. The economic crisis, which enveloped the entire capitalist world, greatly intensified competition for global markets, and Japan was the hardest hit in that competition. During the decade of the Depression, for example, Japanese exports fell 76.5 percent and imports declined 71.7 percent. The sharp reduction in exports intensified the problem of surplus production. This, in turn, led to a steep fall in commodity prices. Many companies went bankrupt, banks collapsed, and industrial production declined along a broad front. Total industrial output value fell 32.9 percent in the years 1929–31. Production in some major industries plunged dramatically. For example, coal production fell 36.7 percent, pig iron was down 30.5 percent, steel dropped 47.2 percent, shipbuilding fell 88.2 percent, and cotton goods declined 30.7 percent. These percentages were calculated by comparing the peak monthly production figures for each industry with their lowest levels during the Depression. Some major industries operated at only 50 percent of capacity.

Agriculture, which had been stuck in a chronic slump, could not evade disaster either. During the Depression, exports of raw silk fell sharply. Plunging raw silk prices then caused a sharp drop in silkworm cocoon prices. As a result, 40 percent of all farm households in Japan that raised silk cocoons were struck with a deadly blow. A bumper harvest in 1930, when added to the impact of the Depression, caused prices for some dry-paddy farm products to be lower than the transportation costs of getting those products to market. All this ultimately resulted in the shockingly paradoxical "bumper crop famine" of 1930.

In order to shift the burdens of this crisis onto the backs of the working class, and to strengthen their competitive ability in foreign markets, Japan's monopoly bourgeoisie used the government to promote a widespread "movement to rationalize industry." The government enacted its Program for Industrial Rationalization on December 2, 1929, established a Provisional Bureau of Industrial Management on June 2, 1930, and promulgated a Law to Regulate Major Industries on April 1, 1931. The new legislation and new governmental agencies strengthened the control that the big finance capitalists exerted over Japan's vital industries, compelled the creation of cartels within fifty industrial sectors, and eliminated many small and medium-sized companies. The new legislation and new governmental agencies also tightened the monopoly bourgeoisie's control over labor, enabling them to dismiss many workers, as well as to lower their wages. By 1931, the number of unemployed workers reached 413 thousand.

The impact of the Depression as well as the offensive waged by the monopoly bourgeoisie sharpened the class contradictions within Japan.

While there were 1,420 labor disputes in 1929 with 170 thousand participants, those figures had increased to 2,289 and 190 thousand, respectively, in 1930. Landlord-tenant disputes in the villages soared from more than 2,400 cases in 1930 to more than 3,400 in 1931. The organizational consciousness of the workers and peasants in these struggles grew steadily, resulting in the establishment of large numbers of industrial and tenant unions. Outside of Japan, the Korean people launched a huge anti-Japanese, national uprising on May 30, 1930. The Gaoshan national minority of China's Taiwan province also launched a huge anti-Japanese uprising in November 1930. Both these actions seriously jeopardized Japanese imperialism's control over its colonies.

Confronted by steadily sharpening economic and class contradictions both within and outside Japan, Japan's landlord class and bourgeoisie made up their minds to institute a system of fascist rule. On March 15, 1928, the Tanaka government put out a vast dragnet for members of the Japanese Communist party. More than one thousand were arrested. On April 10, 1928, the government forcibly dissolved three left-wing, progressive organizations: the Association to Discuss the Composition of the Working Class, the Worker-Farmer party, and the Communist Youth League. On April 16, 1929, the government once again tracked down many members of the Japanese Communist party, arresting more than three thousand. While progressive forces were being suppressed, various types of fascist organizations were being created in large numbers. For example, fascist groups like the Sakurakai (Cherry Blossom Society), Kyushin Aikokutō (Radical Patriotic party), Sokoku Dōshikai (Brotherhood of Patriots), Aikoku Kinrotō (Patriotic Labor party), Sonnō Kyushintō (the Radical Party to Revere the Emperor), Ketsumei Dan (the League of Blood Brothers), Kokusui (the Mass Party to Preserve the National Essence), and the Kokuryūkai (Black Dragon Association) were all established between 1930 and 1931.

Externally, Japan's government once again sought to launch a criminal war of aggression against China. Not long after the prominent militarist Giichi Tanaka assumed the prime ministership in April 1927, the government convened a "Conference on the East" which debated and eventually drafted a policy of aggression against China. In "Japan's China Policy," a speech that he delivered at the close of the conference, Tanaka pointed out that "the three provinces of Manchuria, Mongolia, and especially Shandong" were "of extremely vital interest" to Japan's "national defense and the existence of its people," that they had to be given "special consideration," and that Japan "must be resolved to adopt appropriate measures without losing its opportunities." In other words, Japan regarded its takeover of China's northeastern provinces as the first step in its aggression against China, and it regarded this area as a military base from which Japan could attack the rest of China. Not only did Giichi Tanaka propose this program, but he also began to implement it once he became prime minister. Twice he sent Japanese troops to Shandong province. The first time occurred in May 1927, the second in May 1928. Japan sought to provoke a war when it assassinated Zuolin

Zhang in June 1928. Japan had to postpone its plan of aggression against China only because the European powers intervened and only because of an upsurge in the anti-war struggle within Japan itself.

6. The Rise and Fall of Japan's Militarized Economy (1931–45)

The Shift to a Militarized Economy (1931–36)

After a global economic depression broke out in 1929, Japanese imperialism took advantage of the economic crises that beset the other imperialist powers to launch a war of military agression against China's northeastern provinces on September 18, 1931. It now began to carry out its wild plan to subjugate China and the world. It was precisely at this moment when the reactionary Chinese government of Jieshi Jiang (or Chiang Kai-shek) was carrying out its "third encirclement campaign" against the Chinese Communist party–led people and army. By carrying out the traitorous policy that "domestic pacification must precede resistance to foreign invasion," the Chiang government adopted a policy of nonresistance to Japanese imperialism's aggression. This policy directly caused China's entire northeastern region to fall under the iron heel of the Japanese military within the space of a few months.

After occupying China's northeast, Japanese imperialism rapidly took the path of becoming militarized state monopoly capitalism. In terms of political institutions, Japanese militarism gradually did away with political parties and a cabinet system and established in their places a fascist system directly controlled by the military, the bureaucrats, and the financial and industrial combines (or *zaibatsu*). In terms of economic institutions, it further strengthened the links between these combines and state power, and put military production as the top priority. It established a militarized economy that was preparing to wage a large-scale war.

First of all, the Japanese government issued bonds and paper currency in order to carry out its policy of expanded military procurement. This was done not only to stimulate an economy that had fallen into a serious crisis, but also to promote the development of a munitions industry. State expenditures went from 14.8 billion yen to 22.8 billion yen (an increase of approximately 54 percent) in the years from 1931 to 1936. Military expenditures more than doubled, and their portion of the general budget increased from 30.8 percent to 47.2 percent. In these six years, the state spent almost seven billion yen to develop a military economy. Of this amount, about 25 percent was used to build or expand a series of large-scale, government-run munitions complexes that employed several tens of thousands of workers. The other 75 percent went to private capitalists to pay for the purchase of military goods. Of the 110 companies selected to receive military contracts from the government, almost all were powerful enterprises that belonged to a small number of *zaibatsu* groups, such as Mitsui, Mitsubishi, Sumitomo, Ōkura, and Kuhara. The government doled out vast quantities of financial assistance, handed out subsidies, and provided various favors that enabled these *zaibatsu* corporations to rapidly turn toward military production. For example, the Mitsubishi *zaibatsu* in 1934 merged its shipbuilding and aircraft manufacturing operations and created Mitsubishi Heavy Industries, Limited. Mitsubishi did this in order to squeeze out the high profits that were available in military production. This company became a large military-industrial conglomerate whose purpose was the manufacture of warships, submarines, aircraft, special weapons, and electric motors. As the older *zaibatsu* rapidly turned to the manufacture of weaponry, a group of new *zaibatsu*—or combines focused on the arms industry—began to emerge. These new *zaibatsu* had close ties with the various cliques that existed in the military services, and were involved exclusively in the production of armaments. Among the most important of these weapons combines were Nissan, Nichiden, Nissō, Mori, and Riken.

Second, the government also strengthened its controls over the national economy in order to make it better serve the purposes of waging war. In addition to revising the Law to Control Vital Production at the beginning of 1931, the government also enacted legislation that put controls on industry, agriculture, finance, and commerce. It forced business enterprises in a number of economic sectors to organize and join cartels and trusts, and put a large number of small and medium-sized industries under the control of the *zaibatsu*, ordering them to manufacture goods required by the military. In the years 1931 to 1935, thirty-five different kinds of cartels were organized, and more than fifty industries (including steel, automobiles, textiles, chemicals, railroads, and foodstuffs) were formed into seventeen trusts that belonged to the *zaibatsu*. The Japan Steel Company, a huge trust created in 1934, gobbled up the major steel companies that had previously belonged to Yawata, Mitsui, and Mitsubishi. In the process, Japan Steel came to monopolize 92 percent of Japan's entire production of pig iron, 51 percent of its steel ingots, and 40 percent of its steel products.

Third, the government devalued the yen in order to stimulate exports, expand imports of strategic raw materials, and resolve the difficulties it faced due to domestic shortages of raw materials. Renewed prohibitions placed on the export of gold at the end of 1931 brought about a continuous drop in the foreign exchange value of the yen. In the years 1931–36, the exchange value of the Japanese yen depreciated more than 35 percent. On the one hand, this made the prices of imported goods relatively dear, thereby protecting Japan's weak machine manufacturing industry, and other industries as well, from foreign competition. At the same time, it also made the international price of Japanese goods relatively cheap, strengthened their competitive power, and stimulated exports. Under this kind of "dumping" policy, Japan's export trade rapidly increased, and served as a favorable condition for expanded imports of strategic raw materials.

At this time, the United States was the major source of Japan's strategic raw materials. After 1932, the annual percentage of raw materials imported from the United States was as follows: 90 percent of scrap iron, 45 percent of lead, 90 percent of copper, 65 percent of oil and petroleum products, and 70 percent of the machine tools required to develop the aircraft and tank industries. American imperialism substantially aided the development of Japan's war economy, and thereby abetted Japanese imperialism's aggressiveness.

Finally, the government made greater use of the resources of both Korea and China's northeastern provinces by turning them into bases for Japan's overall war strategy. Using hypocritical slogans such as "Promoting Korea's Industrial Revolution" and "Stimulating Korean Industrialization," Japanese imperialism built a number of factories and mines to extract iron ore, aluminum, tungsten, copper, gold, and other raw materials from Korea. Examples of these huge, monopolistic enterprises were the Korean Smelting Company (originally established by Mitsubishi), the Korean Nitrogen Company (affiliated with the new Noguchi *zaibatsu*), and the Korean Aluminum Company (built jointly by Mitsui, Mitsubishi, and Sumitomo). These companies used semi-slave Korean labor, and unashamedly plundered Korea's resources. In 1935, for example, the daily wage for a factory worker in Japan was 1.83 yen for men and 1.06 yen for women. However, in Korea, men's wages were only equivalent to 0.9 yen, and women's 0.49 yen. These were not even half the wages earned by Japanese factory workers.

In early 1932, Japan created the puppet state of Manchukuo, and installed the previously deposed Qing emperor Pu Yi as head of state. Japan wanted to thoroughly colonize China's northeastern region, and so went forward with a savage policy of plunder. The Japanese government was able to turn this region into its agricultural subsidiary by forcing the peasants there to pay their taxes in agricultural products—such as soybeans, rice, and wheat. Using the South Manchuria Railway Company as its conduit, Japan also made substantial investments in the northeast—ostensibly for the purpose of creating a "Ferrous Metals Center" for "the Greater East Asia Co-Prosperity Sphere." By 1936, the total amount of Japanese investment came to three billion yen, almost double that of the 1930 figure of 1.6 billion. This Japanese investment started up coal, steel, cement, electrical, aluminum, chemical, and military industries at Chinese cities like Anshan, Lake Benxi, Shenyang, Fushun, Dandong, Yingkou, Luda, Jilin, and Mudanjiang. Like thieves, the Japanese plundered the northeast of its iron, coal, aluminum, magnesium, and other resources.

Japan was able to emerge from the Great Depression of 1929 earlier than Europe and the United States because its previously mentioned policies and measures promoted a militarized economy. Moreover, an economic upsurge—based on its military industries—took place after 1933. In fact, Japanese industrial production increased 52 percent between 1929 and 1936. Production of the means of production grew 71.5 percent, and the production of consumer goods rose 25.3 percent. Steel production went from 2.29 million tons in 1929 to 5.8 million tons in 1937. As a result, Japan's industrial structure which had previously rested on light industry as its main pillar now underwent a significant transformation. Heavy industry's share of total industrial production, for example, went from 38.2 percent in 1930 to 57.8 percent in 1937.

Rapid increases in military production, massive support from the government, and soaring corporate profits enabled the *zaibatsu* to extend their control over various sectors of the economy to an unprecedented degree. For example, the total profits of Mitsui's Japan Steel Works came to 5.19 million yen in the five-year period from 1927 through 1931, but doubled in the five-year span from 1932 to 1936, reaching 10.31 million yen. Sumitomo's Industrial Metals Corporation enjoyed profits of 6.03 million yen for the similar period 1927–31, but its profits almost quadrupled to 23.72 million yen during 1932–36. By the first half of 1937, the total capital assets of the venerable "Big Eight" *zaibatsu* (Mitsui, Mitsubishi, Sumitomo, Yasuda, Ōkura, Asano, Kawasaki, and Furukawa) and the five newly emerging *zaibatsu* (Nissan, Nichiden, Nissō, Mori, and Riken) came to 41.7 billion yen, comprising 27.2 percent of the total capital assets of all Japanese companies. These thirteen *zaibatsu* controlled the various sectors of Japan's economy through a network of cartels and trusts.

Intensified exploitation of the working people was the source of the sharply rising profits enjoyed by the *zaibatsu*. For example, although the industrial work force had expanded due to the booming military economy (total factory employment came to 2.6 million in 1936, a gain of 760 thousand when compared to 1929), the workers themselves suffered greater exploitation. In the name of "industrial rationalization," labor intensity constantly increased, and the workday commonly reached twelve or fourteen hours. Wages did not compensate either for increased work-related expenses or the higher levels of production. On the contrary, due to inflation and increasingly higher taxes, real wages in 1937 were down by 12.8 percent when compared to 1930. In the textile industry, for example, even the average daily cash wage fell from 1.06 yen in 1927 to 0.65 yen in 1937.

Although the Japanese worker and peasant movement declined between 1933 and 1935 as a result of brutal fascist suppression, the greater impoverishment of the working people led to renewed militancy on their part, beginning in 1936. Farm tenancy disputes in 1936 reached 5,714 cases, more than double and triple the number that occurred during the 1929 Depression. The fury of workers' strikes in 1937 also set historical records, with the number of participants reaching 214 thousand people. The struggles waged by Japan's workers and peasants strengthened the anti-fascist battlefront, and enabled Japan's anti-fascist forces to gain a great victory in the February 1936 Diet elections. These developments led Japan's militarist forces (spearheaded by elements of its officer corps) to launch a coup d'état on February 26, 1936, thereby pushing Japan further down the road of fascism.

The Complete Control Imposed by Japan's Militarized State Monopoly Capitalism (1937–41), and the Intensification of Economic Contradictions

As early as 1935, Chairman Mao pointed out that "today Japanese imperialism wants to change China from a semi-colony carved up by several imperialist powers into a colony occupied solely by itself."[25] Although Japanese imperialism's policy of seeking to destroy China had been decided upon earlier, it was only after the September 18, 1931 incident that Japan actively prepared to throw in its full power. The complicity of international imperialism (headed by the United States and England) and the signing of the German-Japanese Anti-Comintern Pact in 1936 emboldened Japanese imperialism even more. However, Japan's aggression met fierce opposition and resolute resistance from the Chinese people led by the Chinese Communist party. Especially noteworthy was the historic telegram of February 10, 1937 which the Chinese Communist party sent to the Nationalist party. Advocating an end to the civil war, the creation of an anti-Japanese front, and cooperation between the Communists and Nationalists, the telegram quickly galvanized into action a strong anti-Japanese United Front composed of people from various social strata. People in both rural and urban areas organized anti-Japanese groups. All this produced a new environment in which to prosecute the war against the Japanese.

On July 7, 1937, Japanese imperialism launched a full-scale war of aggression against China. Its aim was to extinguish the flames of Chinese resistance. Within less than a year, the Japanese aggressors had occupied vast parts of northern, central, eastern, and southern China. In achieving this, they were aided by Jieshi Jiang's policy of passively resisting the Japanese and actively opposing the Communists. However, confronted by determined resistance from the Chinese people, Japan's dream of crushing China within a few months ended in failure. The Chinese people now began to fight back heroically in a variety of ways, guided by Chairman Mao's brilliant strategic thinking on how to wage both protracted war and guerrilla warfare. As a result, the Japanese were forced to commit more and more men and material to the China battlefront. Unable to either advance or retreat, the Japanese became stuck in a swamp from which they could not extricate themselves.

As the war expanded and became lengthier, a glaring contradiction arose between Japan's economic strength and the inability of its economy to meet the needs of prosecuting the war. In order to solve this steadily growing problem, Japanese imperialism gradually put its national economy onto a wartime mobilization track. The National Mobilization Law (enacted in April 1938) was a detailed program that militarized the state. It established a compulsory mobilization system in the areas of finance, industry, and even people's everyday lives. The law provided a legal basis for the vast reach of government controls.

Everything from the manufacture of weapons, munitions, aircraft, and communications equipment to the production of ships, industrial equipment, construction materials, fuels, and electrical power—even that of food, animal fodder, and medicine—fell within the purview of state control. At the same time, the government had such powers as to requisition goods, supervise corporate investment, set profit levels for companies, enact laws relating to the hiring and firing of workers, determine wages and working conditions, prohibit strikes, and dissolve unions. In short, the government controlled all the human, material, and financial resources of the nation.

Japan went on a wild rampage of plunder in China. It pursued this policy in order to link the occupied part of China to the Japanese war chariot, and to make China become its dependency, supplying industrial raw materials and agricultural products to the home country. In 1937, Japan began to implement a Five Year Plan for Agricultural Development in China's northeast. In November 1937, Nissan (the new *zaibatsu*) moved lock, stock, and barrel to China's northeast. It created the Manchuria Heavy Industries Company, and—in conjunction with the South Manchuria Railway Company—forced the people living in that region to expand the production of strategic raw materials for Japan. Following in the train of their armies, the Japanese monopoly capitalists also went on a rampage of plunder in the other parts of China they occupied. In April 1938, for example, Japan announced a predatory plan called "The Policy for the Economic Construction of North China." In November 1938, Japanese state capital and private monopoly capital jointly created the North China Prospecting Company and the Central China Development Company. These corporations then began an aggressive and unconstrained policy of acquiring Chinese companies in the industrial sector. Eventually they came to monopolize the transportation, dock facilities, post and telecommunication operations, electric power, mining, salt refining, fishing, and other economic sectors in the areas of China they occupied. In 1938, the Standard United Bank of China was established in Beijing. In 1940, the Reserve Bank of China was set up in Shanghai. Both plundered the Chinese people by issuing vast amounts of nonconvertible bank certificates. In March 1940, Japanese imperialism organized a puppet government in Nanjing led by Jingwei Wang in order to create even more favorable conditions for its plunder of central China.

Japan also stepped up its plunder of Korea after the July 7, 1937 incident. Nichiden (one of the five "new" *zaibatsu*) served as the main organization that looted Korea of the raw materials required by the Japanese army. Between 1937 and 1940, for example, Japan increased its haul of raw materials and military goods from Korea from 670 million yen to 1.65 billion yen. A system of compulsory grain requisitions took away between 70 percent and 80 percent of the peasants' harvests. Not only did Japan squeeze out a great deal of material and financial wealth from Korea, but it also mobilized many Korean youths (more than 1.3 million by 1942, for example) and sent them to northeast China. There they were put to work manufacturing military goods or building secret military installations. Often, however, groups of these workers would be killed after completing their arduous tasks.

Exploitation of the Japanese people as well as plunder of those living in the occupied colonies enabled Japanese military production to expand significantly, and as a result, greatly enhanced its military power. For example, in the years between 1937 and 1941, Japan's production of heavy-duty trucks went from 19,555 to 42,096 units. Aircraft production increased from 3,365 to 5,088 airplanes; naval tonnage went from fifty-five thousand to 225 thousand tons; and annual production of tanks and armored vehicles reached five thousand to six thousand vehicles by 1941. By this time, Japan's air force had achieved parity with England. Its navy ranked third in the world, next only to that of England and the United States. However, the speed of its industrial growth was also slackening in this period. The profound contradictions that confronted the Japanese economy both domestically and on the international level were now coming to the surface.

First of all, in order to pay for the ever-increasing costs of these wars, the national budget totalled fifty billion yen between the years 1937 and 1941. This represented a sixfold increase over the total budget expenditures for the previous five years. Direct military spending accounted for more than 70 percent of this amount, or about one-third of national income. Because only about one-third of these huge expenditures was offset by tax revenues, a budget deficit began to balloon. Japan tried to find a cure by issuing large quantities of paper money, but this only caused inflation. Commodity prices doubled in the five years from 1936 to 1941. The national treasury confronted bankruptcy.

Second, the growth of military industries was seriously hampered by acute shortages in the production of raw materials. By 1941, for example, coal production in Japan, its colonies, and the areas it occupied could satisfy only 88.3 percent of demand. For oil, this figure came to 18.4 percent; for iron ore, 42.4 percent; for copper, 43 percent; for aluminum, 15 percent; and for zinc, 18.4 percent. The United States was a great help in providing the raw materials and equipment needed by the Japanese military. However, the contradictions between the United States and Japan over their respective Asian policies intensified after 1939, and as a result, American shipments to Japan were dramatically reduced. Japan now found itself in a tight spot, confronting shortages in the supply of raw materials and equipment. Like robbing Peter in order to pay Paul, Japan was left with little alternative but to substantially reduce its production of consumer goods in order to guarantee its military needs. Even a crucial export industry such as textiles suffered cutbacks. For example, cotton cloth production fell from four billion meters in 1937 to 1.1 billion meters in 1941.

Third, contradictions between Japan's agriculture and its industry also became more severe. Agricultural production declined year after year after reaching its highest output in 1939. This occurred because 1. large numbers of the agricultural work force were conscripted into the army or sent to work on military projects, 2. arable land was requisitioned for military bases, and 3. fertilizer supplies were reduced. At the same time, exports of Korean and Taiwanese rice to Japan steadily decreased because of the greatly increased demand by the military forces stationed there. As a result, a crisis situation emerged in Japan's domestic supply of grain. A black market began to flourish. After 1939, the Japanese government even compelled farmers to sell the majority of their rice, wheat, maize, millet, sweet potatoes, and sweet potato stalks and leaves to the government at fixed prices.

The Collapse of the Militarized Economy after the Outbreak of the Pacific War

Embroiled on a battlefront in China and faced with gradually accelerating contradictions both domestically and internationally, Japanese imperialism sought a new way out from the war to save itself from destruction. It took advantage of some favorable opportunities that presented themselves, such as a) France's surrender to Germany and Italy in June 1940, b) weakening British and French control over Southeast Asia, and c) America's intoxication with the windfall profits it was earning from the war. Japan now decided to risk everything on a single throw of the dice, and launched the Pacific War on December 8, 1941 in a wild attempt to realize its blind ambition of establishing a "Greater East Asia Co-Prosperity Sphere." Japanese imperialism used surprise attacks to occupy (within the space of six months) the vast lands of the Philippines, Malaya, Indonesia, Vietnam, Thailand, Burma, and India [*sic*]. The outbreak of the Pacific War symbolized the bankruptcy of the evil policy of American and British imperialism. This policy consistently promoted Japanese imperialism as a pawn opposed to the Soviet Union and to communism. Just as in Europe where they assisted Hitler's Germany, the United States and England had once again wounded themselves with a self-destructive policy, like lifting a rock only to drop it on their own feet.

Chairman Mao pointed out in May 1938: "There are only two possible outcomes to the political situation in Japan. Either the rapid collapse of its entire ruling class transfers political power to the people, and the war then comes to an end, which is impossible at the moment; or Japan's landlord class and bourgeoisie become increasingly more fascist and continue the war until the day of their downfall, which is the very path Japan is now taking."[26] In the latter half of 1941, and especially after the Pacific War broke out, Japan's fascist regime established a "New Political Order" and "New Economic Order," further intensifying the fascist process in government and the militarization of the economy. This elevated the policy of military fascism to the highest degree possible.

The New Political Order peeled off the façade of sham bourgeois democracy and put into effect a naked fascist dictatorship of the landlords and bourgeoisie.

In October 1940, Japan's imperial government banned all political parties and dissolved the Diet. The Imperial Rule Assistance Association, a fascist political organization, appeared in early 1942. It was the only national political organization legally permitted to operate, and it was controlled from top to bottom by bureaucrats, fascist military officers, *zaibatsu* officials, landlords, local tyrants, and evil gentry. They brutally suppressed any progressive forces, and recklessly spread ideas of chauvinism and militarism. Japan's cabinets were subsequently composed of *zaibatsu* leaders—with the exception of fascist warlords like Hideki Tōjō and others. For example, Shigeaki Ikeda, the Minister of Finance, was the General Manager of the Mitsui Bank and Chairman of the Board of the Mitsui Holding Company. Ichizo Kobayashi, the Minister of Commerce and Industry, was the Chairman of the Board of Mitsui's Tōkyō Electric Power Company.

After December 1941, the New Economic Order, based on the Law Governing Groups in Vital Industries, established regulatory agencies throughout all the major industrial and financial sectors. This system forced various large, medium, and small-sized companies to engage in military production that was controlled by monopoly capital. The state granted these regulatory agencies broad powers not only to allocate military contracts, raw materials, and labor power among the various industries, but also to set production quotas and prices. The leading personnel of the regulatory agencies were drawn from the *zaibatsu* or were their representatives. For example, the General Manager of the Riken *zaibatsu*, Masatoshi Ōkōchi, chaired the regulatory agency that supervised machine manufacturing. The Chairman of the Board of Mitsubishi Heavy Industries was chairman of the regulatory agency responsible for the aircraft industry. Toyotarō Yūki, the President of the Yasuda Bank, chaired the regulatory agency that handled national finances. These regulatory agencies in reality represented a form of direct fusion between state power and monopoly capital.

To solve the problem of shortages of raw materials and equipment, a Fixed Assets Management Group was set up in December 1941. This agency ordered the closure of many small and medium-sized companies, and turned over their equipment to the monopolies. The government also enacted the Industrial Readjustment Law in 1942. As a result of the law, large quantities of machinery and equipment used in consumer industries were broken up into scrap iron in order to increase the supply of steel. By the end of the war, for example, two-thirds of the textile industry's machinery had been melted down.

The Japanese also created many National Strategic Companies (jointly capitalized and managed by the government and by finance capital) in the colonies and conquered territories. These enterprises were established on the foundations of land, mines, or companies confiscated from local citizens. The presidents and trustees of these companies were all appointed by the government, and focused all their activities on plundering local resources. In the occupied countries of Southeast Asia, for example, these companies looted whatever material wealth was readily available, and justified these actions as conforming to the slogan of

"Giving Top Priority to the Rapid Extraction of Mineral Resources and Guaranteeing the Needs of the War Effort." In China's northeast, they forced the local citizens and students to manufacture strategic goods or work on various construction projects. As a result of using this kind of "volunteer labor" or "hard work," the Japanese dug many mass burial pits where the bleached bones of tens of thousands of people were piled on top of each other, creating countless blood debts they owed to the Chinese people. Like "plucking a lotus flower," they brazenly looted China's northeast of its grain, and deprived its farmers of their right to a minimal standard of living. Even eating too much rice was considered an "economic crime" for which one could be jailed.

As the war expanded, so did the size of the army and navy. In 1937, for example, 1.1 million men were serving in the military. In 1941, this figure had increased to 2.41 million. By the time Japan surrendered in 1945, this number had reached 7.13 million. More than 30 percent of Japan's male population was sent to fight on the battlefield. In order to support this gigantic war machine, government spending reached 93.4 billion yen by 1944, or more than five times the 1941 budget of 16.5 billion yen. To raise the revenue for such colossal expenditures, the government not only boosted taxes, floated bonds, and printed currency within Japan itself, but also did everything it possibly could to shift this burden onto the colonies and occupied territories. There it issued vast quantities of unbacked paper currency and military scrip, which were the direct cause that drove up commodity prices a hundredfold, and even two thousandfold, in the occupied parts of China, Korea, and Southeast Asia in the years from 1941 to 1945.

Extensive conscription brought about a serious shortage of labor power. After the government in 1941 passed the Law to Adjust the Supply of Labor and the Law to Regulate Labor in Major Industries, it also enacted a General Program to Reorganize the Labor Force in 1943. These laws instituted a system of military controls over the work force, abolished any limits on working hours in factories, organized a Women's Labor Corps, and forced high school and college students to work in factories. In 1944, the government put into effect a national mobilization, requiring all males between the ages of twelve and sixty and all females between the ages of twelve and forty to perform some type of uniform labor service. By 1944, there were 8.26 million factory workers in Japan, or more than triple the 2.6 million working there in 1936. Of these, one-fourth were women, and two-fifths were either children or youths under the age of twenty. In addition to these people, 314 thousand workers from Korea and thirty-four thousand from China had been essentially kidnapped and brought to Japan to work in various military industries in the years 1939 to 1944. In short, all of Japan had been turned into a labor camp for the military.

However, Japan's total industrial production declined after 1941, even though the government resorted to such fascist methods. By the end of the war, the economy had virtually collapsed. Not only did Japan confront a shortage of raw materials, but its leading industrial centers were all concentrated in four regions: the Ōsaka-Hyogo area, the Tōkyō-Yokohama area, the Aiichi-Shizuoka area, and the Fukuoka-Nagasaki area. Although these areas constituted only one-tenth of Japan's land surface, they held two-fifths of its population and three-fourths of its large-scale industry by war's end. After 1942, the United States steadily intensified its aerial bombing campaign against Japan. The Japanese islands were also subjected to a tight naval blockade. As a result, Japan could sustain neither its consumer industries nor its military industries. By 1943, the government was left with no choice but to institute a policy that emphasized only the "vitally important" industries. Aircraft production was assigned the top priority, with shipbuilding and heavy weaponry next. The production of other military goods, without any exception, could not be sustained. By 1945, 90 percent of Japan's industrial facilities were lying idle. Total industrial and mining production came to only 28.5 percent of the 1935–37 levels. Production of consumer goods stood at 30 percent, and that of capital goods at 10 percent, of their 1935–37 levels.

Agricultural production, like that of industry, also found itself in a similarly distressed situation. Vast tracts of arable land had been comandeered for use as airfields or military bases. Young workers in their prime had all been either drafted into the military or assigned to work on military-related projects. The majority of those still left in the villages were either elderly or children. One-third of the horses had also been requisitioned for service in the armed forces. When the war ended in 1945, agricultural production came to only about one half that of 1937. After 1941, the daily rice ration for an adult amounted to only eleven ounces. Moreover, the proportion of barley, sweet potatoes, and dried vegetables in the diet grew increasingly large until they became staple foods.

Japanese imperialism, which consistently reaped huge profits from its wars of aggression, nevertheless pushed the country and the people onto the road to ruin. During the war, 6.46 million people became casualties, and of these, 1.2 million lost their lives. Twenty-two million people lost their homes under the American aerial bombardment. More than 45 percent of the national wealth was destroyed in the war. The sufferings inflicted on the people of the colonies and the occupied territories were too numerous to even be recorded. In the eight years between 1937 and 1945, Japanese imperialism destroyed 930 cities in China, killed several tens of millions of Chinese people, and looted or destroyed an incalculable amount of wealth. Japanese imperialism was the common enemy of the Japanese people as well as the peoples of Asia.

However, the war fattened Japan's *zaibatsu.* The capital assets of those companies affiliated with the Mitsui *zaibatsu* grew from 1.18 billion yen in 1937 to 2.82 billion yen in September 1945. Mitsubishi's capital increased from 850 million yen to 2.16 billion yen during the same time span. Sumitomo went from 380 million yen to 2.82 billion, and Yasuda from 260 million yen to 2.09 billion. These increases ranged between 2.5 to eight times their pre-1937 capitalization levels.

As early as 1938, Chairman Mao had pointed out: "Confronted by domestic and international contradictions, Japanese imperialism by the 1930s not only was compelled to launch a risky war on an unprecedentedly large scale, but now has to face the twilight of its total collapse. When we look at the path that its society has travelled, we can no longer regard Japan as a flourishing nation. The war will not culminate in the prosperity sought by its ruling class, but rather will end in its exact opposite: the demise of Japanese imperialism."[27] History has completely confirmed Chairman Mao's brilliant prediction. Japan began to reel under the coordinated attacks from the world's anti-fascist forces. The blows struck by the Chinese people, led by the Chinese Communist Party, in the eight years of their anti-Japanese struggle were especially important. Outwardly strong but inwardly weak, facing grave contradictions everywhere, and increasingly isolated, Japanese imperialism finally accepted the terms of the Potsdam Declaration and surrendered unconditionally on August 15, 1945.

Notes

Note to Preface

1. Mao Zedong, "Cast Away Illusions, Prepare for Struggle," in *Selected Works of Mao Zedong* (Beijing: People's Publishing House, 1967), 1372.

Notes to Chapter 1

1. Marx, *Capital*, vol. 1, in *Collected Works of Marx and Engels* (Beijing: People's Publishing House, 1972), 23:783.
2. Ibid., p. 784.
3. Ibid., p. 784.
4. Marx and Engels, *The Manifesto of the Communist Party*, in *Collected Works of Marx and Engels* (Beijing: People's Publishing House, 1972), 1:252; English translation taken from Marx and Engels, *The Manifesto of the Communist Party* (Beijing: Foreign Language Press, 1970), 31–32.
5. Marx, *Capital*, vol. 1, in *Collected Works of Marx and Engels* (Beijing: People's Publishing House, 1972), 23:784.
6. Ibid., p. 783.
7. Ibid., p. 891.
8. The Netherlands was located in the present-day area of Belgium and Holland. Its southern part is presently Belgium, and its northern part is presently Holland.
9. Marx, *Capital*, vol. 1, in *Collected Works of Marx and Engels* (Beijing: People's Publishing House, 1972), 23:820.
10. Marx, *Capital* (Beijing: People's Publishing House, 1966), 3:373.
11. Marx, *Capital* (Beijing: People's Publishing House, 1972), 23:819.
12. Lenin, *The Development of Capitalism in Russia*, in *Collected Works of Lenin* (Beijing: People's Publishing House, 1959), 3:411; English translation taken from *The Development of Capitalism in Russia*.
13. Lenin, "The Land Program of the Social Democratic Party During the First Russian Revolution," in *Collected Works of Lenin* (Beijing: People's Publishing House, 1959), 13:219.
14. Marx and Engels, *The Manifesto of the Communist Party*, in *Collected Works of Marx and Engels* (Beijing: People's Publishing House, 1972), 1:256; English translation taken from Marx and Engels, *The Manifesto of the Communist Party* (Beijing: Foreign Language Press, 1970), 37.
15. Marx, *Capital*, vol. 1, in *Collected Works of Marx and Engels* (Beijing: People's Publishing House, 1972), 23:679.

16. Marx, "A Resolution Passed at the Meeting to Commemorate the First Anniversary of the Paris Commune," in *Collected Works of Marx and Engels* (Beijing: People's Publishing House, 1963), 17:677. English translation taken from Marx and Engels, *On the Paris Commune* (Moscow: Progress Publishing, 1971), 269.

17. "Minutes of the Speeches on the Paris Commune," in *Collected Works of Marx and Engels* (Beijing: People's Publishing House, 1963), 17:677.

18. The special characteristics of the cartel were as follows: Companies that took part in a cartel made an agreement among themselves to divide up the sales market and to fix the quantity of products that would be made. The cartel would set a standard price. However, each company still preserved its independent management over production and sales. Those companies that participated in syndicates lost their independence regarding sales. The marketing of the commodity was accomplished under the unified management of the syndicate. Each company only retained an independent role in production. Irrespective of production or marketing, companies that had been swallowed up by a trust lost all their independence, and were administered by the trust's board of directors who were responsible for its management.

19. The conglomerate was a comprehensive monopoly corporation that a) had a certain capitalist clique at its core and b) had swallowed up not only numerous companies from different industrial sectors, but also trading companies, transportation companies, banks, and insurance companies.

20. Lenin, *Imperialism, The Highest Stage of Capitalism* (Beijing: People's Publishing House, 1971), 53.

21. Ibid., 80; English translation taken from Lenin, *Imperialism, The Highest Stage of Capitalism* (Beijing: Foreign Languages Press, 1970), 106.

22. Lenin, "A Caricature of Marxism and 'Imperialist Economism,' " in *Collected Works of Lenin* (Beijing: People's Publishing House, 1958), 23:35.

23. "Junker" refers to Prussia's landed aristocracy.

24. Lenin, *Imperialism, The Highest Stage of Capitalism* (Beijing: People's Publishing House, 1971), 114; English translation taken from Lenin, *Imperialism, The Highest Stage of Capitalism* (Beijing: Foreign Languages Press, 1970), 150.

25. As commodity prices fall steeply during an economic crisis, the prices of some products (especially agricultural products) will sometimes decline so far as to go below the costs incurred in their care, warehousing, and transportation. Some monopolies then will take a portion of these products and destroy them, or the government will destroy them after they have purchased them. All this will be done in order to reduce market supplies, prevent prices from continuing to decline, or cause these prices to rise in order to make up for prior financial losses.

26. Lenin, "The Historical Fate of Marxist Theory," in *Collected Works of Lenin* (Beijing: People's Publishing House, 1959), 18:583.

27. Lenin, "The Second Plenary Session of the Communist International," in *Collected Works of Lenin* (Beijing: People's Publishing House, 1958), 31:238.

28. Lenin, *Imperialism, The Highest Stage of Capitalism* (Beijing: People's Publishing House, 1971), 82.

29. The two treaties that Lenin referred to were a) the Treaty of Brest-Litovsk that was imposed by Germany on the Soviet Union in 1918 and b) the Treaty of Versailles which was imposed on Germany by England, the United States, and France after the war.

30. Lenin, preface to the French and German language editions, *Imperialism, The Highest Stage of Capitalism* (Beijing: People's Publishing House, 1971), 7; English translation taken from Lenin, *Imperialism, The Highest Stage of Capitalism* (Beijing: Foreign Languages Press, 1970), 6.

31. Stalin, *Economic Problems of Socialism in the Soviet Union* (Beijing: People's Publishing House, 1971), 45.

Notes to Chapter 2

1. The Normans originally lived in Northern Europe, and in the early tenth century established the duchy of Normandy in Northern France. In 1066, William, Duke of Normandy, led an army across the English Channel and conquered England. History has called this "the Norman Conquest."

2. Marx, *Capital*, vol. 1, in *Collected Works of Marx and Engels* (Beijing: People's Publishing House, 1972), 23:784.

3. "Copyholder" (a peasant whose name was entered on the public register) referred to a serf and his descendants who had become free individuals. Although the land that copyholders farmed still belonged to the aristocracy, the copyholder's rights over that land were recorded on the court documents of the estate. Those documents also stipulated the duration of the agreement (whether it extended from generation to generation, for the lifetime of the copyholder, or only for a fixed time period) and also if the parcel of land could be inherited. A copyholder who wished to alter or extend the length of the rental agreement was obligated to pay a certain tax to his feudal overlord. In general, the copyholder paid a fixed amount of money as rent to his feudal lord. Once the copyholder had fulfilled his other obligations, the feudal overlord—according to tradition and custom—had no right either to increase the rent or to evict the tenant.

4. The "yeomanry" has also been translated as "self-sufficient farmers" or as "middle peasants."

5. The cotter owned only a thatched cottage and three to four acres that he could call his home. He had little choice but to do odd jobs for the aristocracy or for wealthy farmers, and earned a living as a poor peasant by herding livestock on the public lands.

6. Clan was the name of the clan lineage of the Celt family located in the Scottish highlands.

7. Marx, *Capital*, vol. 1, in *Collected Works of Marx and Engels* (Beijing: People's Publishing House, 1972), 23:801; English translation in Marx, *Capital* (Moscow: International Publishers, 1967), 732–3.

8. Engels, "Preface to the English edition" of *The Development of Socialism from Utopian to Scientific*, in *Collected Works of Marx and Engels* (1965), 22, 349.

9. Marx, *Capital*, vol. 1, in *Collected Works of Marx and Engels* (Beijing: People's Pulishing House, 1972), 23:790–91.

10. Under the Norfolk system, the farmer divided his land into four parts. Every year he would plant turnips, barley, clover, and wheat in each segment, and then rotate those crops for the following year. Under the fallow system, the farmer divided his land into two portions, with one segment sitting idle (or fallow) each year.

11. Marx, "The East India Company, Its History and Results," in *Collected Works of Marx and Engels* (Beijing: People's Publishing House, 1961), 9:168; English translation taken from Marx and Engels, *Articles on Britain* (Moscow: Progress Publishers, 1971), 173.

12. Marx, *Capital*, vol. 1 (Beijing: People's Publishing House, 1972), 23:822; English translation taken from *Capital* (New York: International, 1967), 753–54.

13. Jenny was the name of Hargreaves daughter.

14. Engels, "The Condition of England in the 18th Century," in *Collected Works of Marx and Engels* (Beijing: People's Publishing House, 1956), 1:668.

15. Engels, *The Condition of the English Working Class*, in *Collected Works of Marx and Engels* (Beijing: People's Publishing House, 1957), 2:300.

16. Marx, *The Poverty of Philosophy,* in *Collected Works of Marx and Engels* (Beijing: People's Publishing House, 1958), 4:163–64.

17. Approved by Parliament, the Corn Laws represented a policy of agricultural protectionism promoted by England's wealthy landlords in order to increase the income from

their own lands and to prevent competition from foreign agricultural products. The Corn Laws stipulated what could be imported when the price of a quart of wheat passed a certain threshold. Between 1773 and 1815, Parliament frequently increased the trigger price that would permit wheat imports, thereby artificially raising grain prices. This made it more difficult for factory owners to keep wages low, yet cleverly enabled the large landowners to reap even greater profits. In order to repeal the Corn Laws, the industrial bourgeoisie during the first half of the nineteenth century did a great deal of work to publicize the issue and stir things up, and waged a long-term struggle with the landed aristocracy.

18. Marx, "A Speech on Free Trade," in *Collected Works of Marx and Engels* (Beijing: People's Publishing House, 1958), 4:456; English translation taken from Marx and Engels, *Articles on Britain* (Moscow: Progress, 1971 ed.), 86.

19. Engels, preface to the 1892 English edition, *The Condition of the Working Class in England*, in *Collected Works of Marx and Engels* (Beijing: People's Publishing House, 1965), 22:320; English translation taken from *The Condition of the Working Class in England* (Moscow: Progress, 1973), 34.

20. Pressured by the industrial bourgeoisie and the struggles waged by the masses of people, England's Parliament enacted legislation in 1831 that partially reformed the system of parliamentary elections. The reforms either eliminated or reduced the number of parliamentary seats in many "pocket boroughs" and shifted them to the new industrial cities. The legislation also lowered the property qualifications required for eligible voters. For example, the requirements for urban voters were relaxed to include home owners with an annual income in excess of ten pounds sterling and tenants who paid more than ten pounds in rent annually. This legislation enabled the industrial bourgeoisie to send more representatives to Parliament.

21. Engels, *The Condition of the Working Class in England*, in *Collected Works of Marx and Engels* (Beijing: People's Publishing House, 1957), 2:281.

22. Engels, *The Condition of the Working Class in England*, in *Collected Works of Marx and Engels* (Beijing: People's Publishing House, 1957), 2:436; English language translation taken from Engels, *The Condition of the Working Class in England* (Moscow: Progress Publishers, 1973), 188.

23. Marx, *Capital*, vol. 1, in *Collected Works of Marx and Engels* (Beijing: People's Publishing House, 1972), 23:272; English language translation taken from Marx, *Capital* (New York: International Publishers, 1967), 1:243–44.

24. Marx, "Inaugural Address of the Working Men's International Association," in *Collected Works of Marx and Engels* (Beijing: People's Publishing House, 1964), 16:11; English language translation taken from Marx and Engels, *Selected Works* (Moscow: Progress Publishers, 1969), 2:16.

25. Marx, *Capital*, vol. 1, in *Collected Works of Marx and Engels* (Beijing: People's Publishing House, 1972), 23:271; English language tranlation taken from Marx, *Capital* (New York: International Publishers, 1967), 1:242.

26. Cited in Engels, *The Condition of the Working Class in England*, in *Collected Works at Marx and Engels* (Beijing: People's Publishing House, 1957), 2:309; English translation taken from *The Condition of the Working Class in England* (Moscow: Progress Publishers, 1973), 69.

27. Engels, preface to the 1892 English edition of *The Condition of the Working Class in England*, in *Collected Works of Marx and Engels* (Beijing: People's Publishing House, 1965), 22:321; English translation taken from *The Condition of the Working Class in England* (Moscow: Progress Publishers, 1973), 35.

28. Engels, *The Condition of the Working Class in England*, in *Collected Works of Marx and Engels* (Beijing: People's Publishing House, 1957), 2:502; English language translation taken from *The Condition of the Working Class* (Moscow: Progress Publishers, 1973), 251.

29. Lenin, "The Third International and Its Place in History, in *Collected Works of Lenin* (Beijing: People's Publishing House, 1956), 29:276.

30. Cited in Marx, *Capital*, vol. 1, in *Collected Works of Marx and Engels* (Beijing: People's Publishing House, 1972), 23:472.

31. Lenin, "Imperialism and the Split in Socialism," in *Collected Works of Lenin* (Beijing: People's Publishing House, 1958), 23:110; English translation taken from Lenin, *On Britain* (Moscow: Progress Publishers, 1973), 272.

32. Lenin, "Harry Quelch," in *Collected Works of Lenin* (Beijing: People's Publishing House, 1959), 19:370; English translation taken from Lenin, *On Britain* (Moscow: Progress Publishers, 1973), 160.

33. Engels, preface to the 1892 English edition of *The Condition of the Working Class in England*, in *Collected Works of Marx and Engels* (Beijing: People's Publishing House, 1965), 22:322.

34. Engels, preface to the 1892 English edition of *The Condition of the Working Class in England*, in *Collected Works of Marx and Engels* (Beijing: People's Publishing House, 1965), 22:322.

35. Engels, preface to the 1892 English edition of *The Condition of the Working Class in England*, in *Collected Works of Marx and Engels* (Beijing: People's Publishing House, 1965), 22:324–25; English language translation taken from *The Condition of the Working Class in England* (Moscow: Progress Publishers, 1973), *38*.

36. Lenin, "The British Labor Movement in 1912," in *Collected Works of Lenin* (Beijing: People's Publishing House, 1959), 18:460; English translation taken from Lenin, *On Britain* (Moscow: Progress Publishers, 1973), 130.

37. Lenin, *Imperialism, The Highest Stage of Capitalism* (Beijing: People's Publishing House, 1971), 15; English translation taken from *Imperialism, The Highest Stage of Capitalism* (Beijing: Foreign Languages Press, 1973), *17*.

38. Lenin, *Imperialism, The Highest Stage of Capitalism* (Beijing: People's Publishing House, 1971), 15; English translation taken from *Imperialism, The Highest Stage of Capitalism* (Beijing: Foreign Languages Press, 1973), *16*.

39. "Agency Houses" were organizations that represented English capital in their investment activities in India. British capital would frequently utilize an "Agency House" when establishing a new company there and would turn over managerial responsibilities to it after the new enterprise had been established. In addition to receiving an annual fee for managing the company, the "Agency House" would also earn a commission that would be a fixed portion of either the company's production, business volume, or net profit. As a result, "Agency Houses" acted quite literally as the agents of British finance capital in their investment activities in India.

40. Lenin, *Imperialism, The Highest Stage of Capitalism* (Beijing: People's Publishing House, 1971), 57.

41. Lenin, *Imperialism, The Highest Stage of Capitalism* (Beijing: People's Publishing House, 1971), 70; English language translation taken from *Imperialism, The Highest Stage of Capitalism* (Beijing: Foreign Languages Press, 1970), 91.

42. Cited in Lenin, *Imperialism, The Highest Stage of Capitalism* (Beijing: People's Publishing House, 1971), 71; English language translation taken from *Imperialism, The Highest Stage of Capitalism* (Beijing: Foreign Languages Press, 1970), 93–94.

Notes to Chapter 3

1. Marx, *Capital*, in *Collected Works of Marx and Engels* (Beijing: People's Publishing House, 1972), 23:829.

2. The thirteen colonies included Massachusetts, Rhode Island, New Hampshire, and

Connecticut. These four were collectively called New England, or the Northern colonies. Pennsylvania, New York, New Jersey, and Delaware were known as the Middle colonies. Virginia, Maryland, North Carolina, South Carolina, and Georgia were called the Southern colonies.

3. Unable to pay their own passage to North America, the poorest of the European immigrants could do little but sign a contract (or indenture) with either a ship captain or company operating in the colonies that would agree to transport them across the Atlantic. After arriving in North America, the white indentured servant had to work from three to seven years to repay the travel expenses he or she had incurred. After the period of indentured servitude had been completed, the indentured servant gained his freedom. Probably half of all whites who emigrated to North America during the colonial period arrived there as indentured servants.

4. Marx, *Capital*, in *Collected Works of Marx and Engels* (Beijing: People's Publishing House, 1972), 23:836.

5. Mao Tsetung, "People of the World, Unite, and Defeat the U.S. Aggressors and All Their Running Dogs," (Shanghai: Commercial Press, 1971), 9.

6. Lenin, "Letter to American Workers," in *Collected Works of Lenin* (Beijing: People's Publishing House, 1956), 28:43.

7. Marx, *Capital*, in *Collected Works of Marx and Engels* (Beijing: People's Publishing House, 1972), 23:11.

8. Marx, *Capital*, in *Collected Works of Marx and Engels* (Beijing: People's Publishing House, 1972), 23:495.

9. Lenin, "The Land Programme of the Social Democratic Party in the First Russian Revolution," *Collected Works of Lenin* (Beijing: People's Publishing House, 1959), 13:219; English translation in *Collected Works of Lenin* (New York: Progress Publishers, 1972), 13:239.

10. These statistics concerning grain production included seven types of grain (corn, wheat, rice, barley, buckwheat, oats, and alfalfa) as well as potatoes. Four tons of potatoes were calculated as one ton of grain.

11. Marx, *Capital* (Beijing: People's Publishing House, 1966), 3:940.

12. Marx, *A History of the Theory of Surplus Value* (Commercial Press, 1957), 2:402.

13. Marx, *The Poverty of Philosophy*, in *Collected Works of Marx and Engels* (Beijing: People's Publishing House, 1958), 4:145.

14. Marx and Engels, "On the American Civil War" (Beijing: People's Publishing House, 1955), 79.

15. Lenin, "New Material on the Laws of Development of Capitalist Agriculture," in *Collected Works of Lenin* (Beijing: People's Publishing House, 1958), 22:11.

16. Mao Tsetung, "People of the World Unite! Oppose the Racial Discrimination of American Imperialism! Support the Struggle of American Black People Against Racial Discrimination!" (Publication and publisher unknown.)

17. Marx and Engels, preface to the 1882 Russian edition of *Manifesto of the Communist Party* (Beijing: People's Publishing House, 1971), 5.

18. In order to continue working his land, a destitute farmer often mortgaged his property to a bank in return for a loan. While nominally the famer still retained ownership over his farm, in reality he was paying rent to the bank in the form of interest and mortgage payments to clear his loan.

19. Lenin, "New Materials on the Laws of Development of Capitalist Agriculture," in *Collected Works of Lenin* (Beijing: People's Publishing House, 1958), 22:12. Italics in original.

20. Lenin, "New Materials on the Laws of Development of Capitalist Agriculture," in *Collected Works of Lenin* (Beijing: People's Publishing House, 1958), 22:13.

21. Marx and Engels, preface to the 1882 edition of the *Manifesto of the Communist Party* (Beijing: People's Publishing House, 1971), 3.

22. Stalin, "Speech Delivered at a Meeting of Workers of the Stalin Railroad Factory, October Railway Bureau," in *Collected Works of Stalin* (Beijing: People's Publishing House, 1954), 9:158.

23. Marx and Engels, *Manifesto of the Communist Party* (Beijing: People's Publishing House, 1971), 29.

24. Lenin, *Imperialism, The Highest Stage of Capitalism* (Beijing: People's Publishing House, 1971), 12.

25. Engels, "On the Accumulation of Capital in the United States," in *Collected Works of Marx and Engels* (Beijing: People's Publishing House, 1963), 19:337. Italics in original.

26. Ibid.

27. Lenin, *Imperialism, The Highest Stage of Capitalism* (Beijing: People's Publishing House, 1971), 13.

28. Ibid.

29. Lenin, *Imperialism, The Highest Stage of Capitalism* (Beijing: People's Publishing House, 1971), 13.

30. The pool was a short-term agreement reached by a number of companies to fix a common price. The leading officials of the corporations involved would agree either to fix output quotas for each company, or to allocate market shares among themselves. The purpose of the pool was to guarantee monopoly profits to its participants.

31. A holding company would purchase enough shares of stocks in nominally independent companies to acquire control over them.

32. Lenin, "On Ridicule of Marxism and 'Imperialist Economism,'" in *Collected Works of Lenin* (Beijing: People's Publishing House, 1958), 23:35.

33. The Kuhn-Loeb group primarily controlled America's largest railroad system. Having prospered in the manufacture of explosives, the DuPont group later became America's largest chemical manufacturer as the DuPont Company. After the First World War, it also controlled one of America's largest car manufacturers—General Motors. The Mellon group used its banks to control the aluminum industry, a portion of Pittsburgh's coal and steel industries, and various other heavy industries. The Chicago group was composed of Chicago's banking magnates. It controlled corporations in various industries, including oil, agricultural machinery, railroads, and so on. The Cleveland financial group was composed of three groups led by financial magnates from Cleveland (a commercial center west of Pittsburgh). This group controlled iron mines, smelting industries, and various kinds of machine manufacturing operations in the North. The Boston group was composed of several Boston families that had settled there quite early, had come originally from England, and had subsequently become quite wealthy. Boston was the financial center for industry in Massachusetts and throughout northern New England. The Boston group controlled companies which primarily belonged to light industry, such as textiles, shoe making operations, and so on. The Boston group later founded the United Fruit Company, and turned to control of Latin America's fruit products.

34. John Moody, *The Truth About the Trusts* (New York: Moody Publishing Company, 1904), 493.

35. Lenin, "On the State," in *Collected Works of Lenin* (Beijing: People's Publishing House, 1956), 29:443.

36. Lenin, "On the State," in *Collected Works of Lenin* (Beijing: People's Publishing House, 1956), 29:442.

37. Marx, *Critique of the Gotha Programme*, in *Collected Works of Marx and Engels* (Beijing: People's Publishing House, 1963), 19:28.

38. Lenin, "4,000 Rubles Annually and a Six-Hour Workday," in *Collected Works of Lenin* (Beijing: People's Publishing House, 1958), 20:55.

39. Lenin, *Imperialism, The Highest Stage of Capitalism* (Beijing: People's Publishing House, 1971), 55.

40. Lenin, "The Impending Catastrophe and How to Combat It," in *Collected Works of Lenin* (Beijing: People's Publishing House, 1958), 25:334.

41. Lenin, *Imperialism, The Highest Stage of Capitalism* (Beijing: People's Publishing House, 1971), 106.

42. Lenin, "Letter to American Workers," in *Collected Works of Lenin* (Beijing: People's Publishing House, 1956), 28:44–45.

43. Stalin, "Political Report to the 15th Congress of the CPSU (Bolsheviks)", in *Collected Works of Stalin* (Beijing: People's Publishing House, 1954), 10:234.

44. Stalin, "Political Report to the 15th Congress of the CPSU (Bolsheviks)," in *Collected Works of Stalin* (Beijing: People's Publishing House, 1954), 10:234.

45. Marx, "Wage Labor and Capital," in *Collected Works of Marx and Engels* (Beijing: People's Publishing House, 1961), 6:506.

46. Stalin, "Political Report to the 16th Congress of the CPSU (Bolsheviks) Central Committee," in *Collected Works of Stalin* (Beijing: People's Publishing House, 1955), 12:282.

47. Mao Zedong, "The Present Situation and our Tasks," in *Selected Works of Mao Zedong* (Beijing: People's Publishing House, 1967), bound vol., p. 1155.

Notes to Chapter 4

1. The *taille* (or tax assessed on real estate) was a type of perpetual land tenancy. Peasants became so-called "annual taxpayers" (or "*mainmortables*") for generation after generation. They could farm the land by themselves, or could even transfer it to others. However, the aristocrat retained—in perpetuity—ownership rights, and it was on this basis that he claimed his tax payment. The length of the rental period varied, and was contractually stipulated. When the contract expired, the land returned to its owner, the aristocrat.

2. Mao Zedong, "The Chinese Revolution and the Chinese Communist Party," in *Selected Works of Mao Zedong* (Beijing: People's Publishing House, 1967 combined edition), 587.

3. Louis XIV's edict of 1669 divided the nominal "common lands" into three types. One portion was to be given to the aristocracy. One portion was to be given to the peasantry. The third portion was to be retained as "common land." This arrangement had a clearly predatory character because it legalized the actions of the aristocracy after they had forcibly seized "common lands."

4. The *louis* was the name for France's traditional unit of money. One *louis* weighed approximately five grams.

5. The *sou* was the name of a coin denomination in traditional France. Twenty *sou* were equal to one *louis*.

6. The Le Chapelier Law became operative on June 14, 1791 at the Constitutional Convention on a motion offered by Le Chapelier, a member of the assembly. The law declared that all workers' strikes, gatherings, or associations were illegal. Violators could be severely penalized by fines up to five hundred *livre* and be deprived of their political rights for one year. This was a reactionary bourgeois law, extremely inimical to the working class, and was repealed only in 1864.

7. Marx, *Capital*, vol. 1, in *Collected Works of Marx and Engels* (Beijing: People's Publishing House, 1972), 23:810.

8. Lenin, "On the Open Enemies of the People," in *Collected Works of Lenin* (Beijing: People's Publishing House, 1958), 25:41.

9. The *arpent* was the name for a unit of land in France at that time. One *arpent* was equivalent to 0.3 of a hectare.

10. Lenin, "The First Congress of Representatives of Russian Social Education," in *Collected Works of Lenin* (Beijing: People's Publishing House, 1956), 29:334.

11. Mao Zedong, "On New Democracy," in *Selected Works of Mao Zedong* (Beijing: People's Publishing House, 1967 combined edition), 635.

12. Marx, *The Eighteenth Brumaire of Louis Bonaparte*, in *Collected Works of Marx and Engels* (Beijing: People's Publishing House, 1961), 8:220.

13. Engels, "The Problems of the French and German Peasantry," in *Collected Works of Marx and Engels* (Beijing: People's Publishing House, 1965), 22:583.

14. Marx, *Class Struggles in France, 1848–50,* in *Collected Works of Marx and Engels* (Beijing: People's Publishing House, 1959), 7:97.

15. Marx, *The Eighteenth Brumaire of Louis Bonaparte*, in *Collected Works of Marx and Engels* (Beijing: People's Publishing House, 1961), 8:217.

16. Marx, *The Civil War in France* (Beijing: People's Publishing House, 1971), 54.

17. Marx, *The Civil War in France* (Beijing: People's Publishing House, 1971), 54.

18. Engels, *Anti-Duhring* (Beijing: People's Publishing House, 1970), 23.

19. Marx, *The Class Struggles in France, 1848–50*, in *Collected Works of Marx and Engels* (Beijing: People's Publishing House, 1959), 7:13.

20. Lenin, *Imperialism, The Highest Stage of Capitalism* (Beijing: People's Publishing House, 1971), 48.

21. Marx, *The Civil War in France* (Beijing: People's Publishing House, 1971), 112.

22. Marx, *The Civil War in France* (Beijing: People's Publishing House, 1971), 143.

23. For the original documents and more specific information about the resolutions and the decrees of the Paris Commune, please consult *A Documentary Collection of Resolutions of the Paris Commune* (Commercial Press, 1961 and 1963), two volumes; and *Historical Documents of the Paris Commune* (Commercial Press, 1962).

24. Marx, *The Civil War in France* (Beijing: People's Publishing House, 1971), 58.

25. Lenin, "The Lessons of the Paris Commune," in *Collected Works of Lenin* (Beijing: People's Publishing House, 1959), 13:454.

26. Marx, "Resolution at the Meeting to Commemmorate the First Anniversary of the Paris Commune," in *Collected Works of Marx and Engels* (Beijing: People's Publishing House, 1964), 18:61.

27. Lenin, *Imperialism, The Highest Stage of Capitalism* (Beijing: People's Publishing House, 1971), 60.

28. Ibid., p. 56.

29. Ibid., p. 57.

30. Ibid., p. 48.

31. Ibid., p. 57.

32. Lenin, *Imperialism, The Highest Stage of Capitalism* (Beijing: People's Publishing House, 1971), 52.

33. Mao Zedong, "Speech at the Supreme Soviet of the Soviet Union Commemorating the 40th Anniversary of the October Revolution" (date unknown).

Notes to Chapter 5

1. The Hanseatic League was a political and commercial alliance made up of various cities located in northern Germany. Approximately ninety cities were members of the League during the thirteenth century. By the fourteenth century, the League's membership

peaked at 160. The city of Lübeck emerged as its leader. The Hanseatic League had its own armed forces and treasury, and exercised the power to declare war, make peace, and conclude treaties. The Hanseatic League achieved its greatest prosperity subsequent to its military victories over Denmark and Norway in 1370.

2. Mao Zedong, "On Contradiction," in *Selected Works of Mao Zedong* (Beijing: People's Publishing House, 1967 one-volume edition), 277.

3. Engels, "The Mark," in *Collected Works of Marx and Engels* (Beijing: People's Publishing House, 1963), 19:366.

4. Engels, "December 5, 1882 Letter to Karl Marx," in *Collected Works of Marx and Engels* (Beijing: People's Publishing House, 1971), 35:123.

5. Engels, "The Situation in Germany," in *Collected Works of Marx and Engels* (Beijing: People's Publishing House, 1957), 2:635.

6. Marx, "A Bill to Abolish Fedual Obligations," in *Collected Works of Marx and Engels* (Beijing: People's Publishing House, 1958), 5:325.

7. Engels, "Letters from Wuppertal," in *Collected Works of Marx and Engels* (Beijing: People's Publishing House, 1956), 1:497–98; English language translation taken from Marx and Engels, *Collected Works* (London: Lawrence and Wishart, 1975), 2:9–10.

8. Marx, "A Bill to Abolish Feudal Obligations," in *Collected Works of Marx and Engels* (Beijing: People's Publishing House, 1958), 5:331. Italics in original.

9. Lenin, "The Land Program of the Social Democratic Party During the First Russian Revolution of 1905–07," in *Collected Works of Lenin* (Beijing: People's Publishing House, 1959), 13:224.

10. Lenin, "The Land Question in Russia at the End of the Nineteenth Century," in *Collected Works of Lenin* (Beijing: People's Publishing House, 1959), 15:114.

11. Lenin, "The Land Program of the Social Democratic Party During the First Russian Revolution of 1905–07," in *Collected Works of Lenin* (Beijing: People's Publishing House, 1959), 13:219.

12. Marx, "The Situation in Prussia," in *Collected Works of Marx and Engels* (Beijing: People's Publishing House, 1962), 12:729.

13. Engels, preface to the second edition of *Peasant Wars in Germany*, in *Collected Works of Marx and Engels* (Beijing: People's Publishing House, 1964), 16:450.

14. The new German Reich was a federal state composed of twenty-two principalities, three free cities (Hamburg, Bremen, and Lubeck), and one region under direct imperial rule (Alsace-Lorraine).

15. Stalin, "On the Economic Situation in the Soviet Union and the Party's Policies," in *Collected Works of Stalin* (Beijing: People's Publishing House, 1954), 8:114–15.

16. Stalin, "Questions and Answers," in *Collected Works of Stalin* (Beijing: People's Publishing House, 1958), 7:163.

17. Lenin, *Imperialism, The Highest Stage of Capitalism* (Beijing: People's Publishing House, 1971), 60.

18. Lenin, *Imperialism, The Highest Stage of Capitalism* (Beijing: People's Publishing House, 1971), 12.

19. Lenin, "On 'Left-Wing' Infantilism and the Character of the Petty-Bourgeoisie," in *Collected Works of Lenin* (Beijing: People's Publishing House, 1958), 27:314.

20. Engels, "The Ruhr Miners' Strike of 1889," in *Collected Works of Marx and Engels* (Beijing: People's Publishing House, 1965), 21:434.

21. Lenin, "The 8th Congress of the Bolshevik Party," in *Collected Works of Lenin* (Beijing: People's Publishing House 1956), 29:144.

22. Lenin, "Draft of an Outline Statement to the International Socialist Committee and to the Socialist Parties of All Nations," in *Collected Works of Lenin* (Beijing: People's Publishing House, 1958), 23:213.

23. Lenin, "When Faced with Imminent Disaster, Where Can One Find a Solution?" in *Collected Works of Lenin* (Beijing: People's Publishing House, 1958), 25:324.

24. Lenin, "Speech at the Conference of the Administrative Committee Chairmen from the Prefectures, Counties, and Villages of the Province of Moscow," in *Collected Works of Lenin* (Beijing: People's Publishing House, 1958), 31:292.

25. Stalin, "A Summary Report on the Work of the Central Organs of the Bolskevik Federation Delivered to the 17th Congress of the Party," in *Collected Works of Stalin* (Beijing: People's Publishing House, 1956), 13:260–61.

26. Mao Zedong, "A Discussion with Reporters from New China News Agency Concerning the International Situation," in *Collected Works of Mao Zedong* (Beijing: People's Publishing House, 1967 combined edition), 544.

27. Mao Zedong, "A Discussion with the American Reporter Anna Louise Strong," in *Selected Works of Mao Zedong* (Beijing: People's Publishing House, 1967), 1091.

Notes to Chapter 6

1. Marx, *Capital*, vol. 1, in *Collected Works of Marx and Engels* (Beijing: People's Publishing House, 1972), 23:785.

2. Mulberry trees were also used to make paper products.

3. In order to consolidate its control over the *daimyō*, the Tokugawa *bakufu* required each feudal lord to alternate his residence between Edo (the pre-1868 name for Tokyo) and his native fief every other year. *Daimyō* wives and children were forced to live in Edo on a permanent basis as hostages. This "alternate residence" system stimulated the development of cities and towns along the transportation routes to Edo, and also brought improvements in travel and communications.

4. Mao Zedong, "The Chinese Revolution and the Chinese Communist Party," in *Selected Works of Mao Zedong* (Beijing: People's Publishing House, 1967 combined edition), 588.

5. The "legally determined land price" was not the real market price of the land, but the result of a calculation made by the Meiji government to secure a predetermined, fixed tax yield. It was an artificial price based on combining two factors: the average productivity of the land over the previous five years and the average price of rice for that region for that same time period. A reassessment would occur every six years.

6. A labor contractor (ostensibly a master craftsman seeking apprentices) would recruit workers, and then take control over their lives. He would sign a contract with the owners of a mine or some other enterprise, guaranteeing that he would provide the labor power required for their operations. The labor contractor exploited his workers in making such an arrangement.

7. This was also called the "free room" system. A labor contractor (or person who offered housing arrangements) would recruit unmarried workers, then crowd them into shabby rooms (also known as "free rooms" or "eating places") where they would live and eat together and leave to go to work together. Labor contractors would also sign agreements with factory owners to provide them with workers who would be rigorously monitored on the job and cruelly exploited.

8. Destitute peasants would send their daughters to the factories in return for advance wages paid to them by the factory owners. These women factory workers lost their personal freedom after entering the plant. They were forbidden to return home or go outside, and were required to eat and sleep on the grounds of the factory. They worked in order to repay the wages that had been advanced to their parents, and to pay for the room and board charges that they personally incurred. Therefore, they drew no direct wages.

9. The workers' freedom was restricted because they were required to live on the grounds of the factory. The factory owners took advantage of their captive audience and exploited the workers even more by charging them fees when the workers patronized the company dormitories, cafeteria, or store.

10. The original terms of the Treaty of Shimonoseki required China to pay an indemnity of 200 million ounces of silver to Japan. It also required China to cede the Liaodong Peninsula to Japan. However, Japan was forced to relinquish its claims to the Liaodong Peninsula after the cession of hostilties because of the intervention of Russia's allies, Germany and France. These two countries had their own designs on China's northeastern provinces. In the end, China was forced to pay to Japan an additional indemnity of thirty million ounces of silver as compensation for Japan's frustrated take-over of the Liaodong Peninsula.

11. Lenin, "The Second Congress of Representatives of the Communist International," in *Collected Works of Lenin* (Beijing: People's Publishing House, 1958), 31:198.

12. The "unlimited partnership" was an organizational development of the Japanese joint-stock company. Its capital was supplied by various shareholders. As shareholders, each had unlimited liability. In other words, they became jointly liable for all debts when the company's assets were insufficient to clear such debts. This type of joint-stock company was generally a family enterprise inherited from generation to generation. All the shareholders were principal members of the family and its relatives.

13. The "limited partnership" was yet another advanced form of the Japanese joint-stock company. Its main difference with the "unlimited partnership" was the distinction it made between two kinds of shareholders: one carried unlimited liability, the other enjoyed limited liability. Those shareholders who enjoyed limited liability were liable only for the amount of their investment.

14. Mao Zedong, "On Protracted War," in *Selected Works of Mao Zedong* (Beijing: People's Publishing House, 1967 one-volume edition), 416.

15. Lenin, "Imperialism and the Split in the Socialist Movement," in *Collected Works of Lenin* (Beijing: People's Publishing House, 1959), 2:114.

16. Mao Zedong, "On Protracted War," in *Selected Works of Mao Zedong* (Beijing: People's Publishing House, 1967 one-volume edition), 415.

17. Lenin, *Imperialism, The Highest Stage of Capitalism* (Beijing: People's Publishing House, 1971), 88. Italics in original.

18. Lenin, "Speech to a Conference of Activists of Moscow Organizations Led by the Bolshevik Party," in *Collected Works of Lenin* (Beijing: People's Publishing House, 1958), 31:404.

19. In 1902, Japan and England entered into a military alliance aimed at 1) stopping Czarist Russia's aggression against China and 2) promoting their mutual efforts to partition Asia. After Russia's defeat in the Russo-Japanese War, Germany became the principal obstacle to British and Japanese hopes of conquering China and partitioning Asia. As a result, the Anglo-Japanese Treaty of 1902 was subsequently revised and extended twice, the first time in August 1905, the second in August 1911. Its spearhead was now pointed at Germany.

20. Mao Zedong, "On Tactics Against Japanese Imperialism," in *Selected Works of Mao Zedong* (Beijing: People's Publishing House, 1967 one-volume edition), 129.

21. Lenin, *The State and Revolution* (Beijing: People's Publishing House, 1972), 3.

22. After an intense struggle, the United States, England, Japan, France, and Italy signed an agreement in Washington, D.C. on February 16, 1922. This treaty put proportional limits on the naval forces each power could maintain, and essentially forced Japan to acquiesce to a two-tier system of power. The proportions (in tonnage) of capital ships and aircraft carriers permitted to the five countries were as follows: the United

States (5), England (5), Japan (3), France (1.75), and Italy (1.75).

23. Kantō refers to the location of Kanhasshu, or the eight provinces of Kantō in antiquity. It includes the capital city of Tōkyō and six prefectures: Kanagawa, Saitama, Gumma, Tochigi, Ibaragi, and Chiba.

24. The "three detestable laws" were three reactionary bills enacted by the imperial government. They were "the law banning extremist social movements," "the law on labor unions," and "the law on mediating tenancy disputes."

25. Mao Zedong, "On Strategy Against Japanese Imperialism," in *Selected Works of Mao Zedong* (Beijing: People's Publishing House, 1967 combined edition), 129.

26. Mao Zedong, "On Protracted War," in *Selected Works of Mao Zedong* (Beijing: People's Publishing House, 1967), 477.

27. Mao Zedong, "On Protracted War," in *Selected Works of Mao Zedong* (Beijing: People's Publishing House, 1967 combined edition), 415–16.

Index

About the Translator

Uldis Kruze, a graduate of Yale University, received his M.A. in American and European History from Northwestern University and his Ph.D. in Modern Chinese and Japanese History from Indiana University. He has been a research associate for the Center for Chinese Studies at the University of California, Berkeley since 1977 and is currently an associate professor in the History Department at the University of San Francisco.